Marching Off To War

Marching Off To War

The events surrounding the
Men of Chigwell
Killed in
The Great War
1914 – 1918

By

Marc Alexander

First published in 2008

Copyright © Marc Alexander, 2008

All Rights Reserved. No part of this publication may be reproduced, stored in a retrieval system or transmitted in any form or by any means; electronic, electrostatic, magnetic tape, mechanical, photocopying, recording or otherwise, without permission in writing from the author.

This book is sold subject to the condition that it shall not, by way of trade or otherwise, be lent, resold, hired out, or otherwise circulated without the author's prior consent in any form of binding or cover other than that in which it is published and without a similar condition including this condition being imposed on a subsequent purchaser.

The moral right of Marc Alexander to be identified as author of this work has been asserted by him in accordance with the Copyright, Designs and Patent Act, 1988.

Published by Marc Alexander 2008

Printed by Book Printing UK
Remus House
Coltsfoot Drive
Woodston
Peterborough
PE2 9JX

ISBN 978-0-9560032-0-1

Set in Franklin Gothic Book

IN SACRED MEMORY OF THE MEN OF CHIGWELL

WHO DIED FOR FREEDOM AND MANKIND

*"AT THE GOING DOWN OF THE SUN AND IN THE MORNING
WE WILL REMEMBER THEM"*

CONTENTS

ACKNOWLEDGEMENTS	1
GLOSSARY	2
FORMATIONS OF THE BEF	3
AUTHOR'S EXPLANATIONS	4
THE MEN OF CHIGWELL	5
LIST OF ILLUSTRATIONS	6
LIST OF MAPS	9
PREFACE	11
PROLOGUE	13
INTRODUCTION	17
1914	19
THE WAR AT SEA	37
1915	43
GALLIPOLI	59
1916	69
1917	101
PALESTINE	139
1918	149
AFTER THE ARMISTICE	195
EPILOGUE	197
APPENDIX 1 JOHN WILLIAM DRAPER	205
APPENDIX 2 SDGW (CHIGWELL, CHIGWELL ROW AND WOODFORD BRIDGE)	208
APPENDIX 3 WOODFORD BRIDGE - ROLL OF HONOUR	209
APPENDIX 4 ST PAUL'S CHURCH WAR MEMORIAL (WOODFORD BRIDGE)	212
APPENDIX 5 CHIGWELL SCHOOL - ROLL OF HONOUR	214
APPENDIX 6 CHIGWELL MEMORIAL (WW2)	215
APPENDIX 7 CWGC CASUALTIES WITHIN CHIGWELL, CHIGWELL ROW AND WOODFORD BRIDGE.	218
CHIGWELL PARISH MAGAZINE ROLL OF HONOUR	219
CHIGWELL'S VICTORIA CROSSES	221
NOTES	225
BIBLIOGRAPHY	237
INDEX	239

ACKNOWLEDGEMENTS

I would like to thank the following people for their help for without it this book could not have been written.

Firstly thanks to my wife Hilary and sons Sam and Rudy for standing by me whilst I shut myself away writing and for Hilary's help in correcting my numerous spelling mistakes, also my father in law Martin Solomons for taking a keen interest in my subject, helping with format and design and accompanying me on numerous trips to France and Belgium pre kids!. Thanks to Ann Marie Shuttle who has supplied useful information regarding not only her family but various names and numbers of other useful contacts, she was one of the first people I contacted as I embarked on this project. Peter Trendall (at time of writing) the rector of St Mary's Church, Chigwell for all his help and Mac Leonard, Reader at St Paul's Church Woodford Bridge for his assistance in providing photos and answering questions. John 'Mr Chigwell' Redfern - whose father fought in and survived WW1 - for his help in supplying the names and addresses of numerous relatives of those men listed on the Chigwell Memorial and thanks also to Geoff Hamilton for various photographs. Thank you to Mr Leslie Prescott for all his help and for supplying photos of Joseph Samuel George Underwood and Mr David Martin for all his help and for allowing me the use of his picture of Second Lieutenant Harry Walter Jassby. Mr Frank Gapes and his wife for taking the time to sit down and share details of their family history, also Mr H.C. Dunkley, Mrs Alice Frost, Mrs Nina Hanson, Mrs Marjorie Barton and Noeline and Donald McLaren for their help. A Special thank you goes to Bill Oliver for sharing his newspaper cuttings and photographs with me and for all his help in carrying out research.

Thank you to Loranda Morrison at Chigwell School for her help and also thanks to Marian F Delfgou at the school archive department for her help in supplying details on John Leslie Fish, Edwin Ambrose Daniels and Harold Hull Moseley. Thank you to the management and staff of the Kings Head Public House on Chigwell High Road for allowing me access to pictures in their possession and thanks also to Julia Skinner, Photo Library Manager at the Francis Frith Collection. A big thank you to Ian Dowd and the staff of the Local Studies Department situated at Ilford Central Library for all of their help. All the staff at the National Archives at Kew in London and to the late Captain Mason who worked at the archive department of the Guards Museum in Birdcage Walk SW1 for his help in obtaining the service record of Frederick Arthur Bailey.

Thanks to Steve Coe for supplying the computer and helping with arrangements, also Peter Coe for supplying the camera. Thank you to all the staff at Hotel La Basillique in the town of Albert in France and all the staff at both the Ariane Hotel and Best Western Hotel at Ypres in Belgium. I would also like to thank Mr David Tattersfield the author of *'A Village Goes To War'* for his help in answering my questions on the subject of writing a book, letting me use his maps and also for answering many other questions I had regarding research. A big thanks to the authors and publishers of all the books used during the course of my research for their permission to use their material including Gabrielle White at Random House, Peter Sherrott at Harper Collins, Tamsin Johnson at Pen and Sword, Mary Bergin-Cartwright and Ben Kennedy at Oxford University Press, Jessica Purdue at Orion Group Publishing Ltd and Rowena Blackwell at Pearson Educational. Also thanks to Chris Baker and the people behind the website The Long Long Trail/1914-18.net and Chris McCarthy and the staff of the Imperial War Museum at Lambeth in London. Peter Simkins, author of *'Chronicles of the Great War'* and Colour Library Books of Godalming/Bramley Books. Gordon Stuart the administrator of the Old Catton website for his help and Martin Edwards – Roll of Honour webmaster for pictures of the Cromer Memorial in Norfolk, also a big thank you to Ezra Friedlander for taking various pictures of the Jerusalem Memorial. A big thank you to Terry Denham for all his help concerning the CWGC and also to Roy Hemington at CWGC France for his help in correcting the initials on the headstone of Pte Henry John Clark.

I would also like to thank all those who fought and died in two world wars for our freedom and those service personnel who continue to protect us in conflicts around the world.

Whilst every effort has been made to trace and acknowledge all copyright holders I would like to sincerely apologise should there have been any mistakes or omissions.

GLOSSARY

A/Capt - Acting Captain
A/Cpl - Acting Corporal
A/LCpl – Acting Lance Corporal
ACC – Army Cyclist Corps
ADS - Advanced Dressing Station
AEF- American Expeditionary Force
AIF- Australian Imperial Force
AM – Albert Medal
ANZAC – Australian and New Zealand Army Corps

BEF-British Expeditionary Force (Army in France and Flanders)
BRCSM – British Red Cross Service Medal
BWM - British War Medal

CCS - Casualty Clearing Station.
CEF- Canadian Expeditionary Force
CIC- Commander in Chief
CIGS-Chief of the Imperial General Staff
CO- Commanding Officer
COM – Certificate of Merit
Coy - Company
CWGC - Commonwealth War Graves Commission

DCM-Distinguished Conduct Medal
DLI – Durham Light Infantry
DOW- Died of Wounds
DSC- Distinguished Service Cross
DSO-Distinguished Service Order

EEF- Egyptian Expeditionary Force (Army in Egypt and Palestine)

F&F – France and Flanders
F/Sgt – Flight Sergeant

G.C.V.O. – Grand Cross of the Victorian Order
GDSN - Guardsman
GHQ - General Headquarters
GOC- General Officer Commanding

HAC - Honourable Artillery Company
HLI - Highland Light Infantry
HQ – Headquarters

K.C.B – Knight Commander (order of the Bath)
KIA- Killed in action
KOSB- Kings Own Scottish Borderers
KOYLI- Kings Own Yorkshire Light Infantry
KRRC - Kings Royal Rifle Corps
KSLI- Kings Shropshire Light Infantry

L/Cpl - Lance Corporal
Lt - Lieutenant
Lt Col - Lieutenant Colonel
LOC - Line of Communications

MC - Military Cross
MEF – Mediterranean Expeditionary Force (Army sent to Gallipoli)
MGC - Machine Gun Corps
MIC – Medal Index Card
MID – Mentioned in Dispatches
MM - Military Medal

NA – National Archives
NCO- Non Commissioned Officer (Sergeant or Corporal)

OBE – Order of the British Empire
OIC - Officer in Charge
OTC - Officer Training Corps

P.O.-Petty Officer
P/O- Pilot Officer
Pte – Private

QRWS - Queens Royal West Surreys
QWR – Queens Westminster Rifles

RAF – Royal Air Force
RAMC -Royal Army Medical Corps
RASC - Royal Army Service Corps
RE - Royal Engineers
RFA - Royal Field Artillery (served alongside the Infantry)
RFC-Royal Flying Corps
RGA - Royal Garrison Artillery (controlled by Army HQ and held the heaviest guns)
RHA - Royal Horse Artillery (served alongside the Cavalry)
RMF - Royal Munster Fusiliers
RND – Royal Naval Division (63rd)
RNAC – Royal Naval Air Corps
RNAS – Royal Naval Air Service
RPM - Rounds per Minute
RWK- Royal West Kent's

SWB - South Wales Borderers

T/Capt - Temporary Captain
T/Lt - Temporary Lieutenant
TF – Territorial Force
TMB – Trench Mortar Battery
Tpr – Trooper

VC – Victoria Cross (Highest British gallantry award)
VM - Victory Medal

FORMATIONS OF THE BEF

The commanders in chief were:

        Field Marshal Sir John French - August 1914 to December 1915
        Field Marshal Sir Douglas Haig - December 1915 to Armistice

ARMY = Came under the command of a general and was made up of four corps but this number varied depending on involvement. In this book British units are written in numbers e.g. 1st Army and all other nationalities are in word e.g. German First Army.

CORPS = Came under the command of a Lieutenant General and was made up of either three or four divisions. Referred to in this book using Roman numerals e.g. II Corps.

DIVISION = Came under the command of a Major General and consisted of three Infantry Brigades as well as Divisional Troops, artillery, transport, medical services and various other tactical units.

BRIGADE = Came under the command of a Brigadier General and consisted of four infantry battalions however in 1918 this was reduced to three.

BATTALION = Came under the command of a Lieutenant Colonel and was split into four companies, at full strength would contain roughly a thousand men.

COMPANY = Came under the command of a Major or Captain and was split into four platoons, usually lettered A, B, C and D, at full strength would contain in the region of two hundred men.

PLATOON = Came under the command of a Subaltern i.e. First or Second Lieutenant and was split into four sections, a platoons strength varied throughout the war from thirty to forty men.

SECTION = Came under the command of an NCO and consisted in early 1914 of sixteen men later that figure became roughly eight to ten men.

AUTHOR'S EXPLANATIONS

Whilst this book tells the story of the men listed on the Chigwell Village War Memorial some of those men came from nearby Woodford Bridge; this is not surprising as the two villages are less than two miles apart. The parish church at Chigwell is St Mary's – beside whose ground the village war memorial stands - whilst St Paul's Parish Church serves Woodford Bridge. Inside St Paul's Church stands a memorial plaque dedicated to forty five men connected with the church who died in the Great War, a war memorial in the form of a Roll of Honour Plaque also exists at Woodford Bridge, the details of both these memorials can be found at the back of this book in Appendixes 3 and 4. Also in close proximity to Chigwell is Grange Hill, in 1914 - 1918 this came under the parish of St Mary's at Chigwell. Parts of another nearby village called Chigwell Row also came under St Mary's however this village did have its own parish church called All Saints, more details on all these villages can be found in the Prologue.

Started in 1885 the Chigwell Parish Magazine was a booklet produced monthly that recorded the goings on and events in and around Chigwell Village. Amongst other things it recorded Births, Marriages and Deaths therefore during the years of the Great War it was an important source of information in regards to the wellbeing of Soldiers at the front. Copies of the magazine dating from 1910 to 1920 can be viewed in the Local Studies Department at Ilford Central Library.

Every man who joined the army before and during the First World War had a service record in the form of a file kept on him. These records included basic things such as name, address, personal details and army career. These records prove an enormous help when tracing a soldier's journey however in 1941 the building they were stored in at Bermondsey (Southeast London) was bombed in an air raid and in the fire that followed most were destroyed. Those that survived (approximately 20%) are held at the National Archives (NA) in Kew, of the 41 men from Chigwell 14 records have survived, most of those for the men killed during 1916.

Officers Died in the Great War (ODGW) and Soldiers Died in the Great War (SDGW) were first published in 1921 and totalled 81 volumes. These volumes listed regiment by regiment the details of roughly 37,000 officers and 635,000 men killed between 1914 and 1919. The details listed for soldiers include date and place of death, name, rank, army number, birth place, place of residence, place of enlistment and decorations if any, officer's details however contain slightly less information. In recent years a company based in Sussex called Naval and Military Press has transferred all the information from both ODGW and SDGW onto one CD-Rom database. This database has been used to compile information for use in this book however given the size of the task in transferring all the original details the database does contain the odd mistake here and there. In this book all casualty figures from ODGW and SDGW are simply shown as SDGW.

The Medal Index Cards (MIC) can be found at the NA and show a soldier's entitlement to various campaign medals, the cards also contain a reference number which refers to the Medal Rolls. The MIC and Medal Rolls hold basic information regarding a soldier e.g. rank, unit, battalion etc. Those men who served prior to 1916 in most cases will have their date of entry into the theatre of war they served in recorded on their MIC; for those who served after 1916 this information will sometimes appear on the Medal Rolls.

Every battalion that served overseas during the First World War was obliged to keep a war diary that recorded that unit's day to day events. The diaries were usually filled out by an officer and whilst some when writing up went into detail others rather frustratingly were extremely vague. In most cases a battalion war diary will record daily losses, sometimes officers are mentioned by name however it is very rare for men (or other ranks) to be mentioned except in the case of a bravery award. Copies of all the battalion war diaries can be found at the NA in Kew.

Where possible I try not to baffle the reader with science regarding the various units and formations within the British Army of 1914 to 1918 however in some cases in order to tell the story this has proved unavoidable. In such cases I have tried to make these explanations as easy as possible to follow. The term British Army has sometimes been used to include the forces of other countries such as India, South Africa, Australia, Canada and New Zealand whose soldiers fought alongside Great Britain as part of the empire.

Where numbers appear in brackets e.g. (1) please refer to Notes at the back of this book.

THE MEN OF CHIGWELL
1914 - 1918

1914

Cpl Harold Henry Shuttle - 1st Bedfordshire Regiment +
Pte Charles Leonard Harrup -1st Dorsetshire Regiment +
Pte Edwin Bird - 2nd Yorks & Lancs Regiment
Pte Charles Alfred Reeves - 4th (Queens Own) Hussars *+
OS Joseph S G Underwood - H.M.S. Pathfinder +
AB Harry Norman Bailey - H.M.S. Kestrel +

1915

Sgt John William Draper -1/1st Essex Yeomanry *
Pte Thomas George Bird - 2nd West Yorkshire Regiment
Pte Henry John Clark - 6th Queens Royal West Surrey Regiment
Pte James Edward Cox - 9th Essex Regiment
Lt Maurice Austin Murray -11th Essex Regiment
Pte Denham George King -1/4th Essex Regiment +

1916

Pte William Frank Gapes - 2nd Essex Regiment
Pte Frederick William Dunkley - 7th Buffs (East Kent Regiment)
Lt John Leslie Fish - 7th Suffolk Regiment
Capt Arthur John Waugh - R.A.M.C. (1st North Staffordshire Regiment)
L/Cpl Edward Stephen Scott - 11th Rifle Brigade
Pte Alfred Charles Vince -11th Rifle Brigade
Sgt Sidney Hayter MM - 12th Rifle Brigade
L/Cpl Albert Charles Cox - 7th Norfolk Regiment
Capt Edwin Ambrose Daniels - 8th South Lancashire Regiment
Pte Charles Alfred Flack - M.G. Corps (96th Coy)

1917

Pte George Pleasance - 2nd Essex Regiment +
Pte William Harold Hyde - 1/4th Essex Regiment
Pte Harry Mark Brown - 1st Essex Regiment +
Pte Daniel James Trevett - 13th East Surrey Regiment *+
Pte Charles Ernest Bailey - 1/6th London Regiment (City of London) +
Pte Frank M Fogg - 1st Royal Munster Fusiliers
Pte Patrick Fitzgerald - 1/7th Worcestershire Regiment +
L/Cpl George Charles Belcher - 1/17th London Regiment (Poplar & Stepney Rifles)
Pte William Albert Kerry - 13th Royal Fusiliers
Gnr Ernest Herring - Royal Field Artillery (70th Brigade) +
Pte John Arthur Witham - 10th Essex Regiment +

1918

Pte Mathew Amos Wesson Mason - 11th Royal Fusiliers +
Pte James Simpson - 20th Durham Light Infantry +
Pte Frederick Elliot Noble - 13th Yorkshire Regiment
Pte Charles William Day - 9th Norfolk Regiment
Pte Sydney James Bodger - 2nd Essex Regiment +
Pte Frederick Arthur Bailey - 2nd Grenadier Guards +
Sgt Frederick William Barton - 2nd Tank Corps +
Sgt Harold Hull Moseley - 2/5th London Rifle Brigade
Pte John Green - 2nd Royal Fusiliers

* = *Men not listed on Chigwell Village War Memorial*
+ = *Men (also) listed on Woodford Bridge Roll Of Honour*

LIST OF ILLUSTRATIONS

FRONT COVER

The Chigwell Village War Memorial

PREFACE

1, Second Lieutenant Harry Walter Jassby *(Picture courtesy of David Martin)*
2, The gravestone of Harry Walter Jassby inside St Peter's Churchyard
3, The Chigwell Village War Memorial
4, The Royal Fusiliers Memorial at Holborn in Central London
5, The Ilford War Memorial situated at Newbury Park

PROLOGUE

6, The Chigwell Village War Memorial
7, Chigwell Grammar School *(Photograph courtesy of Geoff Hamilton)*
8, St Mary's Church in Chigwell *(Photograph courtesy of Geoff Hamilton)*
9, All Saints Church, Chigwell Row
10, St Paul's Church, Woodford Bridge *(Photograph courtesy of Geoff Hamilton)*
11, Chigwell, The Village 1925 *(Copyright - The Francis Frith Collection)*
12, Chigwell Village Shops and Post Office 1955 *(Copyright - The Francis Frith Collection)*
13, The Prince of Wales Public House *(The Essex Chronicle Newspaper)*
14, The Three Jolly Wheelers Public House at Woodford Bridge *(Photograph courtesy of Geoff Hamilton)*
15, The Old Police Station at Woodford Bridge
16, The Bald Hind Public House

1914

17, La-Ferté-Sous-Jouarre Memorial to the Missing
18, The name of Cpl Harold Henry Shuttle as it appears on the La-Ferté-Sous-Jouarre Memorial to the Missing.
19, Cpl Harold Henry Shuttle's grandparents gravestone situated inside St Mary's Churchyard
20, The name of Pte Charles Leonard Harrup as it appears on the Le Touret Memorial to the Missing
21, The name of Pte Edwin Bird as it appears on the Ploegsteert Memorial to the Missing
22, The 4th (Queen's Own) Hussars at Curragh in 1914 *(Photograph courtesy of the Imperial War Museum)*
23, The Menin Gate Memorial to the Missing at Ypres

THE WAR AT SEA

24, The Chatham Naval Memorial in Kent
25, Harry Norman Bailey as it appears on the Chatham Naval Memorial
26, HMS Kestrel *(Picture courtesy and copyright of Tony Davies)*
27, HMS Pathfinder *(Picture courtesy and copyright of Tony Davies)*
28, Joseph Samuel George Underwood *(Picture courtesy of Leslie Prescott)*
29, The name of Joseph Samuel George Underwood as it appears on the Chatham Naval Memorial

1915

30, The Memorial Plaque dedicated to those killed at the Prince of Wales Pub on the evening of 19th April 1941
31, The gravestone of Pte Thomas George Bird situated at the rear of St Mary's Churchyard in Chigwell
32, The gravestone of Pte Henry John Clark at Cite Bonjean CWGC Cemetery with the initials N J instead of H J
33, The gravestone of Pte James Edward Cox
34, The name of Lt Maurice Austin Murray as it appears on the Loos Memorial to the Missing
35, Lt Maurice Austin Murray

GALLIPOLI

36, Men of the 1/4th Battalion Essex Regiment marching off to war *(Photograph courtesy of the Imperial War Museum)*
37, Essex Battalions landing at Sulva Bay on the Gallipoli Peninsular August 1915 *(Photograph courtesy of the Imperial War Museum)*
38, Trenches held by Essex units inland from Anzac *(Photograph courtesy of the Imperial War Museum)*

39, Anzac Beach 1915 (*Photograph courtesy of the* Imperial War Museum)

1916

40, The gravestone of Pte William Frank Gapes at Serre Road No 1 CWGC Cemetery, Somme France
41, The Thiepval Memorial to the Missing
42, The gravestone of Second Lieutenant John Leslie Fish
43, The name of John Leslie Fish as it appears on the Cromer War Memorial in Norfolk, England
44, The name of Capt Arthur John Waugh as it appears on his parent's gravestone situated inside St Mary's Churchyard in Chigwell
45, The Waugh Family *(Picture taken from a Brief History of Chigwell Hall by Carol Cooper and Tony Durrant)*
46, Second Lieutenant Leonard Victor Waugh
47, The gravestone of Capt Arthur John Waugh at Carnoy CWGC Cemetery Somme, France
48, The name of Pte Alfred Charles Vince as it appears on the Thiepval Memorial to the Missing
49, The gravestone of L/Cpl Edward Stephen Scott at Guillemont Road CWGC Cemetery Somme, France
50, The gravestone of Sgt Sidney Hayter MM at Grovetown CWGC Cemetery Somme, France
51, The Military Medal
52, The gravestone of L/Cpl Albert Hayter at Heilly Station CWGC Cemetery Somme, France
53, The name of Capt Edwin Ambrose Daniels as it appears on the Thiepval Memorial to the Missing
54, The plaque commemorating Capt Edwin Ambrose Daniels situated inside St Mary's Church, Chigwell
55, Flint Cottage
56, The memorial to the officers and men of the Machine Gun Corps on the north side of Hyde Park Corner in Central London
57, The grave of an unknown soldier attached to the Machine Gun Corps

1917

58, The Arras Memorial to the Missing
59, The name of Pte Harry Mark Brown as it appears on the Arras Memorial to the Missing
60, The gravestone of Pte Daniel James Trevett at Fins CWGC Cemetery Somme, France
61, The gravestone of Pte George Pleasance at Bray CWGC Cemetery Somme, France
62, Pte Charles Ernest Bailey's gravestone at Oak Dump CWGC Cemetery, Ypres, Belgium
63, The name of L/Cpl George Charles Belcher as it appears on the Menin Gate Memorial to the Missing at Ypres
64, The plaque outside 59-61 Farringdon Road commemorating the Zeppelin Raid in September 1915
65, The name of Pte Frank Fogg as it appears on the Tyne Cot Memorial to the Missing
66, The Royal Artillery Memorial at Hyde Park Corner in Central London
67, Solferino Farm CWGC Cemetery Ypres, Belgium
68, The gravestone of Gunner Ernest Handy Herring at Solferino Farm CWGC Cemetery
69, The names of Pte Patrick Fitzgerald, Pte William Albert Kerry and Pte John Arthur Witham as they appear on the Tyne Cot Memorial to the Missing
70, The Third Battle of Ypres 1917 *(Photograph courtesy of the Imperial War Museum Ref E Aus 1220)*
71, Muddy shell holes at Ypres *(Photograph courtesy of the Imperial War Museum Ref CO 2241)*
72, The Mud of Passchendaele 1917 *(Photograph courtesy of the Imperial War Museum Ref CO 2246)*

PALESTINE

73, Advance of the 1/4th Essex at the First Battle of Gaza 26th - 27th March 1917 *(Photograph courtesy of the Imperial War Museum)*
74, The Jerusalem CWGC Cemetery and Memorial to the Missing *(Picture Courtesy of Ezra Friedlander)*
75, The name of Pte William Harold Hyde as it appears along with other Essex men on the Jerusalem Memorial to the Missing

1918

76, The gravestone of Pte Matthew Amos Wesson Mason at Grand-Seraucourt CWGC Cemetery, Somme, France
77, The Mason family gravestone situated inside St Mary's Churchyard in Chigwell
78, An unidentified soldier from the First World War whose picture hangs in the Dining Room of the Kings Head Public House in Chigwell
79, An unidentified corporal from the First World War whose picture hangs in the Dining Room of the Kings Head Public House in Chigwell
80, The gravestone of Pte Frederick Elliot Noble at Le Grand Beaumart CWGC Cemetery, Steenwerck, France
81, The name of Pte James Simpson as it appears on the Arras Memorial to the Missing
82, The gravestone of Pte Charles William Day (Far left) along with three other soldiers buried at Pont-De-Nieppe Communal Cemetery northwest of Armentières, France
83, The name of Pte Sydney James Bodger as it appears on the Loos Memorial to the Missing

84, The gravestone of Guardsman Frederick Arthur Bailey at Beinvillers CWGC Cemetery, Somme, France
85, The Guards Division Memorial on Horse Guards Road in Central London
86, The Tank Corps Memorial at Pozieres on the Somme
87, The gravestone of Cpl Frederick William Barton at Heath CWGC Cemetery, Harbonnières, Somme, France
88, The gravestone of Cpl Harold Hull Moseley at Dive Copse CWGC Cemetery Somme, France
89, The private memorial to Harold Hull Moseley that used to exist in the grounds of St Mary's Churchyard in Chigwell
90, The Mission Room and Chapel at Grange Hill - Chigwell Row
91, The gravestone of Pte John Green at Longuenesse (St Omer) Souvenir Cemetery, Pas de Calais, France

EPILOGUE

92, The gravestone of Pte Percy Green of the Labour Corps at St Paul's Church, Woodford Bridge who died of wounds on 29th November 1918
93, The gravestone of Harry Cecil Dunkley who was gassed during the Great War and died in February 1939 aged 44
94, The Oak Screen Memorial unveiled inside St Mary's Church, Chigwell on 14th November 1920
95, The names of the men of Chigwell killed between 1914-1916 as they appear on the Oak Screen Memorial
96, The names of the men of Chigwell killed between 1917-1918 as they appear on the Oak Screen Memorial
97, The names of the men of Chigwell killed between 1914-1918 as they appear on the village war memorial
98, St Mary's Church, Chigwell and the Village War Memorial 1925. *(Copyright - The Francis Frith Collection)*
99, The Cenotaph in Whitehall in London
100, The statue of Earl Haig in Whitehall in London

APPENDIX 1

101, The gravestone of Sgt John William Draper of the Essex Yeomanry at Bedford House CWGC Cemetery near Ypres in Belgium
102, Sgt John William Draper *(Picture courtesy of The Essex Chronicle Newspaper)*
103, Men of the Essex Yeomanry 1914 -1918 *(Photograph courtesy of Caroline O'Neill and Essex-Yeomanry. Org)*
104, The gravestone belonging to John William Draper Senior situated inside St Mary's Churchyard in Chigwell

APPENDIX 3

105, The Woodford Bridge and District Roll of Honour
106, The plaque commemorating the replacement of the Woodford Bridge Roll of Honour situated at the junction of Manor Road and Chigwell Road in Woodford Bridge

APPENDIX 4

107, The St Paul's Church War Memorial Woodford Bridge *(Photograph courtesy of Reader Mac Leonard)*

APPENDIX 6

108, The names of the men of Chigwell killed between 1939-1945 as they appear on the village war memorial

CHIGWELL'S VICTORIA CROSS WINNERS

109, The memorial to Pte Thomas Edwards VC situated inside St Mary's Churchyard in Chigwell
110, Pte Thomas Edwards VC *(Source Unknown)*
111, A Cap Badge of the Black Watch
112, The Victoria Cross

BACK COVER

Poppies on the Somme

LIST OF MAPS

1, Chigwell Area
2, Chigwell, Chigwell Row, Grange Hill, and Woodford Bridge.
3, Europe 1914 – *Source - The origins of the First World War by James Joll - Courtesy of Longman /Pearson Educational Publishing*
4, The Schlieffen Plan – *Source – The Western Front (BBC Books) by Richard Holmes – Reprinted by permission of Random House Group Ltd*
5, The BEF (August 1914)
6, Le Cateau – *Source - Riding the Retreat (Pimlico) by Richard Holmes – Reprinted by permission of Random House Group Ltd*
7, The Western Front – *Source – The First World War by Michael Howard (2003) –Reproduced by permission of Oxford University Press*
8, The Battle of La Bassée – *Source- Atlas of the First World War by Arthur Banks – Courtesy of Pen and Sword Publishing*
9, The Battle of Armentières – *Source – Atlas of the First World War by Arthur Banks – Courtesy of Pen and Sword Publishing*
10, Touquet – *Source – 2nd York's & Lanc's War Diary – NA Reference: WO95/1610*
11, The Ypres Salient – *Source – Tommy © Richard Holmes 2005 - Courtesy of HarperCollins Publishing*
12, Great Britain
13, Aubers Ridge and Neuve Chapelle – *Source – The Western Front (BBC Books) by Richard Holmes – Reprinted by permission of Random House Group Ltd*
14, Le Touquet – *Source – Imperial War Museum*
15, The 9th Essex at Plugstreet – *Source – 9th Essex War Diary - NA Reference: WO95/1851*
16, The 11th Essex at Loos – *Source – Service Battalions of the Essex Regiment Volume 6 by J W Burrows and Son*
17, The Turkish Empire – *Source - The Last Crusade by Anthony Bruce - Courtesy of John Murray Publishing*
18, Gallipoli – *Source – A Village Goes to War by David Tattersfield*
19, Sulva Bay – *Source - A Village Goes to War by David Tattersfield*
20, The Somme Battlefield – *Source - Tommy © Richard Holmes 2005 - Courtesy of HarperCollins Publishing*
21, The 4th Division at Serre – *Source – Imperial War Museum*
22, The 18th Division on 1st July 1916 - *Source – Imperial War Museum*
23, The 12th Division at Ovillers - *Source – Imperial War Museum*
24, The position of the 1st North Staffs - *Source – Imperial War Museum*
25, The Battle of Guillemont - *Source – Imperial War Museum*
26, Area held by 12th Rifle Brigade (September 1916) - *Source – Imperial War Museum*
27, The 12th Division (October 1916) - *Source – Imperial War Museum*
28, Area attacked by 25th Division (October 1916) – *Source - Service Battalions of the Essex Regiment Volume 6 by J W Burrows and Son*
29, Beaumont Hamel and surrounding area - *Source – NA and the Imperial War Museum*
30, The Battle of Arras (April 1917) – *Source - History of the First World War by Liddell Hart – © Cassell Plc, a division of The Orion Publishing Group London.*
31, The 1st Essex at Monchy-le-Preux (April 1917) – *Source – 1st Battalion Essex Regiment by J W Burrows and Son*
32, Villers Plouich – *Source - Imperial War Museum*
33, The Third Battle of Ypres – *Source – (Map taken from 'Chronicles of the First World War by Peter Simkins. © Colour Library Books of Godalming/Bramley Books).*
34, Hollebeke - *Source - Imperial War Museum*
35, The 1st Royal Munster Fusiliers (August 1917) – *Source - Imperial War Museum*
36, St Julien – *Source - Imperial War Museum*
37, Bellewaerde Ridge – *Source - Imperial War Museum*
38, The position of 37th Division on 4th October 1917 - *Source - Imperial War Museum*
39, The position of the 10th Essex (November 1917) - *Source – NA and the Imperial War Museum*
40, Palestine - *Source – A Village Goes to War by David Tattersfield*
41, The First Battle of Gaza (March 1917)
42, The 1918 German Offensives – *Source – The Western Front (BBC Books) by Richard Holmes – Reprinted by permission of Random House Group Ltd*
43, Area held by 18th Division on 21st March 1918
44, Position of 54th Brigade (22nd – 23rd March 1918)
45, Area of Operations of the 20th DLI (21st March – 1st April 1918)
46, The Lys Offensive (April 1918) – *Source - History of the First World War by Liddell Hart – © Cassell Plc, a division of The Orion Publishing Group London.*

47, Bois Grenier – *Source - NA and the Imperial War Museum*
48, Position of the 13th Yorkshire's (11th – 12th April 1918)
49, Position of 9th Norfolk's (15th – 18th April 1918)
50, Area of operation of the 2nd Essex (16th -24th April 1918)
51, Area held by units of the Guards Division (April-June 1918)
52, The Battle of Amiens – *Source - Amiens to the Armistice by J P Harris - Courtesy and copyright of Brassey's Publishing*
53, The 5th Tank Brigade – *Source - 5th Brigade Tank Corps HQ – NA Reference: WO95/112*
54, Area held by III Corps (8th – 10th August 1918) – *Source – Amiens to the Armistice by J P Harris - Courtesy and copyright of Brassey's Publishing*
55, Vieux-Berquin - *Source - Imperial War Museum*

PREFACE

I remember as a child learning about the First World War, there was always something about it that fascinated me. I remember playing with toy soldiers and making trenches for them out of cardboard boxes, at the end of my pretend battles there would always be a few soldiers still standing which I'd cheerfully call the lucky ones. As I grew older my interest in the First World War returned one day as I passed by St Peters Church in Aldborough Road North, Ilford, Essex. As a child I'd lived nearby and I remembered having visited the church on a school trip to do brass rubbings when aged about ten years old. I also remembered that in the churchyard stood a Jewish war grave and was intrigued to take another look. So it was that almost twenty years after I had first seen it I returned, it was quite easy to find close to the front of the churchyard. The grave belonged to a young pilot, the words on the headstone read: Second Lieutenant H W Jassby, Royal Air Force, 6th November 1918, Age 22.

Harry Walter Jassby was a Canadian from Montreal who'd been stationed nearby at 'Training Depot Station 54'. Known also as Fairlop - Hainault Farm Airfield, situated east of London, it played a significant role in home defence during the First World War. Harry was killed in an accident involving another plane whilst flying a Sopwith Camel type aircraft E1442. There was no inquest regarding the incident and his death was deemed just to have been a tragic accident. He was the last man stationed at Fairlop - Hainault Farm to be killed during the Great War with the sad fact being that hostilities ended with the Armistice signed just five days after his death.

It was after seeing this war grave again that I started to see memorials to the Great War that I had passed many times before without ever really taking much notice. These were to include amongst others the Royal Fusiliers Memorial at Holborn in London, the Ilford War Memorial at Newbury Park and another memorial situated on Wanstead High Street. I started also to notice the numerous crosses of sacrifice that generally mark the entrances to most civil cemeteries and finally I noticed a memorial close to where I lived, in the form of a large grey Celtic cross set back from the road beside St Mary's Church in Chigwell in Essex. With this book I try to tell the stories of those men from Chigwell killed in the Great War whose names appear on that memorial. This book covers the stories of forty two men in total although only thirty nine of them actually appear on the memorial, the reasons for this can be found as their relevant stories are told. Aged from eighteen to forty one these men like so many men from villages, towns and cities up and down the land and indeed from across Europe and the world, left their homes, jobs, family and friends to go and fight in the First World War. Some were friends and some were brothers and some even lived in the same street, but all were brave and destined not to return. The men of Chigwell would figure in most of the major actions that made up the events of the First World War. This included such actions as the British Army's retreat from Mons in August 1914, operations at Gallipoli, the battles of the Somme, Passchendaele and the allied advance to victory in 1918.

Where possible I try briefly to explain the events surrounding those men killed however as you will see some stories covered are more conclusive than others. To explain the war in detail is not the intention of this book nor is it my intention as author to give my view on the events of the war. As I write this book the First World War is now almost gone from living memory for those who served in it, therefore it is up to us who remain to keep its interest alive so that its events and stories are not forgotten. As the men featured in this book were killed in the conflict I have taken it upon myself to tell their stories for them as best I can, whilst every effort has been made to ensure there are no mistakes any that do occur are my responsibility alone.

Marc Alexander 2008

1, Second Lieutenant Harry Walter Jassby (Picture courtesy of David Martin)

2, The gravestone of Second Lieutenant Harry Walter Jassby situated inside St Peters Church

3, The Chigwell Village War Memorial

4, The Royal Fusiliers Memorial at Holborn in Central London

5, The Ilford War Memorial situated at Newbury Park

PROLOGUE

The village of Chigwell lies roughly eleven miles northeast of London and falls within the county of Essex, today it is seen as a wealthy middle class area home to businessmen and celebrities alike. Whilst its western side has given way to London's suburbs Chigwell's eastern side has kept its village feel and looks somewhat as it did towards the beginning of the last century. Chigwell's history stretches back to ancient times and is mentioned in the Doomsday Book (1086) as 'Chingelwella' or 'Cingwella' meaning King's Well or King's Weald. The village falls within the district known as Epping Forest, in Tudor times King Henry VIII had a hunting lodge at Chigwell that he used as a base when hunting deer in and around the forest. The register of Chigwell's parish church, St Mary's, dates back to 1555. At the end of the 16th century a man known as Samuel Harsnett came to St Mary's and from 1597 to 1605 took up the post of vicar of Chigwell. Harsnett had an eventful life, at one point he worked for the Bishop of London and was almost sent to the tower for treason. Narrowly escaping Harsnett himself went on to become Bishop of Chichester, Bishop of Norwich and Archbishop of York, he eventually returned to Chigwell and in 1629 set up a boy's grammar school in the village, he died two years later aged 71. One of the schools earliest students was William Penn, today he is recognised as the founder of Pennsylvania in the USA. Chigwell went on to have several famous residents all of whom left their mark on history; Admiral Sir Eliab Harvey lived at Rolls Park at the eastern edge of the village. At the Battle of Trafalgar in 1805 Harvey captained the 98 gun HMS Temeraire, the second ship in Nelsons line. Although Nelson was killed in the battle Harvey and his ship survived. Harvey eventually died in 1830 and the Temeraire was broken up in 1838 but not before she had been immortalised in a famous painting by Turner known as 'The Fighting Temeraire'. The inventor of the Omnibus, George Schilliber was also a Chigwell man. He was born in London in 1797 and went on to work in Paris as a coachbuilder; he eventually returned to England, settled at Grove House in Chigwell Row and on 4th July 1829 introduced the first two Omnibuses on a route between Central London and Paddington. Schilliber went on to design vehicles for undertakers; he himself died in August 1866 and is buried in the churchyard of St Mary's. Arguably the most famous person connected with Chigwell was the writer Charles Dickens, in a letter he wrote to his close friend John Forster he is quoted as saying *"Chigwell, my dear fellow is the greatest place in the world"*. Dickens loved the forest scenery and enjoyed the ride between London and Chigwell, on his many visits to the village he fell in love with 'The Kings Head' public house. Situated opposite St Mary's Church, Dickens used it for inspiration immortalising it as 'The Maypole Inn' in his 1841 book 'Barnaby Rudge'.

By the beginning of the 20th Century much of the forest scenery that Dickens had enjoyed so much still existed however the areas around Chigwell were used mainly as farmland. The ground around the village consists of clay with a subsoil of sand, at the turn of the last century the main crops being grown were wheat, oats and root vegetables, the village covered an area of 4,136 acres and the population according to the census of 1911 was put at 2,742. Many people worked in and around the village however its close proximity to London, and the arrival of the Great Eastern Railway in 1903, meant people were able to commute to the city quite easily. Chigwell High Road had several shops including a post office, grocers, butchers, bakers, blacksmiths and builder's merchants, the station even housed a branch of W H Smiths. Also situated on the High Road was a Workman's Hall, built in 1876 its main function was to provide a space for reading and recreation. Chigwell had three public houses but only two remain to this day, 'The Kings Head' as has been mentioned is by far the oldest and of the Stuart period whilst 'The Bald Hind' on Hainault Road was built towards the end of the 19th Century. The third pub was called the Prince of Wales and although it no longer exists it features several times in this book. Chigwell had three schools, Harsnett's grammar school, known as Chigwell School, was recognised as a public school in 1909 and at that time could accommodate in the region of 150 boys. A council school for boys was built in the village in 1886 and by 1911 that too could cater for roughly 150 boys. The third school that existed was a public elementary school for girls and infants, built in 1837 and enlarged in 1891 this school could accommodate over 200 pupils. Two miles east of Chigwell on the edge of Hainault Forest stands the neighbouring village of Chigwell Row whilst one mile south of Chigwell stands another village called Grange Hill. At the beginning of the 20th Century both these villages came under the parish of St Mary's despite Chigwell Row having its own parish called All Saints. All Saints Church was built in 1867 and its congregation was made up of people from all three villages, within its surroundings was a schoolroom as well as a burial ground which unsurprisingly along with the church remains today. Situated at Grange Hill was a church mission room shared from time to time by both the congregations of St Mary's and All Saints. The 1901 census puts the population of Chigwell Row at 727; surprisingly the 1911 census puts the population at 644, despite both villages being quite small they were served by a train station at Grange Hill. Nowadays totally swallowed by London's suburbs the community of Woodford Bridge is situated one and a half miles southwest of Chigwell and has its own parish called St Paul's. Built in 1854 St Paul's Parish Church served a relatively large community, the census of 1901 puts the population of Woodford Bridge at 2,667. Apart from the usual array of village shops and a public house that still remains called the 'Three Jolly Wheelers' Woodford Bridge, along with the neighbouring area of Claybury, was also home to a Dr Barnardo's boys home and a mental hospital known as the London County Council Lunatic Asylum. The latter housed roughly 3,000 patients whilst the boy's home boasted accommodation for 192 boys. The village also had a small police station as Woodford Bridge, Chigwell, Chigwell Row and Grange Hill all until as recently as 1997 came under the jurisdiction of the Metropolitan Police. Colonel Amelius Mark Richard Lockwood (1847–1928), later the First Baron Lambourne, was the Conservative Member of Parliament for Epping from 1892 to 1917. Brigadier General Sir Richard Beale Colvin MP took over the seat in 1918; Chigwell, Chigwell Row, Grange Hill and Woodford Bridge all fell within the Epping constituency. In the summer of 1914 the people living in cities, towns and villages across the country and around the world found they were propelled into a conflict that appeared to come out of nowhere. The communities around Essex were no exception and it wasn't long before the men of Chigwell, Chigwell Row, Grange Hill and Woodford Bridge found themselves marching off to war.

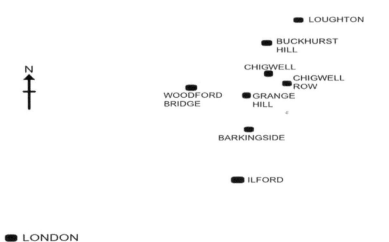

Map 1, Chigwell and the surrounding area

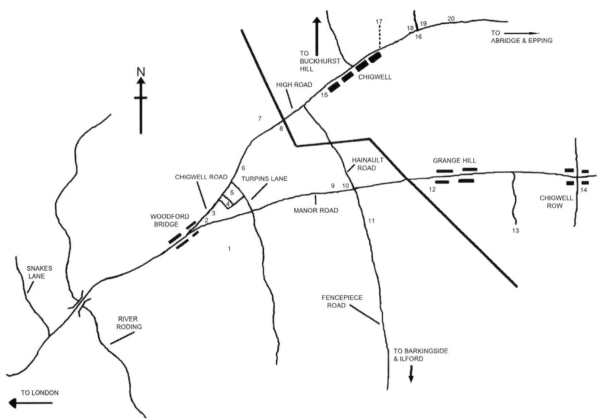

Map 2, Chigwell, Woodford Bridge, Grange Hill and Chigwell Row

1, Claybury Hospital
2, St Paul's Church
3, The Three Jolly Wheelers Pub
4, Brunel Road
5, Smeaton Road
6, Chigwell Convent
7, Flint Cottage
8, Chigwell Station
9, The Prince of Wales Pub
10, The Bald Hind Pub
11, Forest Cottages
12, Grange Hill Station
13, Fairview Hospital
14, All Saint's Church
15, Chigwell Council School
16, The Kings Head Pub
17, Chigwell Hall
18, St Mary's Church
19, Chigwell School
20, Post Office

Railway Line _____

6, The Chigwell Village War Memorial

7, Chigwell Grammar School (Photograph courtesy of Geoff Hamilton)

8, St Mary's Church in Chigwell (Photograph courtesy of Geoff Hamilton)

9, All Saints Church, Chigwell Row (Photograph courtesy of Geoff Hamilton)

10, St Paul's Church, Woodford Bridge (Photograph courtesy of Geoff Hamilton)

*11, Chigwell, The Village 1925
(Copyright The Francis Frith Collection)*

*12, Chigwell Village Shops and Post Office 1955
(Copyright The Francis Frith Collection)*

13, The Prince of Wales Public House on Manor Road Chigwell (Circa 1900), destroyed by a Parachute Mine April 1941

14, The Three Jolly Wheelers Public House at Woodford Bridge (Photograph courtesy of Geoff Hamilton)

15, The old Police Station at Woodford Bridge

16, The Bald Hind Public House

INTRODUCTION

Europe in 1914 was a fragile place made up of two alliances, on one side was Germany the largest of the central powers, ruled by Kaiser Wilhelm II the grandson of Queen Victoria. Born in 1859 the Kaiser was the son of 'Vicky' the Princess Royal of Great Britain and 'Fritz', the crown prince of Prussia. Austria–Hungary was an ally of Germany and ruled by Francis Joseph, his country had annexed Bosnia and Herzegovina in 1908 upsetting Serbia and causing unrest in the Balkans, the heir to the Austro–Hungarian throne was Archduke Franz Ferdinand. On the other side was Russia ruled by Tsar Nicholas II, also related to Queen Victoria and the British Royal Family via marriage. Russia who felt the annexation of Bosnia and Herzegovina to be unfair was an ally of Serbia as well as an ally of France. Russia's alliance with France stretched back to the 1890's when France had supplied her with armaments and also financed the building of her railways. In return France knew that having Russia as an ally was in her best interest whilst Russia saw France as a country that could steady the ship with the central powers should a problem arise in the Balkans. Also in this alliance was Great Britain, ruled in 1914 by King George V he was also a grandson of Queen Victoria, he came to the throne upon the death of his father Edward VII in 1911. Britain's alliance with France originated from both countries protecting their colonial interests in North Africa. In 1906 Germany had tried to provoke a war with France, this did nothing but strengthen British and French relations and opened the eyes of the governments of both countries to the fact that one day a war with Germany might become a reality. At the prospect of this both Britain and France decided secretly that should it become necessary their armies would fight together. As for Britain's alliance with Russia this stemmed from both countries interests in various parts of the Middle East and Asia. With this triple entente of Britain, France and Russia - although it was not written that if individually attacked each would come to each others aid - Germany was made to feel encircled. With Germany only having Austria as an ally it was with the utmost importance that relations were kept strong between Vienna and Berlin. In the Kaisers eyes Austria held the gates to the near east - today known as the Middle East - and gulf of Persia where German interests were centred. During the years before the war Germany had increased her influence on Turkey, if trouble arose she saw the Turkish Ottoman Empire as a possible ally as it was destined to become in October 1914.

On 28th June 1914 a young Bosnian Serb called Gavrilo Princip assassinated Archduke Franz Ferdinand whilst the Archduke and his wife were visiting the Bosnian capital of Sarajevo. Gavrilo belonged to an organization known as the Black Hand Terrorists who sought independence for Bosnia. Austro-Hungary, believing the Serbian government to be involved in the assassination demanded justice for the crime but Serbia refused to hand over those responsible, therefore on 28th July Austro-Hungary declared war on Serbia. It was then that Serbia turned to Russia for help and on the 30th July Russia began mobilizing her armies in support. Germany warned Russia that if she didn't stop mobilization a state of war would exist between them; Russia had backed down to German threats before and had vowed never to do so again. Ignoring German threats Russia continued mobilization; as a result on 1st August 1914 Germany declared war on Russia. As a precaution France was asked to surrender the fortresses along her border with Germany, she was also asked to remain neutral, she refused both requests so on 3rd August 1914 Germany declared war on France. Germany had anticipated a war with France and Russia for some time so in the event of this happening a plan had been compiled. This plan detailed a way of attacking France by crossing through Belgium; this route avoided the heavily defended Franco/German border at Alsace and Lorraine. The French provinces of Alsace and Lorraine had been lost to Germany during the Franco-Prussian War of 1870-1871, by marching through Belgium Germany fully expected to defeat France before the Russians became fully effective. Great Britain had signed a treaty back in 1832 vowing to protect Belgian sovereignty in case of invasion therefore on 3rd August the country's ruler King Albert turned to Great Britain for help. King Albert vowed to fight anyone that invaded his country as best as he could so as German troops entered Belgium on route to France it was expected that British troops would be called on to assist. Respecting the terms of the treaty on 4th August 1914 Great Britain declared war on Germany having first requested, without answer, that German troops leave Belgian soil. The countries of Europe were at war but it would not take long for their conflict to involve other countries from across the world, as a result of a gunshot the First World War had begun.

Map 3, Europe in 1914 (Map taken from 'The origins of the First World War' by James Joll and reproduced courtesy of Longman /Pearson Educational Publishing)

1914

'The outbreak of war has come upon us all and Europe has been plunged into a struggle of nations such as the world has never seen'.

Chigwell Parish Magazine September 1914

During the opening days of war the battle lines were drawn, Russia clashed with Austro-Hungry on her southern borders as German troops moved eastwards to meet Russian troops on their joint frontier, to the west on the 4th August 1914 German troops entered Belgium on their way to France. In 1905 Count Von Schlieffen, the chief of staff of the German Army from 1892-1906, had devised a plan. The Germans would use this plan should there be a war with France and Russia at the same time; this plan was appropriately called 'The Schlieffen Plan'. It consisted of entering France through Holland and Belgium as the French and German border at Alsace and Lorraine was heavily defended as outlined in the Introduction. The Schlieffen Plan was designed to defeat the French before Russia's armies could fully mobilise. By attacking France through Holland and then Belgium, on entering Northern France it was thought that the French armies could be outflanked and surrounded as they fell back and tried to protect Paris. The Kaiser said 'We can be in Paris in a fortnight'. However Helmuth Von Moltke, the Chief of Staff of the German Army in 1914, had tampered with the plan. Instead of bringing the German Army through Holland he avoided it at the same time respecting the wish of the Dutch government to remain neutral. This action however took the German forces longer thus slowing down the pace of their advance. The Belgian Army, like any force trying to protect both its country and citizens, put up a rigid defence of its towns, villages and fortresses but the Germans fought harder. The Belgians were vastly outnumbered by the sheer size of their opponents' army and its superior weapon capabilities, as a result on 20th August the Belgian capital Brussels fell to the Germans.

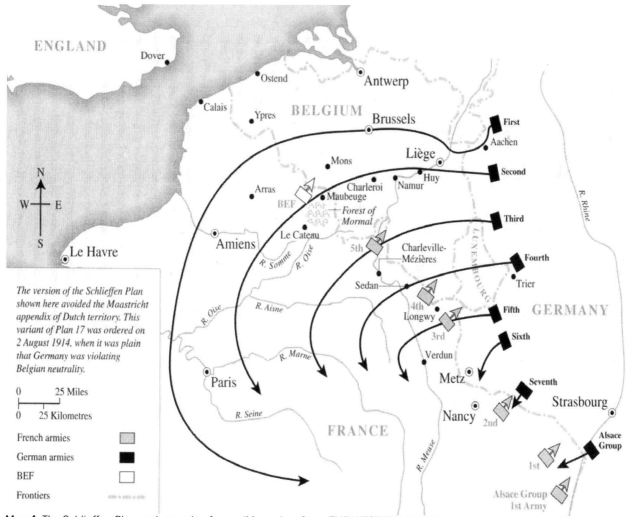

Map 4, The Schlieffen Plan and opposing forces (Map taken from 'THE WESTERN FRONT' (BBC Books) by Richard Holmes. Reprinted by permission of The Random House Group Ltd)

The British Expeditionary Force (BEF) was the name of the British Army in France and Flanders, commanded by Field Marshal Sir John French the BEF was sent to France in great secrecy in August 1914. French was a seasoned soldier and a veteran of both the Sudanese campaign (1884 -1885) and the Boer War (1899 -1902), very much his own man he was 62 years old as the Great War started.

The BEF some 100,000 men strong consisted of a Cavalry Division commanded by Major General Edmund Allenby. The Cavalry Division was made up of five cavalry brigades numbered from 1 to 5, each brigade contained three battalions and also had sections of RHA attached. The infantry of the BEF was divided into two corps initially numbered I and II. Each corps contained two divisions numbered 1, 2, 3 and 5. The divisions were made up of three brigades numbered from 1-9 and 13-15.

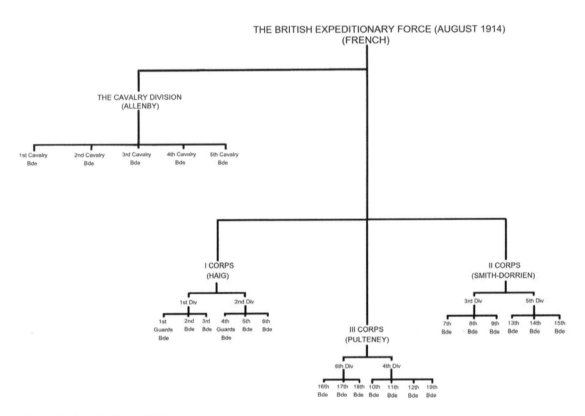

Map 5, The BEF (August 1914)

Each brigade was made up of four battalions and had various units of artillery attached (1). I Corps under the control of Lieutenant General Sir Douglas Haig consisted of the 1st and 2nd Divisions. The 1st Division contained Brigades 1, 2 and 3 whilst the 2nd Division contained Brigades 4, 5 and 6. II Corps consisted of the 3rd and 5th Divisions. The 3rd Division contained Brigades 7, 8 and 9 whilst the 5th Division contained Brigades 13, 14 and 15. Another two divisions, the 6th containing Brigades 16, 17 and 18 and the 4th containing Brigades 10, 11, 12 and 19 and would arrive later to make up III Corps. II Corps initially came under the control of Lieutenant General Sir J M Grierson however his appointment didn't last long as he died of a heart attack on his way to take control; his replacement therefore was General Sir Horace Smith-Dorrien. Grierson's replacement did not sit well with Sir John French as he disliked Smith-Dorrien and doubted his ability to command an entire corps; the decision however had been made by the Secretary of State for War Lord Kitchener. It was a good choice by Kitchener as Smith-Dorrien was an experienced soldier; he had been one of only a few men to survive the Battle of Isandhlwana at the hands of the Zulu's in January 1879.

The BEF crossed the channel between the 14th August and 16th August and on entering the French port of Le Havre moved inland placing itself on the French Fifth Army's left flank (see map 4). The French Army initially had five army groups, commanded by Joseph Joffre; the French were positioned with the First Army group in the south and the Fifth, commanded by General Charles Lanrezac up in the north. As they advanced forward into Belgium to engage the German forces the BEF found itself on 21st August and 22nd August inland as far as the town of Mons. Smith-Dorrien's II Corps held the BEF left flank whilst Haig's I Corps held the right. In early August 1914 the German Army in France and Belgium consisted of seven army groups plus a detachment known as the Alsace group. The German First Army was positioned to the north spreading downwards with the seventh to the south, the

Alsace group being positioned at Alsace and Lorraine. The First Army commanded by General Von Kluck on Sunday 23rd August clashed with Smith-Dorrien's II Corps by the canal at Mons. Involved in this action were 7th, 8th and 9th Brigades from Dorrien's 3rd Division and the 13th and 14th Brigades from his 5th Division. Smith-Dorrien lost in the region of 1500 men in this action but German casualties were higher. British rifle fire had been overwhelming and the Germans said later *"the British were entrenched and hidden, for us it was like fighting an invisible enemy"*. The Kaiser had called the British Army a *"contemptible little army"* he did not think the British could or would pose a problem, the action at Mons had proved the BEF as a force to be reckoned with and for years afterwards the survivors of Mons would be known as the "Old Contemptibles".

During the early hours on the 24th August the French Fifth Army, on the BEF's right, started to fall back without consultation. Therefore in order not to be surrounded on their now open right flank it was left up to the BEF corps commanders Haig and Smith-Dorrien to follow suit. Sir John French was not at all pleased with not being informed of the French Fifth's withdrawal. The BEF fell back reluctantly into France. They had scored a victory at Mons and were disappointed at having to retreat. The Germans were in pursuit. Haig's I Corps fell back easily to the French town of Landrecies then Smith-Dorrien's II Corps retreated; the 3rd Division first and the 5th Division soon after, on 25th August these units found themselves positioned to the west of Le Cateau. That night Haig's 4th Guard's Brigade, part of his 2nd Division, was attacked at Landrecies by elements of a small German force and over reacting the corps commander thought he was under heavy attack. Smith-Dorrien whose orders were to retreat knew the Germans would be on top of him if he fell back immediately; his men were tired so against orders he made the decision to stand and fight (2). By making a stand Smith-Dorrien hoped he could buy some time before continuing II Corps retreat; it was in this action that Chigwell sustained its first casualty of the First World War.

HAROLD HENRY SHUTTLE

Harold Henry Shuttle was born in Chigwell in 1895 the son of Frederick and Emma Matilda Shuttle; his father had been born in 1868 whilst his mother whose maiden name had been Hepburn was born in 1867. Harold had a brother called Edgar and at least one sister we know to be Edith. His grandparents had been Henry and Elizabeth Jane Shuttle, his grandfather had been Parish Clerk for Chigwell for some 20 odd years during which time both lived at the Workmen's Hall in Chigwell. Elizabeth died in August 1899 whilst Henry lived until January 1907; both are buried in St Mary's Churchyard. Frederick Shuttle was known as Fred; in January 1911 he also became Parish Clerk for Chigwell, at this time the family lived at 2 Fern Cottages, Brunel Road, Woodford Bridge. A short time later the Shuttle family moved around the corner to 5 Smeaton Road, Woodford Bridge. Very little is known of Harold's early life but it appears he joined the army quite soon after leaving school, when war broke out he was already a regular soldier. The British Army before the war was made up totally of volunteers, men usually enlisted into its ranks for a period of seven years. It seems Harold joined the army with his friend Frederick William Barton; both men had enlisted at Bedford however it's unclear why they chose this location. Both were posted to the 1st Battalion Bedfordshire Regiment their army service numbers being 9734 and 9762 respectively.

On 4th August 1914 the 1st Bedfordshire Regiment were stationed at Mullingar in Central Ireland and on 5th August received orders to mobilize. This according to the battalion war diary went smoothly and to schedule although the battalion didn't move as early as expected. During this delay the men engaged in route marches, musketry skills and other duties in order to prepare them for what lay ahead. On 15th August at 2:00am the 1st Bedford's boarded a train at Mullingar bound for Belfast, from there the following afternoon they boarded the ship SS Oronsa and then set sail for France; the battalion landed at the port of La Havre later that night. During the early hours of 16th August the men marched into camp, which according to the war diary was described as being on top of a hill and very muddy. The next two days saw more travelling for the men. Eventually around midnight on 18th August they arrived at basic accommodation – known as billets - in the French village of Pommereuil just north of Le Cateau. By this time Harold had been promoted achieving the rank of corporal. The next two days were spent waiting for more units to arrive; the 1st Bedford's would eventually join the BEF as part of II Corps, 5th Division. Commanded by Major General Sir C Fergusson as earlier mentioned 5th Division contained the 13th 14th and 15th Infantry Brigades, the latter commanded by Brigadier General A.E.W. Gleichen contained the following battalions: 1st Battalion Norfolk Regiment, 1st Battalion Cheshire Regiment, 1st Battalion Bedfordshire Regiment and 1st Battalion Dorsetshire Regiment.

On the 21st August Harold's battalion started their advance to Mons and two days later, as the rest of 5th Division were involved in fighting, according to their war diary the 1st Bedford's were ordered to proceed to the village of Wasmes southwest of Mons to reconnoitre the area and dig trenches. At this time no immediate fighting was expected but the men were shelled whilst carrying out these tasks, it was to be their first taste of action. That afternoon the enemy did attack and the Bedford's suffered some casualties. Early next morning Harold's battalion was ordered to fall back holding as long as possible the various houses and bridges on route as they went. So it was that on 25th August the Bedford's and most of II Corps found themselves positioned back at La Cateau. The Bedford's by this time were very tired and footsore although there was no time to rest as they set to work preparing defences. The Bedford's war diary states that the battalion held very good trenches; this would have a tremendous effect over the hours to come.

The Germans attacked from a northerly direction at dawn on 26th August commencing the Battle of Le Cateau, the weather that day was both warm and dry. The main assaults were made by German cavalry corps to the west on the British left flank around the town of Caudry, these positions being held by the newly arrived 4th Division under the command of Major General T Snow. The HQ of 4th Division was based at Haucourt just south of their main positions.

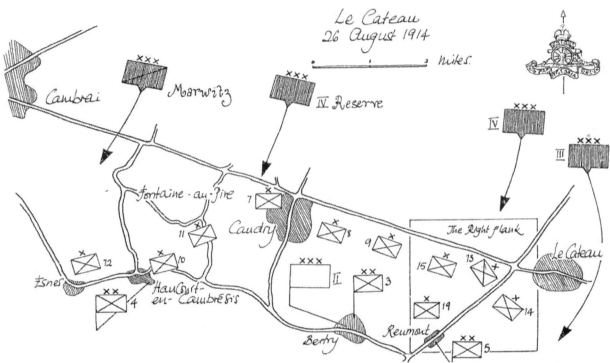

Map 6, Le Cateau (Map taken from 'RIDING THE RETREAT' (Pimlico) by Richard Holmes. Reprinted by permission of The Random House Group Ltd)

II Corps HQ along with 3rd Division HQ had been established in the town of Bertry about 3 miles to the east. 5th Division HQ was situated at Reumont 2 miles east of Bertry southwest of Le Cateau. The 5th Division was deployed a mile north of Reumont with its 14th Brigade on the right flank, 13th Brigade centre and 15th Brigade on the left next to 9th Brigade of 3rd Division. Both the 13th and 14th Brigades came under attack by divisions of the German Third Army. During the battle of Le Cateau battalions of 15th Brigade suffered the least casualties finding themselves away from the main German thrusts. They were however attacked by members of the Eighth Division of the German Fourth Army and SDGW lists the Dorset's as losing 3 men one of whom died of wounds, the Cheshire's had 1 man killed whilst the Norfolk's amazingly suffered no casualties. The Germans had been held back during the morning by British artillery and rifle fire but by mid afternoon the 3rd and 5th Division had been pushed back to the line of Bertry and Reumont. At 5:00pm II Corps retreat was back underway and by midnight it was situated 10 miles southwest of Le Cateau.

During the course of the day's action the 1st Bedford's had suffered little owing to their good trench positions. They had held out long enough to cover the retirement of their guns, eventually they fell back with some difficulty over flat ground and open country reaching the French village of Estrées around midnight. According to SDGW the battalion lost 6 men but their war diary puts casualty figures much higher at 1 officer and 30 men. One of those men lost by the Bedford's that day was 19 year old Cpl Harold Henry Shuttle (3). Like so many men killed in the Great War Harold's body was lost in battle and never recovered, in fact out of the six men SDGW lists as lost by the 1st Bedford's that day not one has a known grave. It is the belief of the CWGC that every man who was killed during the First World War should be commemorated. Throughout the various theatres of war that the conflict covered memorials to the missing exist that list the names of all those who have no known grave. Those men lost in the retreat from Mons and its subsequent battles during the period August to October 1914 are commemorated on the La Ferté-Sous-Jouarre Memorial to the Missing. This memorial includes the name of Cpl Harold Henry Shuttle and lies in a small park on the south side of the River Marne - in the town of La Ferté-Sous-Jouarre - about 65 miles east of Paris.

During the course of the war the Shuttle family lost also two cousins one of whom was awarded the Military Medal. In October 1914 the Chigwell Parish Magazine reported the death of Cpl Harold Shuttle stating that he had died a *"soldier's death in the retreat from Le Cateau"*, it goes on to say *"those who realise what that was know he died a hero"*. Put there by his father shortly after his death, Harold's name appears on his grandparent's gravestone inside St Mary's Churchyard. It seems that even though the parish had called Harold a hero Fred Shuttle felt nobody really cared about the death of his son and the sacrifice he'd made, this is evident as on the gravestone under the name Cpl Harold Henry Shuttle are the words:

IS IT NOTHING TO YOU, ALL YE THAT PASS BY?

Any doubts I may have had about wanting to write this book disappeared on reading those words.

* * *

After Le Cateau the retreat continued. The French Army commander Joseph Joffre met with Sir John French in Paris and the two men decided they would work together in order not to have a repeat of the breakdown in communications that had occurred at Mons, it had been Lord Kitchener who insisted the two men work as a team. At the beginning of September as the German First Army pushed further forward into France it was spotted by an allied aviator turning southwards in front of Paris; the French government by this time had relocated to Bordeaux. General Von Moltke by now made another mistake; when desperately needed in France he'd sent two German corps east to stem the Russian advance. The German Second Army had become nervous and was leaving gaps, Von Kluck's First Army turned to plug these gaps and in doing so it offered its right flank wide open to possible attack. The French had by now formed a new army. The Sixth Army commanded by General Monoury attacked this open flank in the French valley of the Marne. Opening up the two German armies was the job of the BEF however they were slow to respond, the French Fifth Army however along with the newly formed Ninth Army to their right commanded by General Foch also attacked. The Germans had suffered heavily at this point and decided to retreat, the French called this action the 'Miracle of the Marne' and it became the turning point of the war.

Map 7, The Western Front (Map taken from 'The First World War' by Michael Howard and reproduced by permission of Oxford University Press)

The second week of September 1914 saw General Erich Von Falkenhayn take over command of the German Army from the dejected Von Moltke, mainly due to his own decisions the latter was suffering from depression over the losses his armies had sustained. By now the Germans had fallen back to the River Aisne and the allied armies were in hot pursuit. It had been raining after a hot summer, the river was heavily swollen and the Germans had dug themselves in on the far side. Intent on exploiting the gaps between the Germans the allies tried numerous efforts to shift them but all proved unsuccessful, as a result they dug themselves in opposite in an east - west direction. The logical step for both sides was to try to outflank each other by moving positions northward; this was a tactic that had worked before in the course of previous battles. So it was that the allies and the Germans tried to outflank each other and the action became known as 'The Race to the Sea'. The armies of each side moved north digging in as they went through the French countryside. Their path took them over the Somme River, in front of the town of Arras, through Lens and the mining town of Loos and across the Belgian border to Flanders, moving up in front of the town of Ypres they eventually reached the North Sea. The second week of October GHQ for the BEF had been established at St Omer, a French town about 25 miles from Calais, it would remain here until March 1916.

The route to the Channel Ports was of utmost importance for the BEF. This was their line of communication and if it was cut the British Army in France and Flanders would no longer be able to function. As the Race to the Sea continued various divisions of the BEF were withdrawn from their positions in the south and placed in the Flanders area further north. The British felt the Germans could be confronted successfully around the Belgian town of Ypres. The town of Ypres mainly made it's living from textiles and in its centre stood its impressive cloth hall. Ypres would be home to the British Army for the remainder of the war and a scene of bitter fighting. Chigwell would lose three further men in the Flanders area before the end of 1914 and all of the actions that claimed their lives collectively became known as 'The First Battle of Ypres'.

The Belgian Army held most of the area north of Ypres to the coast along with French units. The British Army held Ypres itself and the area south including the border between France and Belgium. The British lines finished at the French town of Givenchy, where after that the remainder of the front was the responsibility of the French Army. Mainly farmland, the countryside of Flanders had one problem; it could become waterlogged and therefore extremely muddy. The third week in October saw Smith-Dorrien's II Corps holding the southern end of the British sector of line around the French towns of Aubers and La Bassée and it was in this area around this time that Chigwell lost its next man.

CHARLES LEONARD HARRUP

In the event of war or in times of national importance any man who had served with the colours after his initial period of seven years service was over could be recalled to the army, in August 1914 this is what happened to Charles Harrup. These recalls were necessary in order to bring various army units back up to full strength. Known as army reservists these men were trained soldiers therefore quite valuable however having been detached from the day to day life of army routine for a while some found they weren't as fit physically as they once might have been. This said on recall they were still required to offer themselves ready for duty, Charles Harrup did just this reporting to a recruiting office at Stratford in East London. Subsequently he was posted to the 1st Battalion Dorsetshire Regiment and given army service number 7001 (4). Charles Leonard Harrup was born in Chigwell in 1886, his mother Mrs Alice Harrup was a charwoman and widowed with five sons. Charles was the third son; his two older brothers were Alfred and Frederick with the two youngest being Ernest and Arthur. The family lived at 5 Watkins Cottages on Snakes Lane in Woodford and when he was 16 years old Charles worked as both a houseboy and general handyman. Although it's not known when he first joined the army Charles met and married his wife Ellen Louisa Harrup, they had two children and lived together – near the Shuttle family - at 37 Smeaton Road, Woodford Bridge, Essex.

The 1st Dorset's had been stationed in Belfast when war broke out but having been strengthened landed at Le Havre on the afternoon of 16th August, like the 1st Bedford's the battalion was attached to 15th Brigade, 5th Division. On joining his unit Charles would have been involved in the fighting that took place on the 24th August as well as the battle of Le Cateau. The Battle of La Bassée as it came to be known was played out between the 16th October and 2nd November 1914. On 16th October Smith-Dorrien's II Corps were positioned on a staggered front that stretched from Givenchy in the south about 2 miles west of La Bassée, to the town of Aubers about 6 miles to the north (see map 8). On 19th October they were about half a mile further east of those positions, and by 20th October their line had been pushed forward again holding a position in the north just to the east of Aubers. Their southern sector was just west of La Bassée, which lay behind the German lines. On II Corps left flank - to the north - the line was held by the French First Cavalry Corps. II Corps 3rd Division held the line in front of Aubers and roughly three miles south to the village of Lorgies. 5th Division held the lines south of Lorgies to a railway line that ran southwest out of La Bassée, beyond that the French Army's Twenty First Corps held the line. The 5th Division (5) were deployed with their 14th Brigade holding Lorgies, on their left was 7th Brigade of 3rd Division. To their right separated by the village of Beau Puits was 13th Brigade who held the lines south to the village of Violaines. 15th Brigade held the southern half of Violaines to a line just west of the village of Canteleux about half a mile west of La Bassée. The 20th October saw fighting all along II Corps front, their opposition being the German Seventh Corps made up of their Thirteenth Division and Fourteenth Division. The 15th Brigade had been involved on and off in the fighting around their section of the line between Violaines and Canteleux although it must be said it was far from serious, their casualty figures on this day according to SDGW were:

1st Dorset's = 1 KIA + 1 Dow
1st Cheshire's = 2 KIA + 1 Dow
1st Bedford's = 1 KIA
1st Norfolk's = 3 KIA

During the day and night of the 21st October the fighting continued but 15th Brigade's losses were not too bad. The war diary of the 1st Dorset's reported, at 5:30am heavy firing in the direction of Violaines. Then at 4:30pm a report was received that the Cheshire's were retreating from the village. At 5:00pm this retirement was checked and then at 6:45pm the 1st Dorset's 'A' Coy were ordered to entrench just west of Violaines. On Thursday 22nd October at 2:30am heavy firing was now reported coming from the direction of Lorgies. 'A' Coy were to support the units falling back from Violaines but by now were coming under fire themselves from Lorgies. Orders were received that they should hold on at all costs. At 5:50am the Germans finally pushed the Cheshire's out of Violaines cheering as they went.

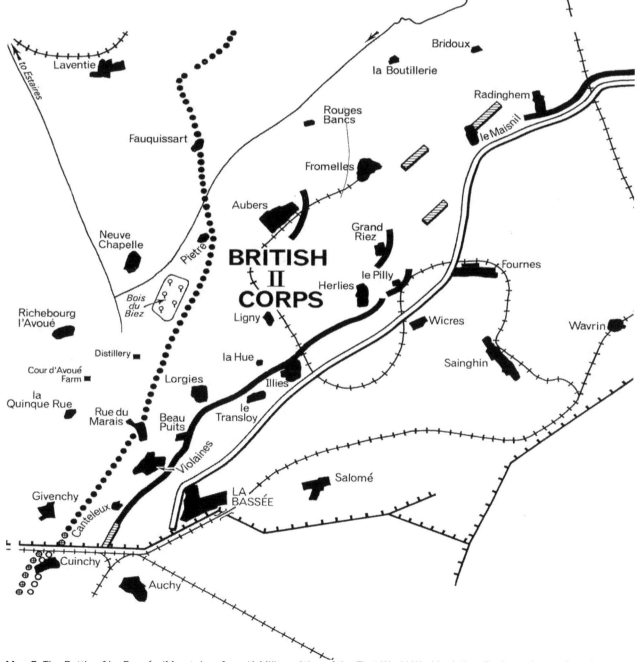

Map 8, The Battle of La Bassée (Map taken from 'A Military Atlas of the First World War' by Arthur Banks and reproduced courtesy of Pen and Sword Publishing)

The Dorset's placed machine guns south of the road west from the village in order to halt any German attack. They also rushed one forward under the cover of darkness to sweep the road leading from the village but were too late losing both the gunner and the gun. The enemy managed to mount a machine gun at the north end of Violaines firing west towards the Dorset's trenches. The Dorset's war diary states that one platoon of 'A' Coy stayed behind holding up the German assault. Managing to hold on till dusk, supported by men of the KOSB on its left, this platoon's action had enabled all other units to withdraw safely. As these units fell back however some of their number held ground taking up positions in front of the village of Rue du Marais. At 7:00am more positions were established further west in front of the village of La Quinque Rue and machine guns were placed in front of the village again to halt possible German attack. As the units of 15th Brigade converged on La Quinque Rue so it was that the Germans tired for the day and their attacks petered out, the rest of the day remained quiet and the 1st Dorset's were withdrawn to billets in Festubert at 8:00pm. Throughout the day the fighting had been intense at times and casualties for 15th Brigade according to SDGW were:

1st Cheshire's = 52 KIA + 1 Dow
1st Bedford's = 15 KIA
1st Norfolk's = 4 KIA + 1 Dow

The 1st Dorset's lost 26 men according to SDGW but their war diary puts that day's casualties at 22 killed and 101 wounded or missing, one of those killed was Pte Charles Harrup most likely attached to 'A' Coy. Out of the 26 men of the 1st Dorset's who fell whilst covering withdrawals on 22nd October 1914 only two have a known grave, the other 24 including Charles Harrup are commemorated on the Le Touret Memorial to the Missing at Le Touret CWGC Cemetery, Pas de Calais France. This memorial commemorates over 13,000 men who were killed in the area before 25th September 1915 and have no known grave. Mrs Ellen Harrup would have received a telegram soon after from the war office informing her of the news that her husband was missing, it would be more than a year before he was officially confirmed as having been killed. In January 1916 the Chigwell Parish Magazine added Charles Harrup to their then growing Roll of Honour. On 11th February 1916 a short obituary appeared in the Woodford Times newspaper reporting that Charles had been killed in France, it also contained this short poem placed by his family:

> "We never knew what pain he had
> We never saw him die
> We only know he passed away
> Without a last goodbye"

* * *

During the course of the next two days the British lines were pushed back with Aubers, Canteleux, Lorgies and La Quinque Rue all falling into German hands. On II Corps left the French First Cavalry Corps was replaced with the Indian Lahore Division (6). II Corps was deployed with its 3rd Division on its left in the north with its 8th Brigade separated from the Indian division on its left by the village of Fauquissart, about a mile west of Aubers. On 8th Brigade's right stood 9th Brigade who were separated from 7th Brigade by the village of Neuve Chapelle. On 27th October the German Fourteenth Division attacked Neuve Chapelle forcing both 7th Brigade and 8th Brigade back. The village subsequently fell into German hands with the British lines stabilizing some quarter of a mile to the west. The 5th Division held the southern sector of II Corps line with the 14th Brigade on its left flank next to 7th Brigade, 3rd Division. The 14th Brigade held the village of Richborg L'Avoué and further south on their right was 13th Brigade .To the right of 13th Brigade the 15th Brigade held the line to Givenchy and beyond that stood the French Army. The British dug in as the fighting in this sector was by no means over.

* * *

Back home in England Lord Kitchener had started a major recruiting campaign to get people to join the army. The popular feeling was that the war would not last long and most people were convinced it would be over by Christmas, this was not a feeling held by Lord Kitchener who felt that the war would last at least three years. Lord Herbert Horatio Kitchener of Khartoum to give him his full title had made his name whilst serving in various colonial campaigns and it had been him who'd brought the Boer War to a successful conclusion. He was looked up to and respected and a hero in the eyes of the British people. He had been in the process of taking up a ministerial position in Egypt when war broke out but was recalled and subsequently made minister for war by the Liberal Prime Minister Herbert Asquith.

The regular British Army numbered a quarter of a million men upon the outbreak of war. It consisted of eight divisions numbered 1 – 8, five of these as we have seen formed part of the original BEF; this figure however did not include the reservists or the Territorial Force.

The Territorial Army was created in 1908, consisting largely of infantry and cavalry (known as yeomanry) units its purpose was mainly to look after defences back home should the regular army be called on to serve overseas. The 'Terriers' or 'Saturday Night Soldiers' as they were sometimes called enrolled for four years service. They attended two week training camps annually as well as other meets at weekends throughout the year. As they were intended for home defence only they had to volunteer for overseas service in times of war. Any man who enlisted into the Territorial Force when war broke out was entitled to an automatic discharge upon its conclusion. The Territorial Force like the regular army was made up of divisions and battalions. Most county regiments had two regular battalions, a reserve battalion as well as a territorial battalion e.g.

The Essex Regiment

1st Battalion = Regular
2nd Battalion = Regular
3rd Battalion = Reserve
4th Battalion = Territorial

Soon after the outbreak of war the Territorial Army received orders to separate those men who had volunteered for overseas service from those who had not. Those men who hadn't volunteered along with new recruits were kept behind to form new battalions that were held in reserve. The idea was that when the main battalion went overseas drafts from this reserve unit would be sent out as and when needed. Known as second and third lines these newly created battalions would take their numbered title from their original so in the case of the Essex Regiment the 4th Battalion became the 1/4th Battalion and the newly created reserve was the 2/4th Battalion. If the 2/4th Battalion were required to head overseas again separation would take place and the small amount of men they left behind would create the 3/4th Battalion. During the course of the war there could be as many as four Territorial battalions in a regiment all having spin offs of each other. Some regiments however were purely Territorial, an example of this was the Cambridgeshire Regiment which had one battalion with four spin offs. Another example was the London Regiment which had up to 28 battalions each having up to three (sometimes four) spin-off battalions. What was special here was some of those battalions had names attached. For instance the 12th Battalion was called the 'Rangers' and the 17th Battalion based in Bow East London were called the 'Poplar and Stepney Rifles' whilst the 8th Battalion initially created from postal workers was called the 'Post Office Rifles'. All territorial battalions were formed into numbered brigades and sometimes named with area affiliations e.g. 162nd (East Midland) Brigade. Originally the Territorial Army had designated divisions of the areas they were from; London for instance initially had two Territorial divisions numbered 1st London and 2nd London. Just like the battalions multiplied these divisions created second lines of themselves in case the first were needed overseas, this was done by using the second line battalions. During the course of the war two more London territorial divisions would be created in this way so the 1st London became 1/1st and 2/1st and the 2nd London became 2/1st and 2/2nd. Another example of this was the North Midland Division and the South Midland Division which both formed a second division of each other using their second line battalions. Although those that had them kept their area titles all territorial divisions were later numbered from 42 – 62 and 64 – 69.

Kitchener did not rate the Territorial Army and he knew that more men would be needed. During the first week of August 1914 he made the first of his appeals for volunteers to join his new army. His request was initially for 100,000 men, posters appeared all over the country with Kitchener on them pointing his finger with the words "Your Country Needs You", wherever you stood whilst looking at the poster his finger seemed to point at you. During the first eight weeks of recruitment more than 750,000 volunteers joined the army, from all over the country men rushed to join what became known as the 'New Armies' or 'Kitcheners Army'. These men enlisted for four years or the duration of the war, after a successful medical they were required to complete a period of basic training. The first 100,000 volunteers had been recruited within two weeks; these men were formed into county battalions just like the regular army but these new battalions were designated 'Service' battalions. The battalions were then formed into six new divisions named K1 (Kitchener 1) and numbered from 9-14.

Just like with the Territorial divisions these New Army divisions also took area titles from where they were created e.g.

9th (Scottish)
10th (Irish)
11th (Northern)
12th (Eastern)
13th (Western)
14th (Light) (7)

Another 100,000 men were recruited and these were to form another six divisions. Named K2 their divisions numbered 15 – 20 also having area affiliations e.g.

15th (Scottish)
16th (Irish)
17th (Northern)

K3 was made up of the next 100,000 volunteers and consisted of divisions 21- 26 these divisions however had no area titles. So many men came forward that another six divisions could be formed. Called K4 and initially numbered from 27 – 32 they were eventually renumbered. The reason for this being that by this time regular army troops had arrived from across the British Empire, they were formed into divisions and numbered 27, 28 and 29 therefore the divisions that made up K4 were re numbered 30 – 35. Rather than use K4 as service battalions it was decided that it would be held as a reserve. A fifth 'New Army' was created in the second week of December 1914 its divisions initially numbered 37 - 42 but as K4 was to be put into reserve this new fifth army became the new K4 and took the original divisional numbers 30–35. The men that made up these divisions had been recruited locally and were known as 'Pals' battalions. Men were recruited from the same towns and sometimes the battalions took the names of these towns as well e.g. 10th East Yorkshire Regiment was also known as the 'Hull Pals'. Also another example of this was the 15th Battalion West Yorkshire Regiment also known as the 'Leeds Pals'. Pals battalions came about as friends were encouraged to join the army together; they were also told they could serve together. Sometimes the men from entire streets or local factories would join up together but the downside of this was if a battalion suffered heavy casualties a whole street or community could be wiped out. The battalions that made up these divisions also took their names from certain professions (like mentioned with the Territorial Army) e.g. 16th Battalion Yorkshire and Lancashire Regiment was also called the 'Transport Workers Battalion'. As the war went on these battalions inevitably sustained losses therefore the 'Pals' battalions were reinforced with new recruits, gradually as time went on their identities changed. The last New Army was created during the first quarter of 1915, designated the sixth 'New Army' it was raised locally and made up of 'Pals' and 'Workers' battalions. Originally its divisions were numbered 37– 42. As the K5 moved to K4 the sixth 'New army' became the new K5 and its divisional numbers changed to those of the original K5 being 36 – 41. Amongst these divisions only two had area affiliations:

36th (Ulster) Division - formed from members of the UVF (Ulster Volunteer Force). The UVF was created to calm tensions resulting from the debate in early 1914 concerning home rule in Ireland.

38th (Welsh) Division – Raised by the Liberal Party MP and future Prime Minister David Lloyd George.

The various divisions of the British Army will be referred to by their numbers, to work out the type of division e.g. Regular, 'New Army' or Territorial consult the following list:-

ARMY DIVISIONS

1 – 8 + 27, 28 and 29 = Regular Army

9 – 26 & 30 – 41 = New Army (Kitcheners Army)

42 – 62 & 64 – 69 = Territorial Force

63 = Royal Naval Division (8)

With this rapid expansion the British Army found that during the first months of the war it was short of uniforms, guns, tools and many other things it needed to operate effectively, in time however this situation was overcome. As you would expect many men from Chigwell and its surrounding areas would become part of the 'New Armies' and Territorial Force during the course of the First World War.

* * *

Whilst the Battle of La Bassée was in progress there was also heavy fighting taking place further north along the British lines. In this early stage of the war the armies of both sides were still staking their claims to the countryside of France and Flanders.

With the 'First Battle of Ypres' in progress our attention is turned to a French town positioned just south of the Belgian border. Armentières made its living mainly from Brewing and Linen production, with the River Lys running through its northern side heading up into Belgium Armentières was a strategic point. Many railway lines ran through the town mainly along its southern edge serving all parts of Northern France including the city of Lille (9). More importantly to the British these rail lines ran to St Omer and the Channel Ports and could therefore serve the BEF lines of supply.

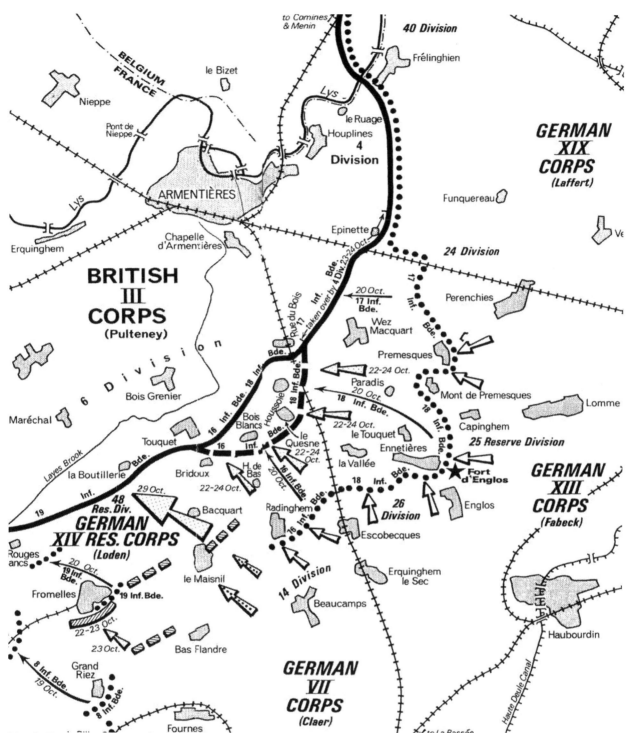

Map 9, The Battle of Armentières 19th October - 2nd November 1914 (Map taken from 'A Military Atlas of the First World War' by Arthur Banks and reproduced courtesy of Pen and Sword Publishing)

Sir William Pulteney was given the command of III Corps which consisted of Major General T Snow's 4th Division (formally attached to II Corps) and the 6th Division - under the command of Major General J Keir - which had arrived in France just prior to the BEF's re-deployment north to Flanders. III Corps commenced its advance to Armentières on 16th October. Holding positions just west of the town its units pushed forward during the course of the 17th October and 18th October finding themselves on 19th October with their left flank positioned two miles to the east (see map 9). From here III Corps line continued southwards before turning southwest eventually ending some three miles south of Armentières. Snow's 4th Division was holding III Corps left and deployed just north of the main Armentières to Lille railway line whilst to the south 6th Division held its positions on III Corps right. Instead of having three infantry brigades attached as was normal in 1914 the 6th Division temporarily consisted of four infantry brigades. They were the: 16th (Infantry) Brigade, 17th (Infantry) Brigade, 18th (Infantry) Brigade and 19th (Infantry) Brigade (10). On 6th Division's left 17th Brigade held the front lines south of the railway to the village of Premesques. During the course of the 20th October their positions were pushed back some one and a half miles to the villages of Epinette and Rue du Bois where they remained until the 23rd – 24th October, their opposition being troops of the German Twenty Fourth Division. This division formed part of the German Nineteenth Corps that in turn formed part of the German Sixth Army under the command of Crown Prince Rupprecht (11).

Alongside 17th Brigade was the 18th Brigade and on the 19th October their positions found them holding the lines between the village of Premesques and a railway line that ran southeast out of Armentières towards La Bassée. On the 20th October their positions were also attacked this time by troops of the German Twenty Fifth Reserve Division, as a result their lines were pushed back to a front stretching from Rue du Bois south to the village of Le Quesne about 2 miles south of Armentières. On 18th Brigade's right flank stood 16th Brigade and on 19th October its units held the front from the Armentières – La Bassée rail line south to the village of Radinghem, serving in one of these units was Chigwell's next casualty.

EDWIN BIRD

Edwin Bird was born at Dagenham in Essex in 1886 the third son of Thomas and Annie Bird. At the turn of the century the family lived in Grange Hill. Thomas worked as a general labourer and at 15 years old Edwin worked alongside his father, as did his two older brothers Herbert and Thomas George. It is not known when Edwin first joined the army but like Charles Harrup it seems he was called up as part of the army reserve reporting to Woodford to re-enlist. Edwin was drafted into the 2nd Battalion Yorkshire & Lancashire Regiment, holding the rank of private he was given army service number 7639. In August 1914, prior to the outbreak of war, the 2nd York's & Lanc's were stationed at Limerick in southwest Ireland however once hostilities began the battalion was ordered back to England to reorganise and refit. On arrival the battalion was temporarily based near Cambridge and whilst there Pte Edwin Bird joined its ranks. The 2nd York's & Lanc's found itself attached to 6th Division as part of 16th Brigade and having been equipped was sent to France landing at St Nazaire on 9th September. The battalions that made up 16th Brigade were: 1st Battalion Buffs (East Kent Regiment), 1st Battalion Leicestershire Regiment, 1st Battalion KSLI (The Kings Shropshire Light Infantry) Regiment and the 2nd Battalion Yorkshire & Lancashire Regiment.

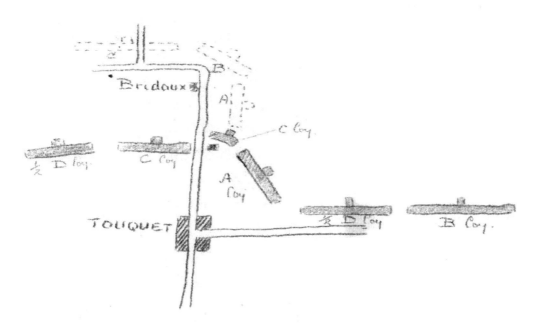

Map 10, Position of the 2nd York's & Lanc's 26th October – 30th October 1914 (NA Ref: WO95/1610)

On the 20th October the positions held by 16th Brigade were attacked by troops of the German Fourteenth Division (part of the German Seventh Corps attached to the German Sixth Army). The men of 16th Brigade fell back to a line that stretched from Le Quesne, due south to just west of the village of Bridoux. Over the next two days however III Corps positions were attacked along its whole front. Between 22nd October and 24th October the 16th Brigade gave more ground losing the village of Bois Blancs that had lay directly behind its frontline. Towards the end of October fighting continued with both sides trying to dominate the areas southeast of Armentières. With Bois Blancs now in German hands 16th Brigade found they were pushed back to the village of Touquet and it was here during the last week of October that Pte Edwin Bird and his battalion found themselves. Positioned to the southwest of the village during the course of 24th October the 2nd York's & Lanc's found themselves under constant enemy shellfire, that evening they were also subjected to small German attacks on their frontal positions.

The worst day during this period for 16th Brigade came on 25th October when the 1st Leicester's lost 38 men and the 1st KSLI lost 15 men. On this day the York's & Lanc's situation was virtually unchanged however whilst still being subjected to enemy shellfire they now found themselves the target of German snipers. It was because of constant shelling and sniping that on 26th October the commanding officer of 16th Brigade decided to withdraw the 2nd York's & Lanc's line slightly - along with a portion held by the KSLI - in order to achieve a better defensive position. This withdrawal was due to start at 9:00pm but was postponed until 11:00pm because some of the KSLI found themselves under attack. Eventually a new position was reached and completed by 12:30am at which point the battalion was met by reinforcements from brigade reserve in case the enemy chose to attack that night. Still situated southwest of Touquet but now occupying primitive trenches the withdrawal proved a waste of time as throughout the 27th October enemy sniping became more active although enemy shelling was just occasional. That evening at 7:30pm the Germans attacked the York's & Lanc's positions to the left and centre however this attack didn't last long and by 8:30pm the Germans had returned to their own positions. The York & Lanc's war diary states that during this exchange one officer was wounded. By mid morning on 28th October any movement out of the trenches became dangerous and that afternoon at about 2:15pm a heavy bombardment started chiefly aimed at battalion HQ situated in a farm to the rear of the frontline. These shells contained high explosive but by 5:30pm the barrage died down. That evening the battalion was again reinforced by units from brigade reserve in case of a night time attack by the enemy. Although shelling that night was heavy the enemy remained in their positions and at dawn the reinforcements moved back into reserve. Although relatively quiet on the morning of 29th October it wasn't long before German guns were active again, a continuous bombardment commenced along 16th Brigade's frontline particularly on Touquet village itself. By late evening extra troops were moved up in readiness for any pending assault by the enemy, in addition rear defensive positions were strengthened. At 10:00pm the Germans left their positions in small numbers and attacked positions held by the men of 2nd York's & Lanc's but once again they soon withdrew back towards their own lines. During this period 19th Brigade had been holding the lines on the extreme right of 6th Division's front, to their right stood French units whilst to the north on their left flank stood 16th Brigade. Throughout the previous week the units of 19th Brigade had suffered the same fate as the rest of 6th Division losing ground to the Germans as the Battle of Armentières ran its course. On the night of 29th/ 30th October their positions were attacked once more by enemy troops and with 16th Brigade to their left it was expected that they too would suffer some casualties. This fact was reported in the 2nd York's & Lanc's war diary and at 3:00am on the 30th October the entry reads: *'Heavy attack on 19th Brigade on our right, an attack expected on our line'.*

Although continually shelled that morning luckily no attack fell on the positions held by the 2nd York's & Lanc's, in fact the main thrust of the attack came about half a mile east of the village of La Boutillerie. On this day however the 2nd York and Lanc's war diary did report that two men were killed in action, although it doesn't say how they died it's most likely they were victims of enemy shellfire. Unfortunately one of the men was 28 year old Pte Edwin Bird; his death was reported in the December 1914 edition of the Chigwell Parish Magazine (12). Pte Edwin Bird has no known grave and his name appears on Panel 8 of the Ploegsteert (known as Plugstreet to the British) Memorial to the Missing. The memorial lies in the grounds of Berks CWGC Cemetery which is situated about 12 kilometres south of Ypres. It commemorates more than 11,000 men killed in the area - mostly in day to day trench warfare - during the course of the First World War. On the last Friday of every month the 'Last Post' is played at the memorial in honour of those men who fell.

* * *

The fighting known as the 'Battle of Armentières' continued for another three days until 2nd November 1914 by which time both sides had established rough trench lines in the area that would remain for the next four years, Armentières however remained in allied hands as did the village of Touquet. Further north, whilst the Battle of Armentières was in progress, the Germans were still trying to breakthrough the allied lines by attacking in strength around Ypres as well as in areas north of the town. The Germans had realised the importance of the Channel Ports to the allies (especially the British) and had attempted an advance towards them during the second week of October 1914 making Dunkirk, Calais and Boulogne their primary targets. As previously mentioned the allied line north of Ypres was held by the Belgian Army. By the 24th October the Belgian Army were not only tired but also running short of supplies. Along the Belgian coast the area consisted of sand dunes where the Belgian forces were entrenched but more importantly to the south towards Ypres the area was made up of a series of canals and ditches, the main canal being the Yser Canal. It was thought that if this area north of Ypres could be flooded this would in turn halt the German advance. The last week of October a series of dams were built, followed by the opening of sluice gates this successfully flooded the area north of Ypres between the Belgian towns of Nieuport and Dixmude (see map 7). This action worked well forming a barrier in front of the Germans; as a result by 30th October they virtually gave up their advance in this area, further south however they were still as active as ever.

The BEF's Cavalry Division during the early part of September and October 1914 underwent a change of formation. The original five brigades were split into two groups each forming a division. The 1st and 2nd Brigades (still consisting of three battalions each) formed the 1st Cavalry Division and were commanded up until October 1914 by Major General Edmund Allenby at which time Major General H de-Lisle took command. The 3rd Cavalry Brigade had been known as 'Goughs Command' during September. The 4th Brigade joined it in October and these two brigades with their battalions formed the 2nd Cavalry Division with Major General Sir Hubert Gough still retaining command. Since its arrival in France despite having been part of the Cavalry Division the 5th Cavalry Brigade had operated independently under its own command. Another cavalry division known as the 3rd Cavalry

Division had been raised in England during September, arriving in Belgium during the first week of October and commanded by Major General Sir Julian Byng it consisted initially of the 6th Cavalry Brigade and 7th Cavalry Brigade with another known as the 8th Cavalry Brigade joining in November 1914.

Map 11, The Ypres Salient – Tommy © Richard Holmes 2005 Reprinted by permission of HarperCollins Publishers Ltd

The cavalry regiments were divided into three main groups, the Household Cavalry mainly responsible for guarding the monarch, the Cavalry of the Line which acted as the main fighting forces and the Special Reserve whose jobs varied but included the training of new recruits. All the cavalry divisions had groups of RHA attached whose job it was to transport, deploy and use the small and light mobile guns that supported the cavalry when in action.

Since the 'First Battle of Ypres' had started on 18th October the Germans had been very active in trying to break the allied lines to the east of Ypres itself. During the last week of October the most northerly British positions were held by Haig's I Corps with its 1st and 2nd Division's doing well to hold their lines in the face of attacks by units of the German Fourth Army. To I Corps right stood IV Corps commanded by Sir Henry Rawlingson consisting of the 7th Division whose positions at this time found them just west of the village of Gheluvelt which lies on the main road from Ypres to Menin. The 7th Division had arrived in Belgium on the 6th October to help with the defence of Antwerp, but as the city was already falling they fell back towards Ypres with the rest of the Belgian Army. To the right of IV Corps stood the three Cavalry Divisions with the 3rd to the north the 2nd centre and the 1st to the south just east of the village of Messines. It was during the last week of October that the Germans came closest to breaking the British lines around Ypres, and it was at the end of that week that Chigwell lost its last soldier killed during the fighting of 1914.

CHARLES ALFRED REEVES

Charles Alfred Reeves is the first of three men whose story appears in this book but whose name does not appear on the Chigwell Memorial. The reason for his inclusion stems from the fact that upon his death his name received an individual mention in the Chigwell Parish Magazine as I discovered whilst carrying out my initial research for this book. Unfortunately very little is known of Charles life. He was born in Chigwell in 1894/5 the son of Alfred and Edith Reeves and had at least one younger brother. The Family lived at Horn Lane Cottages, Horn Lane, Woodford Green and it would appear that Charles had joined the army before the war at Warley in Essex. A private in the 4th (Queen's Own) Hussars, a cavalry of the line regiment; he had been stationed at Curragh in Ireland upon the outbreak of hostilities in August 1914. It is more than feasible to suggest that Charles learnt to ride horses in and around the fields of Chigwell and Woodford therefore making a career in one of the cavalry regiments a good choice. The 4th Hussars was quite a famous regiment and Winston Churchill had once served amongst its ranks. The regiment moved to France with the original BEF as part of the cavalry division arriving at Le Havre on the 18th August having sailed from Ireland on SS Atlantian. During the cavalry re-organisation of September/October the 4th Hussars became part of Gough's 2nd Cavalry Division one of the three battalions attached to 3rd Cavalry Brigade. The battalions that made up 3rd Cavalry Brigade were the 4th (Queen's Own) Hussars, the 5th (Royal Irish) Lancers and the 16th (The Queen's) Lancers. The last week of October after participating in the retreat from Mons and the Race to the Sea the 2nd Cavalry Division found themselves holding a front line that stretched from Hollebeke - about 3 miles southeast of Ypres and located east of the Ypres–Comines Canal between Battle Wood and Zandvoorde - to the village of Messines about 5 miles south of Ypres (see Map 11).

The Cavalry regiments had been trained to fight both mounted and dismounted. The situation they found themselves in at this time made it virtually impossible for them to use horses therefore they held and defended their positions dismounted. The Cavalry would in fact spend most of the war fighting dismounted, the main reasons for this being the state of the ground and the advent of trench warfare. On Sunday 25th October positions held by 2nd Cavalry Division were attacked by members of the German First, Fourth and Fifth Cavalry Corps, part of the German Sixth Army. The 3rd Cavalry Brigade situated on the divisions left flank according to SDGW lost no men in these actions; in fact the brigade suffered no major casualties over the days that followed. The 4th Hussars were positioned on the brigades left flank just north of Hollebeke; to their right were the 5th and 16th Lancers. The battalion was involved in constructing trenches to cover the east bank of the canal as well as a railway that ran northwards out of the village; it can only be assumed that Pte Charles Reeves was involved in this work. On 27th October the Germans formed a new army group to cover their positions in this area relieving their cavalry corps. This new army group called 'Fabeck' consisted mainly of Bavarian divisions and was also part of the German Sixth Army. That morning the 4th Hussars, having been relieved by men of the 129th Baluchis the previous night (13), returned from billets and resumed positions north of Hollebeke. Soon after they reconnoitred the area around their trenches only to find German units were dug in opposite some 800 yards away. In response a decision was made to create a second line of trenches on the west bank of the canal, at the same time a bridge crossing the canal was mined ready for detonation should the Germans attack and force a breakthrough. Over the next two days German attacks were again made against the British lines held by 2nd Cavalry Division but 3rd Cavalry Brigade again suffered little. The 4th Hussars war diary reports that whilst continuing to work on these second line trenches their billets in the village were bombed and shelled. A large chateau stood just outside Hollebeke across the canal from the 4th Hussars positions. It had been used as billets but now stood on dangerous ground, during the morning of 29th October it was shelled along with other buildings that lay close to the front lines, the Germans then moved forward to occupy it.

That afternoon the 5th Lancers and 16th Lancers (and some Baluchis) were moved northeast to support Haig's I Corps leaving Charles and the rest of the 4th Hussars behind, heavy fighting was reported east and northeast of Hollebeke as the Germans launched an attack. On Friday 30th October the 4th Hussars were relieved at 6:00am again by men of the 129th Baluchis. During their time north of Hollebeke the Hussars had kept their horses in the village, that morning however they were called for. The battalion mounted and moved off to meet two other battalions of 2nd Cavalry Division, the 3rd (Kings Own) Hussars and the 2nd Dragoons (Royal Scots Greys). The three battalions were ordered to support I Corps further north but as it turned out this never materialised. Reports were received that the chateau east of the canal had been evacuated by German troops and the 4th Hussars were ordered to retake it, on arrival there they found it was again the target of enemy shellfire however two more battalions, the 10th Hussars and 1st Dragoons (both of 6th Cavalry Brigade, 3rd Cavalry Division), were entrenched in the vicinity. Germans could be seen advancing west from the village of Zandvoorde however two squadrons of the 4th Hussars took over positions from the 10th Hussars and the 1st Dragoons; it is possible Charles was amongst them. If the situation seems somewhat confusing that's because it was, by this time the 4th Hussars found themselves receiving orders from both the headquarters of the 2nd and 3rd Cavalry Divisions as well as the 6th Cavalry Brigade and it was unclear to them exactly which unit their regiment was attached to. That afternoon the 129th Baluchis were driven from Hollebeke by German soldiers of the Sixth Bavarian Reserve Division and fell back to second line positions. The 4th Hussars on seeing this conformed and crossed the canal taking up positions on its west bank in the trenches that they had prepared over the previous few days. On reaching these trenches they were subjected to terrific shellfire however the battalion was supported by a squadron of men from the 1st Life Guards (a Household Cavalry battalion attached to 7th Cavalry Brigade, 3rd Cavalry Division). At the same time the Hussars horses were sent into the safety of woods some two miles away.

The 4th Hussars war diary reports that an officer of the battalion, Captain Kenneth Croft North came in from Hollebeke that afternoon having held off the Germans single-handed for over an hour with a machine gun, it appears he was never decorated for this action. That night an officer of the RE attempted to blow up the bridge crossing the canal but unfortunately this was not totally successful and the girders held, this alerted the Germans who came to investigate but they soon returned to the village. That night the Germans could be heard partying in the village, for the 4th Hussars the day's actions had cost them 2 men killed and 4 wounded. The following morning the 4th Hussars trenches were heavily shelled and German infantry was seen on the canal bridge inspecting what was left of it. A counter attack was ordered on German positions east of the canal however this failed to get very far. Throughout the day the Hussars trench positions were subjected again to heavy shellfire, it appears Captain North tried once more to see off the Germans with his machine gun unfortunately this time though he was killed. In this early stage of trench warfare the Hussars had created two types of trenches, the first were narrow without parapets which made them somewhat immune to enemy shellfire. The others however had parapets with overhead cover, when the shells hit them the damage they caused was severe, it very much looks as though nineteen year old Pte Charles Reeves was positioned in one of these trenches. As the shellfire increased the Germans launched an attack from the village, this action caused a gap to form in the line on 2nd Cavalry Divisions left flank. The 4th Hussars called in a French unit and two squadrons of Life Guards to help strengthen their trench positions and at the same time plug the gap that had been created. With this force they successfully managed to fend off the German assault and the enemy lost heavily, mainly due to accurate rifle fire laid down by the British troops. That evening the battalion received orders to retire and the men of the 4th Hussars withdrew to the village of St Eloi, unfortunately however Pte Charles Reeves wasn't with them. At St Eloi they found the village to be unsafe so they went on to Voormezeele and billeted there. According to their war diary the 4th Hussars had two officers and three other ranks killed that day including Pte Charles Reeves, in addition a further seventeen men were wounded. The diary also states that all of the damage done occurred in those trenches that provided overhead cover.

As the enemy had been active all day when they withdrew the battalion found it was unable to retrieve and subsequently bury the bodies of those men killed. Pte Charles Alfred Reeves has no known grave and his name is commemorated on Panel 5 of the Menin Gate Memorial to the Missing (14). The memorial lists the names of more than 55,000 officers and men who fell in the area around Ypres between September 1914 and August 1917 whose place of burial is unknown. The Menin Gate Memorial, in the form an archway, was unveiled in 1927 and stands across the roadway on the east side of the town of Ypres. Every night at 8:00pm members of the local fire brigade stop the traffic passing through the memorial and the Last Post is sounded in memory of those men killed. It's unknown why Charles name was not included on the Chigwell Village War Memorial however his death was reported in the April 1915 edition of the Chigwell Parish Magazine. In addition around this time, as a mark of respect, the parish sent out a memorial card to his home address. Whilst nothing is known of his family's movements after the war Charles name does appear on both the Woodford Bridge Roll of Honour plaque and the war memorial situated inside St Paul's Church, Woodford Bridge.

* * *

The Germans had succeeded in pushing back the 2nd Cavalry Division throughout the day and on the night of the 31st October the village of Messines, lay directly on the front line (15). Earlier in the day further north the Germans had been attacking Haig's 1st Division and Rawlinson's 7th Division around the village of Gheluvelt and had come perilously close to breaking the British line. Luckily the areas just west of the village were made up mainly of woodland and this served as good cover for the British who punished their attackers yet again with their well practiced musketry skills. The village of Hooge and its chateau which housed 1st Division HQ lay about three miles to the west of Gheluvelt on the Ypres - Menin Road. Inside Hooge chateau were two divisional commanders and as the Germans attacked at Gheluvelt their shells also reached the chateau at Hooge. One commander, Lieutenant General S H Lomax, was mortally wounded and died on 10th April 1915 whilst the other, Major General Monro, was wounded (16). That day Gheluvelt eventually fell to the Germans. As a result of the allied positions a salient was formed around Ypres. A salient quite simply was the term used for a bulge in the enemy's lines. Over the next four days the Germans would try desperately to straighten out the Ypres Salient. They attacked the allied positions to the north and south, to the south Messines was lost but all in all the allied lines held firmly. More attacks were made up until 10th November when the Germans again launched a concentrated artillery bombardment against Ypres itself (17). With still no breakthrough the 'First Battle of Ypres' was effectively over apart from some more artillery attacks on the town in which on 22nd November the Cloth Hall and other buildings were badly damaged. Deadlock was achieved all along the Western Front with both sides occupying 460 miles of trench lines that stretched from the North Sea to the borders of Switzerland. The winter of 1914 was wet and cold, with the mobile war over the soldiers of both sides were now locked in trench warfare and there was no hope that the fighting would be over by Christmas. Unofficial truces occurred up and down the line that Christmas of 1914 but they were soon over and hostilities continued, by the end of the year of the original 100,000 men of the BEF who had landed that August almost 90,000 were either dead, wounded or missing.

17, La-Ferté-Sous-Jouarre Memorial to the Missing

18, The name of Cpl Harold Henry Shuttle as it appears on the La-Ferté-Sous-Jouarre Memorial to the Missing.

20, The name of Pte Charles Leonard Harrup as it appears on the Le Touret Memorial to the Missing

21, The name of Pte Edwin Bird as it appears on the Ploegsteert Memorial to the Missing

19, Cpl Harold Henry Shuttle's grandparents gravestone situated inside St Mary's Churchyard

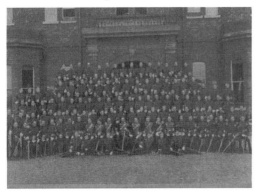

22, The 4th (Queen's Own) Hussars at Curragh in 1914 (Photograph courtesy of the Imperial War Museum).

23, The Menin Gate Memorial to the Missing at Ypres

THE WAR AT SEA
1914 - 1918

The Royal Navy was Britain's most important weapon when it came to protecting her interests around the world, its welfare and security were vital to safeguarding the Empire. The Royal Navy came under the control of two main parties the first being the politically appointed man. Known as the 'First Lord of the Admiralty' this position in 1914 was held by Winston Churchill. The other man in control was the military head of the navy, known as the 'First Sea Lord' this position was held by Lord Fisher. Kaiser Wilhelm II had always envied the Royal Navy, easily the largest and the best in Europe if not the world and had on coming to power attempted to put together a fleet that would rival her. The 'High Seas Fleet' was the name given to the German naval forces operating in the North Sea, on the outbreak of war their commander knew that a direct attack on royal naval vessels in this region would prove futile. The British high command however knew that should their ships be attacked and somehow in the unlikely event be defeated they could not only lose control of the home waters but shipping lanes around the world. This could prove disastrous not only for the country as a whole - Britain relied heavily on most of its food coming from overseas - but also for allied forces in France and Flanders and troops all over the empire who were dependent on receiving supplies. The 'Grand Fleet' was the name given to the main attacking force of the Royal Navy and its commander during the early years of the war was Admiral Sir John Jellicoe. The Grand Fleet had been out taking part in naval exercises in July 1914 therefore when events in the Balkans unfolded and war broke out the following month the navy found itself in a state of readiness. Jellicoe, Fisher and Churchill quickly realised the possible consequences of a full scale confrontation between the British and German fleets therefore they decided that safety first must be the order of the day. This suited the Germans, with no direct attack to contend with they planed to defeat the Royal Navy and British merchant ships by using both mines and submarines. The British had submarines but preferred their Battleships where as the Germans saw submarine warfare as the most effective form of defeating the enemy.

The Chigwell Village War Memorial lists two men who served with the Royal Navy in World War One; both were killed in 1914.

JOSEPH SAMUEL GEORGE UNDERWOOD

Joseph Samuel George Underwood was born on 1st April 1896 at Walthamstow in East London to parents Robert and Emily Underwood. His father had been born at Gardley Hastings Northamptonshire in 1872 whilst his mother was born two years later in 1874 at New Norby in Yorkshire. Having met and married his parents moved south settling in Woodford Bridge, Essex where Robert found work as an attendant at Claybury Hospital. Joseph was the eldest child followed by two sisters Martha and Annie, in time however more brothers and sisters were born. Robert and Emily Underwood were to have eleven children in all, besides Joseph, Martha and Annie their others were Ada, Harry, Emily, Amelia, Robert, Edith (1), Lily and Mary. At the turn of the century the family lived at 2 Rose Cottages, Woodford Bridge, they moved a short time later however to 18 Smeaton Road, Woodford Bridge. After leaving school Joseph worked as a Telegraph Messenger however in April 1912 aged just 16 he decided to join the Royal Navy. His service record states that at the time he was 5ft 6˝ tall with a 32½˝ chest, it goes on to say he had brown hair, blue eyes and a fresh skin complexion. On joining the navy, given service number J/17076, Joseph was made Ship Boy and served from 15th April 1912 to 30th August 1912 on board HMS Impregnable, a training ship based at Devonport near Plymouth. On 31st August 1912 Joseph was transferred to HMS Ganges, the name of a training depot based at Shotley in Suffolk. On arrival he gained promotion attaining the rank of Signal Boy, Joseph remained at Ganges until the 11th April 1913. During the course of the next year Joseph served at several bases and on board several ships. On 12th April 1913 he moved to HMS Pembroke, this was the name of the royal naval barracks based at Chatham in Kent (2). Joseph wasn't there long and on 22nd April he was posted to HMS Juno, a cruiser that would be sold by the navy in 1920. On 1st July 1913 Joseph was transferred onto HMS Sentinel, a Light Cruiser built in 1903 weighing 2,895 tons and armed with 9x4" guns. During the third week of August Joseph returned to HMS Pembroke for a period of four days, on 30th August however he joined HMS Amethyst, a Light Cruiser built in 1902 weighing some 3,000 tons armed with 12x4" guns. On 1st October 1913 Joseph was transferred once again this time to the British Cruiser HMS Pathfinder, having grown an inch taller and gained a little weight, on 1st April 1914 Joseph re-enlisted into the navy for a period of 12 years. It was no coincidence that this was his birthday as re-enlistment on ones birthday was normal procedure. Also on this date he was promoted again, this time to the rank of Ordinary Signalman. At some point however, although it's not clear when, Joseph briefly returned home to Woodford Bridge where he met a young girl and was engaged to be married.

On the outbreak of war the British main concerns were to try to control the German High Seas Fleet in areas in and around the North Sea. The British badly underestimated the range of the German submarines known as U-Boats. The main British naval base at this time was at Scapa Flow on the Orkney Islands, about 18 miles off the Scottish northeast coast.

Map 12, Great Britain

On 1st September 1914 a false sighting - although not known at the time - was made of a U-Boat in Scapa Flow, scaring the British this forced them to move their base firstly to western Scotland and then in October 1914 to Northern Ireland. The U-Boats were far more dangerous than the British gave them credit for, as the crew of HMS Pathfinder was soon to find out. The German U-Boats were numbered and U-21 was under the command of Captain Otto Hersing. U-21 was stationed at the submarine base at Heligoland, an island off the German northeast coast. This base had been established upon the outbreak of war in case the allies made a naval drive towards the German coast. As early as 8th August 1914 U-21 left its base and headed out into the North Sea to look for enemy targets only to be turned back by bad weather. A week later Hersing set out again but no contact with the enemy was made. On 28th August the British tried to lure out some of the German Fleet from their home base at Jade Bay on the German coast, this battle cost the Germans four ships, the British however had four ships damaged. On the 2nd September U-21 was again out on patrol this time around the east coast of Scotland. She passed undetected into the Firth of Fourth and after moving around for a few days she passed out again finding herself on Saturday 5th September back off the Scottish mainland. On this day HMS Pathfinder was returning to Britain having been investigating shipping movements out in the North Sea. HMS Pathfinder was built in 1903 and completed in 1905, a Light Cruiser she was fitted with 9x6" guns and weighed 2,940 tons with a top speed of 25 knots. Her captain was Francis Martin-Leake, an experienced 45 year old from Hertfordshire who had risen through the ranks of the Royal Navy (3). At 4:30pm U-21 encountered HMS Pathfinder off St Abbs Head on the Northumberland coast, she fired a single torpedo hitting Pathfinder square on igniting the cruisers boilers sending shrapnel into the bulkhead and causing an explosion that sank the ship in less than four minutes. HMS Pathfinder was the first British warship to be sunk by a torpedo and the second ship ever to be sunk by a submarine (4). A sailor on board a Scottish trawler witnessed the event and gave his account of what happened to a newspaper reporter from the East Kent Gazette in September 1914:

"Looking in the direction of the boat {HMS Pathfinder} we saw a great cloud of smoke and steam rise up. It was just like a big white mountain, until at the end you would have thought it was an ordinary cloud. We could not see the boat at all. But as the cloud lifted bit by bit, I saw the stern sticking straight up out of the water. It slipped slowly down and disappeared with a great rush. The whole thing had not lasted three minutes from the time I had been admiring her until she sank from sight".

(The above account is reproduced courtesy of the East Kent Gazette)

Pathfinder's casualties were very high and out of a crew of 264 only 58 survived. One of those lost was 18 year old Ordinary Signalman Joseph Samuel George Underwood; he has no grave but the sea and is commemorated on Panel 3 of the Chatham Naval Memorial in Kent (5). Overlooking the town of Chatham the memorial commemorates more than 8,500 sailors of the First World War. In April 1915 the Underwood family received a memorial card from the parishioners of St Mary's Church. Emily Underwood died on 6th January 1940 aged 65 whilst her husband Robert died six months later on 28th June 1940 aged 68, both are buried in the churchyard of St Mary's in Chigwell. After Joseph was killed the family did keep in touch with his fiancé who eventually married someone else, contact was maintained by Joseph's sister Edith for many years until one year no more was heard and it was assumed that the woman had passed away.

HMS Pathfinder's Captain Francis Martin-Leake survived his ships sinking and took control of other vessels throughout the remainder of the war. The wreck of HMS Pathfinder was located off St Abbs Head in 1984. U-21 went on to be the most feared submarine to operate during the course of World War One. Hersing became a hero back in Germany and he and his submarine survived the war. In February 1919 after the Armistice was signed Hersing was due to hand over U-21 to the Royal Navy at Harwich. His pride got the better of him and, under the escort of the Royal Navy, on route across the North Sea he ordered his crew to open the ships valves successfully sinking the ship. The scuttled wreck of U-21 was discovered by British salvage expert Graham Jessop in 1999, in her career she had undertaken 21 patrols sinking a total of 36 ships.

* * *

The main naval confrontation of 1914 occurred a few thousand miles from Europe in waters of the South Atlantic. The Germans had a number of ships stationed in the Pacific when war broke out. The commander of these ships was Vice Admiral Graff Von Spee and he planned to take his fleet back to Germany by way of the Atlantic. After grouping his ships together at Easter Island in the Pacific he set sail for South America (6). On the 1st November Von Spee clashed with the British off the Chilean coast in what was to be known as the 'Battle of Coronel'. This action cost the British four ships, two of which were sunk, in what was the Royal Navy's worst day for over a century. Just over a month later the British got their revenge in 'The Battle of the Falkland Islands'. They managed on 8th December to track down Von Spee and virtually destroyed his entire fleet off the coast of East Falkland. Von Spee was killed in the battle but one of his ships escaped only to be sunk the following year. This action had proved how effective the Royal Navy could be, with the next direct attack between the two sides not occurring until the early summer of 1916.

HARRY NORMAN BAILEY
Harry Norman Bailey was the last man that Chigwell lost in 1914. He was born at Epping (7) in Essex on 5th August 1895 to parents Harry and Charlotte Bailey. His father worked as a Postman and was born in Chigwell in 1863 whilst his mother was also born there the same year. Harry Bailey was the second youngest of five children and the middle eldest of three sons. According to the census of 1901 the family lived at Hainault Road in Chigwell but

shortly before the war they moved to Turpins Lane, Woodford Bridge. Harry Norman Bailey enlisted into the Royal Navy on 6th June 1911 aged 15 years 10 months. It appears that prior to joining, like Joseph Underwood; he too worked as a Telegraph Messenger. Although the two boys lived very close and were of a similar age there is no evidence to suggest that Harry and Joseph knew each other, it's possible they did and it's also possible they'd attended the same school. Harry's service record states that on enlistment he was 5ft 9˝ tall with a 35˝ chest, he had brown hair, blue eyes and a fair complexion. His rating on enlistment was that of Boy Seaman with his service number being J/12442. Harry was posted on 6th June 1911 to HMS Impregnable at Devonport where he remained for just short of a year; like Joseph Underwood Harry Bailey would serve on board numerous ships and at various bases during the next twelve months.

On 3rd June 1912 Harry was transferred to HMS Berwick, a British Cruiser built in 1900 weighing some 9,800 tons and armed with 14x6" guns. He continued to serve on board HMS Berwick until 4th September 1912 at which time he was posted to HMS Pembroke, the royal naval barracks at Chatham. Whilst at HMS Pembroke Harry was described as having very good character, something that would eventually see him promoted. On 2nd October 1912 Harry moved to HMS Thames, an ex Cruiser used as a training ship by the navy, he stayed here for just under two weeks before briefly returning to HMS Pembroke. On 18th October 1912 Harry was sent to serve on board HMS Falmouth, a Light Cruiser built in 1909 weighing 5,250 tons and armed with 8x6" guns (8). Whilst serving on HMS Falmouth Harry was once again described as having very good character, on 5th August 1913 whilst still on board he celebrated his eighteenth birthday. On this date Harry re-enlisted into the navy for a further period of 12 years, gaining promotion at this time to Ordinary Signalman his medical record now showed that he was 5ft 10˝ tall with a 36˝ chest. On 26th February 1914 Harry was promoted again, this time to the rank of Able Seaman. On 6th March 1914 he was posted back to HMS Pembroke for a period of one month and then on 9th April 1914 he was transferred to HMS Kestrel, a torpedo boat based at Chatham. All torpedo boats were classed as Destroyers; Kestrel weighed 335 tons and was capable of a top speed of 30 knots. On the outbreak of war HMS Kestrel was moved a few miles east of Chatham to Sheerness on the Isle of Sheppey. Sheerness not only stood on the south side of the Thames Estuary which leads into Central London but also at the mouth of the River Medway which at that time lead to the royal naval base at Chatham. With regards to the fate of HMS Pathfinder we have seen how dangerous German U-Boats could be, if they could penetrate either of these two areas the consequences could be disastrous. This said it was the Job of HMS Kestrel to patrol the areas off Sheerness and those waters around the east and southeast coast of England in order to guard against possible enemy attacks.

Throughout October and November 1914 HMS Kestrel patrolled these waters constantly searching for enemy activity. Daily duties on board ship included such things as the cleaning of decks and taking on coal in order to fuel the engines, general maintenance was also carried out be it painting or the overhauling of guns. The crew of HMS Kestrel found they were always on action stations and kept alert, all hands on deck was called frequently in order to test their response times. On Friday 27th November HMS Kestrel was in dock at Sheerness whilst her crew attended to duties, the following day saw the boat leave to go out on patrol. That day whilst out Kestrel encountered another ship and assisted her in transferring one of her passengers to the dockside at Margate. Returning to duties Sunday saw Kestrel at sea, a normal day ensued patrolling up and down the east coast. Still at sea on the morning of Monday 30th November the weather was overcast, the wind blew in a southwest direction leaving a cool temperature. At 6:00am all hands on deck was called and routine inspections were carried out amongst the crew, shortly afterwards duties commenced. At 6:30am the upper deck was washed down then almost an hour later the alarm was raised as the shout went up "man overboard". Harry's job that morning had found him working at the forward torpedo tubes of HMS Kestrel carrying out cleaning duties and routine maintenance. Somehow while doing this he fell overboard and everything stopped as the crew tried desperately to save him. The Ships Log records that a lifebuoy was dropped and a search carried out until 8:00am however although every endeavour was made by the crew to save him he was pronounced missing presumed drowned. Harry was wearing sea boots, an oilskin suit and a duffle coat, once wet these items weighed a ton and its no surprise his body disappeared beneath the waves and was never recovered. HMS Kestrel proceeded to Felixstowe where she secured alongside dock at 9:30am; she remained there until the following day when she returned to Sheerness.

A court of enquiry was held on 8th December 1914, it was told the events surrounding the incident and it subsequently concluded that no blame could be attributed to anyone. Harry's death had just been a terrible accident. Harry was just 19 years old when he was lost at sea and like Joseph Underwood his name appears on Panel 2 of the Naval Memorial at Chatham (9). The fact that Harry was not killed in action but in a terrible accident would just add to the grief the Bailey family would suffer not only during the next four years of war, but for the rest of their lives. During the first four months of the war the village of Chigwell lost six men, most of those had lived within a road or two of each other, of course their families still did. Just as tragic is the fact that none of those six men has a known grave. Chigwell was starting to feel the effects of the First World War very quickly and the situation over the following four years would only get worse.

* * *

It is probably a good time, during this chapter, to briefly describe the other events that occurred at sea during the First World War that would have an effect on the men fighting on land.

On the outbreak of war the Germans had two ships operating in the Mediterranean, their job being to disrupt merchant shipping and French troop movements between North Africa and France. Called the 'Goeben' and the 'Breslau' these ships were hunted by the British in early August and they moved up towards northeast Sicily in order to escape. With the British still in pursuit the two ships passed through the Mediterranean into the Aegean Sea and up through the Dardanelles to the Turkish capital of Constantinople - now Istanbul. The British Ships closed in behind waiting at the mouth of the Dardanelles effectively trapping the two ships. Before the war Turkey had placed an order with Britain for two new Battleships. As war began these ships, both in their final stages of completion, were requisitioned by the British much to the annoyance of the Turks. The Germans knowing their two ships now to be effectively useless offered them to the Turkish Navy. This offering mainly influenced Turkey to join the war on Germany's side. The two ships predominantly crewed by German sailors were used on the 29th/30th October 1914 to bombard Russian interests on the coast of the Black Sea, the next day after a British, French and Russian ultimatum went unanswered Turkey entered the war.

In January 1915 the Germans attempted a raid into the North Sea however this was met by the pre warned British at Dogger Bank some 80 miles off the English coast. The British had been alerted by radio intercepts after decoding a German signal book. In February the Germans started a campaign of unrestricted submarine warfare on all merchant shipping vessels around British waters regardless of where they were from in an effort to disrupt supplies reaching the mainland. On 7th May the Germans sunk the passenger liner Lusitania off southern Ireland, more than 1000 people were killed and the event caused outrage especially in America, this event amongst other things eventually brought America into the war. The unrestricted submarine campaign was suspended but British targets were still attacked. Various allied naval attacks occurred around Gallipoli in 1915 and are discussed in that chapter. The main naval confrontation of the war came in late May and early June 1916 when the Grand Fleet and High Seas Fleet clashed in the Battle of Jutland (10). The British came off worst in this battle but did enough to prevent the German Navy from entering into anymore direct clashes for the remainder of the war. The Battle of Jutland however had no direct consequence for the men fighting on land. The German campaign of unrestricted submarine warfare resumed in 1917 with the same plan as before, to disrupt allied shipping and supplies. Later American troop convoys crossing the Atlantic to France were made targets however by this time the Germans had the American Navy to contend with. The last real main action of sea warfare came in April 1918 when the British tried to block German submarine bases in the Belgian Ports of Zeebrugge and Ostend, although not a complete success the German submarine menace was slowly overcome. The main job of the Royal Navy throughout the war had been to keep Britain functioning as well as its armies supplied and its population free from starvation. All these things it managed to do however its other job was to make sure that Germany suffered the opposite fate. Eventually naval blockades were imposed against Germany that by late 1918 saw conditions become extremely harsh for the German people, in addition fuelled by the fact that their army was facing defeat on the battlefield meant that all they wanted was an end to the war.

24, *The Chatham Naval Memorial in Kent*

25, *Harry Norman Bailey as it appears on the Chatham Naval Memorial*

26, *HMS Kestrel (Picture courtesy and copyright of Tony Davies)*

27, *HMS Pathfinder (Picture courtesy and copyright of Tony Davies)*

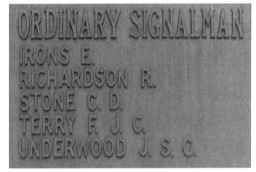

29, *The name of Joseph Samuel George Underwood as it appears on the Chatham Naval Memorial*

28, *Joseph Samuel George Underwood (Picture courtesy of Leslie Prescott)*

1915

As 1915 started it found the men and women of Chigwell trying to go about their normal business, sure there was a war on but life in the Essex village still carried on. The businesses within the village still operated as usual, the post office, the grocer, the farms and public houses, trains still ran at the station and the people went to work just as they'd always done. The villagers however were quick to pull together as money was raised for various funds to help the war effort. The British soldiers were short of clothing and appeals had been made for certain items. The cold winter months of 1915 required warm clothing and socks and shirts were in short supply, the villagers were helpful in providing such items. The adult members of St Mary's Church choir usually took an annual outing and money for this was saved throughout the year however, as there was a war on, a decision was made to cancel the trip and instead the money was sent to the Prince of Wales Relief Fund, a charity set up to help soldiers and their families (1). At the best of times Chigwell really was a quiet place, the parish magazine in its February 1915 edition summed this up perfectly by saying in a piece entitled *'Impressions of Chigwell'*:

'What early hours we keep in Chigwell! No midnight sounds of merry-makers on their way home, who are anxious to keep others merry as well'.

With the coming of war, though tragic, one can't help feel that an air of excitement came to this otherwise quite place. None more so than when, on 3rd January 1915 at 4:00pm what was thought to be an enemy aircraft was spotted overhead. The parish magazine reported: 'At last it seemed as if something would happen to break the monotony of quiet Chigwell'. In a somewhat dramatic report by those who had witnessed the event it went on to say: 'This German raider was coming with the one object of destroying the peaceful and law-abiding Chigwell'. It also described the fear of the onlookers who felt that the aircraft may drop a bomb at any moment and that there was nothing that they could do about it. These fears were realised some 26 years later when on 19th April 1941 a parachute mine, dropped by a German aircraft, fell on the Prince of Wales Pub in Manor Road, Grange Hill where a Saturday night darts match was in full swing. Over 30 people were killed - the exact number is unknown - most of whom are buried in a communal grave to the rear of St Mary's Churchyard (2). In fact the German aircraft seen over Chigwell on 3rd January 1915 turned out to be a British plane on its way to intercept German Zeppelins over the Essex town of Colchester some 30 odd miles away, understandably this mistake was made due to the fact that the people of the village were not used to seeing such things, after all in 1915 the aeroplane was a fairly new invention. Most residents in the village really felt they had a part to play in the war and it seems none more so than the patriotic writer of the parish magazine. He felt it was his job to try to encourage the men of the village who had not already done so to enlist in the 'New Armies' or second best as he called it the Territorial Army. He really praised those who answered the call. "The Chigwell Junior Football Club set a good example, fourteen out of eighteen members of the club enlisted". He also commended a married father of six who joined up. Two older men who had been rejected in place after place because they suffered from varicose veins were prepared to undergo an operation to rectify this and he called them "an example of pluck and typically English". The headmaster of Chigwell council school Mr John Moseley, whose own two sons were to enlist, informed the parish magazine that over seventy of his boys from the past were now with the colours. The writer shunned the shirkers and those who done nothing. In one edition of the magazine he felt that some people who flocked to football matches cared more for goals than the nation's honour. He said there were some families who had done and would do nothing. It was not unusual during the early years of the war for a man if not in uniform to be given a white feather by a female passer by as a sign of cowardice. This happened all over the country, sometimes to soldiers who were home on leave and happened to be wearing their civvies for the day. The feeling over most of the country really was that everyone should be made to do their bit to help the war. The parish magazine requested that relatives send the names of those men serving to the vicar at St Mary's so that gifts could be sent to them and reports regarding progress could be relayed back to the community.

As previously mentioned the war in France at the end of 1914 found the armies of both sides locked in stalemate and as a result of this trench warfare had ensued. The trenches were set out in lines, consisting of a front line, a support line and reserve line. These were connected to each other via communication trenches off of which dugouts, latrines and storage areas would exist. The winter of 1914 and 1915 was particularly bad and the trenches had been constructed hastily as the opposing armies dug in opposite each other. The countryside of Flanders, where the British Army found itself, was mainly soft based and muddy unlike the chalky uplands of the Somme where they would find themselves a year later. This meant that to dig down as little as two feet it was not long before one hit water. It had rained almost constantly from October and it would until early March and as a result the trenches filled up terribly. To construct trenches in this type of situation was nigh on impossible for the British troops. The Germans however had entrenched mainly on high ground that overlooked the British lines and whilst carrying out construction work British soldiers unwittingly became targets for German snipers. The British generals were reluctant to give any ground even if it meant that a better position could be achieved so the troops really had to make the best of it even if that meant paying the price with ones life. As it was hard to dig down without finding water the trenches, especially in Flanders, were raised up with breastwork. This mainly consisted of wooden structures shored up by sandbags - although sandbags in early 1915 were in short supply. Each breastwork had to be quite thick in order to withstand the ferocity of a machine gun. All the time the Germans would be shelling the areas along the British lines and building these structures under those conditions was an extremely hard task, you could build only to find a volley of shells come over and destroy all your hard work. The tools needed to do the work were not exactly in abundance and as the troops were only in certain sections of line for short periods of time they were extremely reluctant to make a serious effort when it came to improving the quality of the trenches. The general feeling amongst many was *'why should we work hard when the next day we may be moved to a different stretch of line'*, when it became apparent however that the situation of trench warfare was a permanent one this attitude soon changed. British trench systems varied but most consisted of three lines split into front, support and reserve. These lines ran parallel to each other and were connected by more trenches called communication trenches. Along the communication trench came supplies, relief battalions, ammunition, rations and anything else soldiers in the frontline may require. In front of the trenches entanglements of barbed wire were erected by the armies of both sides as added defence, this task was mainly carried out by work parties on night patrols. Sometimes positions jutted out from the main frontline trench and these could be used for observation, fortified and manned such positions were known as redoubts. The ground between the allied and German trenches was known as 'no mans land' and generally consisted of muddy grassy wastes. This area sometimes contained the remains of old buildings destroyed by shellfire whilst tree stumps and shell craters mainly littered the ground. Dead soldiers of both sides, killed whilst out on patrol or in small scale attacks whose bodies could not be retrieved by their comrades were also a common sight. No mans land varied in width and in some cases the opposing trench lines were so close that it was possible, if quiet, to hear the sound of the enemy talking. The conditions within the trenches that the soldiers of both sides found themselves in during the early part of 1915, and as it would turn out for much of the war were truly appalling. Imagine standing in a trench waist high in water for maybe two or three days with rats, dead bodies, sniper bullets and shellfire all around you, add to this temperatures somewhere around freezing and your somewhere there. The men were virtually covered with lice from head to toe and as a result its not surprising that illness claimed just as many men as the enemy. If that wasn't enough once relived you had a five mile march probably under shellfire, to a rest area behind the lines and on arrival it was not uncommon to find nowhere to wash or dry your clothes, the possibility of no warm food and no bed to sleep in was also a reality and then within a day or so it was back to the trenches to do it all over again, god only knows how a man survived.

The allies were planning a joint offensive for the beginning of 1915 just as soon as the weather improved, this it was thought would be no sooner than April. Meanwhile to compensate for the addition of more regular and territorial divisions the BEF had been restructured into two armies. Haig commanded 1st Army to the south of the British lines in France and Smith-Dorrien commanded 2nd Army in the north around Ypres. Sir John French felt that British efforts for their part of the offensive should be concentrated in the south around La Bassée, Neuve Chapelle and Aubers and carried out by Haig's 1st Army. This sat well with Haig who like Sir John French was not a fan of Smith-Dorrien and felt he couldn't be trusted, after all he had rightly or wrongly defied orders by deciding to stand and fight at Le Cateau. The French commander General Joffre had asked Sir John French for his help in relieving some of his units north of Ypres. At this time Kitchener had the last regular army division at his disposal - the 29th Division - but instead of sending them to the Western Front he was sending them to Egypt as part of the Gallipoli campaign. Although he was being sent a territorial division instead this annoyed Sir John French who wanted the 29th Division for service in France, the CIC felt he was being left short and therefore denied Joffre his request. This infuriated Joffre who said that without the relief of his units to the north the French Army would not be able to participate in any joint offensive. Joffre tried to compromise requesting fewer units be relieved but French still refused and with this Joffre decided the French Army would play no part in the planned action. He also came to the conclusion that the British could not be trusted or relied upon. With this Sir John French, still determined and wanting to prove Joffre wrong, decided that with or without French assistance the British would carry on with their plans and launch an offensive on their own. Another reason for the CIC wishing to launch an attack stemmed from the fact that with deadlock having occurred on the Western Front various politicians and military personnel back in England had started to look around for other areas of operation - mainly in the east - where a breakthrough could be achieved. Most people fell into two camps; those who favoured an attack in the east were called easterners whilst those who felt the war could only be won in France and Flanders were called westerners. It was because of this that Sir John French, a devout westerner, needed to prove that a breakthrough could be achieved on the Western Front.

At 7:30am on 10th March 1915 the British guns commenced their bombardment signalling the start of the 'Battle of Neuve Chapelle' the bombardment was to be the most intense of the War so far. For one man from Chigwell the action at Neuve Chapelle would be his first taste of action since the conflict begun.

THOMAS GEORGE BIRD
Thomas George Bird was the older brother of Edwin Bird who'd been killed at Armentières back in October 1914. Born in 1884/5 at Dagenham in Essex (3) he was the second of five sons of parents Thomas and Annie Bird. His father had been born at Hempstead Burstead in Essex in 1845 whilst his mother was born at Dagenham in 1850. Their eldest son was Herbert and then Thomas named after his father, next had been Edwin and finally Alfred and John, all the children were born in Dagenham with the exception of John who was born in Chigwell.

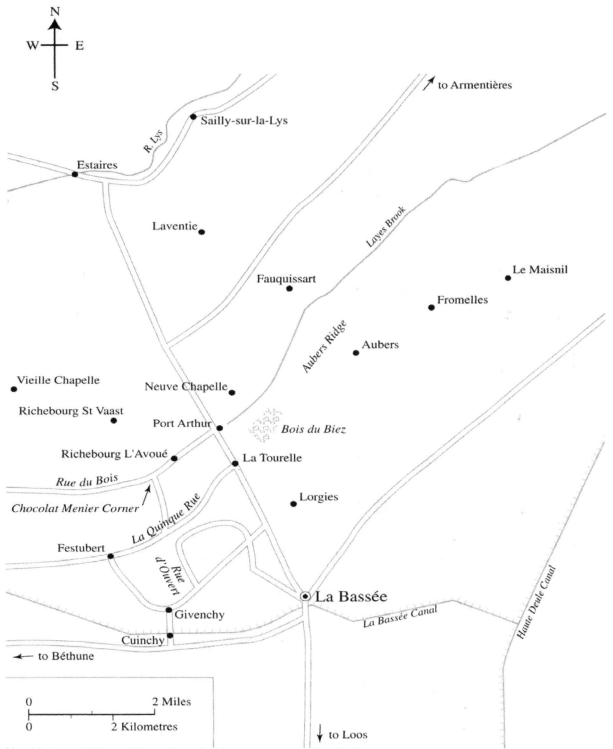

Map 13, Aubers Ridge and Neuve Chapelle (Map taken from 'THE WESTERN FRONT' (BBC Books) by Richard Holmes. Reprinted by permission of The Random House Group Ltd)

As previously mentioned in the story of Edwin the Bird family lived in Grange Hill but where exactly is unknown. After leaving school Thomas George Bird worked as a General Labourer alongside his father and brother before leaving home and joining the army. The date Thomas initially joined is unclear however on the outbreak of war in August 1914 Thomas re-enlisted at Ilford having been recalled with the army reserve. The 2nd Battalion West Yorkshire (Prince of Wales Own) Regiment, the unit to which Thomas was eventually posted, was stationed on the Mediterranean island of Malta when war broke out (4). On 14th September 1914 the battalion left Malta for England arriving at Southampton nine days later. Upon their arrival the 2nd West York's were attached to 23rd Brigade along with the 2nd Battalion Devonshire Regiment, 2nd Battalion Middlesex Regiment and subsequently the 2nd Battalion Cameronian's (Scottish Rifles) (5).

The 23rd Brigade, 24th Brigade and 25th Brigade made up the 8th Division, commanded at the beginning of 1915 by Major General F Davies the division trained at Hursley Park in Winchester. On 4th November 1914 the 2nd West York's received orders that they were to move at once and at 2:45pm the battalion started the roughly 20 mile march from Winchester to Southampton. Thomas having joined the battalion at Hursley Park was with them as they boarded the SS Mount Temple and set sail for France landing at Le Havre at 3:15am on 5th November 1914. The battalion was to spend a very cold and wet new year in trenches ¾ mile north of Neuve Chapelle.

The German lines at Neuve Chapelle formed a small lightly defended salient just west of the village. The ground mainly in this area was flat, but just to the east of the village lay an area of high ground known as Aubers Ridge. The plan was to capture the salient taking the German troops holding it totally by surprise, then to push forwards through any gaps created to Aubers Ridge using waiting cavalry troops. The British attack was to be made by IV Corps, made up of the 7th and 8th Divisions, commanded by Sir Henry Rawlingson with assistance coming from the Indian Corps. The attacks were made with IV Corps to the north and the Indian Corps in the south. The German front line trenches were no further than 2-300 yards away. The attacking British troops went over the top at 8:05am on 10th March taking the enemy, who had been shocked by the preceding artillery bombardment, completely by surprise. In less than half an hour the attacking troops found themselves entering the deserted village of Neuve Chapelle passing though it towards their objectives beyond. They found many positions where they'd expected to find resistance free of Germans. Then a breakdown of communications and hesitation gave the Germans time to regroup, rush up reserves and consolidate new positions. Vital minutes turned to hours and eventually good opportunities to advance were lost. Pte Thomas Bird and the 2nd West York's were part of a second wave that had been supporting the other battalions of 23rd Brigade that day. The 2nd Devon's had supported the 2nd Cameronians who suffered quite heavily due to the fact that an enemy machine gun on the extreme left of their attack front had failed to be put out of action. This was because of a mix up during the preliminary bombardment that had left an entire section of enemy breastwork totally untouched. The guns whose job it had been to destroy this section had been left behind in England; they were rushed to France but arrived to late to take part in the opening bombardment. Although Pte Thomas Bird was to survive the day's battle a lot of men from his battalion and brigade were less fortunate, their losses for 10th March 1915 according to SDGW were as follows:

2nd Devon's = 4 Officers + 25 Other Ranks
2nd Middlesex = 6 Other Ranks
2nd Cameronian's = 13 Officers + 149 Other Ranks
2nd West York's = 1 Officer + 26 Other Ranks

The Battle of Neuve Chapelle lasted until 13th March and had been initially successful - mostly the first day - but a breakdown of communication and missed opportunity were its undoing although the village itself remained in British hands. During the course of the three days of fighting the British had lost some 12,000 men whilst German losses were roughly the same, but if anything it had showed the French that the British were not afraid of a fight.

Back in Chigwell during April 1915 two things happened concerning Pte Thomas George Bird. Firstly his family received a memorial card regarding the loss of Edwin from parishioners at St Mary's Church. The families of all those men from Chigwell killed up until this point also received cards. The second thing that happened was that his father Thomas Bird died suddenly aged 71 and was buried inside St Mary's Churchyard on 22nd April. It was also on this day back at Ypres that the Germans chose to launch a new attack in the hope of once again trying to access the Channel Ports, but this time however they had a new weapon. These actions that lasted from 22nd April until the 25th May 1915 later collectively became known as 'The Second Battle of Ypres'.

With the coming of spring to the Ypres Salient the temperatures rose and the water logged fields started to dry out, flowers started to spring up here and there and the sun shone, for a moment one could forget there was a war on, besides no serious fighting had occurred in the salient since November 1914. On 22nd April however Ypres came under a heavy bombardment from German artillery for much of the morning, a quiet afternoon saw the bombardment resume around 5:00pm. The French Army consisting of a territorial division and French African troops (the 45th Algerian Division) held the area of the Ypres Salient north of the town around the village of Langemarck, on their right around the village of St Julien the line was held by Canadian troops. Just after 5:00pm two green and yellow clouds were seen drifting towards the French held positions with German infantry following on behind, these clouds contained Chlorine Gas. Having been released from cylinders positioned within the German trenches all it required was a favourable wind in the right direction, on 22nd April this was the case. Cylinder gas was released in vapour form, it caused its victims eyes to sting, they became short of breath, liquid built up in the lungs and a man slowly drowned to death whilst coughing up blood. Not surprisingly the French troops scared to death ran for their lives on seeing the gas clouds approaching leaving the Canadian troops dangerously exposed, they had to fight hard to hold their positions which luckily they managed to do. The Germans gained ground but even they couldn't believe how successful their new weapon had been, they had insufficient troops to follow up on their success. Eventually the line of the salient was stabilized after British and Canadian counter attacks during the following few days, once again Ypres and the Channel Ports were saved however now the allied lines were overlooked by German forces on three sides. Sir Horace Smith-Dorrien, whose 2nd Army held the areas around Ypres, had during the attacks requested to shorten his lines in order to gain a better position from which to defend. This request was quite reasonable but for Sir John French it was the last straw, as a result on 6th May 1915 Smith-Dorrien was replaced as commander of 2nd Army by General Sir Herbert Plumer. Sir Horace Smith-Dorrien eventually went on to command troops in East Africa although he was to be dogged by illness for much of his time, the first job of his replacement however was to shorten British lines around Ypres.

After a partial success at Neuve Chapelle and the withstanding of German assaults around Ypres the British decided a fresh assault of their own should be made. The area for the attack would once again be Aubers Ridge and the action was to coincide with a French attack further south in Artois, on a front that stretched from Arras to Lens along an area of high ground known as Vimy Ridge. The allies really felt a major breakthrough could be achieved. Since Neuve Chapelle the German positions at Aubers had been improved quite considerably. Having not been affected by earlier fighting since March the Germans had worked hard by bolstering breastworks with sandbags, constructing dugouts and fortifying machine gun nests. Trenches were dug in such positions that a field of fire could be achieved right across their attack front, barbed wire in front of the trenches also added to their defence. Behind this front a second line of trenches were constructed and further back in the event of a breakthrough machine gun nests were situated. The Battle at Aubers was destined to fail right from the start mainly due to a shortage of artillery shells - over 20,000 had been sent to Gallipoli - and as a direct result the effectiveness of the German machine guns. The plan of the British attack was to assault two different positions north and south of Aubers and on breaking through for various units to then join up on the high ground of Aubers Ridge. As with Neuve Chapelle again the attack would be made by Haig's 1st Army made up of both British and Indian units. The 9th May 1915 was a sunny day and at 5:00am the British guns began to bombard the German lines, the barrage however would in no way compare to the one that preceded the Battle of Neuve Chapelle. Just prior to going over the top as the barrage lifted and the smoke cleared it became apparent, by observers from the British lines, that the German breastworks and machine gun positions opposite were more or less completely intact. German soldiers could even be seen moving about. The British shells had been too light to cause any serious damage to the German positions, whilst some of the shells were dud and did not work altogether worn out guns also caused shells to fall short of their targets. At 5:40am the troops left the trenches and went over the top into 'no mans land', the attack in the south was a disaster as advancing troops were cut to pieces almost immediately by German machine gun fire. Troops tried desperately to return to the safety of their own trenches only to be met by further waves of advancing troops. The mix up made them sitting ducks and easy targets for enemy gunners, some men however did manage to reach the German wire and in some cases just beyond it but these were soon killed. Despite all of this another attack in the south was planned for 7:00am and much of the same followed.

The attack to the north was just as bad and was led by the 8th Division but Pte Thomas Bird and 23rd Brigade would not be part of the main action. Although the battalion commanders within the brigade had been briefed on the planned operations the brigade was to be held in divisional reserve, only the 24th Brigade and 25th Brigade were involved and they suffered terribly. The 2nd West York's had spent the previous night in assembly trenches behind the firing line having had to be ready in case they were called upon. At 6:30am with the battle well underway the battalion received orders to move up to trenches within 500 yards of the firing line, it was there that they stayed for the whole day under continual enemy shellfire waiting and prepared to join the attack. There was talk that evening of a possible night attack that the 2nd West York's may be part of however with things as they were this never materialised and at 11:00pm orders were received to return to their assembly trenches. That day whilst waiting battalion casualties according to the 2nd West York's war diary were 1 officer and 2 other ranks killed, a further 13 men were wounded and 3 more were listed as missing. Fifteen hours after it started the Battle of Aubers was called off, the British had lost 12,000 men with virtually no ground gained compared to the Germans who lost less than 1,000. The Battle of Aubers had been a complete failure, what's more was the fact that in spite of the losses Britain's professional army was slowly but surely disappearing. The French attacks in Artois on 9th May had initially been successful but they failed to gain their objective of Vimy Ridge, in the following month of fighting French losses were to exceed 100,000 men.

The 2nd West York's had been ordered back to the firing line trenches just after midnight on 10th May but these orders were cancelled fifteen minutes later, they did however take over the front line trenches at 8:00pm that evening. As the Germans had first used gas during the Second Battle of Ypres it was now quite common for them to fire over gas shells onto the allied positions. It was because of this that most battalions in the front line were fitted with respirators, the men of the 2nd West York's had been issued with these prior to the Aubers offensive on 7th May. The frontline trenches the battalion now held were described as quite good although a salient existed that brought enemy positions opposite extremely close. Throughout the 11th May both sides were quite active shelling each other with trench mortars in the positions around the salient. The next day was quiet for the battalion and the men spent their time carrying out various duties within the frontline. It rained during the day on 13th May which made the trenches extremely wet and muddy; things were made worse around 1:00am on 14th May as both sides started to exchange rifle and artillery fire. This demonstration went on for quite a while and after a period of quiet it started up once again later that afternoon; it can only be assumed that some of the shells the Germans fired at the West York's positions during this period contained gas. During those exchanges that day the 2nd West York's had 5 men wounded, it is more than likely that one of those men was Pte Thomas George Bird. Although his battalion was fitted with respirators for some reason Thomas was exposed to gas, he and the four other men wounded that day were moved to an aid post towards the rear in order to receive treatment. As for the rest of the 2nd West York's quietness eventually ensued and the following evening they were relieved by men of the 1/6th Battalion Cameronians (Scottish Rifles), the battalion then moved back to billets behind the lines.

As news of the disasters that had occurred on the Western Front started to filter back to the British people a feeling of outrage ensued. Sir John French blamed British losses on a lack of munitions and engineered an article that appeared in The Times newspaper on 14th May with a headline that read: 'Need for Shells'. Changes were needed and Prime Minister Herbert Asquith knew it, soon after he formed a coalition government made up of Liberal, Tory and Labour members of parliament. Asquith appointed cabinet member David Lloyd George as minister of munitions and as a result British factories quickly went to work on producing the shells and munitions that would in future be needed. At this time however French commanders were putting pressure on the British to keep up local offensives to coincide with their continued attacks in Artois. As a result on 15th May, after a three day bombardment, an attack at Festubert - to the south of Neuve Chapelle - towards Le Bassée was made again carried out by Haig's 1st Army. The battle commenced at 11:30pm and was to be the first night time attack made by the British, after heavy fighting initial success was achieved and German trenches were captured. During the course of the first week the British continued to make progress however the amount of ground actually gained was minimal, although casualties were sustained and no major breakthrough achieved the battle continued until 25th May.

Pte Thomas George Bird died from the effects of gas poisoning at a hospital in England on Thursday 27th May 1915, he was 29 years old. He had been sent there from a hospital in France a few days earlier, at least three of the four other men affected by gas that day also died. Annie Bird had her son's body brought back to Chigwell; a funeral service took place for him at St Mary's Church on Monday 31st May 1915. The service was conducted inside the church and a large number of local residents attended, a full choir was also there and sang numerous hymns and psalms. As the coffin left the church the resident organist Mr Henry Riding played the Dead March in Saul. At the graveside gunshots were fired in military salute and the 'Last Post' was sounded. Pte Thomas George Bird is the only man listed on the Chigwell Village War Memorial killed in the First World War to be buried on British soil; his grave is situated behind trees at the northwest end of St Mary's Churchyard. In time the IWGC as it was then (6) where possible allowed the families of the fallen to put a few words at the foot of their loved ones headstone, Annie Bird chose simply *'In Memory Of My Dear Son'*. In less than a year Mrs Bird had lost her husband and two of her sons, soon afterwards she left Chigwell and moved to Hanwell in West London.

* * *

The last week of May and early June saw the first of the 'New Army' divisions start to arrive in France and Flanders; these were the K1, K2 and K3 divisions. In June the British front line was extended south of the La Bassée Canal to the French town of Loos, a distance of just over ten miles this area was controlled by Haig's 1st Army. During July the newly arrived divisions were formed to make a third army group, this 3rd Army was commanded by Sir Charles Monro who had commanded I Corps when Haig took command of 1st Army (7). With the arrival of the 'New Army' divisions came several men from Chigwell.

HENRY JOHN CLARK
Unfortunately very little is known about Henry John Clark other than that he was the eldest son of a local farm worker called Henry Clark who'd been born at Bishops Stortford in 1852 and his wife Annie who'd been born at Epping in 1863. Henry himself was born in Chigwell sometime between 1886 and 1887 and had three younger brothers called Ernest, Alfred (8) and Arthur all of whom had also been born in Chigwell. At the turn of the century and at least until the end of the war the Clark family lived at 8 Hainault Villas, Hainault Road, Chigwell. Whilst nothing is known of his education or profession the young Henry Clark was one of the first 100,000 men to answer Kitcheners request for volunteers enlisting at a recruiting office at Croydon in Surrey in August 1914. Given the location it is reasonable to suggest that Henry was working in this area at the time. After passing a medical examination Henry was given service number 738 and subsequently posted to the 6th Battalion Queen's (Royal West Surrey Regiment) (9). This 'New Army' battalion was formed that August at Guildford in Surrey as part of K1 and assigned to 37th Brigade as part of the 12th (Eastern) Division. Soon afterwards Henry's battalion along with other units of 12th Division were transferred to Purfleet in Essex for a period of basic training. During November the battalion moved to Hythe on the south coast and then in February 1915 to Aldershot to complete training. On Wednesday 2nd June at 5:00pm Pte Henry Clark and his battalion left Aldershot for Folkestone and from there they crossed the Channel to France, sailing on SS Invicta they arrived at Boulogne at 10:35pm that evening.

The next three weeks saw the battalion spending much of their time in billets and training. It was not until late June that they entered the trenches for the first time taking over a stretch of line just east of Armentières.

According to their battalion war diary the 6th QRWS suffered its first casualty on 24th June when a young corporal was killed (10). As July started the battalion was held up in billets in the Plugstreet area just over the Belgian border, then on the 11th July they once again entered the trenches at Armentières. This period was rather quiet for the battalion and the men were mainly involved in strengthening defences and carrying out general repairs along their stretch of line. As August began the battalion, when out of the line, were mainly called on to form working parties. This involved the men being detailed to dig trenches, build roads or carry out general duties such as the loading and unloading of supplies. During this time the battalion were based in billets at Le Bizet, a village which lies directly on the border between Belgium and France. On 3rd August Pte Henry Clark and his battalion moved back to the trenches taking over a stretch of line they had previously held at Le Touquet from men of the 7th Battalion East Surrey Regiment. This relief started at 8:30pm and was completed by 10:45pm. The next day was very quiet although a draft of 40 extra men arrived from the base to join those men already holding the line. During the early hours on 5th August enemy working parties were spotted in front of the QRWS trenches but the battalion suffered no casualties. The following day was relatively quiet however the trenches held by the battalion were hit by German shellfire, no serious damage was caused but one NCO was killed and three other men were wounded. The next day more shells fell but most were aimed at houses beside a main road that ran alongside the QRWS trenches, fortunately the battalion reported no casualties. Each battalion had a HQ and the 6th QRWS had theirs located in a farm just to the rear of their line.

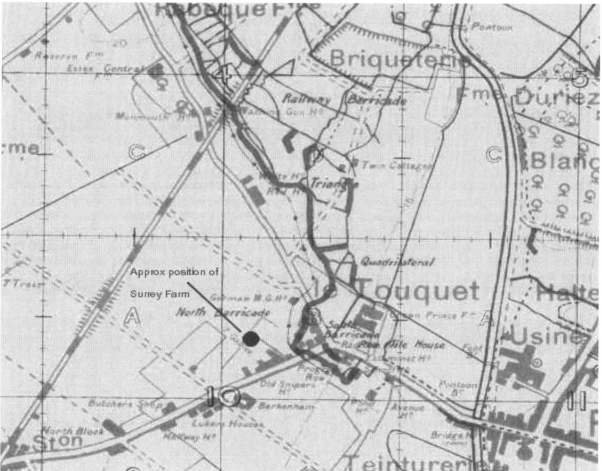

Map 14, Le Touquet (Position of the 6th Queens (Royal West Surreys) August 1915)

Given that the building generally housed senior officers as well as what could be described as secret information regarding troop plans and movements it wasn't uncommon for guards to be posted around the outside of the building. For obvious reasons this farm was known to the men as Surrey Farm and on 8th August it suffered two direct hits by high explosive shells, both landed and detonated on the roof however amazingly little damage was done. The remainder of the day was quiet however the battalion war diary states that three men were wounded when the farm was hit, it is most likely that one of these men was Pte Henry John Clark. It is possible that Henry was standing guard around Surrey Farm or helping to bring up supplies when the shells landed. At 3:50am on the morning of 9th August the Germans heavily shelled the trenches to the right of the QRWS, also hit were the communication trenches to the rear and the Le Touquet Road. This bombardment lasted nearly two hours then a quiet day ensued. At 8:30pm the battalion was relieved by the men of 7th East Surrey Regiment. This relief was completed by 10:45pm and the 6th QRWS returned to billets in Le Bizet. Meanwhile Pte Henry Clark it seems was taken to a makeshift hospital known as a Casualty Clearing Station behind the lines southwest of Armentières.

On entering a CCS a wounded man was classified according to his wounds and sometimes if necessary small operations were carried out. Although the extent of Henry's injuries will never be known it seems they were such that he survived for only a few days. Pte Henry John Clark died of wounds on Wednesday 12th August barely a year after enlisting. His death was reported in the Chigwell Parish Magazine in September 1915, he is buried in Plot IX, Row A, Grave 37 at Cite Bonjean Military Cemetery near Armentières. The next part of the story however is rather interesting as a mix up saw the IWGC mark Henry's headstone with the initials N J rather than H J. This oversight went unnoticed for possibly 87 years until I came across the mistake whilst researching this book. I am pleased to say that having provided sufficient proof of this error it has now been rectified and at last Henry's correct initials appear on his headstone. Although less serious another mistake sees the name of Pte Henry John Clark appear on the Chigwell Village War Memorial with the casualties for 1916 instead of those for 1915.

* * *

Towards the end of August preparations for the next allied offensive were well underway. This assault was to be centred in the area around the French mining town of Loos which lies halfway between La Bassée and Lens. The area around Loos was made up of mining villages scattered with pitheads and slagheaps, this was the industrial area of France and a stark contrast to the farming areas of Flanders. The plan was quite simply to evict the Germans from France by any means possible. Joffre as far back as June had put it to Haig that Loos was a suitable place to launch an attack. After a visit to the area Haig, who before the visit had welcomed the idea, felt it was too heavily defended and not suitable terrain for such an operation preferring instead a renewed attack around La Bassée. A conference held by allied command came to the conclusion that an attack should be made on a large front but the British, because of a lack of men and munitions felt that no such event could take place until the following spring. Joffre disagreed and wanted a fresh assault before the end of the year. Sir John French had agreed to support any French breakthrough around Lens but offered no more, after Joffre met with Kitchener and a subsequent meeting between Kitchener and French he was soon persuaded to change his mind. Bad results on the Eastern Front and at Gallipoli had made Kitchener realise that efforts must be made in order for something positive to be achieved, it was hoped that Loos would be that something. Right from the start Sir John French had his doubts, as did Haig who suspected that heavy losses would be incurred. As planning began and things were arranged however their mood and the mood of their staff changed to one of optimism, although it must be said in their minds they could have done without the whole affair. The plan being worked out once again would involve Haig's 1st Army. It would be carried out in conjunction with French attacks to the south in Champagne and it was initially hoped it would occur in August, it was postponed however several times until it was agreed that 25th September would favour everyone. The Battle of Loos would turn out to be the biggest and most important attack made by the British on the Western Front during 1915; it would also be the first time that divisions of Kitcheners New Army would participate in a major action. In addition to this the Battle of Loos would turn out to be the catalyst for a change of command within the British Army. However before the story of Loos is explained on the same day the battle was due to start an event in Flanders occurred involving a man from Chigwell.

JAMES EDWARD COX

James Cox had arrived in France on 31st May 1915 - the same day that Pte Thomas George Bird was buried - amongst the influx of New Army divisions. James was born at Wickford in Essex in 1893 the eldest son of Albert Edward and Elizabeth Cox. An older sister called Mary was born in 1888 then two years after James another sister named Edith was born. To follow was a brother called Albert Charles, another sister called Ada and eventually two more brothers named Arthur and Richard making seven children in all. At the turn of the century the family were living in Wickford but James's father, a railway labourer, found work on the Great Eastern Railway and the family moved to Grange Hill living at 6 Railway Cottages. It is thought that on leaving school James also found work on the railway. When war was declared James, like Henry Clark, wasted no time in answering Kitcheners call. Having travelled to Chelmsford in Essex in August 1914 to enlist James was posted to the 9th Battalion of the Essex Regiment. This battalion was formed at Warley in Essex during August 1914 becoming part of K1. The 12th (Eastern) Division to which the battalion was attached was made up of the 35th Brigade, 36th Brigade and 37th Brigade; the first of these contained the 9th Battalion Essex Regiment along with the 5th Battalion Royal Berkshire Regiment, 7th Battalion Norfolk Regiment and the 7th Battalion Suffolk Regiment.

After formation the 35th Brigade went to Shorncliffe for a period of basic training. In March 1915 they were transferred to Blenheim barracks Aldershot to continue preparations. As previously mentioned on the last day of May 1915 the battalions of 35th Brigade landed in France joining the other units of 12th Division. The next day saw units of 35th Brigade head for the Hazebrouck area although it wasn't until the second week of June that some of the battalions, including men of the 9th Essex, went into the trenches at Ploegsteert for the first time. The beginning of July saw Pte James Cox and his battalion in billets around Ploegsteert but soon after they entered the trenches again, throughout that month whilst holding the lines a steady flow of casualties were sustained. Some nights the men were used for working parties which saw them strengthening defences or bringing up supplies, throughout August the men regularly continued going in and out the line.

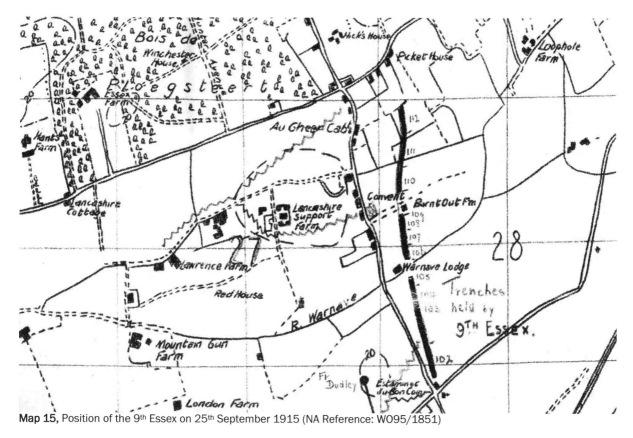

Map 15, Position of the 9th Essex on 25th September 1915 (NA Reference: WO95/1851)

By September the 9th Essex found themselves still holding the lines, positioned southeast of Ploegsteert Wood, on the 25th September they were to take part in a diversion to coincide with events taking place further south. Their battalion war diary takes up the story:

'At 5:55am simultaneously with the launching of French and British attacks at various places south of Armentières, Hooge and Champagne a curtain of smoke was raised to conceal our parapet along the whole of the front. It was preceded at 5:00am by an artillery shoot on the enemy lines. Bundles of wet straw soaked in paraffin were lighted and thrown over our parapet, a bundle to every yard. Smoke bombs were thrown by hand and by the best thrower. A dense cloud of smoke was thus raised in a few minutes, rising to a height of 50ft and drifting slowly toward the enemy lines, the wind being favourable, a similar procedure was also followed by the battalions on our flanks'.

The reason for this smoke screen was that the British intended to use Chlorine Gas during the Battle of Loos; its use is explained in more detail further on in this chapter. The 9th Essex war diary continues:

'The enemy appeared considerably alarmed; a bell was heard ringing, rapid rifle and maxim fire opened on our parapet to which our four machine guns replied. Following the firing of a red rocket his {German} artillery opened steady fire on our fire and support trenches with shrapnel and high explosive shells. Lawrence Farm East was struck by a 15cm high explosive shell and set on fire and burned to the ground, a number of packs and material being lost. The enemy shooting was accurate, several direct hits on our trenches causing a score of casualties. In all about 130 shells were fired to which our artillery replied. By 7:30am all was quiet. In the afternoon (3:00pm to 3:45pm) we annoyed the enemy by short bursts of rapid rifle fire and machine gun fire, to which he replied with little rifle fire but about 30 shells along our line. In the evening (10:00pm onwards) he fired another 30 shells, and in the early morning some trench howitzer "Sausages" to which our artillery replied'.

Throughout the day's exchanges the 9th Essex had 22 men wounded, the battalion war diary states that 2 men were also killed; one of those was Pte James Cox. A report appeared in the November 1915 edition of the Chigwell Parish Magazine stating that James had been killed in action, apparently his cousin had informed James parents before the War Office. Another report in the parish magazine a year later incorrectly stated that James had been killed at the Battle of Loos. The other man of the 9th Essex killed along with James that day was L/Cpl Ely Brown who, according to SDGW lived in Woodford. Pte James Cox and L/Cpl Ely Brown are buried next to each other in graves C4 and C5 respectively at Gunners Farm CWGC Cemetery south of Plugstreet; this cemetery was created by the battalions of 35th Brigade in July 1915.

* * *

The Battle of Loos was to be carried out by two corps of Haig's 1st Army. These were Gough's I Corps and Rawlinson's IV Corps and their objectives were to penetrate the German front line positions, and then push on some 3000 yards beyond to a well prepared German second line creating a gap that could be exploited by waiting cavalry units. I Corps was to attack on the northern sector of the battlefront. Made up of three divisions it was deployed with its 2nd Division to the north attacking south of the La Bassée Canal along the Béthune to La Bassée Road in the direction of Auchy. To the right of 2nd Division stood 9th Division and their line of attack was towards a German position known as Hohenzollern Redoubt and a slagheap beyond known as Foss 8. South of 9th Division stood 7th Division and their attack front consisted of an area of high ground which lead beyond the German first line towards a position known as the Quarries. To the right of 7th Division's line ran the Vermelles to Hulluch Road and this served as the corps boundary. IV Corps was positioned with 1st Division to its north attacking on a front towards the village of Hulluch (see map 16). In its path stood two wooded areas known as Bois Carre and La Haie, although mainly destroyed these areas still concealed German observation posts. To the south of Bois Carre and also on 1st Division's front stood the remains of a cherry tree known to the British as Lone Tree, despite sustaining rifle fire and bombardments the tree still flowered during the spring of 1915. On 1st Division's right stood the brigades of 15th Division and their objectives were the Loos Road Redoubt, Lens Road Redoubt and Loos village itself, at this point the German positions in front of the village were protected by two trench lines, beyond Loos lay Chalk Pit Wood. Success on the southern sector of IV Corps front fell to units of the Territorial Force. The objectives set for 47th Division were the southern half of Loos village and ground beyond towards a large metal structure, used by the Germans for observation, known to the British as Tower Bridge. The metal structure was in fact the winding gear for a coal mine in the area but its outline resembled Tower Bridge. On the far side of their front and east of Loos stood Hill 70 which took its name from its height in contours on local maps, to its left was positioned a redoubt beyond which was the German second line. Positioned on the right of 47th Division stood the French Army. In General Reserve stood the Guards Division and two 'New Army' divisions all of which were attached to IX Corps under the command of Lieutenant General Haking. It was thought that the two New Army divisions, although having never seen action, could be used along with the guards and cavalry to consolidate the front once success was achieved. The two divisions in question were the 21st Division and 24th Division; the latter contained a young officer from Chigwell.

MAURICE AUSTIN MURRAY
Maurice Austin Murray was born at Stone in the county of Kent on 4th January 1895, for many years his grandfather was the cannon at the church in the village. Maurice's father was Frederick Auriol Murray, also a clergyman he too was born at Stone on 27th November 1865. Fredrick met Maurice's mother Jessie Styles and the couple were married on 4th January 1893, Jessie had been born at Swanscombe in Kent sometime during 1869. By the turn of the century Frederick had taken up the post of Vicar at St Peters Church in the Hertfordshire village of Mill End (11), the family lived at the vicarage there situated in Church Lane. Jessie gave birth to another son soon after called George; he was born at Rickmansworth on 2nd April 1900, in later life he was referred to by his middle name of Ronald. Maurice was educated at Eagle House Sandhurst eventually gaining a classical scholarship at Haileybury College. Whilst there he would spend four years as a sergeant in the Officer Training Corps as well as becoming head of Colvin House and captain of the school football team. Whilst Maurice was enjoying life at Sandhurst his father was offered the job of vicar at St Mary's Church in Chigwell, a replacement for the then vicar Reverend Thomas Marsden who was retiring due to ill health (12). Reverend Frederick Auriol Murray readily accepted the position and he and his family moved into Chigwell Vicarage between December 1911 and January 1912. Meanwhile Maurice continued his studies and the following year won an open Rustat scholarship to Jesus College Cambridge, he was due to start there in October 1914 but world events intervened.

It was only natural that Maurice would have wished to join the army, no doubt all his friends were doing just that and luckily his service record has survived for us to follow his story. On 19th August 1914 he filled out an application form at Warley applying for a temporary commission in the regular army for the duration of the war requesting to serve in either the Essex Regiment or a Scottish Regiment. According to a medical carried out on this date Maurice had good hearing and vision and weighed 149lb. This form was then taken on 22nd August to the master of Haileybury College to be signed in order to vouch for Maurice's good character, it was then returned to Warley on 23rd August. Maurice underwent another medical examination in London on 4th September and from this we know that he was 6ft ½˝ tall with 38˝chest, he had fair hair and a healthy complexion, he also states that he was born of Scottish decent and this would explain his earlier request.

Then on 11th September it seems Maurice changed his mind and he walked in to the recruiting office of the 16th Battalion Middlesex Regiment (Public Schools Battalion) at 24 St James Street London (13), at that time he was just 19 years and eight months old. On that date he became Private 484 Murray and was posted to the battalion based at Kempton Park in Surrey. Then just fifteen days later on 26th September he was discharged to take up a temporary commission as a Second Lieutenant in the 11th Battalion Essex Regiment (14). The 11th Essex had been formed at Warley in early September becoming part of K3. They moved to Shoreham to begin training and by the late spring of 1915 were practicing their skills at Blackdown Camp on Salisbury Plain. On the 21st August they received orders that a probable move to France was in the offing and were moved to Cobham Common in order to practice the art of trench warfare. The battalion, along with the rest of their division, finally received orders to move overseas a few days later and on 30th August they landed at Boulogne.

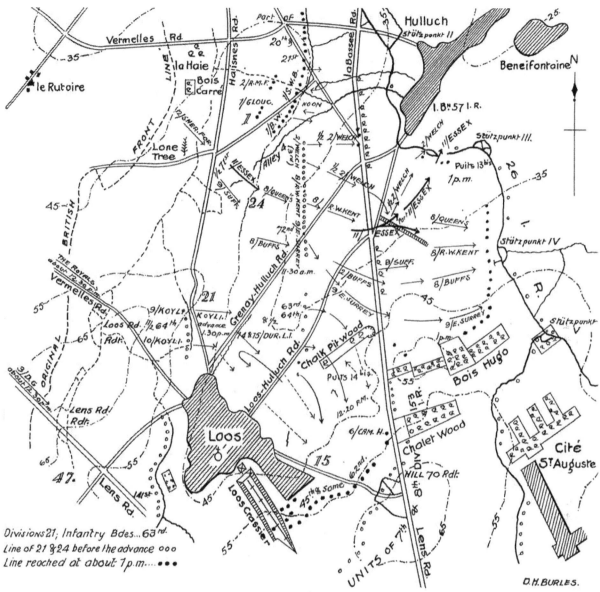

Map 16, Attack by the 21st and 24th Divisions at Loos on 26th September 1915 (Map taken from 'Service Battalions of the Essex Regiment' Volume 6 by J W Burrows and Son)

A lack of artillery was a major concern for the British commanders at Loos and to compensate for this it was decided that Chlorine Gas would be used as a weapon for the first time, after all the Germans had used it at Ypres back in April. Prior to the day of the battle trenches were dug along the British front line and under the cover of darkness gas cylinders were placed in them ready for release, on the day it was hoped that the wind needed to push the gas towards the German positions would be favourable. The British troops were issued with gas helmets in the form of a hood worn over the head, not the most comfortable garment it had eyeholes to see through although these tended to steam up making vision extremely difficult. On the 21st September the allies began a preliminary bombardment of the German lines ahead of their main attack, for the British it was by far their largest battle front yet however their concentration of guns, although strong, turned out to be not as effective as hoped. At just after 5:00am on the 25th September Haig consulted his meteorological officer on the wind conditions and was told they weren't great. He tried to find out if the battle could be stopped but was told that it wasn't possible as preparations were well under way, this being the case he decided to proceed with the plan of attack. At 5:51am as British artillery continued to pound enemy lines the order to release the gas was given and the taps on cylinders were opened right along the British front, like the 9th Essex had done further north at Plugstreet, smoke was also released in order to confuse German troops. The gas formed a greenish yellow coloured cloud and drifted slowly eastward towards the enemy, as they saw it their machine guns sprung to life and bullets flew towards the British positions. The assault troops were massed in the front line trenches, on what was a cold and slightly rainy morning, as they awaited the order to advance. At 5:40am the gas cylinders were turned off by which time more than 150 tons of gas had been released, the whistles blew and the British troops in attack dress and gas helmets climbed their trench ladders and advanced into a somewhat misty no mans land.

To the north on 2nd Division's front the gas was completely ineffective as it failed to reach the German lines. On 9th Division's front around the Hohenzollern Redoubt the gas worked quite well, but unfortunately it moved slowly as it drifted towards the German front and there was not enough of it. It was the same story in front of Loos although it did assist in the advance of the 15th Division and 47th Division. To the centre of the attack front, in positions held by 1st Division, around the Vermelles-Hulluch Road the gas at first drifted towards the German trenches but then started to drift back towards the British frontline, as a result some casualties were sustained. As for the battle itself the 47th Division on the far right of the attack front initially made good progress but at a heavy price, having made gains they then proceeded with caution adopting defensive positions when they should have pressed on. Some of the troops on the divisions left did however manage to enter the southern outskirts of Loos and push beyond the village towards Chalk Pit Wood but German troops entrenched there inflicted terrible enfilade fire upon them. The Scottish battalions that made up 15th Division, after overcoming lingering pockets of gas managed within the first hour of attack to take both enemy trench lines in front of Loos and the village itself. However confusion ensued as the battalions now short of officers - they had been either killed or wounded - became mixed up around the village, eventually though they did manage to sort themselves out and push on towards the lightly defended Hill 70. Ascending with ease once at the top they made down the slope towards the German second line were they became sitting ducks for waiting enemy machine guns and were virtually wiped out. The Germans were reinforced throughout the day and as counter attacks were mounted Hill 70 was eventually retaken. Although ground had been gained on the southern sector to the north on the front of 1st Division things were not so good. Some units of the division after suffering severe casualties from the German positions concealed in the copses of Bois Carre and La Haie – that had been left unaffected by either the gas or the artillery barrage - did manage to breakthrough the enemy lines and reach the southern edge of Hulluch and area beyond to the German second line. However the troops needed to reinforce them and help consolidate the ground gained got held up in futile attacks around the position of Lone Tree. These attacks were deemed futile because at this point the positions around Lone Tree could have and should have been outflanked. As the minutes ticked away the Germans brought up reinforcements and the advanced elements belonging to 1st Division became more desperate. Meanwhile more unsuccessful frontal attacks at Lone Tree saw any chance of help fade and by nightfall the men in Hulluch were forced to retire back to the Lens-La Bassée Road. The 7th Division and 9th Division were successful in taking positions along their front, capturing both the Quarries and the Hohenzollern Redoubt but as German resistance intensified their advance was soon halted. The 2nd Division however, due to their unsuccessful gas attack made no gains. As with most battles mounted by the British in 1915 the first day of Loos had initially been one of success but by nightfall it had turned once again to one of failure.

On the morning of the 26th September Haig, now short of troops, requested from Sir John French that the General Reserve, Haking's IX Corps, be put under his control. It must be said that the two commanders did not see eye to eye on the exact involvement of these untried and tested troops however after much debate French agreed and the 21st Division and 24th Division - the Guards Division was too far back behind the lines and not used - were put at Haig's disposal. By this time these two divisions had only been in France for just over two weeks. After the various units that made up these divisions arrived they were assembled and concentrated around St Omer, the second week of September saw them receive orders to head south to Béthune. The 24th Division was made up of the 71st Brigade, 72nd Brigade and 73rd Brigade, the first of which contained the following battalions: 8th Bedfordshire Regiment, 9th Norfolk Regiment, 9th Suffolk Regiment and 11th Essex Regiment.

The next three days would have been a testing time for the young Lieutenant Murray trying to keep order in his ranks as his men marched southwards covering many miles in the hot summer weather. Their route took them along country lanes, through villages and towns and on the 23rd September they reached Lilliers west of Béthune. Their journey was made that little bit harder due to the confusion that existed behind the lines prior to the battle however the men, although exhausted pressed on towards Béthune. At 9:00am on the 25th September the battalion CO called a meeting of all officers to brief them on the forthcoming operations; they were instructed that during the attack they were not to get held up by light enemy opposition but to push on with their assault. At 11:00am the battalion moved southeast out of Béthune halting near the village of Noyelles where they rested up for three hours taking on rations and filling water bottles, from there they turned east and headed towards Hulluch. That night the 21st Division and 24th Division were ordered up towards the front line amid a congested flow of wounded men and ambulances headed in the opposite direction. By now it had started to rain heavily and the exhausted men became soaked, they lacked warm food as their mobile kitchens had been left behind but in spite of it all their moral remained high. Whilst this was going on the Germans were all the time bringing up reinforcements and restoring their second line, it would be so that by the time the British attacked the following morning their positions would be stronger defended than had been the case on the previous morning when the battle had first started. That night the artillery belonging to the 21st Division and 24th Division advanced too far ahead as a mist had formed making their exact position confusing; when the mist cleared the guns were in full view of the Germans who almost immediately silenced them. Both divisions by this time were totally confused as they had no maps and no knowledge of their immediate area however they still managed to reach their starting positions.

Their line was just east of Loos west of the Lens-La Bassée Road. The front to which they would attack was between Hulluch and Hill 70. The German second line ahead of them stretched in an outward shaped semi-circle from Hulluch to Cite St Laurent, at intervals contained within were concrete machine gun bunkers known as Stutzpunkt each of which was defined by a numeral - as shown on Map 16. Throughout the night the Germans occupied two copses to the front of their position known as Chalet Wood and Bois Hugo. These woods should have been held onto by the British the previous afternoon but were not and from them the enemy had a perfect field of fire. Small scale German attacks throughout the night only helped to improve their position. Haig's plan was for the men of the 21st Division and 24th Division to continue the battle and push forward beyond the German second line, he was unaware that divisional commanders were under the false impression that German forces were almost beaten and that their task would be simple. In fact their task was impossible, harder than the previous day when experienced troops had had gas and artillery for support.

At exactly 11:00am on the 26th September the two divisions started off in the direction of the German positions unbeknown to them in full view of their enemy. As they moved they found themselves stepping over the dead from the previous day and had been ordered to ignore the cries of those wounded men still lying out in areas of no mans land. The 21st Division was situated to the south of the front attacking mainly in the direction of Chalet Wood and Hill 70, as they advanced they were massacred. As for the 24th Division their attack front was between Hulluch and Bois Hugo. The 72nd Brigade attacked first with battalions of the 8th Royal West Kent's and 9th East Surreys leading the charge through long grass towards the German second line. As they advanced in rows, downhill towards the Lens-La Bassée Road and then up hill towards the German line, they were systematically cut to pieces by machine gun fire coming not only from Bois Hugo but also from the various Stutzpunkt defending the main German positions. They also took fire which came from the direction of Hulluch. At 11:25am the 71st Brigade led by the 9th Suffolk's on the right and the 11th Essex on the left followed in the same direction but by this time the Germans were waiting for them (15). The commanding officer of the 11th Essex, Lieutenant Colonel Radclyffe led the men of the battalion, they advanced in lines of platoons roughly 600 yards south of the Vermelles-Hulluch Road as German machine guns rattled away and artillery shells burst all around. The battalion's objectives were not clear; they were just to attack the German Line ahead of them. The officers of the battalion including Lieutenant Murray encouraged their men forward as the troops of the 11th Essex pushed on. Within a few minutes Colonel Radclyffe was seriously wounded and it appears from a report in the January 1916 edition of the Chigwell Parish Magazine that Lieutenant Murray had tried to help him by rendering first aid. Continuing the advance downhill towards the Lens-La Bassée Road it was soon after that Murray was hit, four soldiers later reported their versions of the event:

Private Albert Ernest Gosling (16) on 15th February 1916 at a hospital in Etaples said:

'On Sunday 26th September I saw him {Lt M A Murray} lying on the ground when I passed him both on the advance and afterwards on the retreat. I did not see where he was hit but I heard it was in the head, he was laying face foremost on the ground. I was wounded myself just afterwards so did not see what happened to the ground where he was lying but the Germans probably occupied it because several men lying around Lieutenant Murray where reported missing later'.

Private B J Gerrod on 2nd March 1916 at the Canadian hospital in Etaples said:

'I saw him hit and then I saw him put his hand to his head and exclaimed "I'm done". It was terrible machine gun fire. Then we advanced and left him behind. We came back over the ground on retirement but I did not see him'.

Corporal Palmer on 18th March 1916 at Boulogne said:

'Pte J W Hartley 'B' Coy told me that he saw Lieutenant Murray lying on the ground opposite Hill 70 face downwards shot through the head and apparently dead. I think the place where the Lieutenant was lying was between the English and German lines and could not be examined'.

Private Loftus on 20th March 1916 at the Anglo American hospital at Boulogne (described as a most reliable witness) said:

'I was attached to HQ (Battalion) at the time of the action on 26th September 1915 and so I was only about 20 yards from Colonel Radclyffe when he was hit. Mr Murray was wounded either 10 minutes before or after the Colonel, I can't remember which and it was very much in the same place. It was in the dip in the road going towards Hill 70 on the Hulluch Road. This was beyond where we crossed the Lens-La Bassée Road. From the way in which he fell I fancy he must have been killed'.

During the next hour the men of the Essex and the rest of 21st Division and 24th Division found themselves gaining no advantage as German troops withstood their attack. Some men reached the wire in front of the enemy but could find no way through, the artillery had not touched it and it remained intact. Eventually one by one they were hit by bullets from the German machine guns. At around 12:30pm, with no more units left to come up in support the only option left was for the remaining men to fall back towards their own lines and the order to retire was given. The slaughter had been such and their victory so overwhelming that German troops on seeing the men withdraw didn't fire another shot for the rest of the day as a show of compassion. During the actual assault made by the 21st Division and 24th Division they gained no ground that hadn't already been held prior to their advance, added to this they sustained casualties in excess of 8,000 (17). In spite of this it must be said that no one could deny the bravery shown that day by these inexperienced but gallant men of Kitcheners Army. Over the next few days German counter attacks slowly clawed back the ground that had been won during the action of 25th September with the Battle of Loos effectively fizzling out into the first week of October.

On 2nd October 1915 the Murray family received a telegram, at the vicarage in Chigwell, informing them that their son was reported wounded and missing from the period 25th September to 27th September. After mixed reports filtered back it was hoped Maurice may have been taken prisoner therefore on 17th November Frederick Murray wrote to the War Office to enquire if this was in fact the case. Meanwhile around this time Jessie Murray became very active in helping send supplies to the prisoners of her sons regiment known to be held by the Germans. In January 1916 the Chigwell Parish Magazine stated that still no news of Maurice had been received at the vicarage and admitted that hopes of finding him still alive were fading. The War Office wrote again on 13th May saying they still had received no news although by this time the soldier's reports outlined on the previous page had been made. Then again on 7th August Frederick received a letter from the War Office saying they had no further reports of his son and did he know anything. Frederick wrote back on the 12th August saying he did not, that letter was received by the War Office on 14th August. Therefore on the 19th August 1916 they wrote back to him saying they regretfully constrained to conclude that Lieutenant Maurice Austin Murray was killed in action on 25th September 1915 - we know it was 26th September - and that they expressed their sympathy. The body of 20 year old Lieutenant Maurice Austin Murray was never found and his name is commemorated on panel 85 of the Loos Memorial to the Missing at Dud Corner CWGC Cemetery. The memorial lists the names of more than 20,000 officers and men who fell in the area between the 25th September 1915 and the end of the war. It includes the name of Lieutenant Colonel Charles Edward Radclyffe, the commanding officer of the 11th Essex who Lieutenant Murray had helped prior to being killed himself. Frederick Murray enlisted the help of Cox & Co - a firm of solicitors - to look after affairs as Maurice had left no will, on 13th November Reverend Murray collected his son's effects. Around this time an obituary appeared in The Times and Essex newspapers reporting the death of Lieutenant Maurice Austin Murray, contained within was this quote from another of his commanding officers: *"He was loved by his men and all who knew him, he was a character that was an example to all,"* he added, *"We share your anxiety as your son was the most popular officer in the Regiment"*. Reverend Frederick Auriol Murray died on 12th February 1939 aged 73 whilst Jessie Murray lived until April 1955, their second son George eventually married and had children; he died on 8th November 1961.

* * *

The disaster of Loos did not sit well with the public or the politicians back home in England as wounded soldiers had arrived home and told of the impossible task they had been set. With a string of disasters and another winter fast approaching it was decided a change of command was needed if the war was ever to be won. Therefore after much infighting and subsequent pressure placed upon him, on 8th December 1915 Sir John French resigned as CIC of the BEF. His replacement was to be the 55 year old Scottish born General Sir Douglas Haig. Although he would not be promoted to the rank of Field Marshal until late 1916 Haig's appointment as CIC became effective on 19th December. With a large number of the regular army now either killed or wounded it would be him who would decide the fate of those men who had rushed to the recruiting offices back in late 1914 and early 1915 to become part of the British Army.

30, The Memorial Plaque dedicated to those killed at the Prince of Wales Pub on the evening of 19th April 1941

31, The gravestone of Pte Thomas George Bird situated at the rear of St Mary's Churchyard in Chigwell

32, The gravestone of Pte Henry John Clark at Cite Bonjean CWGC Cemetery with the initials N J instead of H J

33, The gravestone of Pte James Edward Cox

34, The name of Lt Maurice Austin Murray as it appears on the Loos Memorial to the Missing

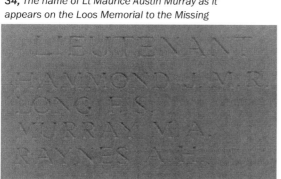

35, Lt Maurice Austin Murray

GALLIPOLI

In order to tell the story of the last man from Chigwell to die in 1915 it's necessary to go back in time to events that occurred towards the end of 1914 and consequently the beginning of 1915. At this time a plan had been devised which if successful would shorten the war and bring victory to the allied armies. With deadlock having occurred between both sides on the Western Front other theatres of operation were looked at in the hope of finding a successful solution and an end to the war. Russia badly needed supplies and the allies could not afford to see her defeated, with her land borders to the west forming the Eastern Front a fresh approach was needed in order to assist her. Assistance could only be given by sea and the route to the north was long and too dangerous, especially in winter. Therefore the plan, the idea of the then First Lord of the Admiralty Winston Churchill, involved forcing a passage, by way of a naval bombardment, through the Dardanelles whilst at the same time knocking Turkey out of the war. The stretch of water known as the Dardanelles Straits is bordered on its western or European side by a stretch of land known as the Gallipoli Peninsular. The land on the eastern or Asian side of the Dardanelles which today makes up most of mainland Turkey in 1915 connected much of the Ottoman Empire. Quite simply the Dardanelles links the Aegean Sea with the Sea of Marmara and in turn this leads some 170 miles up to the Bosphorus River. On the west bank of the Bosphorus where it meets the Marmara lays the Turkish capital Istanbul known in 1915 as Constantinople. The river leads into the Black Sea on whose northern edge lays the southern coast of Russia. It was hoped that if the allies could force the Dardanelles and keep the waterway open and at the same time capture Constantinople Turkey would be defeated. Then the allies would not only have access to Turkey's Empire but they could also supply Russia and in turn reinforce the Eastern Front and defeat Germany. Turkey was known as the Ottoman Empire and at the outbreak of the Great War she owned much of the area which today makes up those countries of the Middle East (see map 17). With an area so vast and such a mixed population it was impossible for Turkey to control every quarter of her Empire and inevitably tensions in some parts ran high. Ruled by Sultan Abdul Hamid II (also know as Abdul the Dammed), until a revolution in 1908 saw a group known as the Young Turks have a say in how things were run, Turkey was known as the sick man of Europe. The Young Turks upset at how Turkey seemed to be losing its grip and social standing had gained military support in order to challenge the Sultan and in 1909 he was removed. The next few years saw Turkey lose more of its land due to a succession of conflicts and by 1914 she was looking for some kind of stability; Germany saw this and realised her potential as an ally. Two days before war was declared the two nations agreed an alliance although, as previously mentioned elsewhere in this book, Turkey would not officially enter the war until 31st October 1914.

The Gallipoli plan it was hoped could be achieved one of two ways. The first was by naval bombardment alone and the other was for the combined use of naval and ground troops. The latter however didn't sit well with the westerners who felt troops were required for actions in France and Flanders. So it was that a naval operation would be tried first and on 3rd November 1914 Churchill ordered the navy to shell the forts on both sides at the mouth of the Dardanelles. A direct hit on one of the forts inflicted terrible damage and loss of life but the action proved counter productive as it alerted the Turks to allied intentions in the region. Turkish forces around Gallipoli came under the leadership of Liman Von Sanders, a German general his influence saw the Turks strengthen their position by improving defences. Therefore on 19th February 1915 when a fresh attempt was made to destroy by way of naval bombardment the Turkish forts and defences that lined the entrance on both sides of the Dardanelles it achieved little. A further attempt to clear the way again by way of bombardment was made with the help of small landing parties on 26th February however this proved more successful. The next hurdle, as well as the need for the continued destruction of Turkish guns, for the allies to overcome was the mine's that the Turks had now laid at the narrowest part of the Dardanelles since the first attack on 3rd November. Over the next few weeks the allies tried several attempts to put ashore small landing parties, made up of naval forces, but by now these were suffering casualties due to stiffer Turkish resistance. At the same time minesweepers crewed by civilians were trying unsuccessfully to clear a passage whilst coming under intense fire from Turkish guns. Several attempts were made at this and all proved futile. Back in England the First Sea Lord – Lord Fisher - who had initially been in favour of the idea was getting cold feet over the lack of success the Navy was having. It was looking more and more likely that in order to silence Turkish defences a ground invasion would have to take place, Kitchener sent for the mild mannered General Sir Ian Hamilton whom he wanted to command forces in the Dardanelles. On 18th March a last attempt to force the Dardanelles was made by the Royal Navy with assistance from French ships, this combined force pounded the Turkish defences harder than ever. That day the allies lost three ships to mines and had at least five more damaged by Turkish guns which unbeknown to the allies were by now running short of ammunition. If they had continued their attempt the following morning the allies would have more or less gone unopposed, however they didn't and their attentions turned from that of a naval operation to that of a ground invasion. In the hope of misleading Turkish forces it was decided that the main landings would be made at two different locations on the peninsular together with several diversionary landings on both the peninsular and Asian side of the Dardanelles. The landings on the peninsular were to be made by units of the 29th Division and those of the Anzac Corps with the diversions, on the peninsular at Bulair, being made by RND units and, on the Asian side at Kumkale, by French forces. By the time the landings took place on the early morning of

25th April 1915 Liman Von Sanders had had almost a month to prepare himself and his forces, a good tactician he had spread his forces in such a way that all areas for invasion were now covered.

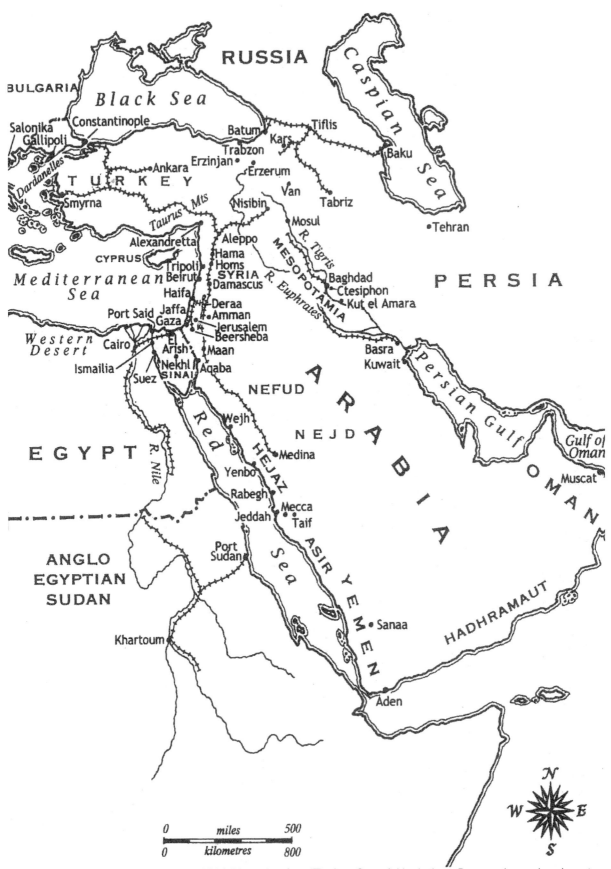

Map 17, The Turkish Ottoman Empire in 1914 (Map taken from 'The Last Crusade' by Anthony Bruce and reproduced courtesy of John Murray Publishing)

The Gallipoli peninsular was not exactly the best place for such an operation and today it's changed little to the way it was in 1915. With no major towns existing on the peninsular just settlements, the two main ones being Krithia to the south and Bulair on the Dardanelles side to the north, the area consists mainly of prickly shrub covered rocks and steep hills that give way to deep gullies and ravines. Further inland and more central high peeks and valleys make up the landscape enabling the defender to gain clear advantage over his attacker. The summit of Achi Baba, some 2km east of Krithia, overlooks the area of Cape Helles and it was here that Hamilton had decided the 29th Division would land on the beaches. Cape Helles surrounds the southern tip of the peninsular and formed the best place for a landing. It was hoped that on securing a beachhead 29th Division could then move inland and link up with the Anzacs to their left, if successful together the two groups would then move north and eastward pushing the Turkish forces north as they went.

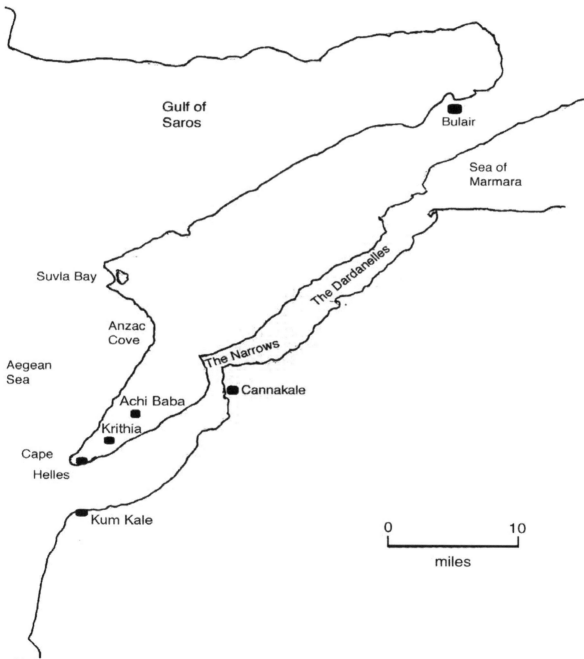

Map 18, Gallipoli (Map taken from 'A Village Goes to War' by David Tattersfield)

The Anzacs had been recruited from Australia and New Zealand at the outbreak of war in much the same way as the men of the New Armies had been and were made up mainly of volunteers. After undergoing a period of basic training it was expected they would be sent to the Western Front. It was while the Anzacs were completing training in Egypt that the Gallipoli plan was conceived and a decision was taken to send them there instead. The Anzacs it was decided would land at beaches situated on the western side of the peninsular that looked out towards the Aegean Sea.

On the morning of 25th April the 29th Division landed on the beaches around Cape Helles with a mixture of success and failure. Some units went unopposed while others met strong Turkish resistance as some beaches were better defended than others. Falling well short of their objective - to take Achi Baba - however the division managed to gain a defensive position some 4km inland and it was hoped that this could be improved upon over the following days. That morning on the western side of the peninsular the men of the Anzacs were making their landings also with some degree of success and failure. Unfortunately they had been swept north by strong tides therefore instead of landing at their intended position, a large beach, they found themselves on a narrow beach in a small cove at the foot of steep cliffs, in time this small beach would come to be known as Anzac Cove. Undeterred however with all their enthusiasm the Anzacs scaled the cliffs pushing inland fighting the Turks as they went. With the confusion that ensued high casualties were sustained and a breakdown of communication between men on the ground meant the assault soon petered out. With such high casualties General Birdwood, the Anzac Corps commander, requested an immediate evacuation, this however was denied by Hamilton who ordered the Anzacs to take up defensive positions and dig in. Apart from a costly and unsuccessful attack by Turkish troops that came during the middle of May throughout June and July not much happened along the Anzac positions, at Cape Helles however it was a different story. Hamilton determined to take Achi Baba decided to launch an attack from his positions around Helles in the direction of Krithia. On 28th April what was to be known as the 'First Battle of Krithia' took place. The 29th Division with help from other British and French units as well as naval support at 8:00am made an attempt for Achi Baba. Making it to the forward slopes before midday the Allies soon encountered strong Turkish resistance that eventually forced them back with little in terms of ground gained and roughly 3,000 casualties to show for their efforts. On 6th May the Turks launched a night attack at Helles against the centre of the allied line however this too proved unsuccessful. The 6th May also saw Hamilton once more try to take Achi Baba signalling the start of the 'Second Battle of Krithia'. At 11:00am now joined by the 42nd Division and additional Anzac units the British, assisted by a naval and artillery barrage, made a fresh attempt to take the heights. This attempt was to last three days with ground gained but then lost. With this Hamilton now burdened with heavy casualties informed Kitchener he needed substantial reinforcements if the peninsular was ever to be captured. Gallipoli was now starting to resemble the Western Front with both sides locked in trench warfare, added to this were the omnipresent additions of heat and disease. Just under a month later Hamilton along with the help of the Royal Navy and French forces again tried to take Achi Baba – in what became the Third Battle of Krithia - but this time a different method was tried. Spreading the battle over several days and without reinforcements it was hoped that the Turks could be taken trench by trench. In most places the machine guns massacred the advancing troops of both sides and little if any fresh ground was actually gained. Although it must be said that the Turks lost more men during the few days of fighting at the end of the battle they still held Achi Baba.

By now things looked bleak especially back in England. Following the disasters at Aubers and the shells scandal that had erupted in its wake the generals on the Western Front and some newspaper reporters had started to undermine the efforts of those involved in the Gallipoli campaign. It would not have been so bad if things were actually going well for forces based in the Dardanelles. Lord Fisher now totally disenchanted and constantly fighting with Winston Churchill resigned as First Sea Lord (1) on 15th May forcing Asquith to yield to pressure from Conservative leader Andrew Bonar Law and form the coalition government. Kitchener lost some of his power to the new minister of munitions David Lloyd George in addition to slowly losing support from those around him. It was felt Winston Churchill could in no way figure in the new government so he was dismissed and replaced as First Lord of the Admiralty by Conservative Arthur Balfour (2). With Kitchener's hand in things limited and Churchill gone the fate of the Gallipoli campaign now fell to a new group known as the Dardanelles Committee.

A deep ravine ran along the western side of the peninsular known as Gully Ravine. On 28th June the British made an attack on this ravine in order to extend their positions in the area. After just over a week of intense fighting ground was gained denting Turkish moral however in the grand scheme of things not a great deal had changed.

Hamilton had been asked by Kitchener what he felt was needed in order for success to be achieved in the Dardanelles and his answer had been more troops and a new plan. So it was that the Dardanelles Committee agreed to send fresh divisions for a renewed attack that Hamilton planned to carryout some 8km north of the Anzac positions. The plan was to land these divisions on three beaches around an area know as Sulva Bay whilst at the same time launching a diversionary attack around Helles to confuse the Turks. It was also planned for the troops positioned around Anzac to break out ultimately cutting the peninsular in half and trapping most of the Turkish forces in the southern sector.

The area around Sulva Bay formed a perfect place to launch such a landing (see map 19). At its northern end stands Sulva Point beyond which stands the slopes of Karakol Dagh that forms the western end of a stretch of high ground known as the Kiritch Tepe Ridge. As the bay swings round the first of the three proposed landing beaches is encountered. Known as 'A' Beach directly beyond it stands the position known as Hill 10 that in turn leads inland towards the flat ground of Sulva Plain. Just south of the beach lays an area known as 'The Cut' and this at the time led inland towards a large dry Salt Lake, east of here stood the positions of both Chocolate Hill and Green Hill - the former named after the burnt shrub that covered it and the latter named for precisely the opposite reason. At the southern tip of the bay stands Nibrunesi Point and beyond it lays the heights of Lala Baba. The two other landing beaches known as 'C' Beach and 'B' Beach both lay south of Nibrunesi Point and east of these the southern end of Sulva Plain is found, as you head inland from here you hit the position of Hill 60. The main point of the Sulva Bay Landings was for the troops to move inland and capture the high ground of Kavak Tepe and Tekke Tepe which lay beyond the Sulva Plain; from here they could control the Peninsular, unfortunately this would never happen. The landings at Sulva Bay were to be carried out by IX Corps under the command of Lieutenant General Sir Frederick Stopford. At 61 years old it's now agreed by most historians that Stopford was totally the wrong man to command such an operation. IX Corps consisted of the 10th Division and 11th Division and the plan was to land at Sulva Bay on the night of 6th - 7th August. Confusion would unfortunately dog the operation as troops would land in the wrong places, those in command would be unsure of their objectives and all the while the enemy would be rushing its forces towards the area to strengthen its positions.

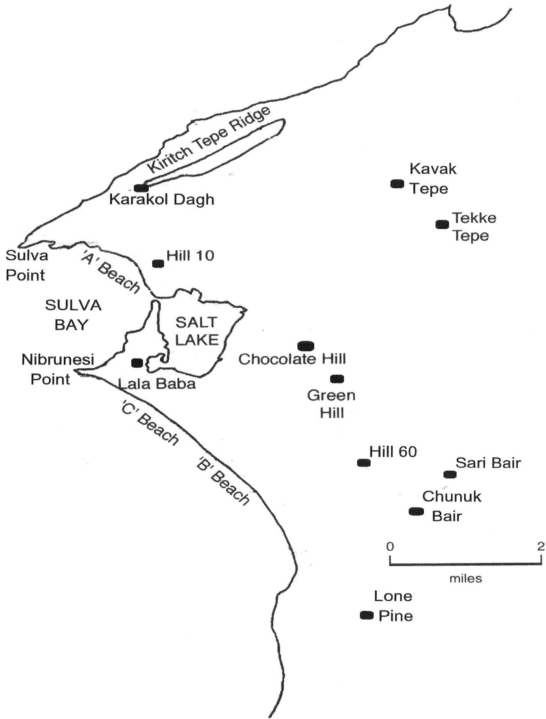

Map 19, Sulva Bay (Map taken from 'A Village Goes to War' by David Tattersfield)

That night two brigades of 11th Division landed at 'B' Beach unopposed, they then moved inland and managed to capture both Nibrunesi Point and Lala Baba but in doing this took many casualties even though they substantially outnumbered their enemy. The last remaining brigade of 11th Division was supposed to land at 'A' Beach but ended up too far south making its objectives of taking Karakol Dagh and Hill 10 that much more difficult. The first elements of this brigade to land eventually found their bearings and moved in along the Kiritch Tepe Ridge capturing some 3km of it, the remaining units however found themselves stuck out at sea as the boats bringing them in hit sandbanks. Once these units did land they came under fire that meant that some of them had to land at 'B' Beach instead. Eventually the following afternoon the brigades of 11th Division captured Hill 10 and that evening troops there began to dig in. A few hours after 11th Division landed the troops of 10th Division started to arrive, their objective was to reinforce the 11th Division at Karakol Dagh then push on and take Kiritch Tepe Ridge itself. The division was supposed to land at 'A' Beach however complete chaos ensued. Some of their commanders had no idea of where they were or what they were supposed to do. Again boats got stuck then 'A' Beach was ruled out as a landing site so the first battalions ashore were landed at 'C' Beach instead, completely on the other side of the bay from their objectives. Eventually a landing position was found further west around the bay a lot closer to Karakol Dagh but by now the brigades of 10th Division were all over the place, just three battalions remained to help assault Kiritch Tepe Ridge, these battalions managed to link up with those units of 11th Division already there but then advanced no further. The next action that faced 11th Division was to take both the heights of Chocolate Hill and Green Hill, it had been wrongly reported that the southern slopes of the former were heavily defended by Turkish troops. Instead of a frontal assault the attacking troops took a detour of some 8km in the hot sun around the Salt Lake but in spite of everything they still managed to capture both positions.

It should be remembered how the Sulva Bay Landings were to coincide with two diversionary attacks at Helles and Anzac. The Helles diversion commenced by way of a heavy bombardment of the Turkish trenches at midday on 6th August. At 4:00pm the 29th Division and 42nd Division yet again attacked towards Krithia although only one brigade - the 88th Brigade - of the 29th Division was supposed to actually advance, it tried and it failed and its casualties were worse than ever. Fighting here continued between the two sides for just under a week, the Helles diversion had failed and if the Turks were confused they certainly didn't show it, as losses mounted the game at Helles was finally up. Anzac was a slightly different story; firstly a tunnel was dug under the Turkish lines around their southern positions in an area known as Lone Pine. This would enable the attacking forces to emerge virtually on top of their enemy, it was hoped this would grab the Turks attention whilst other pushes at Anzac were attempted further north. Like with the Helles diversion Lone Pine was bombarded prior to the assault, at 5:30pm on 6th August attacking troops rushed Turkish positions opposite and after heavy fighting at close quarters they eventually fell to the Anzacs. In the central positions along the Anzac line the famous Australian Light Horse Regiment went over the top and suffered appalling casualties at the hands of Turkish machine guns however by now Turkish attention had well and truly been turned towards the Anzac Front. The high ground of Chunuk Bair lay ahead and this became the focus of the troops positioned on the left - or northern - flank of Anzac, the fighting for the heights was later known as the 'Battle of Sari Bair' and it lasted for almost a week. After reaching the position the attacking troops fought a tough fight but failed to hold on and were eventually driven from the heights by Turkish counter attacks. Although the left flank of Anzac managed to link up with the right flank at Sulva making one continuous front line a total of 12,000 allied casualties were sustained during the Sari Bair battle.

Back at Sulva Bay amazingly in spite of all the upsets that had occurred during the landings the troops there had managed to gain a foothold. By the night of 7th August they'd taken Karakol Dagh and gained part of the Kiritch Tepe Ridge whilst Hill 10, Lala Baba and both Chocolate and Green Hills had also been captured. Now they needed to push inland and capture the high ground of Tekke Tepe before the Turks. Wasting no time at all Liman Von Sanders had ordered two of his divisions based at Bulair to head for Sulva, at the same time he ordered his troops based on the Asian side of the Dardanelles to cross over to Gallipoli where they came under the control of Mustafa Kemal, a 'Young Turk' turned army commander, this took the whole of the following day. Whilst this was happening the allies rested and on 9th August when units of 11th Division resumed their attack Turkish reinforcements had arrived and were in position. Having gained the high ground Turkish troops were yet again able to inflict heavy casualties upon their attackers, as a result the allies were brought to a standstill.

Although the Sulva Bay Landings were turning to failure fresh units continued to arrive. They'd set off several days before the landings fully expecting that by the time they arrived the whole of the peninsular would more or less be in allied hands. The 54th (East Anglian) Division was one such unit and although not immediately it would eventually contain the only man listed on the Chigwell Village War Memorial to die as a result of the Gallipoli campaign.

DENHAM GEORGE KING
Denham George King was born at Navestock in Essex in 1881, his father George had lived in the village his whole life having been born there in 1842. George worked as a Horseman on a farm and in time met and married Denham's mother Emma who was born in the neighbouring village of Southweald in 1844. Denham it seems was an only child and the family continued to live in Navestock until moving to Epping during the late 1890's. On leaving school Denham found work as a machine hand in a factory specializing in cordite, a kind of explosive. He

met his wife to be Blanche Marguerite Lagnaz and the couple set up home in Claybury near Woodford Bridge. When war broke out Denham enlisted at a recruiting office in Gordon Road, Ilford; this was the local office as well as the main headquarters of the 4th Battalion Essex Regiment. The 4th Essex was split into eight companies lettered from A to H, each had its own HQ in districts roughly within a 10 mile radius of battalion headquarters at Ilford; Gordon Road although being the main HQ was also home to 'C' Coy. As previously mentioned in August 1914 the territorial battalions were ordered to form three lines and Denham - possibly even a pre war territorial - found himself attached to the 2/4th Essex. In August 1914 however the 1/4th Essex formed part of the Essex Brigade; commanded by Lieutenant Colonel A R Meggy it was attached to the East Anglian Division (3). Towards the end of August the 1/4th Essex moved to Norwich in preparation for any part it might have to play in the coming months, in April 1915 it moved once again, this time to Colchester where training continued. The 2/4th Essex at this time were also in training, stationed at Great Yarmouth in Norfolk a month later they moved across the county to Thetford, whilst here Denham was granted leave to return home to Claybury and marry Blanche. The ceremony took place on Tuesday 4th May at St Mary's Church in Chigwell officiated by Reverend Frederick Auriol Murray, soon after Denham rejoined his battalion at Thetford.

By now the 1/4th Essex was attached to 161st Brigade and the East Anglian Division had been numbered the 54th Division under the command of Major General F Inglefield. The division and its battalions were moved yet again this time to St Albans in Hertfordshire. It was not long before they received orders to move overseas, the 1/4th Essex sailed from Devonport - near Portsmouth - for Alexandria at 6:00pm on 21st July 1915. The battalion arrived at Malta on 29th July and from there it headed for Alexandria in Egypt. Arriving during the morning on 1st August once at Alexandria it received orders to head for the Aegean, after a rough crossing it arrived in Mudros harbour on the Greek island of Lemnos on 3rd August. The battalion remained at Lemnos until the afternoon of 12th August when it set sail for Sulva Bay, the men of the 1/4th Essex landed at 'C' Beach at 10:30pm that evening.

Another unsuccessful attempt to move inland was made on this day; it did not involve the 1/4th Essex although it did involve another territorial battalion of 54th Division. The 1/5th Norfolk's had been stationed at East Dereham in Norfolk. On the outbreak of war the battalion set about recruiting men to its ranks, one company of 250 officers and men was drawn entirely from the staff of the King's country estate at Sandringham in Norfolk. Known as King George V's Own Sandringham Company it had only arrived two days previously when it took part in the attack on 12th August, as the men advanced they seemed to disappear, mystery has surrounded their fate ever since.

As for the 1/4th Essex the battalion settled down to life on the peninsular taking over trenches along the front line in areas in around Hill 10, the trench lines at Gallipoli being now very similar to those in France and Flanders. On 18th August the battalion was involved in operations to straighten their stretches of line however this turned out not to be as successful as it was hoped it would be (4). Later that month the battalion moved to trench positions east of Lala Baba, they would remain here for the rest of August and throughout September. At the end that month they received a new commanding officer in 40 year old Lieutenant Colonel Edmund James Jameson DSO - formally of the 5th Battalion Leinster Regiment. The 1/4th Essex had initially arrived at Sulva with a force of 29 officers and 671 other ranks, by the end September they were just 9 officers and 337 other ranks strong. This decrease of 20 officers and 354 other ranks was mainly due to men falling ill due to the conditions they were forced to endure, only 3 officers and 22 other ranks had actually been killed in action. As October started the men of the battalion found themselves at rest in reserve trenches, a bombardment could be heard some miles away in the direction of Achi Baba. On 5th October the men received mail from England; it had taken roughly two to three weeks to arrive. Desperately in need of reinforcements on 7th October eight officers arrived from England to join the battalion, the 2/4th Essex was sending replacements to its first line battalion. The following day these officers were joined by two more plus a draft of 83 other ranks, among them was Pte Denham George King.

The battalion war diary states that these reinforcements had sailed via Gibraltar on H.M.S. Mars; they arrived fully equipped and clothed for winter, that day the original men of the battalion were also fitted out swapping their drill kaki for winter clothing. On the evening of 10th October Denham and the rest of the battalion prepared to take over front line trenches in the vicinity of Hill 60, they were to relieve the men of the 1/5th Essex. This relief was completed by 6:00am the following morning, by now the heat and humidity that had existed on the peninsular had given way to a cool breeze. As the men settled in sentries were posted and the battalion made itself at home, for Denham this was his first experience of life in the front line. Their brigade commander Brigadier General F Daniell visited their front line daily accompanied on his rounds by the battalion CO. The war diary notes that the Turks opposite seemed to be getting the upper hand when it came to sniping therefore the battalion's snipers consisting of three officers and three NCOs were instructed to win back the advantage. This they did by changing loopholes - a position used for sniping - regularly, marking enemy sniping positions for future reference and tunnelling under their own parapet to gain a better position in which to have a shot at the enemy. As the days past the men of the battalion carried on manning their section of line, small patrols were sent out regularly in order to keep an eye on what the enemy was up to. The Turkish soldiers mainly being Muslims respected their Sabbath day, the men of the battalion noticed that on this day enemy activity became very quiet. 'Stand To' was the name given to the action that saw men of the battalion man their positions in case of attack, during October this took place every morning between 5:00am and 5:30am. The most likely time the enemy might launch an attack was just before it got light, therefore 'Stand To' was performed depending on the hour of sunrise. The men continued to spend their time mainly improving trench positions, sandbags that made up the parapets were noticed to sink somewhat after it rained and had to be built back up again. With the coming of rain the men found it was becoming difficult to keep dry, no materials existed in which to erect roofing over their positions. It was noted in the war diary that the Turks who used to expose themselves continuously along their lines were now keeping their heads down due to the battalion's successful sniping exploits, however they still managed to send over the occasional shell to keep the Essex men on their toes. By the 24th October the men had been in their trenches for two weeks straight, their effective strength was 18 officers and 337 other ranks, the remainder had gone sick. Dysentery and stomach troubles dogged the men due to a lack of clean water, germs spread by rats, dirty latrines and the poor conditions that troops were forced to live under. The officer commanding the battalion thought that these illnesses also stemmed from the fact that his cooks hadn't been trained properly whilst back in England, he concluded they didn't know how best to operate a field kitchen or oven in order to feed the men. The battalion was losing between 5 and 7 men a day due to sickness and it was hard for them to man all their positions effectively. Measures were put in place to try and keep the men healthy, they were encouraged to wash and shave regularly in order to prevent sickness and also keep active as much as they could. As the rest of the battalion set about constructing dugouts for winter Denham could not help but fall ill, due to the conditions around him it was not long before he too had contracted dysentery. By the last day of October having served three weeks straight in the trenches 83 men of the battalion had contracted the disease in some form or another, the exact same number that had joined on the day Denham arrived.

Unable to continue with their duties these men were sent to aid posts behind the lines; from there they found themselves evacuated to places such as Lemnos and Alexandria. Pte Denham George King found himself placed on a boat amongst other sick and wounded men bound for Alexandria, those men who died on the way were inevitably buried at sea whilst those that survived were admitted to hospital upon their arrival. Although we don't know the exact date that Denham arrived in Alexandria he was admitted to hospital, unfortunately he died there of dysentery on Monday 22nd November making him the first territorial soldier listed on the Chigwell Village War Memorial to die during the Great War. He is buried in Row C, Grave 137 at Alexandria (Chatby) Military War Memorial Cemetery, Egypt. Pte Denham George King had only been at Gallipoli for roughly a month before he became ill, he saw no major action nor was he involved in any real fighting. His death was reported in the January 1916 issue of the Chigwell Parish Magazine the article stated that another married man - Denham George King - from Claybury had been lost and that the sympathy of all goes out to his widow in her hour of trial and sacrifice (5).

* * *

Since the Sulva Bay Landings back in August and the unsuccessful attempts by the allies to push inland which followed soon after stalemate once again existed on the Gallipoli Peninsular with both sides locked in trench warfare. Back in early October Sir Ian Hamilton had been asked by the Dardanelles Committee for his opinion on whether an evacuation of the peninsular was possible; his answer in not so many words was 'not a chance'. A few days later he was sacked and replaced by Sir Charles Monro. At the end of that month Monro arrived at Gallipoli and after visiting Helles, Anzac and Sulva decided that evacuation was his only option. In a carefully planned operation that took place during December 1915 and January 1916 all three fronts were evacuated without the loss of one allied life, if only the rest of the campaign had been managed with such efficiency (6).

36, Men of the 1/4th Battalion Essex Regiment marching off to war. Photograph courtesy of the Imperial War Museum.

37, Essex Battalions landing at Sulva Bay on the Gallipoli Peninsular in August 1915. Photograph courtesy of the Imperial War Museum.

38, Trenches held by Essex units inland from Anzac. Photograph courtesy of the Imperial War Museum.

39, Anzac Beach 1915. Photograph courtesy of the Imperial War Museum.

1916

By the start of 1916 Britain had been at war for almost a year and a half, up until now the list of casualties as far as Chigwell was concerned stood at some ten men however this figure was to double over the next twelve months. Back in late 1915 Reverend Frederick Auriol Murray had erected a Roll of Honour for the parish inside St Mary's Church, described in the parish magazine as simple and dignified it consisted of a Union Jack draped and attached to a pillar facing the south door of the church (1). Beneath the flag stood a framed list of Chigwell's fallen that was altered month by month to include the names of any more parishioners killed for king and country. The year started quietly for the people of Chigwell in terms of casualties sustained but on the home front things still happened from time to time. On 28th March 1916 a storm hit in a two mile radius of the village up rooting almost sixty giant elm trees that lined the main roads to the north and east. All roads to and from the village were blocked except in the direction of Buckhurst Hill, a neighbouring village to the northwest. The war came closer to home in early May; police regulations insisted that the church clock in the village should not strike nor should the church bells be rung after 7:30pm in case this gave Chigwell's whereabouts to passing enemy aircraft. This measure was a kind of forerunner to the blackout that would be enforced during the Blitz some 25 years later.

In England by the spring of 1916 a slowdown had occurred in the amount of men heading to the recruiting offices to enlist, therefore in order for the army to remain supplied with men something had to be done. Back in October 1915 Lord Derby introduced a scheme that was to eventually make conscription law however before this was implemented under the terms of the 'Derby Scheme' men were given a last chance to enlist voluntarily which many chose to do. In January 1916 conscription became law but initially only applied to single men, once registered a man would be called up as and when needed, towards the end of May conscription was extended to include married men. The 'Derby Men' as they were known and those men recruited by conscription would make up the armies of 1917 and 1918 however 1916 would be the year of Kitchener's volunteers, the New Armies.

Meanwhile for the Allies on the Western Front the year started relatively quietly and it was hoped that 1916 would prove more successful than the previous year. Joffre and Haig met during the second week of February and the two men agreed on a joint offensive to be carried out at the end of June beginning of July. This offensive would concentrate on the areas north and south of a river that ran through the Picardy region of the French countryside. Known as the River Somme it must be said an attack in this area held no real strategic value for the allies other than to wear down German forces in the area, in fact that was Joffre's plan, a war of attrition. Then just a week after that allied meeting the quietness was shattered as the Germans launched a surprise attack on the French positions around the town of Verdun. The battle was to last for most of the year as French and German losses spiralled out of control. Success at Verdun became a matter of pride for the French Army in a feud that dated back to the Franco-Prussian War of 1870-1871. The Germans saw Verdun as a weak spot they could exploit in order to defeat the French and they knew France would pull all her resources in order to protect the town. With most of their army heading towards the Verdun area many of the trench lines previously held by the French now became the responsibility of the British, none more so than in areas around Arras and to the north of the River Somme. As allied plans had now been thrown into disarray by the German attack at Verdun Joffre hoped that the British could launch an attack to take pressure off the French Army. Although eager to offer his services in his new role as CIC of the British Army Haig however felt his units, now mainly made up of New Army volunteers, were not yet ready to fulfil such a role especially if they were to fight with minimal French co-operation. Joffre insisted that if something wasn't done and soon the French Army would cease to exist. During April 1916 GHQ for the British Army moved from St Omer to Montreuil about 20 miles south of Boulogne. With the influx of New Army volunteers arriving in France almost daily a 4th Army had been created, this now meant the BEF consisted of four armies controlling some 80 miles of front line. The British lines to the north around Ypres were the responsibility of Plumers 2nd Army, then south from Armentières to Lens stood 1st Army commanded by Sir Charles Monro. Allenby's 3rd Army held positions from Lens to the village of Gommecourt and to the south of that, after a gap of about a mile, the front was held by 4th Army. Incorporated within the four armies were those units that came from the various countries throughout the British Empire such as Canadian and Anzac troops. However it was the 4th Army in the south and its commander Sir Henry Rawlingson that Haig turned to when planning the first phase of the British offensives of 1916, the names of which would all go down in history as 'The Battles of the Somme'.

The Somme battles would last from July to November and all casualties sustained by Chigwell during 1916 occurred in the Somme region. The attack front for the first phase of the Somme battle stretched some 15 miles from Gommecourt in the north to Maricourt in the south on the north banks of the Somme. In stark contrast to the waterlogged landscape of Flanders or the solid ground of Loos the countryside over the Somme front was made up mainly of rolling farmland above a chalk base. Many wooded areas littered the landscape and there was an area of high ground that stretched from the village of Thiepval southeast to the village of Guillemont - this in early 1916 lay in German hands. In summer months the woods and fields of the Somme were very green making the area an ideal place to conceal men and equipment in order to fight a battle. Apart from the Somme another river flowed through the area. The River Ancre was smaller than the Somme and ran north through the countryside splitting the area of the front to be attacked almost in half. This you could say created two sectors the northern sector and southern sector. Numerous villages were dotted around the Somme and all were quite similar to each other. Like the villages in the countryside of England they all had their churches, shops, farms and houses; many of these lay on the front lines.

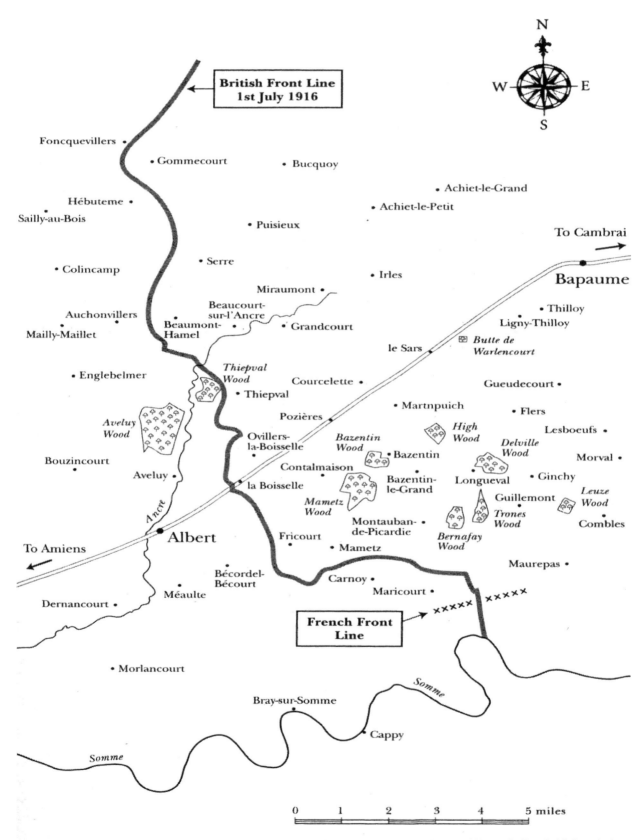

Map 20, The Somme Battlefield - Tommy © Richard Holmes 2005 Reprinted by permission of HarperCollins Publishers Ltd

The chalk landscape of the Somme made perfect ground for the construction of trenches, there was no danger of collapse and all water drained away which was completely the opposite to the trenches further north in Flanders, to be in the trenches on the Somme before July 1916 was in contrast quite cushy. Since trench warfare had begun at the end of 1914 the Somme had been a quiet sector of the front and this had given the Germans time to prepare defences in the area at their own pace. Their trench positions on the Somme consisted of three lines, the first of which made up the frontline trenches. These were constructed in a zigzag pattern stretching the length of the front and were protected by numerous belts of barbed wire in places sometimes up to 50 yards thick. The frontline trenches were connected to the rear positions by communication trenches whilst machine gun nests were scattered along the front allowing, with the help of the open countryside, an almost perfect field of fire on attacking troops over an enormously wide front. Various villages positioned along the frontline had also been fortified to add to the defence of the forward positions. The second line was situated about two miles behind the first and was just as well protected, whilst the third line was still under construction. On some sectors along their frontline the Germans had constructed deep dugouts into the chalk with living areas that housed hundreds of men at a time; these were to provide them with excellent cover just prior to the Somme battle. However French soldiers in trenches opposite the Germans had been lazy in comparison and their positions were of a poor condition. The opposing trench lines were roughly 300 yards apart but no more than half a mile although the Germans, having occupied the high ground, had excellent views over the French positions. As it transpired these were the trenches that the British took over in readiness for the July offensive. In preparation for the coming battle the British went to work on improving their lines, supplies were brought up and men poured into the area. This build up alerted the Germans that the British planned to attack on the Somme and they improved their positions further still. The town of Albert lay just behind the British lines and many troops passed through it on their way to the front. The town would become synonymous with the British troops much in the same way Ypres would, however unlike Ypres the town of Albert would briefly fall into German hands during the spring of 1918. Like with the cloth hall at Ypres in the centre of Albert stood a church called the Basilique on top of which stood a statue of the Virgin Mary. The statue could be seen for miles around; the Basilique although virtually destroyed during the war was eventually rebuilt after the Armistice.

Planning for the forthcoming attack had pretty much been left up to Rawlinson and his staff officers at 4th Army HQ situated about 12 miles behind the front line at Querrieu. The 46th Division and 56th Division attached to Allenby's 3rd Army however were to make a diversionary attack at Gommecourt in an effort designed to mislead the Germans as to the position of 4th Army's main assault (2). Rawlinson had developed a method where his attacking troops would assault the German frontline positions in extended lines then consolidate any ground gained before continuing to push on towards the German second line. This method would be carried out under cover of a preliminary artillery bombardment lasting several days. This bombardment was designed to destroy all the German defences, most importantly the barbed wire that lay in front of their trenches. The plan however did not sit well with Haig who preferred a more straightforward approach consisting of short bombardments followed by masses of troops going over the top. Any gaps that were created would then be exploited by waiting cavalry and infantry troops of Gough's Reserve Army in an effort to roll up the German line and head north towards Arras (3). Rawlinson saw problems with Haig's idea regarding short bombardments but the CIC eventually agreed a large scale preliminary bombardment would be necessary if all the German defences were to be destroyed. Rawlinson however saw no problems with the cavalry exploiting gaps as and when his infantry had broken through the German lines. After much planning the British generals and especially Rawlinson felt their plan for the Somme battle was well conceived and really believed that it would be an overwhelming success, unfortunately they were wrong.

Just before the story of the Somme battle is told an event occurred during June that involved the man who had done so much, and was chiefly responsible for Britain's now mainly volunteer army holding positions in France and Flanders. Lord Kitchener as we have heard was a hero in the eyes of the British people, however since the coalition government had been formed and the disaster that had been the Gallipoli campaign his influence and standing had been somewhat curbed. Regardless of this it was hoped he could undertake a trip to Russia in order to boost the war effort there. Lord Kitchener set sail on HMS Hampshire but whilst on route across the North Sea his ship hit a mine and Kitchener along with most of the crew was killed. It is quite ironic that the man who had done so much for Britain's volunteer army was killed the month before it was due to face its first major test (4).

The artillery bombardment that signalled the start of the Somme offensive commenced on 24th June. Intensive shelling of the German lines was planned to last for five days with the assault itself due to take place on the 29th June, this however was delayed due to bad weather therefore a further two day bombardment ensued making Saturday 1st July 1916 the first day of the Battle of the Somme. The preliminary bombardment employed 200 heavy guns and 1,800 light guns, they fired some 1.5 million shells throughout the week but the barrage was to prove ineffective. Following the shell scandal of 1915 minister of munitions David Lloyd George made sure there was no shortage of shells preceding the Somme offensive, this said due to the rate these shells were churned out many were badly made and consequently turned out to be duds. In addition some of the heavy guns, manned by inexperienced officers and men, were worn out and very few of the shells fired actually reached their intended targets. The lighter calibre guns with their light shells failed to cut the German wire or destroy enemy defences.

Machine gun positions remained intact ready to meet the attacking British infantry once it started its push across no mans land. Also untouched were the German batteries and these remained poised and ready to rain down a murderous fire onto British troops as and when they crossed the open fields in front of them. On the night of the 30th June the British sent out patrols to inspect the German lines. When the reports came back that the enemy defences were still intact and virtually untouched they were unwisely dismissed by those in command. The French divisions due to take part in the battle at the southern end of the front, and south of the River Somme, insisted that the troops should attack as soon as it was light, this they said would give their artillery good observation in which to operate therefore zero hour was set for 7:30am.

Prior to the battle the British had dug tunnels towards the German lines and at the end of these tunnels explosives were placed ready to be detonated on the morning of the battle. At 7:28am a total of seventeen mines were blown killing those Germans occupying positions above, many German soldiers in positions nearby were shaken so badly they were in no state to oppose the attacking troops. In some cases however German troops were able to occupy some craters before British troops could get there. Two minutes later the whistles blew and British troops, wearing steel helmets for protection, climbed the trench ladders and went over the top into no mans land (5). They were under the impression that they would be capturing then occupying the German positions so with them they carried masses of equipment weighing in some cases as much as 90lb. This equipment consisted of packs, spades, rifles, ammunition, grenades, food, water and anything else which may have been needed when reaching the enemy lines. The men had been told to fix bayonets and walk in extended lines slowly towards the enemy in the belief that all the Germans in front of them had been killed by the week long artillery bombardment. As we know this wasn't the case, the Germans simply sheltered in their dugouts and emerged to take up positions once the barrage had lifted. They manned their machine guns and carnage ensued as fire was poured into the British infantry as it advanced at walking pace across no mans land, at the same time enemy gunners rained down shrapnel shells onto the numerous New Army battalions heading towards them. Within minutes whole battalions were wiped out as their men walked into the murderous fire directed at them. In places the British found it impossible to advance especially when they reached sections of German wire only to find it intact. A total of 5 Corps made up of 12 Divisions - 18 were available - attacked that morning and wave after wave of men were cut down by enemy machine gun and shellfire.

To the north the 46th Division and 56th Division of Allenby's 3rd Army in a successful diversion managed to take Gommecourt but at heavy cost. A mile south however on 4th Army's left flank no gains at all were made. Two men listed on the Chigwell Memorial were killed on the first day of the Somme battle and one of those was in this northern sector close to the village of Serre.

WILLIAM FRANK GAPES

William Frank Gapes was born in Chigwell in December 1897 and was named after his grandfather on his father's side. His father Frank Gapes was born in Ongar in 1870 whilst his mother Harriet was born in Barkingside in 1872, the couple were married at All Saints Church in Chigwell Row sometime between 1894 and 1895. William was their only son but Frank and Harriet had at least four daughters. The eldest was Lily followed by Mary, Eliza and Annie (6). All the children were born in Chigwell and at the turn of the century lived with their parents in a small house at 2 Forest Cottages, Fencepiece Road, Grange Hill. Frank Gapes had various jobs; he worked in a coal yard and worked as a farm hand on Wilkins Farm in Grange Hill, eventually on leaving school William worked alongside his father helping out on Wilkins Farm. When war broke out William saw it as his chance to leave quiet Chigwell and fearing the conflict wouldn't last long he travelled to Warley to enlist, the problem was that William was too young. In August 1914 the age of enlistment in the volunteer armies was 19 but William was only 16 years old, this didn't stop him however and like many boys during this period he lied about his age in order to be accepted (7). After several attempts William was accepted and soon after was posted to the reserve battalions of the Essex Regiment, once there he was made Private 19687 and underwent a period of basic training before being sent to France sometime in early 1916. Unfortunately William's army service record no longer exists and his MIC at the NA in Kew yields little information regarding his movements, with this being the case it's impossible to know the exact date he landed in France. Upon his arrival however William was posted to the ranks of the 2nd Battalion Essex Regiment as a much needed replacement. The 2nd Essex was a regular battalion and first crossed the Channel to France as part of the BEF in August 1914, since that time the battalion had suffered substantial losses so by late 1915 early 1916 it was reinforced by volunteers from Kitcheners New Armies. The 4th Division was made up of the 10th Brigade, 11th Brigade and 12th Brigade; the 2nd Essex were attached to 12th Brigade along with the 1st Battalion Royal Lancaster (Kings Own) Regiment, 2nd Battalion Lancashire Fusiliers and 2nd Battalion Duke of Wellington (West Riding) Regiment.

On the 28th June Pte William Gapes and the men of the 2nd Essex, commanded by Lieutenant Colonel G Stirling DSO, were in billets at Bertancourt and whilst here they came under shellfire from German artillery. At 4:30pm that afternoon the men were informed that the proposed attack would be postponed for a period of 48 hours due to bad weather. The following day whilst still in billets the battalion received orders that the following night they'd move forward in readiness, at 11:10pm on 30th June the men of the 2nd Essex proceeded towards allotted assembly trenches. On the morning of 1st July 1916 the 4th Division was part of VIII Corps and holding a stretch of frontline just west of Beaumont Hamel and Serre, to their left stood the 31st Division whilst to their right stood 29th Division. Opposite their frontline stood a German strongpoint known as the Quadrilateral, the men of 4th Division would have to capture this position first if they were to push on to their objectives of Serre and beyond. The 11th Brigade was to lead the first wave of 4th Division's attack although several battalions of 10th Brigade were also involved (8). At 7:30am the leading battalions of both brigades left their trenches followed ten minutes later by further battalions in support. Immediately coming under machine gun and shell fire the leading waves, although having lost heavily, managed to reach the Quadrilateral however once there they continued to be hampered by machine gun fire from the direction of Serre.

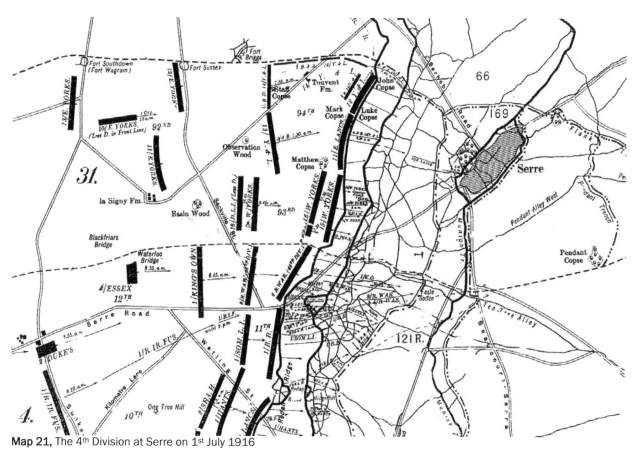

Map 21, The 4th Division at Serre on 1st July 1916

Those units on the right also took fire from Beaumont Hamel. Despite this however some men did manage to penetrate beyond the Quadrilateral towards a trench line known as Feste Soden. The 12th Brigade were to be in support and their objectives, like the leading brigades of 4th Division, were to reach and hold enemy trenches on the Grandcourt - Puisieux Ridge some two miles away. The brigade formation was to be the 1st Royal Lancs on the left and the 2nd Essex on the right leading the attack whilst in support were the 2nd Duke of Wellington's and 2nd Lancashire Fusiliers. The 2nd Essex was deployed with it's 'A' Coy on the left and 'D' Coy on the right leading their attack whilst 'B' Coy and 'C' Coy were to remain in support.

The battalion war diary tells us what happened:

'At 8:36am 'A' Coy and 'D' Coy advanced from their assembly trenches and immediately came under very heavy machine gun fire and artillery barrage. At about 9:30am the 10th Brigade was holding a line about 50 yards short of the German second line and some parties had forced their way through and got as far as Pendant Copse'.

The German second line in this area was known as Munich Trench and was situated about half a mile behind the first line. Incorporated within Munich Trench stood the fortified village of Serre itself, the wooded area known as Pendant Copse however stood some half a mile beyond southeast of the village.

The battalion war diary continues:

'The main line tried to consolidate themselves in a line of craters but this work was virtually impossible owing to the intense machine gun fire brought to bear on them from the direction of Serre on the left flank and Beaumont Hamel on the right. Later a screen of German bombers advanced against them and the brigade on the left (93rd Brigade, 31st Division) retiring left their left flank in the air'.

This action had left the survivors of the 2nd Essex and the surviving men from battalions of both 10th Brigade and 11th Brigade totally exposed. At roughly 4:00pm these survivors now desperately short of officers were forced to retire back to the German front line, any man who had penetrated as far as Munich Trench or Pendant Copse was by this time either wounded or dead. Two surviving officers of the Essex, a captain and second lieutenant rallied this mixed group and together these men made a long stand in the trenches of the Quadrilateral. These men kept German counter attacks at bay by throwing bombs and sniping at the enemy, eventually though a lack of ammo became a problem and fresh supplies were required from the British lines. With the intensive fire sweeping no mans land it proved virtually impossible to get the supplies across, luckily enough the men found German bombs stored in the Quadrilateral and used these against the enemy. Whilst holding out the surviving men also came under friendly fire from British artillery, by signalling back to the British front line however this was soon stopped before any real damage was done. After holding out all night at 10:00am on the 2nd July those survivors in the Quadrilateral were relieved by men of the Royal Irish Fusiliers, the attack carried out by 4th Division on the first day of battle had been a total failure.

During the attack the commanding officer of the 2nd Essex, Lieutenant Colonel G Stirling DSO, was wounded, it appears however that 'B' Coy and 'C' Coy seeing the attack faltering never left the frontline trenches. According to their war diary the 2nd Essex lists casualties for 1st July 1916 as 33 officers and 400 men, of these according to SDGW, 4 officers and 135 men were actually killed. Although it's not known with which company he served or exactly how far he advanced that morning among those killed was 18 year old Pte William Frank Gapes, he is buried in Plot V Row D Grave 12 of Serre Road No.1 CWGC Cemetery, Somme France. William's death was reported in the October 1916 edition of the Chigwell Parish Magazine and after the war his parents not only received his medals but also a small pension to compensate for their loss. For many years a memorial scroll and picture of William hung in his parents living room however when they died their house was cleared out and these items disappeared, Frank and Harriet Gapes are buried to the rear of St Mary's Churchyard in Chigwell.

* * *

Some success was achieved by 4th Army that morning further south along the attack front although very little. Just north of Thiepval the 36th (Ulster) Division managed to gain entry to a German strongpoint known as the Schwaben Redoubt but lack of success by the divisions on either side of them and subsequent German counter attacks meant that come late afternoon they weren't able to hold on to ground gained. Further south a huge mine was exploded just before zero in front of La Boisselle and as a result the 34th Division positioned there managed a small advance southeast of the village (9). The furthest advances were made on the southern sector of the front by units of the 7th Division, 18th Division and 30th Division who, along with the French Army south of the Somme, managed to fulfil all their objectives. It was 18th Division that contained the other man from Chigwell to be killed on the first day of the Somme.

FREDERICK WILLIAM DUNKLEY

Frederick William Dunkley was born Alfred William Dunkley in Chigwell sometime in 1897. His father Joseph was a Policeman and had been born in Northampton in 1862. Joseph moved south where he met his future wife Lucy Dudley who lived in the village of Rivenhall Oak in Essex. Once married the couple moved around a lot because of Joseph's job, eventually they had five sons and settled in Chigwell. The family then moved a few miles away to Victoria Cottages, Victoria Road in Ilford and here they stayed until the early 1900's before returning to Chigwell. Alfred or Frederick as we will now call him was their youngest son whilst their eldest was Joseph - named after his father – who was born at Vauxhall in South London in 1890. Then there came Fritz, Louis and Harry who was three years older than Frederick (10). Nothing is known of Frederick's early life however on the outbreak of war he travelled to Warley to enlist, once accepted he was posted as Pte G/3745 to the 7th Battalion East Kent Regiment (11). The regular battalions of this regiment were more commonly known as 'The Buffs' and its New Army battalions also adopted the name. The regular battalion's famous rallying cry 'Steady the Buffs' was also adopted, although confusion surrounds its origin this cry is usually credited to Rudyard Kipling and his book 'Soldiers Three'. The 7th Buffs were formed at Canterbury in Kent in September 1914 eventually becoming part of K2. The battalion moved to Purfleet in Essex to begin training and was attached to the 18th (Eastern) Division. This division contained the 53rd Brigade, 54th Brigade and 55th Brigade; the latter contained the 7th Buffs along with the 7th Battalion Royal West Surrey (Queens) Regiment, 8th Battalion East Surrey Regiment and the 7th Battalion Royal West Kent (Queens Own) Regiment.

The 18th Division like many New Army divisions was very short of trained officers and supplies during its first few months of existence and the men had to make do as best they could. In April 1915 the division moved to Colchester to continue training then in May moved again this time to Salisbury Plain. It was also around this time that the division was considered ready for service in France and the first elements began to move at the end of the month. Frederick and his battalion however remained in England; it was July before they crossed the Channel to France. The battalion set sail from Folkestone on SS Golden Eagle and landed at Boulogne during the early hours of the 28th July 1915. Like most battalions recently arriving in France the 7th Buffs were introduced to trench warfare, they first entered trenches in the Somme area that August mainly holding the line and providing men for working parties. Slowly the men became accustomed to life on the Western Front; after almost a year spent in the trenches the battalion would take part in the Somme offensive.

The 18th Division found itself on July 1st 1916 attached to XIII Corps and holding the frontline just north of the village of Carnoy, the opposing trench lines in this area ran east to west as opposed to north to south. To their left were 7th Division and that morning they successfully took the village of Mametz, to the right stood 30th Division whose objective, the village of Montauban was also taken successfully. The objective set for 18th Division was to take the German first line known as Breslau Trench on a front of 200 yards then move up the communication trenches capturing the second line positions named Pommiers Trench and Train Alley. Once these were successfully taken a third line just north of Montauban and known as Montauban Alley was to be captured. These objectives would see the division advance over ground in the direction of a small copse that lay beyond Montauban known as Montagnes Wood, commonly known to the British as Caterpillar Wood because of its long thin shape. The division was deployed with its 54th Brigade on the left (next to 91st Brigade, 7th Division), 53rd Brigade centre and 55th Brigade on the right (next to the 21st Brigade, 30th Division).

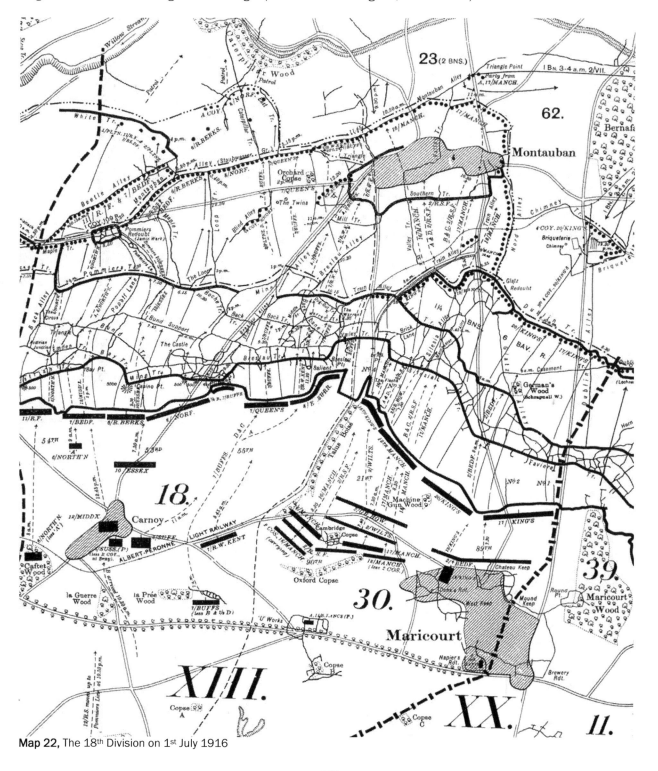

Map 22, The 18th Division on 1st July 1916

The leading battalions of 55th Brigade that morning were the 7th Queens on the left - supported by 'B' Coy of the 7th Buffs minus two platoons on their left flank - and the 8th East Surreys on the right. The 7th RWK were to support the 7th Queens whilst the remaining companies of the 7th Buffs were to provide support for both of the leading battalions. It was also their job to mop up any enemy resistance that still held out once the leading battalions had passed over the main German trenches, unfortunately we don't know to which company Pte Frederick Dunkley was attached that morning.

At 7:30am the leading battalions went over the top in the face of heavy German shell and machine gun fire as did those men of 'B' Coy of the Buffs (12). Known as the Crater Party it was their job to clear a heavily cratered area of any Germans just east of the main road that ran northeast from Carnoy towards Montauban (see map 22). Meanwhile the 7th Buffs 'A' Coy, 'C' Coy and 'D' Coy moved forward to occupy those assembly and frontline trenches now vacated by the leading battalions. These trenches soon came under shellfire and 'C' Coy reported heavy casualties to two of its platoons whilst moving into position, it is possible that Fredrick Dunkley was one of these. As for the actual assault 'B' Coy reported difficulties in clearing the cratered area and the 7th Queens as well as the 7th RWK as their support found it hard to advance over Breslau Trench due to an active enemy machine gun situated in no mans land. As the 30th Division on their right pushed on the 8th East Surreys made ground, two platoons of the Buffs 'A' Coy were sent over in support and the men successfully bombed their way up the communication trenches between the German first and the second line positions of Pommiers Trench and Train Alley.

At 8:45am the Buffs received a message from brigade HQ informing them that the 7th Queens were having trouble taking some craters on their right flank, they were ordered to make contact with the battalion and assist them in overcoming the problem. At 8:50am this order was passed on to 'C' Coy and they were given the job of supporting the Queens and helping them push on towards Pommiers Trench. Just before 9:00am a message was received at the Buffs battalion HQ by the CO of the Crater Party, they had successfully cleared their area except for one machine gun that was providing considerable resistance. Orders were sent to 'D' Coy to reinforce the Crater Party, clear the gun and help them push forward on the left flank, by 9:30am this task had been successfully completed. By this time the East Surreys were requesting urgent help in dealing with a number of Germans who still held out on their right flank at Valley Trench - a continuation of Breslau Trench. It reported this resistance was holding up the advance of the battalions of 21st Brigade. The Buffs found themselves stretched thinly and unable to spare a company so they passed on the message to the 7th RWK. Less than twenty minutes later the East Surreys reported back that the problem had been dealt with and that they had taken Train Alley, unconfirmed reports were also received that Pommiers Trench had also been occupied. Meanwhile the 7th Queens situation was a mixed affair, some elements were held up at Back Trench whilst others made progress moving up and clearing communication trenches, these successful parties also found themselves arriving at Train Alley where they linked up with men of the East Surreys. The battalions of 55th Brigade were indeed making progress and the brigade commander decided that the 7th RWK should undertake the consolidation of Pommiers Trench whilst the other battalions pushed on. The Buffs CO however, Lieutenant Colonel W F Elmslie, needed to know the situation of his companies, a message was sent out for them to report back. The officer commanding 'A' Coy reported that he was at Dug Out Trench - in front of Train Alley - with two platoons plus one platoon of 'C' Coy, they were preparing to bomb their way up Breslau Alley and Mine Alley to take Mill Trench. These trenches ran parallel to the main road from Carnoy and virtually led straight into Montauban. At this time the Buffs were surprised to see two companies of the 8th Suffolk's arrive in their front line trenches, although attached to 53rd Brigade the Suffolk's had been sent up to help 55th Brigade with their advance. Apart from the OIC of 'A' Coy reporting back the CO of the Buffs was growing impatient as to the exact situation regarding the assault therefore he and two fellow officers set off to find out the situation for themselves. They moved forward via craters in search of the CO of the East Surreys, making their way up Mine Alley they stopped just short of Montauban without success, on route however they had met parties of East Surreys, RWK's and Buffs. On his return down Mine Alley Lieutenant Colonel Elmslie met the OIC of the Queens near the junction of the Carnoy–Montauban Road; at this point the two battalion commanders decided to set up an Advanced HQ. After reaching Train Alley the Queens had pushed forward towards the Mametz–Montauban Road but in doing so had lost heavily on their left flank, as a result their CO doubted if they were strong enough to maintain their advance. The Buffs CO ordered two platoons of 'D' Coy forward under a 31 year old Captain called Gerald Neame, his job was to reinforce the Queens left and fill any gaps existing between them and the 8th Norfolk's - the right flank battalion of 53rd Brigade. That afternoon the Buffs and Queens advanced together and occupied their final objective of Montauban Alley, unfortunately in doing so Captain Neame was killed. The East Surreys consolidated their positions east of Montauban whilst the RWK's also reached Montauban Alley, both the 54th Brigade and 53rd Brigade reached their objectives making the assault by 18th Division a complete success.

The Buffs battalion war diary does not list its casualties for 1st July 1916 but according to SDGW they lost 4 officers and 47 other ranks, without his service record it's impossible to know the exact part 19 year old Pte Frederick William Dunkley played in the days events. Like most of the men of the 7th Buffs killed that day Frederick's body was never found, his name is commemorated on Panel 5D of the Thiepval Memorial to the Missing. This memorial bears the names of over 72,000 men - British and South African - who were killed on the

Somme between July 1916 and March 1918 and have no known grave. Built between 1928 and 1932 the Thiepval Memorial is the main British memorial to the missing on the Somme, the names of those men from other commonwealth nations with no known grave are commemorated on memorials elsewhere.

* * *

Saturday 1st July 1916 was the worst day in the history of the British Army before or since. Apart from the limited successes north of Thiepval, around La Boisselle, at Mametz and Montauban the first day of the Somme had been a total failure that saw casualties in excess of 57,000 officers and men, 30,000 of those occurring before midday. Over 19,000 officers and men had been killed mainly by the German machine guns positioned opposite them on the other side of no mans land. Those men of the Regulars, Territorial and New Armies had gallantly gone into battle that morning only to be faced with an almost impossible task; no one can deny their courage or their bravery. It took several days for the scale of the first day's losses to be realised so much so that after 48 hours Haig still felt the attack had been a success. Meanwhile the Somme battle continued and from his HQ at Querrieu General Rawlingson decided to consolidate the ground he had gained. Using reinforcements he would push on in those areas of frontline where his attack had failed, mainly north of the River Ancre. Haig however disagreed and handed Gough command of the two northern corps in this area, he then insisted that Rawlingson should concentrate on the southern sector where he had already achieved success. On the left of Rawlingson's southern sector lay the village of Ovillers and as it had not been captured on the first day it was decided that on 3rd July a fresh attempt would be made to take it. It was this attempt on Ovillers to be carried out by III Corps that would claim the life of the next man from Chigwell to be killed during the 'Battle of the Somme'.

JOHN LESLIE FISH

We are very fortunate as quite a lot is known about the life of John Leslie Fish. He was born at Wanstead in Essex on 1st August 1892 to parents Frank and Ellen Maria Fish. His father, a Mechanical Engineer, had been born at Hackney in East London in 1860 whilst his mother was born at Loughton in Essex sometime during 1862. Frank and his wife were quite wealthy and lived in a large residence called Gordon House situated on Woodford Road in the then village of Wanstead (13). It was at Gordon House that all of their three sons would be born. The oldest named William was born on 5th March 1889; next there came John and then finally Frank - named after his father he was born on 23rd July 1894. On the census of 1901 the Fish family had three servants all living and working at Gordon House and of those one was a nurse another a cook and finally a housemaid. The family eventually moved to the Chigwell area and set up home in a large house called Millbrook situated on the north side of Manor Road to the west of Grange Hill Station. The three brothers attended Chigwell Grammar School and whilst there from 1905 to 1907 John became active in various activities including the school Gymnastics team. Although not much is known about John's life after he left school, we do know that in 1913 he was a member of Chigwell Rifle Club also based at Grange Hill. During March of that year the club played Leyton Rifle Club and beat them with John scoring most of Chigwell's points, he was awarded a prize for his part in the game. The following month the team played again this time against the eastern district of the Post Office, again they were to win but only just by a margin of 2 points. Being quite active as well as a good shot when war broke out John seemed like a perfect candidate to join the army, he was and he did but not right away. It wasn't until the 26th May 1915 that he walked into the recruiting offices of the Honourable Artillery Company based at Armoury House on City Road in Finsbury in London to offer his services. The HAC was a territorial battalion with a long tradition of voluntary enlistment and a lengthy history of which it was very proud. At the time John was 22 years and 9 months old when he volunteered for overseas service for a duration period lasting four years. His medical record states that he was 5ft 10˝ tall with a 37˝ chest that measured 39½˝ when fully expanded; John had perfect vision and his physical development was described as fair. Once accepted John was given army service no 3553, the rank of private and posted to the HAC's second battalion. He was not based in England for long and on 1st July 1915 he crossed the Channel to France as a replacement joining the 1st Battalion HAC in the field on 4th July. His previous experience with weaponry as a member of Chigwell Rifle Club can only have helped his speedy deployment to the front. On 18th September John was promoted to the rank of Lance Corporal whilst with his battalion in positions just south of Ypres, six months later on 18th March 1916 he was promoted again, this time gaining a commission to the officer's rank of temporary second lieutenant. It was whilst gaining promotion that John was transferred to a 'New Army' battalion joining the 7th Battalion Suffolk Regiment. The paperwork for John's discharge from the HAC was completed in London and finally approved on 25th April 1916 by which time he had served 298 day's in the Territorial Army. The 7th Suffolk's were formed at Bury St Edmonds in August 1914, after training they'd crossed to France on 30th May 1915. As previously mentioned in the story of James Edward Cox the 12th (Eastern) Division (14) consisted of the 35th Brigade, 36th Brigade and 37th Brigade, like the 9th Essex the 7th Suffolk's were attached to 35th Brigade.

III Corps front stretched from just south of the village of Authuille to just south of La Boisselle. With the former under British occupation and the latter almost having been taken during the action on the first day the village of Ovillers now stood in III Corps path. The 12th Division had not been involved in the actions of the first day but had found itself held in reserve west of Albert therefore it was selected for the assault to take Ovillers.

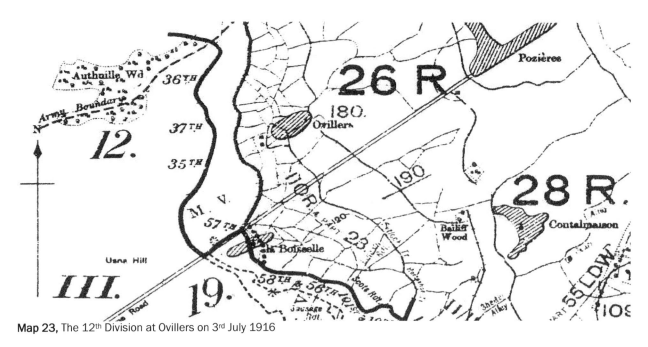

Map 23, The 12th Division at Ovillers on 3rd July 1916

On 2nd July the battalions of the division received orders that they were to attack the village during the early hours of the following morning and proceeded to move up towards their assembly positions on the British frontline. Although Ovillers lay just behind the German frontline it was protected by a further two lines of smaller trenches, if the 12th Division could capture these trenches as well as the village it could then clear a path for an attack on the village of Pozières further east and the main German second line positions beyond it. The 12th Division was to attack with 37th Brigade taking the left flank and 35th Brigade the right flank, 36th Brigade would be held in reserve. 35th Brigade was deployed with the 7th Suffolk's on the left and the 5th Royal Berks on the right, two companies of the 9th Essex were to follow up each battalion in support whilst the 7th Norfolk's were held in reserve. The distance between the British frontline and the German lines was some 800 yards however the British had prepared assembly trenches out in no mans land which they proceeded to occupy under cover of darkness thus shortening this distance to some 500 yards. At 2:15am the artillery of 19th Division situated just south of 12th Division commenced a preliminary bombardment on the German positions around Ovillers, exactly an hour later 12th Division launched its attack.

The 7th Suffolk's war diary takes up the story of their part in the assault:

At 3:15am the battalion made a frontal attack on Ovillers on a frontage of 200 yards; the disposition of the battalion was as follows: 'D' Coy on the right, 'C' Coy on the left, supported by 'B' Coy on the right, 'A' Coy on the left. The battalion assaulted in eight successive waves, the first four (D + C Coys) penetrated to the enemy's third line and portions of them into the village itself, but owing to the darkness they lost touch with succeeding waves and with the 5th Royal Berks on the right. This meant that the leading waves were not supported closely enough thus allowing the Germans to get in between the waves and cut off the leading ones at the third line of resistance, it was at this third line that the chief casualties occurred and the assault was brought to a standstill. The two companies of the 9th Essex moving up in support were too far behind and were practically annihilated by machine gun fire during their advance across the open.

The 7th Suffolk's assault on Ovillers ended in failure with casualties numbering 21 officers and 458 men either killed, wounded or missing, confusion initially surrounded the fate of Lieutenant John Fish. His parents received a telegram at Millbrook from the War Office on 7th July 1916 informing them that their son Second Lieutenant John Fish of the 7th Suffolk Regiment was reported missing on 3rd July. The telegram went on to say that it did not necessarily mean that he had been killed or wounded and any further information would be wired to them as soon as it was received. Frank Fish wrote back the same day thanking the War Office for their immediate response on informing him of the situation regarding his son. He also asked if the other officers of the regiment had any information regarding John, the letter was received at the War Office in Whitehall on the 9th July. However the day before on the 8th July the Fish family had received another telegram:

'Regret to inform you that Second Lieutenant John Leslie Fish reported missing on 3rd July 1916 is now reported wounded and missing as of 5th July 1916. Further details will follow when received'.

It was not until the 24th August 1916 that a wounded and missing report was filed by Pte Arthur Bradford No 20027 of the 7th Battalion Suffolk Regiment. While recovering at Gower Street Hospital in London he was able to report to the staff there what had happened to Lieutenant John Fish on 3rd July 1916.

Informant states: *that Lieutenant Fish was in front of him during an attack on enemy trenches between Ovillers and Pozières. He saw the Lieutenant struck by a bullet and fall; he got up and was killed almost at once by another bullet.*

Although we don't know with which company John attacked that day the above report does shed some light on this question. If he was positioned between Ovillers and Pozières when killed this makes it the third line where the battalion reported most of its casualties occurred. If one ties this up with the war diary report it must be assumed that he was part of the leading waves that reached this position thus making him part of either 'D' Coy or 'C' Coy.

The War Office received official confirmation on 7th October 1916 that Lieutenant John Fish had been killed in action on 3rd July 1916; they sent a telegram to the Fish family at Millbrook the same day (15):

'Deeply regret to inform you Second Lieutenant John Fish 7th Suffolk Regiment previously reported wounded and missing now reported killed in action 3rd July. The Army Council express their sympathy'.

On 14th October 1916 the War Office was informed that Lieutenant John Fish had been buried by the commanding officer of another regiment - The Yorkshire Dragoons. This information was passed to the Fish family however although at the time the place of burial was unknown they were told it would follow. It did and on 15th November 1916 the Military Secretary wrote to Frank Fish to inform him that a report had just been received from Army HQ in the field stating that John had been buried just west of Ovillers. In fact John is buried in Plot VII Row K Grave 3 of Ovillers CWGC Cemetery along with over 3,400 other servicemen of whom almost 2,500 are unidentified (16). On 18th November Frank Fish wrote back to the Military Secretary at the War Office in Whitehall thanking him for information regarding his son's final resting place. A chequebook and advance book was the only items recovered from John's body and these were eventually returned to his parents. Cox & Co was instructed to deal with his estate estimated at around £4,000. For his time with the 7th Suffolk's John was entitled to 124 days pay at 7/6d a day making a total of £46.10. The Fish family received a plaque and scroll in memory of John some time in early 1919 along with the medals that he was entitled to. In 1924 the headmaster of Chigwell Grammar School (1912-1939) Mr Ernest Stuart Walde M.A. erected a memorial chapel in honour of all former pupils who fell in the Great War. This chapel situated inside the school contains 79 names each on brass plaques, these names are followed by different mottos especially chosen by Mr Walde (17). The name of John Fish appears on this memorial followed by the Latin motto *'Libenti Animo'* meaning *'the Free Man of the Mind'*. Mysteriously the name of John Leslie Fish also appears on the Cromer War Memorial in Norfolk, there is no mention of this place in John's service record and I have found it impossible to find a connection between John and the town. The Fish family were very active around Chigwell during the war especially Frank and Ellen. A large building stood on land they owned just to the east of Grange Hill, known as Fairview the building served as a military hospital from early 1915 until the early summer of 1916 at which time another location was found. Ellen was mentioned in despatches and in 1922 was awarded the BRCSM for her services to the wounded during and after the war. Frank died on 16th March 1923 aged 62 whilst Ellen lived until 31st March 1933 when she died aged 70, both are buried in the churchyard of St Mary's and the name of their son, Lieutenant John Fish appears on their headstone.

By 9:00am on 3rd July the battalions of 12th Division had reported total failure in their attempt to capture Ovillers, their fate had been similar to that of the Suffolk's and total losses for the division were put in the region of 2,500 officers and men. As for those surviving men of the 7th Suffolk's over the following days they fell back to positions along the British front line, on the 6th July they were relieved and moved back to billets in Albert.

* * *

During the course of the next week Rawlinson's corps commanders continued to push their divisions forward on the southern sector of the Somme front. Many obstacles remained in their way and would have to be moved if a successful starting position was to be gained for an attack on the German second line. Several woods and copses lined the path to be cleared but during that first week Mametz Wood proved to be the biggest obstacle; it was eventually taken by XV Corps on 12th July. This now left the way clear for Rawlinson to attempt an assault on the German second line positions. In the southern sector the German second line stretched from just west of Grandcourt diagonally down east of Pozières round to Longueval and down in front of Guillemont. A night attack was planned for the early hours of 14th July however two days before a preliminary bombardment ensued and was successful in destroying the German defences. Once the night attack got underway success was achieved on a 5 mile stretch of the German line between Bazentin-le-Petit and a point just east of Longueval. Delville Wood to the northeast of Longueval however became the scene of bitter fighting over the following week, men from four South African regiments suffered appalling losses and the wood was not wholly taken. In the centre of this attack front but some mile and a half distant lay High Wood. The infantry of 7th Division managed to secure the ground in front of High Wood and was amazed to find the wood itself virtually empty of Germans. They were halted from entering the wood by corps commanders and told to wait for cavalry units to come up in support, this delay was to prove disastrous as it gave the Germans time to regroup and mount defensive positions. When the cavalry finally charged the wood that evening they were cut to pieces by machine gun fire as German counter attacks retook the wood. The Germans now reinforced their line from Delville Wood to High Wood and this stretch of line found itself the focus of attention for the next two months. To the west Ovillers, that had claimed the life of Lieutenant John Fish and caused the 12th Division problems on 3rd July, was finally captured in a successful attack carried out on 16th July by 25th Division, the next village in the path of the British on this southern sector was Pozières. From 23rd July to 7th August Australian divisions fought a bitter battle for the village, they eventually took it but lost more men in doing so than they had in the whole of the Gallipoli campaign. As the fighting continued on the Somme it was not until 17th August that Chigwell lost its next man.

ARTHUR JOHN WAUGH

Most men from Chigwell who fought during the First World War it must be said served in either the infantry or as part of an attacking unit. This however was not true in the case of Arthur John Waugh although he did serve alongside them as a member of the Royal Army Medical Corps.

The R.A.M.C. was a non-combatant unit whose job it was to evacuate and then care for those men unfortunate enough to become casualties. There follows a basic chain of the different stages a wounded man could expect to follow although sometimes some of the stages were missed out. Firstly a man injured on the frontline would be dealt with by his battalion Medical Officer. Known as the M.O. this was usually an officer of the R.A.M.C.; if he was not at hand one of his orderlies or the battalion stretcher bearers would deal with the casualty. This assistance would usually be carried out at a Regimental Aid Post situated in one of the forward support or communication trenches, the treatment a wounded man would receive here would be very basic indeed. The next stop for a wounded man would be the Advanced Dressing Station, how he got there would depend on not only the nature of his wound but also the terrain over which he had to travel. The ADS were usually set up close to the front by divisional Field Ambulance units (18). These units provided makeshift medical areas also positioned close to the frontline but their lack of facilities meant they were only able to offer limited help, sometimes however small operations might be performed. Next a wounded man would arrive at a Casualty Clearing Station, the first medical facility most equipped to treat or operate on his wounds. The CCS's were usually set up in tents but sometimes they were housed in buildings. If a man required it his next stop was a General Hospital, situated behind the lines in France and Flanders they were usually located near to the Channel ports or near to main army bases. The hell of the trenches saw most men looking for a wound that would take them home and this was known as a 'Blighty'. If a man found he was lucky enough to receive a 'Blighty Wound' he would usually be treated at a Hospital back in England either in one of the cities or like the one situated at Fairview in Chigwell. Depending on the nature of his wound and its healing process once a man was fit and well enough he would then be expected to report for duty, this was the first step in returning to his battalion at the front. It is the very first stage of the above chain that concerns Arthur Waugh as he was the M.O. attached to the 1st Battalion North Staffordshire (The Prince of Wales's) Regiment.

Arthur John Waugh was born at Leytonstone in East London in 1887 the third son of Walter and Annie - formally Marshall - Waugh. His parents were born in London and Walter worked as a Chemical Merchant which made him a very wealthy man. Walter and Annie had eight children in all, their three eldest children were: Walter C (b.1883 Hackney), Frank (b.1885 Hackney) and Arthur (b.1887 Leytonstone). Their first daughter was Ethel (b.1888 Leytonstone) followed by Lillian (b.1890 Leytonstone). Their three youngest children were Leonard (b.1893 Leytonstone), Stanley (b.1896 Leytonstone) and finally Hubert (b.1899 Wanstead). The Waugh family lived at Southbury House in Bulwer Road Leytonstone towards the latter part of the 19th Century and moved to Chigwell in 1905. Walter Waugh acquired Chigwell Hall - a large red bricked mansion house set in 40 acres of land - for £14,000 from the family of estate agent and auctioneer Alfred Savill. Built by Norman Shaw in 1876 Chigwell Hall was commissioned by Savill whose brother was in business with Shaw. At the turn of the century Arthur Waugh found himself away at boarding school but not too far attending Forest School in Walthamstow (19). After leaving school Arthur trained in medicine and during the years leading up to the war worked at St Bartholomew's Hospital in the City of London before joining the R.A.M.C. An intelligent man of good education he was soon promoted and by the time war broke out he held the rank of Captain. What is interesting here is that Arthur's sister Ethel in July 1915 married a Lieutenant Newman F Norman of the R.A.M.C. Whilst its not known if he or Arthur ever trained or served together it is reasonably possible, as far as is known Lieutenant Norman survived the war. Unfortunately the army service record of Arthur Waugh was destroyed in 1941 but from the Medal Rolls at the NA we know he joined the 1st North Staffs on the 19th August 1914. Upon the outbreak of war this battalion had been stationed at Buttevant in Ireland, they arrived back on the 17th August and headed to Cambridge where Arthur joined them two days later. The 1st North Staffs crossed the Channel to France on 12th September 1914 to join the BEF as part of 17th Brigade, 6th Division. The battalion spent the first year of the war in trenches in and around the Ypres Salient where inevitably it suffered substantial losses. By the autumn of 1915 the 1st North Staffs found itself being reinforced with men from the 'New Armies', as a result that October the battalion was transferred to 72nd Brigade, 24th Division. Arthur and his battalion remained in the salient right up until the summer of 1916, in early July Arthur left the Staffordshire's briefly. The brigades and battalions of 24th Division had been informed they would be moving south to the Somme area and it is possible that Arthur went ahead to help with the casualties generated in the opening days of the Somme offensive. The 1st North Staffs came out of the trenches at Ypres on 19th July, the following day they received orders they should prepare to move southwards however it was not until

24th July that they actually started the journey. The rest of the month was spent moving from village to village and by the beginning of August the 1st North Staffs found themselves in billets at Morlancourt south of Albert, it was here that Captain Arthur Waugh rejoined the battalion.

It should be remembered how the Germans had reinforced their lines from Delville Wood to High Wood towards the end July and then two further months of fighting ensued. Well the 24th Division were positioned in this area and took part in actions south of Delville Wood during early August. Its various brigades held the lines east of Longueval southwards to positions east of Montauban. On 9th August the 72nd Brigade received orders it should be ready to leave billets and move up towards the frontline areas. As a result the following day men of the 1st North Staffs found themselves in support line trenches and dugouts situated south of Bernefay Wood - southeast of Montauban; this area was known as the Briqueterie. During the night of 11th August the battalion was ordered to form working parties for duties on the front line, their task was to improve trenches about a mile west of the Briqueterie on a line stretching northwards from Trones Wood to the Guillemont Road. At the same time that the 1st North Staffs were forming working parties a neighbouring battalion launched an attack on German positions nearby; as a result the Staffordshire's work was delayed until after midnight, once completed however they returned to the Briqueterie. At 11:00am the following morning the 1st North Staffs received orders they were to relieve the 8th Royal West Kent's - also of 72nd Brigade - in frontline trenches just east of Trones Wood, this relief despite the battalion suffering a few casualties was completed by 9:30pm. The 1st North Staffs were to spend the next four days in the frontline, it rained most of the time but the men still had to perform their duties which included improving their frontline trench as well as the communication trenches connected to it. During this time enemy artillery was very active, as battalion M.O. Captain Arthur Waugh would have had his work cut out as a steady number of men fell victim to German shellfire. On the evening of 15th August the battalion was relieved by men of the 8th Royal West Kent's and the 1st North Staffs moved back to support lines at the Briqueterie, during their time in the frontline their casualties were 18 men killed , 60 wounded and 5 missing. The next day saw the battalion ordered back to a cratered area just east of Montauban, two companies were to remain here and two were to man defences in Montauban village itself. A failed attack by British units on the frontline however upset this plan and most of the Staffordshire's remained at the Briqueterie in case of an enemy counter attack. The 17th August was a fine bright day apart from the odd shower here and there; the Staffordshire's remained in their positions at the Briqueterie awaiting further orders.

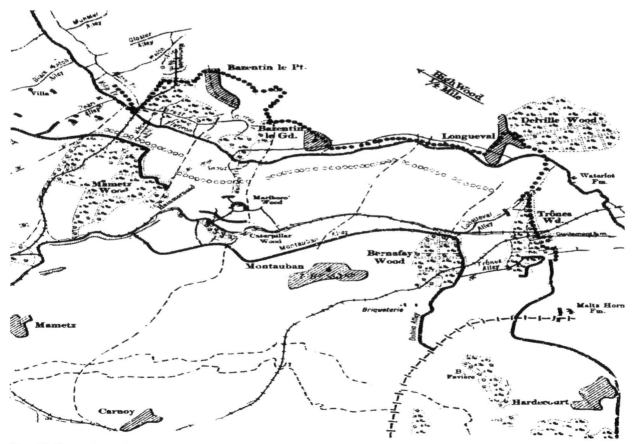

Map 24, The position of the 1st North Staff's (August 1916)

These arrived at 2:30pm ordering the battalion to take up positions they should have occupied the previous day in the cratered area east of Montauban, the Staffordshire's were supposed to be relieved by the 9th Royal Sussex (73rd Brigade, 24th Division) but they failed to show so the 1st North Staffs moved off unrelieved. As the battalion commanders were leaving their HQ a stray shell landed nearby killing their M.O. Captain Arthur John Waugh, he was 28 years old. This event is clearly recorded in the 1st North Staffs battalion war diary and as Arthur had served with this unit since November 1914 his death was considered a huge loss. The battalion CO who was extremely fond of his M.O. described Arthur as someone who'd set a fine example of devotion to duty. Over the weeks that followed the brigades and battalions of 24th Division remained in the areas around Montauban and Trones Wood, their division would be one of those involved in the next phase of the Somme offensive.

Captain Arthur John Waugh is buried in Row C Grave 25 at Carnoy CWGC Cemetery Somme France, started in August 1915 this cemetery contains over 850 casualties of the First World War (20). Two of Arthur's brothers served in the army during the First World War, Leonard as an officer with the 3rd Essex and Stanley as a member of the Essex Yeomanry, both survived the war (21). As far as medals were concerned Arthur was entitled to the 1914 Star, the BWM and the VM, these were sent out and received by his family between 1919 and 1921. Walter Waugh died on 7th April 1925 aged 65, during the war years he had helped out arranging the transport of wounded soldiers from the main station at Ilford to Fairview Hospital in Chigwell. Annie Waugh died on 7th June 1931 aged 73, like her husband she too was an active member of the Chigwell village community connected especially with various events arranged by the parish. Both Walter and Annie are buried inside St Mary's Churchyard; Captain Arthur John Waugh is mentioned on their headstone as is his sister Lillian who died in 1968. As for Chigwell Hall it remained with the Waugh family but was leased out from time to time, eventually in 1938 it was sold to the Metropolitan Police for £30,000, they still own it.

* * *

As the actions around Delville Wood came to an end another battle was set to start for a village situated southeast of Longueval. Guillemont had briefly been occupied at the end of July by a battalion of Scots Fusiliers but was not held onto as the battalion was forced to fall back. Then in early August more skirmishes were fought in the area but were not successful in taking the village although troops remained in the area for most of the month. The main battle for Guillemont fell to XIV Corps and took place between the 3rd September and 6th September although it had been due to start on the last day of August but was postponed due to bad weather. It was the first day of this action that claimed the lives of two friends from Chigwell.

EDWARD STEPHEN SCOTT & ALFRED CHARLES VINCE

Despite there being an age difference of 12 years between them it did not stop these two young men from joining the army together when war broke out. Edward Stephen Scott was born in Chigwell in 1886 to James and Ellen Scott the second youngest of six children. James died very young leaving Ellen to bring up their large family alone. The Scott family had lived in Chigwell their whole lives with all the children including Ellen herself having been born there. At the turn of the century the family lived at 2 Forest View Cottages situated on Chigwell High Road. All the children attended the village school and upon leaving the boys William, Herbert and Edward found employment within the village as gardeners and grooms, by 1914 however Edward had changed his job to that of grocer. Edward was known to help out at St Mary's Church when parties or events were held there; he was also a member of the church choir. Shortly before the outbreak of war the Scott family moved to 1 Prospect Terrace on Hainault Road in Chigwell. Alfred Charles Vince had been born at Gillingham in the county of Kent in 1897 to parents Isaac and Elizabeth Vince. Unfortunately very is little is known of his family background although he did have an older sister Rosina who was born in 1877. The family eventually moved to Chigwell Row living at 2 Tinouth Cottages and after leaving school Alfred worked at the Butcher shop in the village almost next door to the grocery shop where Edward Scott worked. Once war was declared both Edward and Alfred like so many young men saw their chance to do their bit for king and country and on 11th January 1915 they travelled to London to enlist. Both underwent a medical examination, Edward was 5ft 5˝ tall with a 36˝ chest, he had perfect vision, weighed 128lbs and had an indentation on his right shoulder blade but all in all was of a good physical development. Alfred's medical showed that he was 5ft 7½˝ tall with a 36˝ chest; he weighed 196lbs had perfect vision and a scar above his left eyebrow and like Edward was of a good physical development. On acceptance both Edward and Alfred were given army numbers S/7941 and S/7939 respectively and posted as Riflemen to the 11th Battalion Rifle Brigade. On 22nd January they arrived for training at Winchester, the battalion had been formed there in September 1914 as part of K2 and was part of the 20th (Light) Division. This division consisted of the 59th Brigade, 60th Brigade and 61st Brigade; the 11th Battalion Rifle Brigade was attached to 59th Brigade along with the 10th Battalion Kings Royal Rifle Corps, 11th Battalion Kings Royal Rifle Corps and the 10th Battalion Rifle Brigade.

The 59th Brigade moved to Blackdown Camp near Aldershot in late January and its various battalions undertook their first courses in musketry, further training followed and in February they marched in wet weather to Whitley Camp on Salisbury Plain. The camp at Whitley was virtually a sea of mud when the brigade arrived and the tents erected to house the men were damp and leaked constantly. A lack of khaki at this time saw the men dressed in blue uniforms - known as 'Kitcheners Blue' - and thin overcoats were all that was available to protect them from the winter weather. Whilst at Whitley on the 26th March Alfred got into trouble for talking back to an NCO, consequently he was docked 14 days pay. A few days later the battalions of 59th Brigade were moved once again undertaking a four day march to Hamilton Camp near Stonehenge, on arrival training continued that included another course in developing the unit's musketry skills. Over the next two months the brigades that made up the 20th Division were inspected and considered ready for overseas service, the various battalions received orders to this effect and were equipped ready to move at short notice.

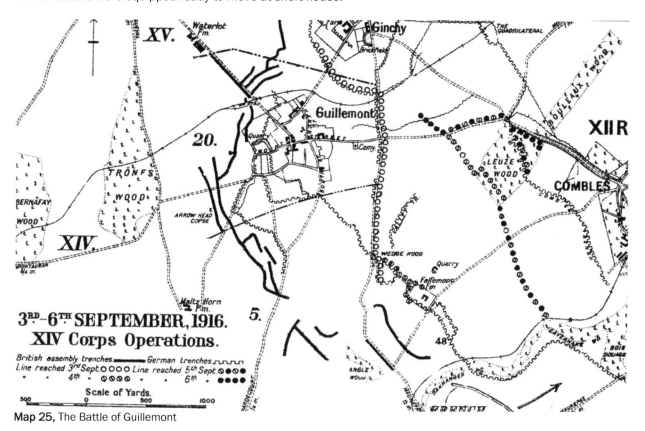

Map 25, The Battle of Guillemont

So it was that on 21st July 1915 with just six months of training behind them Edward and Alfred and the rest of their battalion crossed the Channel to France landing at Boulogne early the following morning. Early August saw the battalion enter the trenches for the first time taking up positions in the frontline at Laventie north of Neuve Chapelle; they would remain in this sector doing regular tours in the frontline for the rest of the year. The start of 1916 saw the battalion and the rest of 20th Division move northwards holding positions in various parts of the Ypres Salient. Alfred found himself in trouble again on 3rd March 1916 for destroying property in the field and he was deprived 3 days pay. Edward on the other hand being older than Alfred stayed out of trouble, on 5th April he was promoted to acting Lance Corporal, this promotion lasted three months until 24th June when it became permanent and he was made a full Lance Corporal. At the end of June the brigades and battalions that made up 20th Division were moved south to the Somme area although they would not be involved in the first phase of the Somme fighting. Having been placed in reserve the division was eventually brought forward to support the assault on Delville Wood, once this objective was taken it was then selected for what would be its first major test, the attack on Guillemont.

XIV Corps consisted of the 5th Division, 16th Division and the 20th Division although only one or two brigades from each would take part in the 'Battle of Guillemont'. Two brigades of 5th Division – the 13th Brigade and 95th Brigade - were allotted the area south of the village attacking in a north easterly direction through a valley towards a copse known as Leuze Wood - Lousy Wood to Tommy. Farm buildings and various enemy positions stood in their path. The 16th Division was mainly held in reserve however its 47th Brigade was brought forward with its battalion's objectives being the northern part of the village and the immediate area beyond. The 20th Division were to attack the southern end of the village and 59th Brigade was to lead the charge supported by the 6th Battalion Oxford & Buckinghamshire Light Infantry (60th Brigade) and 7th Somerset Light Infantry (61st Brigade). The first main objectives for 59th Brigade were two sunken lanes that ran directly in front of its position as well as the enemy trenches situated between them (22). Once these were cleared the brigade could then push on through the village crossing their next objective the Hardecourt Road - known as South Street - towards another objective the Ginchy-Wedgewood Road, from here they could then head for the area west of Leuze Wood in the direction of Morval and Lesboeufs.

Final preparations were carried out on the night of 2nd September as the battalions took up positions in assembly trenches along the frontline; Alfred and Edwards's battalion were in position by 8:00pm on what was to be a quiet night. The 11th Battalion Rifle Brigade was under the command of Major A. E. Cotton, an officer from the 10th Battalion Rifle Brigade (23). Both 'A' Coy and 'B' Coy were selected to lead the assault with 'C' Coy and 'D' Coy in support. Both Edward and Alfred were attached to 'B' Coy commanded by a 19 year old Second Lieutenant called Andrew Munro Hepburn however at one time Alfred had been part of 'D' Coy until he was transferred. The battalion was to attack on the right of the 10th KRRC along with the 6th Ox & Bucks; zero hour was set for 12 noon. The 3rd September was a fine morning and the ground over which the attack would take place had dried up considerably after the rain of the previous few days, the temperature was in the 70's. At noon a preliminary barrage started up on the German positions in and around Guillemont and a few minutes later the battalions of 59th Brigade attacked. The two assaulting companies of 11th Rifle Brigade quickly took the first sunken lane however the German trenches beyond it proved more difficult, enemy machine guns swept the area and the battalion lost heavily. It was here that both 'B' Coy lost its CO Second Lieutenant Hepburn and 'A' Coy its 21 year old CO called Captain Robert Donner (24) as well as several NCOs with possibly L/Cpl Edward Scott amongst them. However the trenches and second sunken lane were soon captured and those Germans that occupied the positions were mostly killed. With the leading companies now short of officers they found themselves attacking alongside the men of the 6th Ox & Bucks however their battalions supporting companies - 'C' Coy and 'D' Coy - were now arriving on the scene. The assault pushed on as the men took machine gun fire from their right as they approached the Hardecourt Road, the few Germans that were encountered were dealt with although little fighting at close quarters actually took place. Approaching the Ginchy–Wedgewood Road the battalion came under further machine gun as well as shellfire and it is possible that it was here that Alfred Vince was killed. Meanwhile further north the 47th Brigade of 16th Division had swept through the village clearing all before them as they went, the 5th Division however having swept comfortably through the valley south of Guillemont were now having difficulty in clearing a ridge on their left that ran southwest out of Leuze Wood. Many Germans could be seen positioned on this ridge and it became clear to the right flank battalions of 59th Brigade that until this position was clear no further advance could be made on their front. The 11th Rifle Brigade concentrated Lewis Gun and rifle fire towards the ridge and to quote their war diary 'many Germans were seen to fall' however in their opinion no advance could be made whilst the ridge remained in enemy hands. So it was that by 2:30pm the battalion and the rest of 59th Brigade took up positions along the Ginchy–Wedgewood Road and started consolidation of the ground they had gained, groups of men known as battle patrols were pushed out in order to fend off any counter attacks by the enemy that may have materialised. Towards late evening enemy counter attacks did occur however they were successfully dealt with, consolidation continued throughout an uneventful night. The following day the battalion held their line although under shellfire most of the time, that evening on their right 5th Division attacked and managed to gain a foothold in Leuze Wood, at 6:30am on the morning of 5th September the men of the 11th Rifle Brigade were relieved of their positions and moved back to camp at Carnoy.

Casualty figures for the battalion on 3rd September according to a document entitled 'History of the 11th Rifle Brigade' were put at 3 officers killed and 6 wounded, as for other ranks 22 are listed as killed and 171 wounded, 11 are listed as missing. SDGW on this date puts casualties for the battalion at 2 officers and 52 other ranks killed. Guillemont had successfully been captured by the divisions of XIV Corps when other divisions had tried and failed. In an address on 8th September, whilst in billets at Corbie, the GOC 20th Division congratulated the battalions of 59th Brigade on their achievement and called Guillemont the *"Place that had been holding up the whole of the British Army"*.

Edward Scott's death was reported in both the October and November 1916 editions of the Chigwell Parish Magazine. The October article stated that he'd initially been reported as wounded by the War Office but that comrades within his battalion had written to his family to say he'd actually been killed on 3rd September. The War Office finally confirmed his death on 20th October on receipt of a casualty report filed by the officer in charge of the 11th Battalion Rifle Brigade. It stated Edward had been killed in action in the field on 3rd September although his place of burial was as yet unknown. L/Cpl Edward Stephen Scott is buried at Guillemont Road CWGC Cemetery in Plot VI Row B Grave 5 (25). On 7th February 1917 a request was sent from the War Office to the HQ of the Rifle Brigade for any of Edward's effects to be sent to Ellen in Chigwell, this request was complied with but it wasn't until 28th August 1918 that Ellen finally received her son's belongings. On 23rd March 1919 she also received on Edward's behalf the 1915/16 Star war medal followed in August 1920 by the British War Medal and Victory Medal, soon after a memorial scroll was also received in memory of her son along with a small war pension. Ellen Scott died on 19th March 1928 aged 84 and is buried in the churchyard of St Mary's in Chigwell; Edward is mentioned on her headstone. The death of Alfred Vince was also reported in the October 1916 issue of the Chigwell Parish Magazine, the article using Alfred's middle name reported that 'Pte Charles Vince' had been killed instantaneously by a shell on 3rd September 1916. The article went on to say that Charles was just 19 years old and had enlisted under age whilst proudly protesting he was not going to be fetched! i.e. would not wait to be called up. Isaac and Elizabeth Vince had learned of the death of their son via the War Office shortly after the 18th September 1916. A casualty report dated 10th September had been made by the officer in charge of the 11th Battalion Rifle Brigade at CCS 22 - located at Bray south of Albert - stating that on 3rd September Alfred Vince had been killed in action in the field, it also reported that Alfred had not been buried. In fact the shell must have been such that Alfred's body was never found therefore he is commemorated on Panels 16 B and C of the Thiepval Memorial to the Missing (26). It is a shame that both Alfred and Edward who had gone through so much together could not be buried side by side. Rosina Vince signed a statement as next of kin on behalf of her parents at Chigwell Row on 27th May 1919 in order that Isaac and Elizabeth should receive a small war pension in compensation for the loss of their son. In August 1920 Isaac collected the 1915/16 Star and would during the following year also receive both the BWM and VM on Alfred's behalf.

* * *

With the Somme battles just three months old Chigwell had lost six men, this put the total loss for the village since August 1914 at seventeen men. As the news of the mounting casualties filtered back to this small Essex village one can only imagine the mood must have been one of sorrow. But Chigwell was not alone, all over the country and indeed from nations around the world communities whether large or small were also suffering such losses. The German commander Erich Von Falkenhayn shortly after the Somme battles begun had insisted that no ground should be lost and if it was steps should immediately be made to retake it. This was all well and good but these counter attacks proved costly and by this stage German formations were losing just as many men as the allies. As the smaller scale battles continued more and more shells were fired by the artillery units of both sides scarring parts of the Somme landscape forever. Throughout that summer it had rained constantly turning the battlefields of the Somme into a muddy waste, not exactly the best conditions for the opposing armies to fight each other. The attacks and counter attacks continued with both sides gaining little, a stalemate was again beginning to exist.

In Britain however with her casualties mounting and success on the battlefront appearing to be making slow progress it was not long before the politicians were looking to Haig for a solution. They sent for Sir William Robertson, the Chief of the Imperial General Staff, to find out what Haig's plans were. The post of CIGS was the most senior position in the army; it was Robertson's job to advise the government on all military maters (27). At their meeting Haig told Robertson he had just the answer to break the latest stalemate situation - The Tank. The War Office had been working on this top secret idea since 1915 and after a period of successful trials in England by the end of August beginning of September 1916 almost fifty had been sent to France to be used on the Somme. Sir Henry Rawlingson was not as optimistic as the CIC was about this new weapon; he was not exactly sure what the Tank could achieve whilst Sir Hubert Gough was of the same mind. The Tank was so named because it looked like a water tank, equipped with guns and able to cross trenches these armoured machines it was hoped could be used to force a breakthrough on the Somme. As the Tanks were a new concept their reliability was questionable however on the night of 14th September over thirty of them were assembled near Trones Wood to the west of Guillemont, they were to take part in the action that would come to be known as the 'Battle of Flers – Courcelette'. It was from this starting position that they were spread out along the southern sector of the front for an attack early the next morning. The Tank attack of the 15th September was to initially prove a great success although only eighteen Tanks actually took part alongside the infantry of various corps participating in the battle. That morning the British managed to advance as far as the villages of Flers, Martinpuich and Courcelette taking with them parts of the German third line. The Germans holding these positions had been terrified at the sight of these huge armoured machines heading towards them closely followed by attacking infantry troops. It did not take long for this British success to be reported back home, the press had a field day and briefly the pressure was lifted off Haig. However on the battlefront after the initial shock of the Tanks had died down it was not long until the armies of both sides again settled down to the same kind of fighting that they had endured over the previous three months. Some people felt that the Tanks had been used too early, no major strategic gain had been made, no breakthrough had been achieved and the element of surprise had inevitably been lost, the Somme battle continued.

SIDNEY HAYTER MM

The story of Sidney Hayter is an interesting one, at times it is complicated but it is certainly one that captures the imagination, with the help of his army service record we are lucky enough to be able to follow his journey. Sidney Hayter was born in the Essex village of Epping on 19th December 1893 to parents Frank and Eliza Hayter. Frank a Domestic Coachman had been born in the Wiltshire village of Hindon in 1864, this village lies on the southern edge of Salisbury Plain. Frank had a brother called Thomas and it seems likely that as children they moved with the rest of their family to the Norfolk area. Eliza had been born in the Essex village of Oisley sometime during 1863, where and when she met Frank is unknown. By 1890 the two were married and that same year their first child Violet was born at Great Yarmouth in Norfolk, soon after the Hayters moved to Epping and in 1892 their second child Albert was born. Sidney was their next child and then in 1897 Eliza gave birth to another daughter she named Lily. Frank and Eliza had two more sons Stanley born in 1898 and finally Ernest born in 1900, this made six children in all. The Hayters connection with the village of Chigwell is one of mystery, it is not clear if they actually lived in the village although they do appear to have moved from Epping to nearby Loughton. Sidney however attended the council school in Chigwell run by Headmaster John R Moseley and he was also a member of the choir that met at St Mary's Church. Sidney also helped out with the various events in the village that were organised by the church, at a concert held in the garden of the vicarage in August 1913 Sidney and Edward Scott both sold programmes to mark the event. After leaving school Sidney worked as a Shop Assistant, here he remained until war was declared in August 1914 and once the call came he wasted no time in responding to Kitcheners request for volunteers. Enlisting in London on 9th September 1914 for a period of three years or the duration of the war Sidney underwent a medical examination, this showed he was 5ft 10˝ tall weighing 138lbs, he had a 38˝ chest 40½˝ when fully expanded. Sidney had perfect vision and was of a fresh complexion; he had blue eyes, brown hair and stated his religion as Church of England. That same day after a successful examination Sidney was posted as Rifleman S/2696 to the 12th Battalion Rifle Brigade based at Winchester, two days later however he was transferred to the 9th Battalion (28). Almost a month later whilst still at Winchester and undergoing the standard period of basic training Sidney was transferred back to the 12th Battalion. This battalion was attached to the 20th (Light) Division therefore its journey is very similar to that as described in the stories of Edward Scott and Alfred Vince (29). The 12th Rifle Brigade however was attached to 60th Brigade along with the 6th Battalion (Service) Ox & Bucks Light Infantry, 6th Battalion (Service) KSLI and the 12th Battalion (Service) KRRC.

During October Sidney was inoculated against disease but this did not stop him contracting tonsillitis and he was admitted to hospital for thirteen days from 30th October until 11th November. After spending Christmas and New Year training on 3rd February 1915 Sidney was promoted to A/Cpl, around this time as previously mentioned the 20th Division were moved to Blackdown Camp near Aldershot and then on to camp at Whitley. The following month Sidney received another inoculation and soon afterwards he once again became ill, he was admitted to Tidworth Hospital on Salisbury Plain for three days between the 17th April and 21st April. Although the cause of his illness cannot be identified the damp conditions within the camp at Whitley could not have helped his situation. During April the 60th Brigade were posted to the village of Larkhill still on Salisbury Plain. It seems that whatever Sidney was suffering from had not been cured as his commanding officer wrote to the medical officer at the hospital and was advised that Sidney should be readmitted, he was on 30th April for a further period of six days finally being discharged on 5th May. The next two months saw the battalions of 60th Brigade spending their time preparing to head overseas, on 2nd July Sidney was promoted to Lance Corporal and twenty days later during the night of 21st/22nd July his battalion along with the rest of the 20th Division crossed the Channel to France. While Sidney had been training his older brother Albert had also enlisted in the army at a recruiting office at Chelsea in southwest London. By this time Albert had been living in Norfolk near his uncle - Thomas Hayter - and had married a woman called Lily, the couple had set up home in the Old Catton area to the north of Norwich. After a successful medical Albert was posted as Pte 12377 to the 7th Battalion Norfolk Regiment; he was 22 years old.

Having landed in France the 12th Rifle Brigade headed, along with the rest of their brigade and division, towards the frontline where they were quickly introduced to life in the trenches. L/Cpl Sidney Hayter, like Edward Scott and Alfred Vince, found his battalion holding trench positions in the Laventie Sector whilst at the same time providing men for work parties on those days when they found themselves out of the line. Towards the end of September 1915 the battalion went back into the trenches at Lavantie. On the 25th September in conjunction with events taking place further south at Loos the 12th Rifle Brigade found themselves supporting an attack being carried out by battalions from the Indian Meerut Division. During this attack the battalion did manage to gain ground but lost touch with the Indian battalions who'd advanced too far ahead of them. The men of the 12th Rifle Brigade had to admit failure and fall back due to enemy counter attacks but not before suffering casualties according to SDGW of 4 officers and 95 men, many more were wounded however including Sidney Hayter who received a gunshot wound to the buttock. This wound for reasons unknown was not reported by the OIC of the battalion until 28th September - maybe Sidney had been trapped out in no mans land - however two days later Sidney found himself heading back to England in order to recover. His wound healed quickly and just over a month later Sidney was posted to the 15th Battalion Rifle Brigade, a reserve unit based on the south coast at Seaford in Sussex. On 18th November he was posted back to the 12th Battalion arriving in France the following day, it took him a further five days however to actually reach and rejoin his battalion whom he found in billets at Fleurbaix south of Armentières. The battalion stayed in this area for the remainder of the year. As previously mentioned the brigades and battalions of 20th Division were moved north and spent the first half of 1916 holding positions in and around the Ypres Salient, it was whilst here that Sidney was awarded the Military Medal. The MM was a gallantry medal first introduced in March 1916; it was mainly awarded to just NCOs and other ranks. Unfortunately the British - unlike the Australians - never kept records on MM recommendations therefore it can be hard to find details behind the award or the date the deed occurred. Sometimes battalion war diaries record the event but in the case of Sidney Hayter the 12th Rifle Brigade's diary sheds no light on his award, surprisingly neither does his army service record (30). Recipients of gallantry awards such as the MM, DCM and VC were mentioned in the London Gazette Newspaper but unlike VC's where an account of the action is recorded MM awards just give the name, rank and battalion of the recipient. Sidney Hayter's award appeared on the 3rd June 1916.

The various units that made up 20th Division had begun to move southwards towards the Somme area at the end of June; however it was not until the third week of July that Sidney's battalion followed. By the third week of August they found themselves stationed behind the lines at Méaulte just south of Albert. Over the next week the battalion moved forward and Sidney found himself resting in the old British frontline trenches at Carnoy and Montauban that Frederick Dunkley had been in on the morning of 1st July. From here they moved forward for their first spell in the Somme frontline occupying trenches in front of Guillemont as yet to be captured. On 8th September whilst still in the line Sidney found himself promoted to the rank of Sergeant attached to 'A' Coy, then having completed their spell at the front three days later his battalion moved back to billets at Méaulte joining the rest of 60th Brigade. Whilst here the battalion paraded by companies and after having equipment checked their mornings were spent practicing activities such as bayonet fighting and bomb throwing, their afternoons were spent playing sports such as football and cricket. The 13th September saw the 12th Rifle Brigade celebrating its second birthday having been created on this date back in 1914, that evening a dinner was held for all those original members of the battalion which included Sgt Sidney Hayter. With the 'Battle of Flers - Courcelette' taking place the 20th Division were moved forward in order to relieve the Guards Division based in trenches east of Ginchy. Leaving Méaulte on the 14th September the 60th Brigade headed east towards the frontline finding itself the following evening bivouacked in heavy rain southeast of Carnoy.

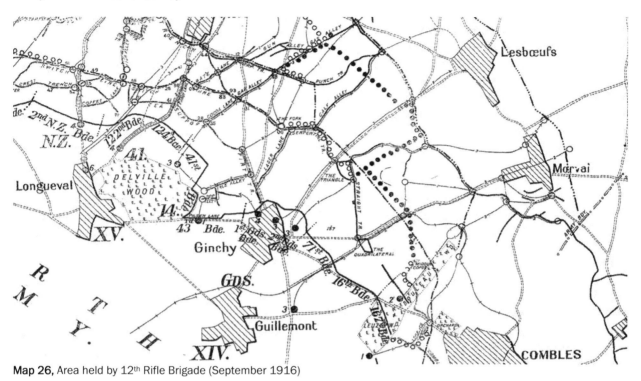

Map 26, Area held by 12th Rifle Brigade (September 1916)

That day two officers from the 12th Rifle Brigade - one of whom was the second in command - were taken ill causing a staff officer from 60th Brigade HQ to be temporarily attached to the battalion, this rendered its total fighting strength at 7 officers. At 5:00am on the 16th September the battalions of 60th Brigade moved off at fifteen minute intervals towards a sugar refinery southwest of Ginchy known at Waterlot Farm, from there they would disperse to take up their positions in the frontline. The battalions of 61st Brigade had gone into the frontline trenches several days earlier to support the Guards Division and 60th Brigade were due to relieve them in a position known as 'The Triangle' just south of the Ginchy–Lesboeufs Road, the 12th Rifle Brigade were due to take over positions vacated by the 7th KOYLI. On their way up the line that evening the men of the 12th Rifle Brigade were subjected to heavy shellfire in pouring rain, they were met by an orderly coming the other way who informed them that the battalion HQ of the 7th KOYLI had just been knocked out by a shell wounding their CO and killing his adjutant (31). Eventually Sidney's battalion reached their allotted positions only to find a state of confusion existed, parties of three different battalions were encountered within their section of trench in addition to men of the 7th KOYLI, added to this the battalion also found a stretch of trench some 300 yards long left totally undefended. Despite all of this the battalion relief was eventually completed by 3:00am on the morning of 17th September. As the day broke enemy shelling quietened down on 12th Rifle Brigades front however their neighbours, the 6th Ox & Bucks were not so lucky, the shelling was so heavy on their line a company of them were forced to move into the Rifle Brigades trenches in order to take cover. With no let up in the wet weather that afternoon the two other battalions of 60th Brigade - 12th KRRC and 6th KSLI - based in 'The Triangle' were attacked by German bombing parties, 12th Rifle Brigade sent up a section of bombers and a Lewis Gunner in support and eventually the enemy attack was driven off. The men of the 12th Rifle Brigade found that their section of line faced south towards a position known as 'Straight Trench' and an area known as the 'Quadrilateral' that lay on the Morval–Guillemont Road (32). The battalion received orders that these two positions were due to be attacked by the neighbouring 6th Division at dawn the following day.

On Monday 18th September it rained all day, after a short barrage at 5:50am 6th Division attacked taking their objectives without difficulty. Many Germans could be seen retiring towards Morval from their positions in the areas around 'Straight Trench' by men from 12th Rifle Brigade and it was decided that the battalion would send out two patrols in order to cut them off. One patrol from 'A' Coy under Lieutenant Breckon including Sgt Sidney Hayter and one patrol from 'C' Coy under Second Lieutenant Reginald Ruddle were given this task, they left their trenches and pursued the fleeing Germans towards a valley 300 yards away that ran south in front of Morval. Their battalion war diary records that these patrols were very successful and many Germans were killed whilst running down the valley, it also states that over forty prisoners were captured. According to SDGW the 12th Rifle Brigade had one man killed during this action but several more were wounded, unfortunately one was Sgt Sidney Hayter who received a gunshot wound to the abdomen. The men of 'A' Coy and 'C' Coy eventually returned to their trenches having brought in their prisoners and those who'd been wounded, Sidney was passed back to the regimental aid post and examined by the battalion MO before being sent to an ADS behind the lines. That afternoon reports were received that German troops had been spotted moving in their lines opposite the other battalions of 60th Brigade possibly preparing a counter attack. A young corporal from 12th Rifle Brigades 'C' Coy - but attached to 12th KRRC - positioned in an advanced bombing post took it upon himself to leave his position and launch a single handed bombing attack, inflicting considerable loss on the Germans and breaking up any threat of counter attacks for his bravery he was later awarded the Military Medal (33). The rain continued to fall during the morning of 19th September however the battalions of 60th Brigade received orders that they were to be relieved that night by a brigade from the Guards Division, the men of 12th Rifle Brigade spent the afternoon clearing mud from their trenches caused by the bad weather over the previous few days. Some battalions were relieved that night however not the men of 12th Rifle Brigade, they themselves relieved 12th KRRC further up the line and were to remain in these positions throughout the following day. It was not until 5:00am on the morning of 21st September that the 3rd Battalion Coldstream Guards finally relieved the battalion and a wet and tired 12th Rifle Brigade marched back to camp near Carnoy.

Meanwhile the wounded Sgt Sidney Hayter had been sent back to the 2/2nd London CCS known as Grovetown near Bray sur Somme south of Albert. He was to die of wounds there on 21st September 1916 aged 22. The death of Sidney Hayter was reported twice in Chigwell Parish Magazine the first report appearing in October 1916. This article stated that it was only recently that the village was congratulating him on winning the Military Medal and being one of the first soldiers to do so, it went on to say that he had given his life for king and country, for right and for god (34). The next report appeared the following month just repeating what had been said before. The OIC of the 2/2nd London CCS had filed a casualty report of Sidney's death on 11th October 1916 and forwarded it to the War Office, at that time Sidney's actual place of burial was unknown. It is not known exactly when the Hayter family first learned of their loss but it was probably during late September 1916, what is more confusing is that by this time the Hayter family had left Essex and moved to Marie Cottages in the village of Holmbury St. Mary near Dorking in Surrey. On 8th February 1917 the War Office contacted the Rifle Brigade HQ at Winchester asking them to send any items they had belonging to Sidney Hayter to his father Frank at his home in Surrey. They complied and two days later on the 10th February several letters, a pocket book, writing pad, a whistle and medal ribbons were returned to the Hayter family. At the time of his death although Sidney had been awarded the Military Medal he had not yet received it. Therefore on 2nd March 1917 the OIC of the Rifle Brigade wrote to Frank Hayter informing him that the medal was in his possession and would he like it sent to him or presented to him in public during a parade. Frank wrote back the next day asking that the medal be presented to him in public. On 8th March the OIC of the Rifle Brigade at Winchester contacted the OIC of the Queens (Royal West Surrey) Regiment at Guildford via memo asking if he would present Sidney's father with the award. Frank Hayter was not only presented with the Military Medal, on 16th March 1920 he received the 1915/16 Star on his son's behalf. On 25th February 1921 Frank Hayter also received the BWM and six months later on August 9th 1921 he received the Victory Medal. Sgt Sidney Hayter MM is buried in Plot I Row F Grave 49 of Grove Town CWGC Cemetery. This cemetery lies in the fields outside the village of Méaulte just south of Albert, in my opinion it is one of the most beautiful and tranquil places I have ever visited (35).

* * *

With the French Army still tied down at Verdun and the British still very much active but making slow progress on the Somme the Germans found themselves stretched very wide indeed, after all they were also fighting the Russians on the Eastern Front. Back in August the German General commanding the forces on the Western Front Erich Von Falkenhayn had been replaced. Two commanders who had achieved success on the Eastern Front against Russia took his place; they were Field Marshal Paul Von Hindenburg and General Erich Von Ludendorff.

By late September early October conditions on the Somme were appalling and the men were literally living like animals in the mud. They found themselves holding waterlogged trenches and shell holes with another winter not too far away, there appeared to be no end in sight to the fighting and it continued day after day, ground continued to be gained by the British but it never came cheap. Remaining with the efforts on the southern sector of the Somme front the action known as the Battle of Morval took place between the 25th September and 28th September. It involved units from three different corps of Rawlinson's 4th Army and during this action the villages of Combles, Morval, Lesboeufs and Gueudecourt all fell to the British. They were still however a little over three miles from Bapaume and an area of high ground now lay in front of them known as the Le Transloy Ridges. This high ground if captured would provide the British with a good place to spend the coming winter rather than the valley they currently found themselves in. So it was that an attempt to take the ridges was planned. The Battle of Le Transloy as it came to be known involved divisions from III Corps, XIV Corps and XV Corps and lasted from the 1st October until the 18th October. This action was to claim the life of the eighth man from Chigwell to die in the Somme battles.

ALBERT CHARLES COX

Albert Charles Cox was born at Wickford in Essex in April 1896, the second son of Albert Edward and Elizabeth Cox. The Cox family history has already been mentioned elsewhere in this book as Albert's older brother James was killed south of Ypres in September 1915. It should be remembered how Albert senior had worked on the railway, well after leaving school Albert Charles also found work on the railway becoming a station porter. With the war nine months old and his brother already in France on 3rd June 1915 Albert decided to join the army, he was just 19 years old. That day at a recruiting office in Ilford he underwent a medical examination the results of which we have (36). Albert was 5ft 7˝ tall weighing 135lbs, he had a 37˝ chest as well as having brown hair and hazel eyes, his vision was excellent and skin was of a fresh complexion. Albert was accepted and was told to report to Norwich, he was to join the reserve battalions of the Norfolk Regiment that were in training there and this he did arriving at the depot on 7th June. His training began the next day and was to last for the next six months. On 16th December 1915 Albert was posted to the 7th Battalion Norfolk Regiment as a replacement, this battalion had been formed at Norwich in August 1914 as part of K1 and was by now already in France. The 7th Norfolk's have previously been mentioned in the stories of James Edward Cox and John Leslie Fish as the battalion was attached to 35th Brigade as part of the 12th (Eastern) Division. Just to recap the other battalions within this brigade were the 5th Royal Berks, 9th Essex and the 7th Suffolk's whilst the other brigades within this division were the 36th Brigade and 37th Brigade.

As mentioned Albert arrived in France during the third week of December. The 12th Division had moved south to the Somme area during the third week of June after having held various positions further north around the French - Belgian border. As has already been mentioned this division as part of III Corps was not involved in the actions on 1st July 1916 but took part in the battle for Ovillers two days later. It was then held in reserve for the Battle of Pozières that lasted from the end of July throughout August until the beginning of September, by October however 12th Division was attached to XV Corps and brought forward along with the 30th Division and 41st Division to participate in the Battle of Le Transloy. During the first week of the battle the British managed to push forward gaining ground as they went, on the left the villages of Le Sars and L'Abbaye d'Eaucourt were captured by divisions of III Corps and on the right German trenches were also taken by divisions from XIV Corps. XV Corps were situated in the centre area north of Flers with its 41st Division on the left and 12th Division on the right holding positions in front and to the northwest of Gueudecourt. That first week had seen both 36th Brigade and 37th Brigade holding the 12th Division front with the 35th Brigade being held in reserve. Albert Cox and the rest of his battalion found itself during this period based at a makeshift camp near Bernafay Wood situated part way between Montauban and Longueval.

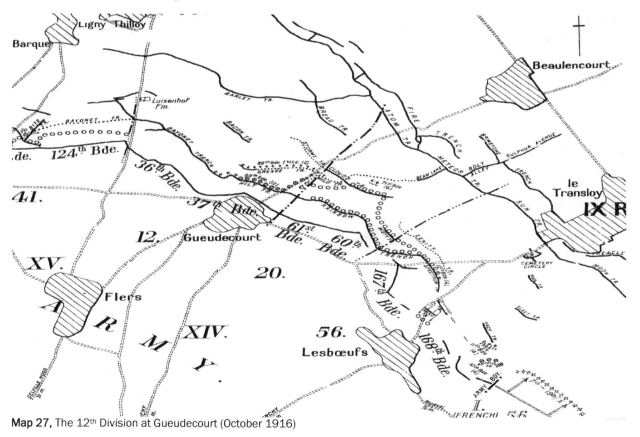

Map 27, The 12th Division at Gueudecourt (October 1916)

Their battalion war diary points out that this camp had no shelters or huts but consisted of old trenches with coverings erected above them. The early part of the week saw the battalion cleaning up and improving their surroundings however towards the end the week they found themselves providing men for both working and carrying parties. The carrying parties were necessary in order to keep those soldiers in the frontline areas supplied with items such as ammunition, food and anything else they may need. A man attached to a working party would mostly find himself carrying out hazardous jobs within the frontline areas such as digging trenches and erecting or repairing barbed wire entanglements, these duties were mostly carried out at night under the cover of darkness.

On 7th October whilst still in camp at Bernafay Wood Albert found himself promoted to the rank of Lance Corporal, unfortunately although part of his service record still exists it doesn't tell us to which company he was attached. The next two days again saw the battalion providing men for working parties however orders were received that further British attacks were in the offing. During the evening of the 10th October L/Cpl Albert Cox and the 7th Norfolk's moved forward with the other battalions of 35th Brigade to relieve the 36th Brigade in the frontline trenches northwest of Gueudecourt. The 7th Suffolk's and 7th Norfolk's found themselves positioned in the frontline trenches whilst the 9th Essex held the frontline support trenches, the 5th Royal Berks were placed in reserve. With the 7th Suffolk's on their right the companies of the 7th Norfolk's were positioned with 'D' Coy on the right and 'A' Coy - next to 41st Division - on the left in the extreme frontline trenches, 'C' Coy were placed in support with 'B' Coy in reserve (37). A large scale British attack was planned for the afternoon of 12th October that would involve amongst others various units attached to XV Corps. The battalions and men of 35th Brigade were due to attack the German frontline positions opposite them known as Bayonet Trench (see map 27). Upon their arrival in the British frontline the men of the 7th Norfolk's along with the 7th Suffolk's on their right straight away set about the digging of assembly trenches in preparation for the assault. These trenches were positioned out no mans land with the aim of shortening the distance the men would have to cover once the attack started, work on these positions could only be carried out at night due to enemy observation. Completed during the night of 11th October by 5:00am on the morning of 12th October the men of the 7th Norfolk's moved forward to occupy the newly created positions ahead of the attack. Their objectives along with those of the 7th Suffolk's were to capture Bayonet Trench and the trenches immediately beyond it then to push on and establish a line north of a position known as Luisenhof Farm that was situated just to the right of the main road leading from Flers through Ligny-Thilloy to Bapaume.

Thursday 12th October was a dull but dry day and zero hour was set for 2:05pm, on schedule the British artillery came to life in order to cover the infantry as it advanced, seconds later the whistles blew and the men of 35th Brigade along with those other British units attacking that day climbed up and over their parapets and advanced in the direction of the German frontline. The 7th Norfolk's attacked Bayonet Trench with all four of its companies dispersed in depth one platoon behind the other; their battalion war diary explains what happened:

After advancing about 50 yards the Hun {Germans} opened fire with machine guns from both flanks and from the front. Our troops continued to advance but before reaching the enemies trench ran into barbed wire which had not been cut. This wire coupled with the machine gun fire prevented any further advance and our men lay down in shell holes from where they brought rifle fire to bear on the Germans who were standing up in their trenches shouting at them.

After dark the battalion made further attempts to advance but the barbed wire in front of Bayonet Trench proved too strong and no way through could be found, with no alternative the order to retire was given and those surviving Norfolk's crawled back to their own lines to reform, unfortunately L/Cpl Albert Cox was not amongst them. The 9th Essex then moved forward to relieve those survivors of both the Norfolk's and Suffolk's in the frontline trenches who then moved back to reserve positions. It was a similar story for those other British units involved in the attack on 12th October, German machine guns and uncut wire being the chief cause of failure. The situation was very similar to that which had occurred on 1st July however this time on a much smaller scale, where ground was gained it was quickly lost due to enemy counter attacks. According to their war diary the 7th Norfolk's suffered casualties of 4 officers and 36 men killed; SDGW however puts the latter figure much higher at 89 in a casualty list that includes Albert Cox aged 20 and the two remaining men he had enlisted with at Ilford back in June 1915. L/Cpl Albert Cox has no known grave and is therefore commemorated on Panels 1C and 1D of the Thiepval Memorial to the Missing. Albert's death was reported in the Chigwell Parish Magazine in November 1916 but the first of several mistakes were made, the article for some reason uses Albert's middle name of Charles and lists him as having served with the Suffolk Regiment and not the Norfolk Regiment. Another mistake for some reason would, like Alfred Charles Vince, see Albert's initials on the Chigwell Village War Memorial engraved as AG and not AC and his battalion listed as the 1st Norfolk's and not the 7th Norfolk's. One can only imagine what it is like to lose two sons virtually within a year of each other but that is something that Albert and James parents had to endure. It was not until 8th May 1917 that Albert's effects consisting of 5 letters, 2 photos and 2 postcards were returned to his parents; in January 1920 they also received a memorial scroll and the relevant medals in memory of their son.

At this point it should be pointed out that although the 7th Norfolk's had over eighty men killed during the attack on 12th October they also had many more men wounded. Their battalion war diary puts this figure at 4 officers and 125 men. It should be remembered how Sgt Sidney Hayter's brother, Albert Hayter, had also joined the army and on enlistment was posted to the 7th Norfolk's. Unfortunately he was one of the 125 men wounded during the attack that day. Like Albert Cox, Albert Hayter also held the rank of Lance Corporal although he was attached to 'C' Coy. After being wounded L/Cpl Albert Hayter found himself evacuated by ambulance train to a CCS at Heilly situated halfway between the village of Albert and Amiens. Unfortunately his wounds were such that he died five days later on 17th October aged just 24. He is buried at Heilly Station CWGC Cemetery in Plot III Row C Grave 24. Unsurprisingly as the Hayter's links with Chigwell are confusing Albert's name does not appear on the Chigwell Village War Memorial alongside his brother, it's possible his name appears on a war memorial elsewhere.

* * *

Over the following week further units took up positions in the Le Transloy area, they remained there until the end of October. The job of holding the frontline was then given to Australian units however as far as further advances were concerned they were limited. The ground gained during the Battle of Le Transloy saw virtually the limit of the British advance on the southern sector of the Somme front during 1916. Up until now all of Chigwell's casualties on the Somme had been sustained with its men serving in units attached to Rawlinson's 4th Army, this however is not the case for the last two of Chigwell's men to be killed on the Somme in 1916. It should be remembered how after the disastrous events of the first day of the Somme battle Haig had handed Gough the command of the two northern corps on 4th Army's front. On 1st October however a general reshuffle of corps and divisions took place and all units now attached to the Reserve Army under Gough's command were renamed 5th Army. These units were now responsible for an area of frontline that stretched from the village of Hebuterne in the north to the region of Thiepval in the south. The first major action of the newly formed 5th Army was a series of battles that would collectively become known as the 'Battle of the Ancre Heights', these battles occurred between the 1st October and 11th November.

EDWIN AMBROSE DANIELS
Edwin Ambrose Daniels was born in Chigwell on the 1st February 1891 to parents William and Elizabeth Letitia Daniels. A surveyor by trade William had been born at Worcester in 1847 whilst his wife Elizabeth had been born in the Essex village of High Easter sometime around 1850. Once married they set up home in Chigwell in an old house situated on the High Road known as Flint Cottage, eventually they started a family. They were to have six children in all consisting of three girls and three boys, Edwin was their youngest son and their second youngest child overall (38). As far as growing up was concerned the Daniels family were quite privileged and Edwin attended Chigwell Grammar School from 1901 until 1909, during his time there he won many awards including a prize for grammar, he also became a Prefect. After leaving school Edwin worked for a short time in Malaya, unfortunately it has not proved possible to determine his exact profession although it is possible that he followed in the footsteps of his father and became a surveyor, when war broke out however he returned home to enlist. Edwin - like John Leslie Fish would a month later - chose to join the HAC and enrolled at Armoury House on City Road in Finsbury, London on 26th April 1915. Enlisting for the duration of the war Edwin volunteered for overseas Service; he was given Army Service No. 3418 and also underwent a medical examination. He was 5ft 7˝ tall with a 35˝ chest; he had perfect vision and was of a good physical development. Having been passed fit Edwin was posted that same day to the 2nd Battalion; he then began three months of training with this unit in areas around London. On the 15th August the 2nd Battalion detailed a group of men to join the 1st Battalion as reinforcements. This group included Edwin and as a result three days later he found himself crossing the Channel to France, on arrival it took him a further four days to reach his unit in positions around Ypres. Edwin served with the 1st Battalion until 12th December 1915; it was around this time that he accepted a temporary commission with the 8th Battalion South Lancashire Regiment (39). By the time he left the HAC Edwin had served a total of 230 days with the regiment, his discharge papers were approved on 4th January 1916. Obtaining the rank of Second Lieutenant Edwin actually joined the 8th South Lancs in billets south of Ypres on 20th December 1915; the battalion had just come out the line having held trenches around Plugstreet, as a new officer Edwin was attached to 'A' Coy. The 25th Division commanded by Major General E Bainbridge was made up of the 7th Brigade (40), 74th Brigade and 75th Brigade; the latter contained the following battalions: 11th Battalion Cheshire Regiment, 8th Battalion Border Regiment, 2nd Battalion South Lancashire Regiment and the 8th Battalion South Lancashire Regiment.

The 25th Division moved south during the spring of 1916 in readiness for the Somme offensive, by the end of June 1916 the fighting strength of the 8th South Lancs was put at 41 officers and 985 other ranks. The 25th Division did not take part in the action on 1st July however it was held in reserve, as a result 75th Brigade found itself positioned at Hedauville northwest of Albert. On the evening of 7th July the 8th South Lancs moved to positions south of Ovillers north of La Boisselle, at 4:00am the following morning along with several other battalions they took part in an attack on the German frontline trenches opposite and were successful in taking the position. During the attack the various battalions had met little opposition however the 8th South Lancs suffered several casualties, amongst those men wounded was Lieutenant Edwin Daniels. A telegram arrived at Flint Cottage on 10th July addressed to Mr and Mrs Daniels informing them that their son had been admitted to hospital at Le Touquet with a slight bayonet wound to his right hand. Unfortunately an event had occurred at home that must have made the arrival of that telegram a most awful experience for Elizabeth Daniels. On Saturday 1st July whilst the British offensive on the Somme was underway back in Chigwell William Daniels had passed away aged 70, he is buried in the churchyard of St Mary's in Chigwell. It appears that Edwin knew nothing of his father's death until he was convalescing in hospital, after making a full recovery Edwin rejoined his battalion still in positions around Ovillers. August was spent in and out the line in trenches known as the Leipzig Redoubt just east of Authuille, the following month saw much of the same however the battalion did take part in the odd small scale engagement; on 28th September 1916 Edwin was promoted to Acting Captain in charge of 'A' Coy.

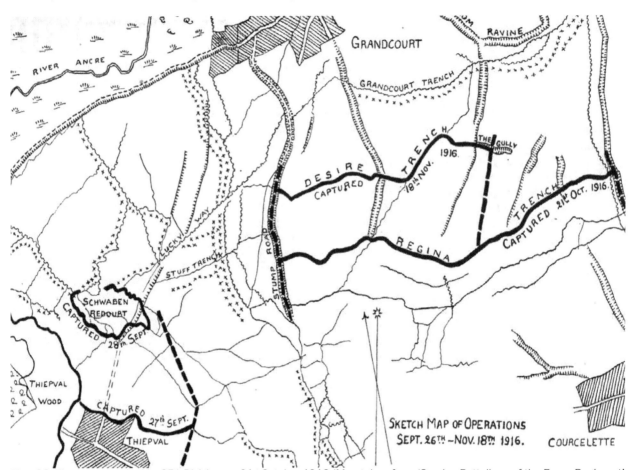

Map 28, The area attacked by 25th Division on 21st October 1916 (Map taken from 'Service Battalions of the Essex Regiment' Volume 6 by J W Burrows and Son)

The village of Thiepval had fallen to the British on 26th/27th September but just to its north lay the Schwaben Redoubt; the German strongpoint that the 36th (Ulster) Division had entered on 1st July but had to retire from due to lack of support. This position was entered again by units of 18th Division and 39th Division on 29th September however it was not totally captured until two weeks later. To the east of the Schwaben Redoubt and south of the village of Grandcourt lay another German strongpoint known as Stuff Redoubt. Incorporated within the German second line this position was attacked and captured by battalions from 7th Brigade, 25th Division on 9th October. A few days after the capture of Stuff Redoubt 7th Brigade went into reserve and the two other brigades of 25th Division were detailed to take over the British frontline from Stuff Redoubt in the west to the Courcelette–Grandcourt Road in the east. The 74th Brigade held the right flank - next to 53rd Brigade, 18th Division - whilst the 75th Brigade held the left flank including Stuff Redoubt itself. In an effort to keep up pressure on the German forces over the following week commanders of 5th Army ordered their divisions to carry out further attacks on enemy positions. In the case of 25th Division during the second week of October both 74th Brigade and 75th Brigade were detailed along with neighbouring units - mainly the 18th Division, 39th Division and 4th Canadian Division - to attack enemy trenches opposite their frontlines; although these trenches were known as Stuff Trench and Regina Trench this action came to be known as 'The Capture of Stuff Trench'.

Prior to taking up forward positions and in preparation for the coming attack during the night of 10th/11th October the 8th South Lancs provided men for working parties, their job was to dig assembly trenches in the areas around Stuff Redoubt. On the 15th October the battalion moved into Danube Trench, the support line behind Stuff Redoubt, the next three days saw a mixture of rain and sunshine with temperatures in the mid 50's. In readiness for their attack on the 18th October the battalions of 75th Brigade moved into frontline positions known as Hessian Trench however due to heavy rain that fell the following day the British assault was postponed. This would have been a testing time for Captain Edwin Daniels; with the attack delayed he would have to keep his men occupied as well as making sure they remained focused. The brigade was deployed with the 8th Border Regiment plus one company of 11th Cheshire's holding the right flank - next to 74th Brigade - the 8th South Lancs holding the centre and the 2nd South Lancs holding the left flank, the remainder of the Cheshire's were held in reserve. Finally with the weather easing off and everyone in position the attack on Stuff and Regina Trenches was scheduled for 12:06pm on 21st October. At zero hour the British attacked, battalions of 75th Brigade made for Stuff and Regina Trench supported by artillery that pounded the German lines, the 8th South Lancs advanced in four waves the first two of which moved off in extended lines. 'A' Coy commanded by Captain Edwin Daniels led the charge as men advanced towards the enemy lines. The Germans had been sitting out the artillery barrage and were slow to react to the British infantry heading towards them, on reaching the enemy frontline the 8th South Lancs were surprised to find the German infantry still in its dugouts however some had manned the parapets and were firing on the British troops as they approached. On entering Stuff and Regina Trench fighting ensued and many Germans were shot as they emerged from their shelters, another trench known as Stump Road ran north from Stuff and Regina Trench in the direction of Grandcourt. Battalion bombers moved along Stump Road attacking the enemy as he emerged from his dugouts positioned there however British artillery which was still firing away at the enemy lines prevented them from pushing on towards Grandcourt. It was a similar story for the other battalions of 75th Brigade, British artillery prevented further advancement, as for the neighbouring brigades and divisions all managed to reach their objectives successfully capturing both Stuff and Regina Trenches thus pushing the British frontline forwards. After spending the afternoon and evening consolidating the ground they had gained later that night the 74th Brigade and 75th Brigade were relieved by units of 19th Division. The 25th Division over the following week left the Somme and moved northwards towards Armentières, in time they once again served in the Ypres Salient. During the capture of Stuff and Regina Trench the 8th South Lancs took in the region of 175 Germans prisoner, the casualty figures for the battalion according to their war diary were 1 officer and 25 men killed, that officer was Captain Edwin Daniels (41).

The Daniels family received a telegram sent to Flint Cottage by the War Office on 26th October:

'Deeply regret to inform you Captain Edwin Daniels, of the South Lancashire Regiment, was killed in action 21st October, the army council express their sympathy'.

Secretary War Office

The officer in charge of the battalion, Lieutenant Colonel AJ Richardson who himself was wounded in the attack felt it his duty to write to Edwin's parents informing them of the circumstances surrounding the death of their son. The Colonel unaware that William Daniels had passed away started the letter *'Dear Sir'*.

Dear Sir,

It is with deepest regret that I write to inform you of the death of your son in the attack of 21st October as he went forward with his company. He was killed by a wound in the head before reaching the German trench that we took and held, his death must have been instantaneous. He was buried the next night by a party of his men at the spot where he fell, about half a mile south of the village of Grandcourt which is on the River Ancre. In him the battalion has lost an officer of untiring energy and of a wonderful witness of temper and disposition and one without fear. To me his loss is great, I had learnt to place implicit confidence in his judgment and calmness and officers of whom one can say that are not numerous and I felt for him both admiration and liking. To his mother and yourself I can only offer sympathy that would seem commonplace to those who have lost a son worthy of all the love a father and mother have to bestow.

Yours Sincerely
A J Richardson
Lieutenant Colonel 8th South Lancs

Although Edwin's death had been reported and his mother notified an official Casualty Report was not filled out by the relevant people until 3rd November. This report, received by the War Office on 7th November stated that Edwin's place of burial was not forthcoming. Although buried by his comrades the grave of Captain Edwin Daniels was lost in later fighting therefore his name appears on Panels 7A and B of the Thiepval Memorial to the Missing. In May 1918 an article appeared in the Chigwell Parish Magazine reporting that a plaque had been erected inside St Mary's Church to the memory of a former parishioner who had made the great sacrifice. That plaque was in memory of Captain Edwin Daniels and it still hangs inside the church today, it contains the following inscription:

'Deathless the Fame That Fearless Deaths Have Won'

To The Glory of God and In Ever Loving Memory Of
EDWIN AMBROSE DANIELS.
Captain 8th South Lancashire Regiment.
Youngest and Dearly Loved Son Of
WILLIAM and ELIZABETH DANIELS, Of This Parish
Killed In Action Near Grandcourt, France.
21st October 1916, Aged 25 Years.

'For The Crown of Life Well Won, We Thank Thee, Lord'

As a former pupil of Chigwell Grammar School the headmaster Mr Ernest Stuart Walde saw that Edwin's name appeared in the school memorial chapel, he also chose a Latin motto to follow Edwin's name:

'Fortitudo et Fidelitas' meaning 'The Strength and the Faithfulness'.

After Edwin's death his mother instructed a firm of solicitors based in the City of London to deal with all his affairs. In time Elizabeth received all of her sons' effects plus his medals and memorial scroll, she died on 19th December 1931 aged 80 and is buried beside her husband in St Mary's Churchyard, the name of Captain Edwin Ambrose Daniels appears on their gravestone.

* * *

The last main attack to be carried out by the British on the Somme during 1916 commenced on 13th November, it would last until 18th November and was known as 'The Battle of the Ancre'. After a postponement of several days due to bad weather seven divisions of 5th Army supported by artillery attacked two villages that lay just north of the River Ancre. Beaumont Hamel and Beaucourt both fell, the former on 13th November the latter the following day, it was hoped however that these could have been taken on the first day of the Somme offensive. Another 1st July objective that had proved impossible to capture throughout the Somme battle was the village of Serre. Situated at the northern end of the front it had been during an attack south of this village on 1st July that Pte William Frank Gapes the first of Chigwell's casualties of 1916 had lost his life. It was in the area south of Serre and north of Beaumont Hamel that Chigwell's last casualty of the year would also be killed.

CHARLES ALFRED FLACK

Charles Flack was born at Chelsea in southwest London sometime during October 1894 and was the second son of Henry and Adah Flack. Henry worked as a butcher and had been born in Chiswick in 1853; he and Adah were married at St Mary's Church in Chigwell on the 23rd July 1889. Their first son named Herbert Arthur was born in Chelsea sometime in 1890 and by the time Charles was born four years later the family were living at 137 Kings Road. It seems that Henry Flack either died or disappeared resulting in Adah being left to bring up her two sons alone. Adah had been born in Chigwell in 1864 the daughter of widower Daniel Heard, by the turn of the century he ran the Post Office situated on Chigwell High Road. The Post Office also sold groceries and really was a family run business, no fewer than three of Mr Heard's daughters and two of his sons worked there. So it was that by 1901 Herbert and Charles moved to Chigwell to live with their grandfather, Adah accompanied her sons and worked as a Clerk behind the counter at the Post Office. Growing up Charles attended school in Chigwell and was a member of the church choir, after leaving school he also worked as a clerk behind the counter at the Post Office. When war broke out Charles wasted no time in joining the army and travelled to London enlisting in the London Regiment (42).

As previously mentioned elsewhere in this book the London Regiment was purely territorial and had as many as 28 battalions all with at least three spin off battalions attached, some even had four. It also had at least six battalions numbered 29-34 with no spin offs. The London Regiment with so many battalions had offices all over the capital. The 7th Battalion were based at 24 Sun Street in Finsbury and it was at these offices that Charles enlisted on 7th October 1914. That day he underwent a medical that determined he was 5ft 6˝ tall weighing 130lbs, he had a 33˝ chest that measured 36˝ when fully expanded, the examiner described his vision as good. Once accepted Charles enlisted for four years provided he was not required longer and signed a notice that stated the conditions he was entering into, given Army No. 3066 he was posted to the 2/7th Battalion. This second line reserve battalion was already in training at Burgess Hill in Sussex when Charles joined and it was whilst here during January and February 1915 that he received inoculations for typhoid. Charles continued to train with his battalion for much of the next year as they moved to various bases in and around Suffolk and Norfolk. During this time the 2/7th London Regiment formed part of 174th (2/2nd London) Brigade part of 58th (2/1st London) Division. This division would remain in England until early 1917 but by early 1916 a new army unit which was formed a few months earlier had caught Charles attention.

On the outbreak of war all battalions had machine guns however they were not easy to handle and required a certain amount of training in order to use them effectively. Many guns were lost and the men trained to use them killed during the first year of the war and it was soon realised that a more solid formation trained in the use and handling of these weapons was needed. The Machine Gun Corps was formed on 14th October 1915 by order of His Majesty King George V. Prior to the formation of the MGC each infantry battalion had four heavy Maxim or Vickers guns plus four Lewis Guns that were lightweight in comparison. The MGC would deal with the tactical handling of these heavier guns leaving the Lewis Gun as the standard weapon of the infantry battalion. Most machine guns could fire from 450 to 600 RPM and were the equivalent of 50 ordinary riflemen; this said it is hardly surprising that they were responsible for most of the casualties that occurred when masses of infantry went over the top during an attack. The British Vickers Gun - use of the Maxim gun fizzled out in 1915 - fired belt ammunition and weighed 73lbs, situated on a tripod it was water cooled as its barrel when firing became extremely hot, the gun was usually operated by a team of six men. Successful use of the gun depended on everyone working together. The first man was the main gunner and he was responsible for carrying the mountings, firing the gun, the direction of fire and observation. The second man carried the gun and was in charge of loading the ammunition. The third and fourth man both carried ammo however the fourth man was also responsible for the water cooling system, the fifth and sixth man acted as scouts and projected required range and distances. In comparison the Lewis Gun sat on ones shoulder, was air cooled, weighed 26lbs, could fire up to 700 RPM using drum fed magazines and required a team of two to operate. As the infantry battalions received Lewis Guns this freed up their heavier guns and at the same time the MGC expanded. The MGC was divided into companies and various tactical units within the army such as the Cavalry, Infantry and Motor Machine (cars, motorcycle and later tank units) would all have these companies attached. In the case of the infantry these companies were assigned to brigades, each company taking the number of the brigade it was attached to: e.g. 53rd Brigade = 53rd Coy MGC (43). At the end of 1914 a machine gun training centre had been established at Grantham in Lincolnshire, when the MGC was formed the following October it set up home here. The MGC base depot in France was based at Camiers, a small village on the coast situated a few miles north of Etaples (or 'Eat Apples' to Tommy). In addition to this a training school also existed at Wisques a few miles west of St Omer.

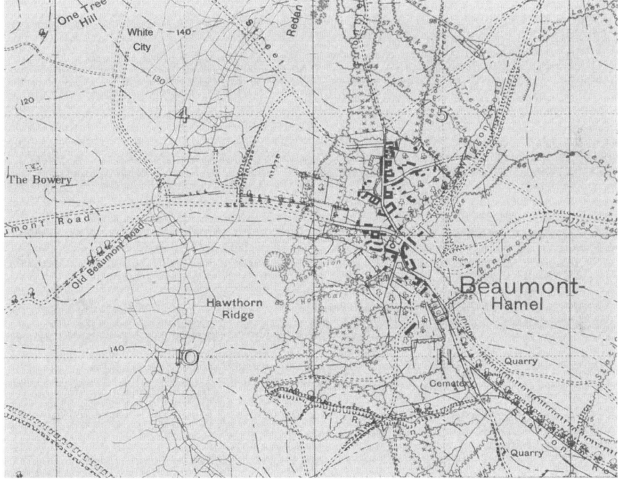

Map 29, Beaumont Hamel and surrounding area

Charles Flack was officially discharged from the Territorial Force in London on 27th May 1916, in all he had served 1 year and 234 days. In that time he had kept a clean regimental conduct sheet except when just 25 days before on 2nd May 1916 he was found absent without request and fined 8 days pay. Charles returned his uniform consisting of: 2 pairs of Boots, 1 Cloak, 1 Cap, 2 Woollen Draws, 2 pairs of Trousers, 2 Jackets, 1 pair of Puttees and 1 Waistcoat. On his discharge papers the reason given for Charles leaving the Territorial Force was that he had enlisted in the MGC. Charles joined the MGC at Grantham on 28th May 1916 and on that date undertook the following oath:

'I Charles Alfred Flack swear by almighty god, that I will be faithful and bear true allegiance to his Majesty King George V, his heirs and successors and that I will, as in duty bound honestly and faithfully defend his Majesty, his heirs, successors, in person, crown and dignity against all enemies and will observe and obey all orders of his Majesty, his heirs and successors, and of the generals and officers set over me so help me god'.

Posted as Private 42234 the following day Charles underwent another medical examination, he was to stay at Grantham for the next month training in the use of machine guns. Embarking for Folkestone on 9th July Charles arrived at Boulogne. Two days later he presented himself at the MGC base depot at Camiers, on 14th July Charles found himself posted to 96th Coy MGC. It took Charles four days to reach the Somme area where his company were stationed, 96th Brigade were part of 32nd Division commanded by Major General W Ryecroft.

This division had been heavily involved in the fighting on the first day of the Somme battle and Charles was joining as a much needed replacement, he would serve with 96th Coy MGC for the next four months although unfortunately we do not know his exact job within the unit. The 32nd Division was moved north after the opening Somme battles and found itself positioned mainly in the areas around Béthune and La Bassée. The beginning of October had seen Charles and the rest of his company positioned on what was at times a very active section of the line near Cuinchy. Known as the 'Brickstacks', it had been here in 1915 that the poet and writer Robert Graves was introduced to life in the trenches whilst serving as an officer with the Royal Welch Fusiliers. The 96th Coy MGC remained in this area for two weeks before heading back south to the Somme area, early November found them in billets at Rubempre about 12 miles west of Albert. Charles Flack and the rest of his unit remained in billets at Rubempre until the 14th November, during their time there they received reinforcements and practiced using their weapons as well as maintaining them, various drills and route marches were also carried out.

At 12:00pm on 14th November the men of 96th Coy MGC marched east from Rubempre to Warloy, they remained here until the following morning at which time they received orders to move east and occupy dugouts known as 'South Bluff' on the slopes between the villages of Authuille and Aveluy north of Albert. They remained here in reserve for two days and two nights before 9:00am on the 17th November saw them moved northwest to billets in the village of Mailly-Maillet. Like most infantry battalions had companies the MGC was split into sections lettered A to D, it appears that Charles Flack was attached to either 'C' or 'D' section. During the afternoon of 18th November the section officers of 96th Coy MGC were sent out to reconnoitre communication trenches that lead to a chalk covered area of steep embankments to the northwest of Beaumont Hamel known as 'White City'. The unit was to relieve men of 97th Coy MGC in positions there as well as positions in and around Beaumont Hamel itself the following afternoon. At 7:30pm that evening 'C' and 'D' sections left Mailly-Maillet and proceeded up communication trenches towards dugouts at 'White City', this took all night and much of the following morning. During the afternoon of 19th November both 'C' and 'D' section relieved men of 97th Coy MGC in positions at Beaumont Hamel, whilst this relief was carried out however enemy shells fell amongst the men and as a result 96th Coy MGC had 1 officer and 4 men killed, unfortunately one of these men was Pte Charles Alfred Flack (44). Although the 'Battle of the Somme' had officially ended the day before soldiers in the area still carried on as usual, they continued going in and out the lines and small scale fighting still occurred; as a result men were still killed. By 6:00pm that evening 96th Coy MGC were in position, they would remain in the area around Beaumont Hamel for the next five days before once again being relieved and moved back to billets at Mailly-Maillet.

The death of Pte Charles Alfred Flack was reported in the January 1917 edition of the Chigwell Parish Magazine, the article stated that he had been killed by a shell. Enemy shellfire was responsible for all the deaths suffered by 96th MGC that day and of the four men killed only one has a known grave, the others including Charles are commemorated on Panel 5 C of the Thiepval Memorial to the Missing (45). The article that January went on to say that Charles officers had written highly of him and that in the eyes of the parish he had made the great sacrifice and given his life for his country. On 15th March 1917 the War Office wrote to the OIC of the MGC requesting that any effects or belongings of Pte Charles Flack be returned to his mother at her home in Chigwell, over the next few years Adah received the medals her son was entitled to and in time a memorial scroll. Charles brother Herbert joined the army and fought in the war, it appears he also served with the MGC although he was to survive the conflict, in 1919 Adah Flack left Chigwell moving to 28 Elliscombe Road, Charlton, London SE7. On the north side of Hyde Park Corner in Central London - opposite Park Lane - stands a memorial to the men of the Machine Gun Corps. It states that a total of 13,791 officers and men were killed during the war whilst serving with the MGC in all its theatres of operation.

* * *

With the Somme battle officially over and with it the allied efforts of 1916, all hope of a breakthrough and end to the war had disappeared, they would have to try again the following year. The 'Battle of the Somme' as far as the British were concerned really belonged to those brave men of Kitcheners Army who had so readily answered his call and volunteered back in August and September 1914, tragically for one reason or another many of them still lie on the Somme battlefield. For those men who survived they inevitably became hardened soldiers, they had fought in and experienced things no amount of training could ever have given them, they were no longer volunteers they were the army. The battle had achieved its objectives of firstly pushing back the German lines, agreed not as far as was hoped, but at a cost ground had never the less been gained. The other thing the Somme fighting had done was to divert German forces from their attack at Verdun thus successfully relieving the pressure off of the French Army. The 'Battle of Verdun' eventually ended during December, both the French and Germans lost so many men in the fighting that exact casualty figures will never be known. As far as the French were concerned the town had been saved and a new man, the English speaking General Robert Nivelle came out of the battle a hero, in December he took over from Joffre as CIC of the French Army. Another change also occurred back in England, on 7th December Herbert Asquith was succeeded as Prime Minister by his former minister of munitions and Secretary of State for War David Lloyd George; it now fell to him to decide Britain's future part in the conflict. So it was that the allies were destined to remain in their trenches and as for their enemy, they remained opposite. For the men and their families of both sides the war was to span yet another Christmas that would inevitably be followed by another new year.

40, The gravestone of Pte William Frank Gapes at Serre Road No 1 CWGC Cemetery, Somme France

41, The Thiepval Memorial to the Missing

43, The name of John Leslie Fish as it appears on the Cromer War Memorial in Norfolk, England

42, The gravestone of Second Lieutenant John Leslie Fish

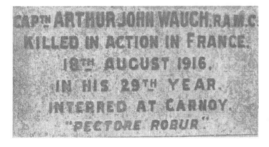

44, The name of Capt Arthur John Waugh as it appears on his parent's gravestone situated inside St Mary's Churchyard in Chigwell

45, The Waugh Family (Picture taken from a Brief History of Chigwell Hall by Carol Cooper & Tony Durrant)

46, Second Lieutenant Leonard Victor Waugh

48, The name of Pte Alfred Charles Vince as it appears on the Thiepval Memorial to the Missing

47, The gravestone of Capt Arthur John Waugh at Carnoy CWGC Cemetery Somme, France

49, The gravestone of L/Cpl Edward Stephen Scott at Guillemont Road CWGC Cemetery Somme, France

50, The gravestone of Sgt Sidney Hayter MM at Grovetown CWGC Cemetery Somme, France

52, The gravestone of L/Cpl Albert Hayter at Heilly Station CWGC Cemetery Somme, France

51, The Military Medal

53, The name of Capt Edwin Ambrose Daniels as it appears on the Thiepval Memorial to the Missing

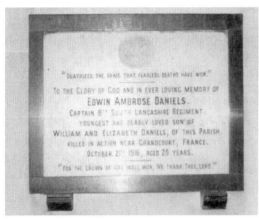

54, The plaque commemorating Capt Edwin Ambrose Daniels situated inside St Mary's Church, Chigwell

55, Flint Cottage

1917

At the beginning of 1917 with the disasters and disappointments on the Somme now common knowledge and the families of those men killed coming to terms with their losses the mood of the country it must be said was still behind the war. The residents of Chigwell were no exception working together in times of crisis however like most people deep down they still longed for peace. The January 1917 edition of the Chigwell Parish Magazine started the year with the following message:

'The year 1917 will be upon us before these lines are in our readers' hands. The war being as it is and so many homes being under the shadow of death – to wish a Happy New Year would be a mockery – but that it may be a year in which peace may come to the warring nations is the wish in everybody's heart'.

In all respects 1917 should have been a year of new hopes and fresh ideas for the allied forces, David Lloyd George was the new British Prime Minister, Haig although already CIC of the British Army received his promotion to Field Marshal and the French Army had a new CIC in Robert Nivelle, unfortunately it was to be a year like the previous two, one of high casualties and limited success. As far as the Germans were concerned during the previous two and a half years of war they had inflicted serious losses on their enemies. Although they too had suffered enormous casualties since the start of the war they were entrenched on French and Belgian soil and were there to stay, this fact alone promised that 1917 would be anything but peaceful. It would be an eventful year for many reasons; the British and French would both launch fresh assaults against German positions on the Western Front and Turkish forces in Mesopotamia and Palestine. Revolution in Russia would eventually lead to the Russians seeking peace terms with Germany ultimately seeing an end to fighting on the Eastern Front. The year would also see America enter the war on the side of the allies however her troops would not arrive in France until early summer and not in any force until the following year. Quite simply 1917 would be another year in a war that was nowhere near over and seemed as if it would last forever.

The allied leaders met in January and amongst other things discussed a plan put forward by Nivelle for a surprise offensive on German positions along the Chemin des Dames (1). Nivelle promised his idea would provide a knock out blow and win the war however although the main thrusts would be made by French divisions he required British troops to take over areas of French frontline south of the Somme and carryout attacks on German positions in and around Artois. Haig however found himself in the same position he had a year before, he still favoured an assault in Flanders designed to capture the Belgian ports of Ostend and Zeebrugge but found himself once again being swept along by French ideas. Lloyd George also backed Nivelle's plan which didn't make Haig's life any easier. Around this time the British Prime Minister was also looking east at the possibility of attacking Turkey, the plans to break out of Egypt and up into Palestine will be covered in the following chapter. On 1st February the Germans resumed their campaign of unrestricted submarine warfare in an attempt to starve Britain out of the war. No distinction would be made in the nationality of those vessels targeted and all merchant ships became vulnerable. The main threat was to those ships crossing the Atlantic, this outraged America and two days later American ties with Germany were broken.

Meanwhile the troops in the trenches carried on as usual holding the lines. They still found themselves the victims of shell and sniper fire as well as participating in the odd small scale engagement with the enemy. Troops still relieved each other as normal and working parties were still required at night to strengthen defences and bring up supplies, day to day life on the frontline continued which ultimately meant that soldiers still died.

GEORGE PLEASANCE

Born at Hampstead in North London in 1889 George Pleasance was the second son of Congressional Minister James Pleasance and wife Ann (2). In all George had two older sisters Edith and Ellen and an older brother called Frank, he also had a younger sister called Mary and two younger brothers Archibald and Herbert (3). Unfortunately very little is known about George other than at the turn of the century he lived with his parents at 38 Rendlesham Road in Clapton, East London before moving to Avondale Cottage, Woodford Bridge with the family a few years later. Nothing is known of his schooling or his profession before he joined the army. George enlisted at Warley probably in early 1916, as his service record has not survived and the Medal Roll at the NA holds virtually no information at all it is impossible to know the exact date. Pte George Pleasance was given army service number 32353 and posted to the Essex Regiment, after completing a period of basic training in England he was sent to France. George arrived just after Christmas and was posted to the 2nd Battalion in positions on the Somme. The 2nd Essex as has been explained in the story of Pte William Frank Gapes was attached to 12th Brigade, 4th Division (4). In late January 1917 the battalion was stationed behind the lines at Bray about three and a half miles southeast of Albert. Whilst there like most units when out the line it found itself training, refitting and often providing men for work details. The winter of 1916-17 was bitterly cold and the conditions the men were expected to live under created their fair share of problems, the 2nd Essex were losing in the region of two to six men a day due to sickness of one form or another. These men were sent to the Field Ambulance units for treatment, some returned to the battalion and some did not. Whilst at Bray on the 26th January the battalion received a draft of 8 other ranks, the following day 1 officer and a further 199 other ranks joined the unit providing much needed reinforcements.

In all respects as George had only arrived in France a month earlier he should have been fitter than most however due to the conditions around him he contracted Pneumonia. On 30th January the 2nd Essex received orders it was to provide relief for the 1st East Lancashire Regiment (11th Brigade, 4th Division) and would be moving up to reserve line positions on the night of the 1st/2nd February. As the battalion moved off two days later George was left behind as by now he was gravely ill. Pte George Pleasance died of Pneumonia on Saturday 3rd February aged 28; he is buried in Plot 1 Row D Grave 25 at Bray CWGC Cemetery, Somme, France. No article reporting the death of Pte George Pleasance ever appeared in the Chigwell Parish Magazine however on Friday 2nd March 1917 a short notice appeared in the Woodford Times. Placed their by his parents it thanked those people within the community who had expressed support at the loss of their son. James Pleasance died in April 1932 whilst Ann lived until March 1945, both are buried in the churchyard of St Mary's in Chigwell.

* * *

The allied leaders met again in Calais on 26th February in an effort to discuss further plans and ideas for their joint offensive. Haig was concerned at the part the British were being expected to play in the upcoming assault; it appeared Nivelle was to have complete control over the entire operation. Haig however argued for a right of appeal which he asserted a few days later when signs of a German withdrawal were realised on his Somme front, he felt the enemy may be moving troops north in an attempt to attack his forces in Flanders.

When the German commander Erich Von Falkenhayn was replaced by Paul Von Hindenburg and Erich Von Ludendorff in August 1916 it became apparent that Falkenhayn's policy of regaining every inch of ground lost by mounting counter attacks was costing the Germans dearly. In order to free up some of their divisions and save on manpower the new commanders came up with a plan of building a new defensive system situated some 25 miles behind their present frontline. It was to cover an area roughly 90 miles long that started just south of Arras and stretched southwards running down in front of Cambrai, St Quentin and its canal then over the River Oise heading west of Laon crossing the Chemin des Dames and the River Aisne finishing just south of Vailly east of Soissons. The Germans agreed that this new system of defence would shorten their existing lines leaving them with less area to defend. Work begun on this new position in September 1916, the Germans named it the Siegfried Line; the British would call it the Hindenburg Line. The Hindenburg Line consisted of concrete machine gun posts positioned at intervals from which the Germans could achieve an excellent field of fire, added to this it was made up of deep and wide trenches protected by masses of barbed wire. The trenches within the Hindenburg Line were littered with concrete bunkers as well as command posts linked together by tunnels. Where the Hindenburg Line met the St Quentin Canal at Bellicourt, a village approximately six miles north of St Quentin, a tunnel existed some three miles long. This was incorporated into the main defence system and modified to house troops, to allow for this however at this point the frontline trenches ran west of the canal. Minimal soldiers were required to hold the forward positions, any sign of attack would alert troops stationed in rear areas and they could then man positions along support lines in readiness, to the Germans the Hindenburg Line was impregnable. Preliminary withdrawals by German troops to their new position began in late February, some British units noticed in areas of the Ancre Valley and further north at Serre that the enemy opposite them had disappeared. As Haig protested to Nivelle about his fear of an enemy attack in Flanders the main withdrawals were yet to take place, they would not occur until the middle of March and would last into early April. The Germans intended to leave nothing of use to the allies when they fell back to their new line of defence, they would leave a virtual desert behind them. Houses were blown up, roads and railway junctions rendered unusable, trees cut down and orchards destroyed, bridges were blown and wells were polluted. Added to this booby traps were placed everywhere from trenches to town halls, if the Germans were to give up ground they would make it hard for the allies to occupy it.

Meanwhile the plans for Nivelle's offensive continued as the allied leaders met again, this time in London during the second week of March (5). The French commander briefed Haig on how things would be done however the German withdrawal to the Hindenburg Line would throw a spanner in the works. A British attack at Arras had first been thought of back in June 1916 to run in conjunction with operations on the Somme, however due to the overwhelming casualties the Somme battles generated the plan was put on hold. The allied commanders looked at the plan a few months later and decided to make it part of their strategy for 1917. When Nivelle became CIC of the French Army he revised it yet again and decided it should be carried out as a diversionary attack. His plan was that it should commence a week before the main attack by his armies on the Chemin des Dames and the areas around Soissons; this he hoped would draw German troops away from the main action. When reports first came in to allied HQ's that the enemy was falling back they were received with scepticism; Nivelle never thought the withdrawals would extend as far south as his front, he was wrong. Stubbornly he refused to change his plans insisting that he could breakthrough the German positions defying all reports from his commanders on the ground, his blatant disregard to look facts in the face would doom his plan to failure. Another event occurred that would also hinder Nivelle's attack, on 4th April the Germans managed to capture a copy of the French commander's plans during a raid on French positions; from these they would know his every move.

For a brief moment it is necessary to turn our attentions to two separate events that would over the following year change the course of the Great War. Harsh conditions in Russia were causing unrest amongst the people, as a result on 15th March Tsar Nicolas II abdicated. He was replaced by a provisional government however for now Russia remained in the war. In December 1916 the American president Woodrow Wilson had invited all those involved in the conflict to state their terms for peace however no agreement could be reached. Then in January it became apparent that the Kaiser had tried to persuade Mexico to start a war with America. Added to this with Germany's resumption of unrestricted submarine warfare in early February and losses now starting to mount up Wilson found he could no longer sit by as if nothing was happening. With diplomatic ties already broken a month earlier on 2nd April Wilson delivered a war address to congress, four days later America declared war on Germany.

The British Army on the Western Front during the spring of 1917 was bigger than it had ever been totalling some five armies made up of nearly one and a half million men. In the north Plumer's 2nd Army was controlling the areas around Ypres with Sir Henry Horne's 1st Army positioned across the border covering the area south to Vimy just north of Arras (6). 3rd Army under Allenby controlled the areas around Arras and south to Gommecourt where Gough's 5th Army and Rawlingson's 4th Army looked after interests in and around the areas of the Somme. Although the Battle of Arras was to be a diversion it still had immense purpose. The Somme battles of 1916 had pushed the British front lines eastwards with Gommecourt and Arras now situated west of a bulge in the lines that those actions had created. It was hoped a push from Arras and the areas north and south of it could move the front forward therefore straightening out the lines. When the Germans withdrew to the Hindenburg Line however this threw British intentions into disarray, therefore abandoning their attack south of Arras where the Hindenburg Line started the British concentrated their efforts where the German lines remained unchanged, chiefly in front of Arras itself and to its north along the high ground of Vimy Ridge. The Arras battlefield consisted mainly of open terrain; very few trees existed unlike the woods of the Somme although rolling fields were to be found. Its two main features were firstly Vimy Ridge to the north whose heights commanded several miles of clear views over the flat fields of a landscape known as the Douai Plain; these fields spread eastwards towards the town of Douai some 15 miles northeast of Arras. The other main feature of the Arras battlefield was the Scarpe; a river that runs east out of Arras that in 1917 cut the battlefield in two in much the same way the Ancre divided the battlefield of the Somme. The town of Arras itself should not be forgotten; a market town famed for its tapestries its houses led virtually up to the frontlines, beneath the town tunnels and caves existed that allowed British troops to move forward without fear of detection by enemy observers. On a front roughly 12 miles long the Arras offensive would be carried out mainly by corps and divisions of Allenby's 3rd Army however Horne's 1st Army to the north - which included the Canadian Corps - and Gough's 5th Army to the south would also be involved. The plan was to be similar to those tried on the Somme back in 1916. Preliminary bombardments would be followed by infantry assaults on the German trenches, once big enough gaps were created it was hoped the cavalry could then push through and successfully roll up the German lines. As plans developed the Arras offensive became much more than just a diversion. It was hoped that if followed by a successful French attack on the Chemin des Dames both assaults would push the Germans back up across the French border and into Belgium following in reverse pretty much the same path the BEF had taken in their retreat from Mons back in August 1914. The Hindenburg Line defences were such that a full on frontal attack was futile, a successful push from Arras however would bring the British east in line with the position where they could then attack it from the right flank and moving southeast also from the rear. The Germans however were not foolish and had noticed this possibility therefore another defensive position roughly five miles east of Arras had been created known as the Drocourt – Quéant Switch. A continuation of the Hindenburg Line defences this position although not fully completed was named after the two towns that stood at each end. The British would have to breakthrough the Drocourt – Quéant Switch if they were to have any chance of attacking the main Hindenburg Line defence system. The British offensive in and around Arras commenced on Easter Monday 9th April and lasted until the 15th May; like with the Somme battle it consisted of several different actions that after the war were each given their own name; collectively these actions are known as 'The Battle of Arras'.

The British attack at Arras commenced at 5:30am on 9th April following a five day bombardment of the German lines. In terrible weather consisting of freezing rain, sleet and snow the Canadian Corps to the north under the command of Sir Julian Byng managed to fulfil its objectives by capturing the strategic position of Vimy Ridge, a feat that had eluded the French Army back in May 1915. Further south the infantry of Allenby's 3rd Army attacked signalling the start of the action that came to be known as The First Battle of the Scarpe. Within the first hour the British pushed forward managing to take the German first line trenches. Situated on 3rd Army's left and north of the Scarpe lay XVII Corps whose divisions managed to push forward as far as Fampoux; all that lay in front of them now was the German defences of the Drocourt – Quéant Switch. South of the river however things did not go as well, German resistance slowed down the advance of both VI Corps in the centre and VII Corps on the right but eventually their various divisions did manage to push on. The main stumbling block came from a heavily defended German line that linked the villages of Feuchy and Wancourt, situated between these two on high ground further east stood the village of Monchy-le-Preux and German machine guns positioned there were also responsible for halting the British advance. Throughout that day Arras itself became congested, fresh divisions found it hard to move forward in support as wounded men headed back from the frontline; the cavalry had pushed up too hoping to be sent into action but lack of progress by the attacking infantry saw this wasn't to be. It soon became clear that the Arras Offensive would not be the big breakthrough it was hoped it would be; the use of tanks to break the German lines might have changed things however not enough were available in order to prove effective.

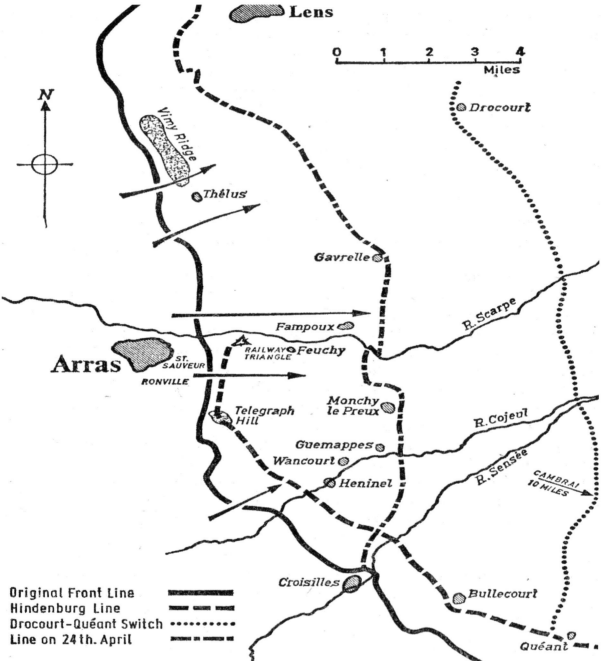

Map 30, The Battle of Arras April 1917 (Map taken from 'History of the First World War' by Liddell Hart © Cassell Plc, a division of The Orion Publishing Group London).

Overnight the Germans were able to bring up reserves, the following day as the British attacks continued it became harder and harder for 3rd Army to push forward however on the 11th April Monchy-le-Preux was finally captured. That same day further south several units of Gough's 5th Army attacked the northern end of the Hindenburg Line defences in and around the village of Bullecourt but were unsuccessful in making any lasting gains on the position. The attacking troops had found it hard to cross the torn up ground recently vacated by the Germans and because of this their guns also struggled to move forward in order to provide them with adequate artillery support, again tanks were supposed to provide support but were too few in number to make any real impression. Meanwhile further north The First Battle of the Scarpe continued; it would last until Saturday 14th April. It was on this day south of the Scarpe that the Germans regrouped and launched a counter attack in an attempt to retake the village of Monchy-le-Preux; it was in this action that the only man listed on the Chigwell Memorial to die during the Arras Offensive of 1917 was killed.

HARRY MARK BROWN

Harry Mark Brown again is someone we know little about, the fact that he has a common surname makes the task of finding information on him very difficult. He was born in Chigwell in 1897 the second son of Luke and Charlotte Brown. His father worked as a Domestic Gardener in the grounds of a big house on Manor Road and at the turn of the century the Brown Family lived in lodgings on the estate. Harry had three older sisters Beatrice, Hilda and Annie and at least one older brother called Edward (7), after Harry was born his parents had another daughter called Ella. Harry was educated at the council school in Chigwell; his profession on leaving is unknown. The Brown Family eventually moved to a small cottage at 8 Brunel Terrace, Brunel Road, Woodford Bridge. Harry enlisted at Woodford in early 1916 probably as a conscript but possibly under the terms of the Derby Scheme; unfortunately his service record no longer exists. After passing his medical Harry was given army service number 23218 and placed in reserve as part of the Essex Regiment, he underwent the standard period of basic training before being sent to France in late 1916. On arrival Harry was posted as Private to the 1st Battalion and attached to 'D' Coy. The 1st Essex was attached to 29th Division commanded by Major General H. de Lisle; the ranks of this once regular division were by this stage of the war mainly made up of both volunteers and conscripts; men just like Harry Brown (8). Upon the outbreak of war in August 1914 some regular battalions referred to their companies not as A, B, C and D but as W, X, Y, and Z, the 1st Essex was one such battalion within 29th Division. Although by the end of 1916 this division bore little resemblance to its former self this policy was still upheld therefore with this in mind although Pte Harry Brown was attached to 1st Essex 'D' Coy he was in actual fact a member of 'Z' Coy. The 29th Division as has been explained in the Gallipoli chapter had landed at Cape Helles in April 1915, after the evacuation of the peninsular it headed to Egypt and eventually to France where it landed in early 1916 arriving in time to participate in the Somme battles. At the beginning of 1917 the 29th Division consisted of the 86th Brigade, the 87th Brigade and the 88th Brigade; the latter contained the following battalions: the 4th Worcestershire Regiment, the 2nd Hampshire Regiment, the 1st Essex Regiment and the 1st Royal Newfoundland Regiment.

The beginning of the year had found the 29th Division and particularly its 88th Brigade holding positions in and around various sectors of the Somme. By early March however 88th Brigades four battalions found themselves out of the line and in billets at Méaulte carrying out various details and training exercises. At the end of the month the fighting strength of the 1st Essex, commanded by Lieutenant Colonel Halahan was 31 officers and 892 other ranks, although some men were lost to sickness the 88th Brigade as a whole was pleased to report that it had not had one man killed as a result of enemy action during the whole month of March. The start of April saw the brigade march northwards as 29th Division was to take part in the Arras Offensive. By the 10th April the 1st Essex arrived at Fosseux about 20 miles west of Arras where they remained for the next two days. On the morning of 12th April they continued on to Arras where they arrived that afternoon rejoining the other three battalions of their brigade. There was very little time for rest, shortly after arriving at Arras the 88th Brigade received orders it was to move four miles east and relieve the 37th Brigade (12th Eastern Division) in positions in and around the village of Monchy-le-Preux.

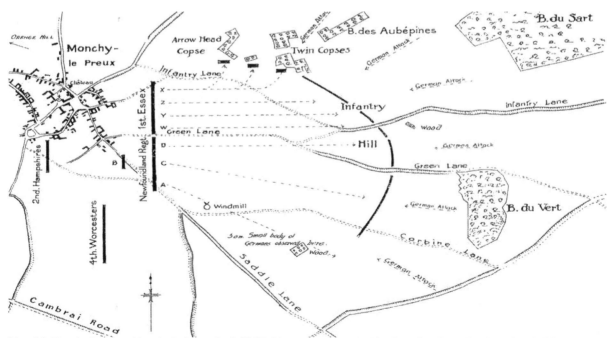

Map 31, The 1st Essex at Monchy-le-Preux April 1917 (Map taken from the '1st Battalion Essex Regiment' by J W Burrows and Son)

The brigade found its route to the village congested and did not arrive there until 3:00am the following morning, on leaving Arras the battalions had been told they were to carry out an attack on German positions east of Monchy-le-Preux. As has been briefly explained the village of Monchy-le-Preux stood on high ground east of Arras, about a thousand yards east of the village lay another piece of high ground that came to be known as Infantry Hill. In a semi-circle east of the village from right to left lay the Cambrai Road to the left of which stood a track known as Saddle Lane, a ruined windmill stood north of this track beyond which lay a small wood. Beyond Infantry Hill stood a large wooded area known as the Bois du Vert and left of this heading directly eastward from the village was another track known as Infantry Lane. North of this stood another large wooded area known as the Bois du Sart. Finally the left hand side of the semi-circle consisted of sloping ground on which three smaller wooded areas existed; the furthest being the Bois du Aubepines then the Twin Copses and finally Arrow Head Copse. All these wooded areas to the east of Monchy were occupied by Germans; virtually from its eastern side the village was surrounded. It was hoped that 88th Brigade could push eastwards out of Monchy and capture Infantry Hill which in itself held views over the Douai Plain; if possible the brigade was also to capture the Bois du Vert and the smaller woods to the left however German troops in position there had other ideas.

The battalions of 88th Brigade were scheduled to attack during the morning of 13th April however this was postponed twice; finally their assault was timed for the early morning of 14th April with zero hour set for 5:30am. The leading battalions were to be the 1st Essex on the left and the 1st Newfoundland on the right; these battalions positioned themselves in assembly trenches on the eastside of the village prior to zero. In support on the Newfoundlanders right flank would be the 4th Worcester's, the 2nd Hampshire's remained in the village as reserve. The companies of the 1st Essex were positioned as follows: 'X' Coy commanded by Captain H.B Foster held the left flank with 'Z' Coy under Captain C.R Brown MC and 'Y' Coy under Captain J Tomlinson centre, the right flank was held by 'W' Coy commanded by Captain R E G Carolin. The 1st Newfoundland was positioned with its 'D' Coy next to the Essex, 'C' Coy centre and 'A' Coy on the right, 'B' Coy was placed behind these three in support (9). On the morning of the attack a mist covered the area; the ground was also wet from recent snow and rain. At 5:30am under the cover of a creeping artillery barrage the leading battalions moved forward (10). The Essex pushed on in short rushes and after an hour had managed to dig in east of the village having taken a few prisoners. The battalion sent patrols forward to see if the Bois du Sart, the Bois du Aubepines and the Twin Copses were occupied by the enemy; a short while later reports came back that Germans could be seen moving about within the woods preparing to counter attack. By now enemy artillery was shelling the areas east of Monchy and the village itself; this had cut the signal wires between the Essex and their guns. With communication lost no shells could be brought to bear on the German formations within the woods, the Essex sent back runners to brigade HQ with messages for the artillery but these failed to arrive as the messengers were killed by enemy shellfire. On the Essex left flank 'X' Coy started to take machine gun fire from the direction of Arrow Head Copse. Several platoons within the company were pinned down as others outflanked the German gunners successfully ejected them from their position and captured their guns, these platoons then continued into Twin Copse. Several platoons from the other companies including Pte Harry Brown's 'Z' Coy pushed forward some reaching as far as the down slope of Infantry Hill but that was as good as it got. Enemy artillery continued to pound the village as well as the area east where the main bulk of the Essex and Newfoundlanders were dug in; as a result many men from these battalions became casualties. The barrage was used to cover a German counter attack by men of the Third Bavarian Division that started from Bois du Sart and several other areas northeast of Monchy, those men of 'X' Coy who had advanced into Twin Copse were literally wiped out by this attack. By 7:00am the frontline companies of the 1st Essex came under attack as the Germans pushed on, by 7:30am no more messages were received at battalion HQ - situated on the eastern edge of the village - by men from the 1st Essex, as a result barricades were manned in Monchy. Meanwhile the Newfoundlanders had problems of their own, at zero hour they had pushed forward and 'A' Coy captured the ruined windmill on their right as well as the small wood beyond it. Platoons of their 'C' Coy and 'D' Coy had also moved forward and dug in, some moved over and down Infantry Hill reaching as far as the Bois du Vert but they soon met German resistance and were wiped out. Those remaining men found themselves the target of German attacks as the enemy rolled down the Essex line onto the Newfoundland front, by 10:35am it was reported that no unwounded man of the Newfoundlanders lay east of Monchy (11). Although the two leading battalions suffered appalling losses they still managed to save Monchy from being captured, what started as a British attack quickly became a game of defence. Later that morning the Worcester's held their positions in front of the village as the enemy continued to attack, the Hampshire's were moved forward to help with defence. That afternoon with the help of the 88th Brigade MGC these battalions managed to halt the German assault on Monchy; that evening the survivors of 88th Brigade were relieved by 86th Brigade.

Although we will never know the exact part Pte Harry Brown played in the actions east of Monchy-le-Preux it is likely he was killed on the slopes of Infantry Hill. His battalion and that of the Newfoundlanders put up one hell of a fight in both attack and defence; the day's casualty figures are testimony to that. The 1st Essex went into action with a fighting strength of 31 officers and 892 men, at the end of the battle they reported losses of 17 officers and 644 men killed, wounded or missing, of their four company commanders Captain Brown and Captain Foster were killed and Captain Tomlinson and Captain Carolin were wounded. The 1st Newfoundland had started the day with a combined strength of 591 officers and men; of that number 487 were reported as killed, wounded or missing (12). That day the Germans took 203 men of the 1st Essex prisoner along with 100 Newfoundlanders, at first it was hoped Pte Harry Brown was among this number. The War Office wrote to Harry's parents informing them that their son was missing and this was reported in the June 1917 edition of the Chigwell Parish Magazine, just over a month later the War Office confirmed that Pte Harry Brown had been killed. Harry's death was reported in the August 1917 edition of the Chigwell Parish Magazine, the article extended the community's prayers and sympathy to his parents. Pte Harry Mark Brown has no known grave and is commemorated on Bay 7 of the Arras Memorial to the Missing. Situated in the Faubourg-d'Amiens CWGC Cemetery on the western side of Arras this memorial commemorates almost 35,000 men who fell in the area between the spring of 1916 and the 7th August 1918 whose place of burial in unknown.

* * *

On 16th April Nivelle launched his offensive on the Chemin des Dames, it came to be known as the Second Battle of the Aisne; it was a total disaster. The Germans sat out the French bombardment in their dugouts then as it lifted and the French Army pushed forward they emerged to man their guns and cut them to pieces. As wave after wave came forward they were cut down, by nightfall on the first day it was obvious the French attack had failed. The defences of the Hindenburg Line were very strong in this area and Nivelle had stubbornly refused to change his plans, the Germans also knew his every move that meant the result could only have gone one way. Over the days that followed French soldiers were ordered to continue attacking against uncut wire and machine guns, it didn't take them long to realise their task was impossible. As a result some units refused to carryout orders, mutinies then broke out within the French Army; soldiers stated they were prepared to defend their positions but were no longer prepared to attack. Meanwhile the British continued their Arras offensive against an ever strengthening enemy. Despite this further attacks were carried out; the main thing now was for Haig to pin down German troops in order to keep them away from the demoralised French armies further south. The third week of April - north and south of the Scarpe - the villages Gavrelle and Guemappe were captured in an action known as the Second Battle of the Scarpe. During the first two weeks of May the villages of Fesnoy and Roeux were also taken - Third Battle of the Scarpe - but they didn't come cheap, with casualties starting to mount on 15th May Haig finally brought the Arras offensive to a close. As the month wore on because of the disasters involving the French Army Nivelle's position became untenable, on 15th May he was replaced as CIC by General Philippe Pétain. It was up to the new French CIC, who had started the war as a Regimental Colonel before climbing the ranks, to try and restore order and morale amongst his troops; this could not be achieved overnight. He toured the lines talking to commanders and their men in an attempt to improve conditions. As a result the French Army was in no position to carryout further attacks preferring instead to sit the year out and wait for American troops to arrive in France. Any further attempts to win the war on the Western Front in 1917 would have to be made by British forces, this suited Haig as it left him free - subject to approval by the War Cabinet - to carryout his preferred choice, an attack in Flanders. Owing to the large number of casualties the British had sustained in recent months it was no surprise that Lloyd George and the rest of the War Cabinet were not keen on committing British forces to another offensive on the Western Front that may or may not win them the war. Other theatres where looked at and it was hoped that one of these may hold the answer. The Prime Minister liked the thought of sending troops to Italy in order to help the Italians. Italy had joined the war on the allied side in May 1915 and quickly her armies moved northwards to meet the Austrians, fighting ensued and both sides suffered terribly over the following two years. Lloyd George was not supported in his views over Italy and naturally Haig as a devout westerner was less than impressed with the idea; as a result the Prime Minister's idea remained just that. It should be pointed out however that the Austrians had turned to Germany for help in early 1917 and consequently in October Italy was almost defeated in an action known as 'The Battle of Caporetto', as a result both Britain and France sent troops out to help her although not in the force Lloyd George would have liked. In order to convince the War Cabinet that the only way forward was an attack in Flanders a meeting was arranged where Haig discussed details of his plan to break out of the Ypres Salient. It consisted of a two stage attack the first part of which would to be carried out by Plumer's 2nd Army with the aim of capturing the high ground south of Ypres known as Messines Ridge. This high ground had been held by the Germans since April 1915; it afforded them perfect observation over the allied positions and would have to be captured if any break out from Ypres itself was to prove successful. This would be followed with an advance made by Gough's 5th Army from the areas east and northeast of Ypres towards Passchendaele Ridge and the village of the same name. Once successful with Passchendaele in British hands the troops would then sweep northwards towards the sea and capture the Belgian ports under German occupation, this would be assisted by an amphibious landing made by units of Rawlingson's 4th Army. If all went to plan and the two stages of the operation were successful a third phase would come into play designed at pushing the Germans deep into Belgium and destroying their lines of supply.

The War Cabinet failed to give Haig the green light for a full scale offensive in Flanders however preparations for the preliminary phase of the operation - the capture of Messines Ridge - had been discreetly underway for the previous two years. Since the end of the Second Battle of Ypres the British had begun tunnelling under the German lines. Miners had been recruited and tunnelling companies established and together with the Royal Engineers on a ten mile front from Hill 60 in the north to Plugstreet in the south the men dug eastwards towards the enemy lines through layers of earth, sand and clay. At the same time but on a much smaller scale the Germans were countermining, both sides used listening devices to try and locate each others tunnels and once discovered efforts were made to destroy them. Sometimes the two sides would stumble upon each others positions and furious fights would develop deep underground, it took a brave man to work and fight in those conditions. The key to the plan of capturing Messines Ridge involved placing mines under the German lines like had been done on the Somme in 1916 however at Messines it was done on a much bigger scale. The German positions at Messines consisted of four lines of trenches three of which sat on top of the ridge itself. A total of 24 mines were placed at intervals along the length of the enemy frontlines ready to be detonated; immediately after the explosions the infantry of 2nd Army would go over the top. The Germans came very close to discovering a mine placed under Hill 60, if it had been found British plans would have suffered a major set back but fortunately this didn't happen. More seriously the Germans had sensed something was up and briefly considered a withdrawal from Messines Ridge altogether, luckily they decided against this which meant that efforts by British miners since April 1915 were not in vain. On 26th May the British launched an artillery barrage that lasted for five days, during that time more than 3 million shells were fired at enemy trenches. At 3:10am on 7th June the action known as the 'Battle of Messines' started. A total of 19 mines were detonated beneath German lines on top of Messines Ridge, the sound of these explosions could be heard as far away as London and the effects so spectacular that enemy positions were blown to pieces (13). Immediately after detonation and protected by a creeping artillery barrage nine divisions of Plumer's 2nd Army advanced out over no mans land towards the German lines, resistance was weak and by 7:00am that morning virtually the whole of Messines Ridge lay in British hands. That afternoon further attacks were made by British units who successfully fended off all German resistance to capture their third line positions, for the days actions British casualties were in the region of 16,000 with roughly 13,000 Germans either killed or wounded and a further 7,000 taken prisoner. Over the days that followed the village of Wytschaete ('*White Sheet*' to Tommy) was captured by Irish divisions. Despite German counter attacks Messines Ridge remained firmly in British hands but what Haig needed now was to quickly follow up on the success of Messines with the next phase of his plan. Without permission from the War Cabinet he was in no position to do so however he was given permission to continue preparations. In fact it would be six weeks before the British launched the next phase of the Flanders offensive, this delay gave the Germans plenty of time to reorganise themselves in readiness. After Messines Haig switched control of operations from Plumer's 2nd Army to Gough's 5th Army, as British troops and munitions began pouring into areas behind the salient in preparation for the second phase of action the Germans struck a blow that disrupted British plans. On 10th/11th July they bombarded the allied defences at Nieuport at the northern end of the Ypres Salient; ground was lost that made preparations for an amphibious landing by Rawlinson's 4th Army that much more difficult however preparations continued. It was around this time at British held lines further south that Chigwell suffered its fourth casualty of 1917.

DANIEL JAMES TREVETT
Daniel James Trevett is the second of three men whose story is told in this book but whose name does not appear on the Chigwell Memorial, like Charles Reeves his inclusion stems from the fact that upon his death his name received an individual mention in the Chigwell Parish Magazine. Daniel was one of the eldest men from Chigwell to be killed during the war; he was born in the village of Epping in 1879 the eldest son of John and Elizabeth Trevett. Both parents were born and grew up in Dorset however John a Wheelwright and Elizabeth a Laundress moved to Essex around 1870. Daniel was educated locally and after leaving school worked as a foreman on a farm, he had two elder sisters Ellen and Millie and a younger brother called William. By the turn of the century the Trevett family were living at 10 Wallers Cottages, Smeaton Road, Woodford Bridge and here they remained when war broke out. It is unlikely that Daniel joined up right away although he did enlist at Woodford possibly under the terms of the Derby Scheme; unfortunately his army service record no longer exists. On enlistment Daniel was posted as Private 20105 to the 13th Battalion East Surrey Regiment, by this stage of the war a man could rarely chose the battalion he was attached to. This battalion had been raised in June 1915 by the Mayor and Borough of Wandsworth, taken over by the war office soon after the next year saw the battalion in training at Aldershot and at camps on Salisbury Plain. Towards the end of February 1916 the battalion was attached to 120th Brigade, 40th (Bantam) Division (14). This division commanded by Major General H Ruggles-Brise crossed the Channel to France in early June 1916, its battalions moved south and by the middle the month the men of the 13th East Surreys found themselves in camp at Sailly–Labourse east of Béthune. The battalion was instructed in the art of trench warfare and during this period was temporarily attached to 44th Brigade, 15th (Scottish) Division; training took place in trenches on a sector of front line at Hulluch. The 13th East Surreys rejoined their division and first went into trenches on their own during the second week of July, they remained in the Hulluch/Loos area taking part in small scale engagements and line holding duties until November 1916 at which time they were moved south to the Somme area. Soon after the battalion found itself holding lines at the northern end of the Somme front around the village of Hebuterne, by Christmas they were out of the line at the southern end of the front in billets at Maricourt. The New Year saw much of the same with line holding, training and working parties taking up most of the East Surreys time. In March when it became apparent that the Germans were withdrawing to the Hindenburg Line all battalions in frontline trenches were ordered to occupy positions vacated by the enemy, the 13th East Surreys were no exception and the British line moved forward.

On 24th April the 40th Division were ordered to attack German positions around the village of Villers-Plouich some eight miles southwest of Cambrai, during this action which saw the village captured Cpl Edward Foster won the 13th East Surreys only Victoria Cross of the First World War (15). The beginning of June saw the battalion holding support lines around Gouzeaucourt but two weeks later they found themselves back in camp behind the lines, as July started the battalion was once again in positions near Villers-Plouich. For Pte Daniel Trevett and the 13th East Surreys life in the frontline meant carrying out various duties and details, the most dangerous of these must have been the nightly foray into no mans land usually carried out by a group of 1 officer and 20 men. These patrols were necessary in order to check on enemy movements and at the beginning of July the East Surreys were making these trips on a regular basis. Daniel and the men of his battalion remained in the frontline until the night of 5th/6th July at which time they were relieved by the 11th Battalion Kings Own (Royal Lancashire Regiment) (16).

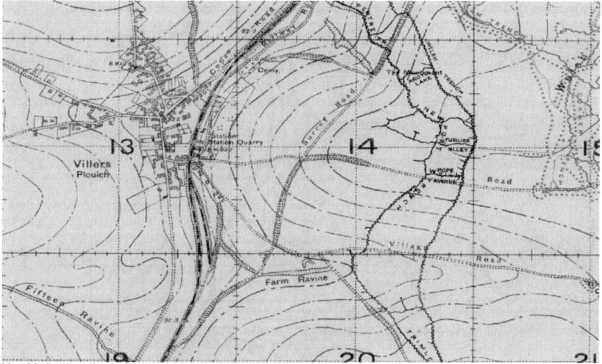

Map 32, Position of the 13th East Surreys near Villers-Plouich (July 1917)

The East Surreys moved back to brigade support in an area known as Fifteen Ravine southwest of the village, one company however remained in an advanced position on the road to Trescault west of Villers-Plouich. Over the days that followed the East Surreys set about improving conditions at 15 Ravine, shelters were built and a new aid post was constructed, at night the battalion provided working parties for duties on the frontline. On the night of 13th/14th July Pte Daniel Trevett and the East Surreys relieved the 11th Kings Own in the frontline trenches east of Villers-Plouich. The battalion companies were deployed with two in the front line, one in support and one in reserve, on the East Surreys left were the 14th Argyle and Sutherland Highlanders and on their right stood the 12th SWB (119th Brigade,40th Division). During this relief Pte Daniel Trevett was wounded, this was more than likely as a result of shellfire that always seemed to fall when battalion reliefs were in progress. It probably came from German guns situated a mile east of Villers-Plouich at La Vacquerie as these guns were very active over the days that followed. The 13th East Surreys would remain in the frontline until the night of the 21st/22nd July, as for Pte Daniel Trevett he was evacuated back to an aid post behind the lines, possibly the newly constructed one at Fifteen Ravine, unfortunately he died of wounds on 15th July (17).

In August 1917 a small article recording the death of Daniel Trevett appeared in the Chigwell Parish Magazine adding his name to the growing list of those men killed. For some reason his name doesn't appear on the Chigwell Village War Memorial however it does appear on both the Woodford Bridge Roll of Honour plaque and war memorial inside St Paul's Church, Woodford Bridge. Pte Daniel Trevett was 38 years old when he died and is buried a few miles southwest of Gouzeaucourt in Plot I Row C Grave 11 of Fins New British CWGC Cemetery. The cemetery was begun in July 1917 by men of the 40th Division, 61st (South Midland) Division and 9th (Scottish) Division. Daniel Trevett's headstone is unique; it's the only one that carries the words: *'Chigwell Essex England, Gone But Not Forgotten'*.

* * *

Since Haig had first mentioned his plan for an attack in Flanders the War Cabinet had made it clear they were not keen on a British offensive carried out without support from the French Army. Although pleased with the success of Messines the British politicians, like the French, were happy to sit the year out and wait for the Americans to arrive; it was up to the CIC to convince them otherwise. Back in May Haig had met the War Cabinet and at that time his argument for an attack had hinged on three main lines of defence all of which by July held no real weight behind them. He had argued that the Germans must be kept occupied and away from the demoralised French Army, by July however with General Petain's influence the French forces were making good progress and on their way to recovery. Another argument saw him insist that the Russians needed help in tying down German troops in the west however by July with their forces and country on the brink of revolution it wouldn't be long before the Russians threw in the towel altogether. The last point his argument hinged on and by far the most important as far as the government was concerned was the losses in terms of food and supplies the British were suffering due to the submarine war. Losses had been heavy and it had been feared Britain may be starved out of the war, the Royal Navy had introduced a convoy system in order to protect merchant vessels, it had proved successful and by July losses were far from critical. Haig had insisted that German submarines were operating out of the Belgian ports of Ostend and Zeebrugge and his Flanders attack was designed to capture them, in fact these submarines were operating out of bases on the German coast.

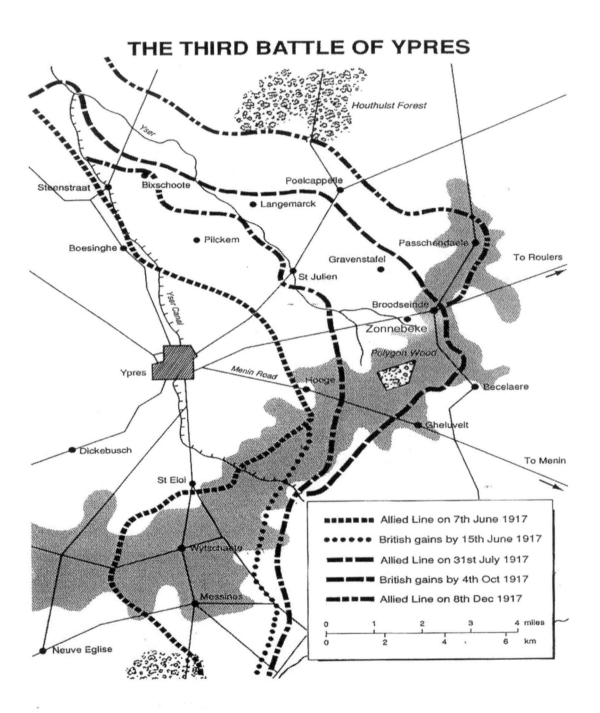

Map 33, The Third Battle of Ypres (Map taken from 'Chronicles of the First World War by Peter Simkins. © Colour Library Books of Godalming/Bramley Books).

The CIC persuaded the Admiralty to back up his beliefs, as naval commanders insisted things were worse than they were the War Cabinet finally buckled and gave Haig the green light he'd longed for. The various actions that made up the next phase of the Flanders offensive collectively became known as 'The Third Battle of Ypres' although most people call it 'The Battle of Passchendaele' (18).

The German forward positions east of Ypres consisted of several lightly held lines of defence protected by concrete pillboxes armed with machine guns; this meant their frontlines could be held with a minimal amount of men. The main bulk of German troops - positioned in case of a breakthrough and ready to deliver counter attacks if necessary – were situated a few miles east of the frontline in three more heavily defended lines known as Flandern I, II and III. Like with most battles during the First World War the allies, in order to clear a path for an attack by the infantry, relied on preliminary bombardments to destroy enemy frontline positions and defences. The Flanders offensive of 1917 was no exception and on 22nd July on a front 10 miles long from Warneton in the south to Bixschoote in the north the British guns opened up on the enemy lines. During the course of the next nine days with their highest ever concentration of guns, virtually one for every six yards of front, the British artillery fired more than four million shells at the German lines. As well as destroying enemy positions these shells were also successful in destroying the intricate drainage system so important to the Flanders landscape, this was to have disastrous effects on the coming battle. During the course of this nine day bombardment Chigwell lost another man.

CHARLES ERNEST BAILEY
As previously mentioned in the chapter entitled 'The War At Sea' Harry and Charlotte Bailey were parents to five children and their second son Harry Norman Bailey was killed tragically whilst serving aboard HMS Kestrel back in November 1914. Charles was their eldest child and was born in Chigwell in 1887, he was followed by two daughters Annie and Ada who were then followed by Harry and finally a younger brother called Frederick. As the children grew up the family lived at Texas Villas on Turpins Lane in Woodford Bridge, having attended school locally on leaving Charles found work as a Telegraph Messenger, he eventually married a lady called Annie and he and his wife moved to Twickenham (19). On the outbreak of war it appears that Charles didn't enlist right away, being married and a possibly a father, its more likely he was attested into the Territorial Force under the terms of the Derby Scheme sometime towards the end of 1915. According to SDGW Charles enlisted at Twickenham and it appears that soon afterwards he was drafted to the reserves of the London Regiment as Private 5630. It should be remembered how the London Regiment with so many battalions had offices right across the capital, the 6th Battalion were based in the City of London at 57a Farringdon Road and during the war they became known as the 'Cast Iron Sixth' (20).

Like with most territorial battalions the outbreak of war saw the 6th London's create both a second and third line formation to supply reinforcements as and when needed. In March 1915 however having been trained and equipped the 1/6th London's were sent to France whilst its two reserve units remained in England. Unfortunately the service record of Pte Charles Bailey no longer exists so we can't tell exactly when he enlisted however the Medal Rolls at the NA tell us for sure that he didn't serve overseas until the late summer of 1916. This being the case we can only conclude that between enlisting and leaving for France Charles was probably attached to the 2/6th London's. Initially created in August 1914 the 2/6th London's remained in England for the first half of the war but as was expected when required the unit still sent out drafts to its first line battalion. Throughout 1915 the 2/6th London's spent much of their time training at various camps in and around Norfolk and Suffolk however in July 1916 the unit was posted to Sutton Veny Camp on Salisbury Plain. Although the 2/6th London's themselves were destined to serve on the Western Front before this occurred Charles was sent out to France as a replacement (21). Pte Charles Bailey crossed the Channel and headed south to the Somme region joining the 1/6th London's in billets at Albert on 30th September 1916. The 2nd London Division had been designated the 47th Division in May 1915 and consisted of the 140th Brigade, 141st Brigade and 142nd Brigade (22). The 140th Brigade contained the following battalions: 1/6th (City of London) Battalion, the London Regiment, 1/7th (City of London) Battalion, the London Regiment, 1/8th (City of London) Battalion, the London Regiment and the 1/15th (County of London) Battalion, the London Regiment (23).

The 47th Division under the command of Lieutenant General Sir George F Gorringe DSO had spent the spring of 1916 in positions around Vimy before moving southwards to see action on the Somme, when Charles arrived however the unit had been involved in various actions in and around High Wood. Throughout October the 47th Division was moved northwards exchanging the Somme battlefield for the awful and much feared Ypres Salient. In March 1917 due to the weight of numbers being conscripted the Territorial Force underwent a series of alterations concerning army service numbers, most soldiers found themselves renumbered and the service number belonging to Pte Charles Bailey changed from 5630 to 322774. The first half of 1917 saw the 47th Division holding various positions south of Ypres so not surprisingly in early June it played its part in the Battle of Messines, by the start of July however the 1/6th London's under the command of Lieutenant Colonel W F Mildren DSO found themselves away from the fighting enjoying a brief spell behind the lines. Hence the name Ontario Camp was initially created by Canadian units and was situated southwest of Ypres close to the village of Reningelst. Whilst based here Pte Charles Bailey and the rest of his battalion spent much of their time refitting, training and resting. The men played cricket and concert parties were also held to help improve moral, on the afternoon of 4th July his majesty King George V passed close to the camp and the men went out to greet him. Over the following days training continued including amongst other things bayonet and musketry practice, during the London's time in camp enemy aircraft constantly patrolled the skies overhead and the battalion had one of its observation balloons shot down. The morning of the 8th July was filled with thunderstorms as Pte Charles Bailey and his battalion prepared to pack up and head back to the trenches. That afternoon the weather improved and at 7:00pm the 1/6th London's left camp and marched to trenches south of Ypres relieving the 21st London's (attached to 142nd Brigade) in support lines at Spoilbank to the east of Voormezele. The battalion war diary describes their journey as quite difficult because the roads and tracks leading to the trenches were broken up by the bad weather and enemy artillery; this said however the relief was finally completed by 11:30pm but the Germans greeted the 1/6th London's arrival with heavy shellfire. Immediately on arrival the battalion was expected to provide men for work and carrying parties in the forward areas, there was no time for rest and the next day Charles and the men not only set about improving their trenches but also erected shelters, gun posts and dugouts along their stretch of line. The following days and nights were spent doing much of the same with the weather a mixture of sunshine and showers, enemy aircraft continued to be active overhead whilst artillery from both sides constantly fired shells across no mans land.

Map 34, Hollebeke

On the night of 14th July the 1/6th London's left the support trenches to relieve the 1/8th London's in front line trenches just south of the Ypres-Comines Canal to the northwest of Hollebeke, in some places the frontline consisted of nothing but fortified shell holes and craters connected by shallow communication trenches. The battalion positioned itself with 'C' Coy on the left and 'D' Coy on the right; both 'A' Coy and 'B' Coy were in support, unfortunately it has not been possible to determined which company Charles was attached to. That night the leading companies sent out patrols to assess the strength of the enemy opposite, advanced posts were to be located and the identity of their occupants were to be established. The following couple of days were spent yet again improving positions, due to the bad weather the trenches and shell holes were flooded and had to be not only drained but deepened and strengthened. In addition yet again where possible further gun posts and shelters were erected however whilst this work was in progress the London's came under constant artillery fire with the Germans firing a mixture of high explosive and gas shells at the British lines. On the right of the 1/6th London's stood units of 19th Division who following the Battle of Messines felt the need to improve their lines before the next major push could begin. On the 17th July the division made a small advance and some units of the 1/6th London's were sent out to help, the London's returned soon after having suffered no casualties but in the days that followed, after several attacks and counter attacks, the 19th Division conceded all of its gains. The night of 20th July saw the 1/6th London's carryout a company relief in the frontline as 'A' Coy relieved 'C' Coy on the left and 'B' Coy relieved 'D' Coy on the right, the following morning was a fine day weather wise as the men yet again set about improving the condition of their trenches.

It should be remembered that on the 22nd July the British began their preliminary bombardment for the Third Battle of Ypres and for the 1/6th London's still in the frontline they really felt it as the enemy retaliated. During this time German aircraft, aware that something big was happening, were constantly overhead trying to keep an eye on not only the British guns but also allied troop movements in both the forward and rear areas. That afternoon several NCO's led by a Second Lieutenant left their trenches and crossed no mans land entering enemy support trenches opposite known as Optic Trench. These support positions in turn led to the main German frontline position known as Oblique Trench. On entering the support trench they found it was held in strength and on meeting the enemy a hand to hand bombing fight took place. This engagement lasted a while and whilst no prisoners were captured the attackers inflicted many casualties among the German garrison. Eventually the London's supply of bombs ran out and they were forced to withdraw, during this exchange however they had no men killed but four men were wounded. As a result of the relative success of the raid, but due to the fact that no enemy prisoners had been captured, the following evening the brigade commander decided a more elaborate plan should be carried out by the 1/6th London's. In conjunction with other units of their brigade the battalion sent out two small groups each under the command of a Second Lieutenant to once again raid Optic and Oblique Trenches as well as a small wood situated in front of the Ypres-Comines Canal. Under the cover of a creeping barrage the two groups took up forward positions and as the barrage lifted they rushed the enemy trenches. The group attacking Oblique Trench met with success taking the enemy by surprise, many casualties were inflicted and 29 German prisoners were secured before the group, having themselves had 5 men wounded, were ordered to withdraw. Those men attacking the small wood however had a more difficult time as the enemy seemed to be prepared for their arrival. Strong resistance was met in the form of rifle and bomb fire as the group neared their objective; they did manage to reach the wood and fighting ensued but by the time they withdrew they'd captured no prisoners; 3 men were killed and 4 were wounded. It is not known whether Pte Charles Bailey took part in the raid but if he did it would appear he came through it unscathed. On the morning of 24th July as the battalion remained in the frontline the enemy artillery continued to pound the British trenches with again a mixture of high explosive and gas shells. In the sector held by the London's the shelling was particularly heavy possibly in retaliation for the raid of the previous night. The battalion received orders that following its exploits it was to be relieved that evening however until the relief arrived the men were still expected to hold their section of frontline. Charles no doubt along with his fellow soldiers after having spent almost two weeks in the frontline would have been gearing up to leave the trenches and looking forward to a well deserved rest, the German guns however kept firing and shells kept raining down. As the men waited unfortunately several casualties were sustained due to hostile artillery pounding their position, some men suffered the effects of gas inhalation whilst others fell victim to flying shrapnel; it appears that one of the men killed during this period as a result of the enemy shellfire was Pte Charles Bailey. In total the battalion war diary puts the 1/6th London's losses that day at 4 men killed and 6 men wounded (24), the battalion was finally relieved by men of the 11th Royal West Kent's (122nd Brigade, 41st Division) at 2:30am on the morning of 25th July and proceeded on foot to huts at Curragh Camp to the west of Ypres.

No individual mention of the death of Pte Charles Bailey appeared in the Chigwell Parish Magazine, its possible however that a report appeared in a paper close to his home in Twickenham. After her husbands death Mrs Annie Bailey moved back to Essex and settled in the village of Alresford near Colchester. Pte Charles Ernest Bailey is buried in Grave E.8 at Oak Dump CWGC Cemetery south of Ypres; this small cemetery contains the graves of just over a hundred men killed between 1914 and 1918. As well as being commemorated on the Chigwell Village War Memorial the name of Pte Charles Bailey also appears on the Roll of Honour Memorial Plaque at Woodford Bridge (25). It is also worth mentioning that in the City of London directly outside the Royal Exchange at Bank Junction stands a rather fine memorial commemorating all battalions of the London Regiment that served in the Great War.

* * *

At 3:50am on Tuesday 31st July the British guns stopped their preliminary bombardment and provided a creeping barrage as whistles blew and in pouring rain twelve divisions of attacking troops supported by tanks went over the top. Although the main attack was entrusted to Gough and 5th Army units of Plumer's 2nd Army provided a supporting roll at the southern end of the attack front, in the north a single French Corps also supported the British attack. This action numbered the first phase of Third Ypres and became known as 'The Battle of Pilckem Ridge', Chigwell suffered no casualties on the first day however several of its soldiers were involved in the event. In the north ground was gained as Pilckem Ridge, Bixschoote and Pilckem itself all fell to the British, most of St Julien was also captured and roughly two miles was covered as troops reached the Steenbeek River in front of

Langemarck. In the centre of the front although the village of Frezenberg was captured and troops reached Westhoek they were unable to push deep into the main area east of Ypres known as the Gheluvelt Plateau. The capture of this area was vital if success was to be achieved, it was the key to the German defences and it needed to be taken quickly however the enemy as well as the weather would see this wouldn't happen. The tanks and their crews found it hard to cross the shell torn ground and therefore were unable to support the infantry to the level it was hoped they would. Some machines were knocked out by enemy shellfire but more frustratingly as the rain got heavier and heavier it caused others to get bogged down in the Flanders fields that were now quickly turning to mud. As the British pushed into the German lines they became disorganised as losses started to mount, shellfire and machine guns situated in carefully placed pillboxes causing most of the casualties. That afternoon as the units of 5th Army were coming to terms with their position the Germans launched counter attacks using specially trained troops, in some places the British were pushed backwards however defensive positions were adopted and eventually the enemy was held. As for the weather the rain did not stop, it poured and poured and the ground got worse and worse, the mud was turning the battlefield into a swamp, it was the worst weather that Belgium had experienced for over seventy years. As the first day came to an end it was clear the battle was not going to be easy, if it was up to Gough he would have ended it there and then, when he suggested this to Haig the CIC would hear no such thing and so it continued. Over the next five days it rained every day making conditions on the battlefield extremely harsh however with enormous effort reliefs took place the wounded were evacuated and supplies were brought forward. A few dry days followed as well as days where rainfall was minimal which allowed the ground to dry out ever so slightly. On the 10th August British troops captured the village of Westhoek, it then continued to rain heavily for the next week. The next major push made by 5th Army came at 4:45am on the 16th August following a three day preliminary bombardment of the German lines. This action would last two days, was titled the second phase of Third Ypres, and referred to later as 'The Battle of Langemarck'. It was during this action that the next man whose name appears on the Chigwell Memorial lost his life.

FRANK M FOGG
Whilst trying to tell the stories of those men listed on the Chigwell Village War Memorial some men more than others have proved difficult to find information on especially regarding their backgrounds, added to this sometimes finding their link to Chigwell itself has proved just as tough. One such man is Frank Fogg and the situation here gets more frustrating as during my research he was one of only a few men of whom I found a living relative, unfortunately however due to ill health they were unable to shed any light on his story which landed me back where I started. With this being the case I can only write what I know. Frank M Fogg (26) was born in the Essex village of Ramsey near Dovercourt sometime around 1896/7. His father called Thomas worked as a yardman on a farm and was born in the village of Writtle west of Chelmsford in 1867 whilst his mother called Mary was born the same year at Ongar in Essex. Frank had two older sisters called Phoebe and Eliza and a younger brother called William, nothing else is known of Frank's early life and we can only assume he or his family moved to either Chigwell or Woodford Bridge shortly before the war. One other clue however does exist that may or may not provide us with an answer regarding his residence and profession. A publication known as 'Kelly's Directory' existed that for a small fee would list the names and addresses of residents and businesses in a said area. The Kelly's Directory usually covered a whole county and the names and addresses within it were listed under the different villages within that county. In the Essex edition of Kelly's Directory for 1912 under Woodford Bridge an entry exists for a business called F & J Fogg Coal Merchants, their address is listed as 6 Waltham Road. Although Frank would have been too young to own this business it is possible it was owned by a relative and at some point he lived and worked there. We do know Frank married a woman called Kathleen however where and when this ceremony took place is unknown, it's also unknown whether or not the couple had children. To make matters worse however according to SDGW it would appear that on the outbreak of war Frank and his wife were living in the Essex village of North Fambridge southeast of Chelmsford and this just adds to the confusion regarding any link to Chigwell. Frank wasted no time in joining the colours enlisting at Colchester sometime during August or September 1914, after successfully passing a medical he was posted as Private 4227 to a Lancers of the Line battalion based in England.

On mobilization in August 1914 fourteen Reserve Cavalry of the Line regiments were created each regiment containing two battalions, only the 7th and 8th Reserve Regiments contained Lancer battalions so Frank must have been attached to one of these two, his service record no longer exists therefore its impossible to tell which one. In the early summer of 1915 along with many other men Frank was transferred from the Lancers to a reserve battalion of the Royal Munster Fusiliers (27). Following this transfer his army service number changed to 5656 and he continued training whilst awaiting orders for a posting overseas. The 1st Battalion Royal Munster Fusiliers were stationed in Rangoon in Burma in August 1914 and arrived back in England in January 1915. The battalion left for Egypt in March as part of 86th Brigade, 29th Division and landed at Cape Helles on the Gallipoli Peninsular on 25th April. Over the following days 86th Brigade suffered heavy casualties and temporarily the 1st RMF and another battalion within the brigade, the 1st Royal Dublin Fusiliers were amalgamated into one composite battalion known as the 'Dubsters'. On 19th May 1915 the battalion resumed its identity and awaited reinforcements, a draft arrived on 11th July that included amongst others Pte Frank Fogg. As previously explained on the outbreak of war some regular battalions designated their companies not 'A' to 'D' but 'W' to 'Z', the 1st RMF was one such battalion. According to the records of the CWGC they show that Pte Frank Fogg was attached to 'B'

Coy which under this system translates as 'X' Coy. After the evacuation of Gallipoli in January 1916 the battalion moved back to Egypt before heading for France landing at Marseilles on 22nd March 1916. In May the 1st RMF, under the command of Lieutenant Colonel R H Monck-Mason, were reinforced with men from the disbanded 9th RMF and became part of 48th Brigade, 16th (Irish) Division (28). The battalion served on the Somme until mid September and during that time took part in the Battle of Guillemont, later that month 16th Division moved northwards and by October held positions at the southern end of the Ypres Salient. Late November saw the 1st RMF yet again absorb men from a disbanded battalion, this time the 8th RMF, and with that the battalion was transferred to 47th Brigade which contained the following battalions: 6th Battalion, the Royal Irish Regiment, 6th Battalion, the Connaught Rangers, 7th Battalion, the Prince of Wales Leinster Regiment (Royal Canadians) and the 1st Battalion, Royal Munster Fusiliers. In June 1917 the 16th Division took part in the Battle of Messines and along with the 36th (Ulster) Division were responsible for capturing the village of Wytschaete, so it was that two months later as the Flanders Offensive started the two divisions once again found themselves in the thick of the action.

The action known as the Battle of Langemarck was not just a push for the village itself but was also an effort to improve British positions on a front roughly six miles long. The area to be attacked stretched from just south of the Menin Road - east of Hooge - northwards to just west of Langemarck. Although the battle lasted for two days most of the action occurred on the first day and involved nine divisions from four different corps. At the southern end stood one brigade from 18th Division (II Corps), they failed to make any advance south of the Menin Road in the direction of Inverness Copse; their failure to take this heavily defended position was mainly due to well concealed enemy machine guns existing amongst the shattered tree stumps and brush. On their left stood 56th Division who were positioned with two brigades north of the road. One was due to attack a German strongpoint known as Glencorse Wood but made no worthwhile gains, instead it suffered heavy casualties whilst the other, on the divisional left flank gained minimal ground east of Westhoek.

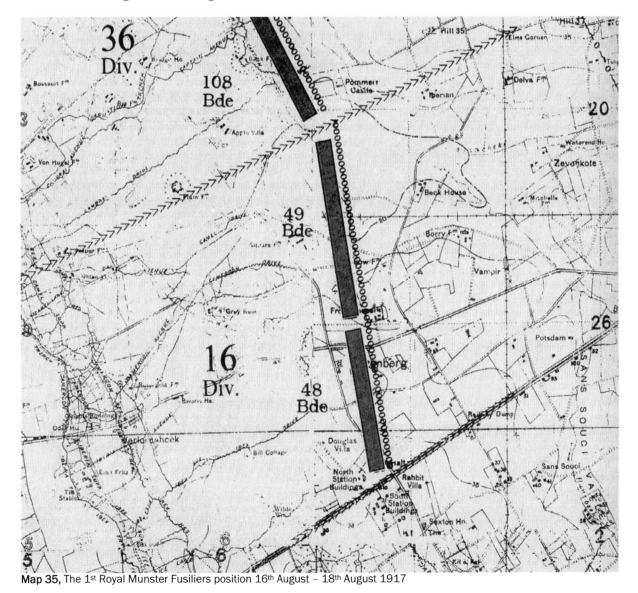

Map 35, The 1st Royal Munster Fusiliers position 16th August – 18th August 1917

It was hoped that if both brigades were successful they could have pushed on to capture Polygon Wood; another enemy strongpoint sited further east. On 56th Division's left stood 8th Division who made little advance north of Westhoek towards Frezenberg. At the northern end of the front the 29th Division and 20th Division (XIV Corps) crossed the heavily swollen Steenbeek River - using bridges hastily constructed under dangerous conditions by men of the Royal Engineers - to successfully capture the ruins of Langemarck. On their right the 11th Division (XVIII Corps) secured the ground south of the village whilst further south the 48th Division captured what was left of St Julien. In the centre of the front between St Julien and Frezenberg the area on the left was held by 36th Division (XIX Corps), two brigades attacked at zero hour however only the left flank gained any ground. The centre right was held by 16th Division and as part of this unit its here that Pte Frank Fogg found himself.

At zero hour 16th Division attacked on the Frezenberg Ridge with two brigades, 49th Brigade on the left flank managed to capture the enemy position of Beck House however troops attacking a position known as Borry Farm failed in their objective. Some units on the brigade left reached as far as Delva Farm but as they passed over enemy positions they failed to clear them properly, as a result these troops came under fire from the rear. As their number got less and less the men were forced to fall back and inevitably this meant that no ground was held. The 48th Brigade on the right flank consisted of the 7th Royal Irish Rifles on the left and the 9th Royal Dublin Fusiliers on the right. In support stood a combined force of the 2nd and 8th Royal Dublin Fusiliers and in reserve stood one battalion of 47th Brigade; the 1st Royal Munster Fusiliers. As the whistles blew under cover of the creeping barrage the leading battalions advanced over the muddy battlefield - still covered with the dead bodies of those men who'd attacked over the same ground on 31st July - towards the enemy held positions of Potsdam and Vampir Farm. On reaching these positions the troops dug in as best they could. However due to the lack of success by the troops of 49th Brigade on the left and 23rd Brigade (8th Division) on the right the battalions of 48th Brigade found their position became precarious. Under heavy machine gun and shellfire the men made do the best they could however as was not unexpected that afternoon the Germans launched counter attacks. After a tough fight the order to retreat was given and the surviving men of 48th Brigade were forced to fall back to their start line.

The 1st RMF had moved into support positions, known as the old German frontline, roughly two hours before zero and awaited further orders. According to their war diary in order to support 48th Brigade the battalion positioned itself as follows: Both 'Y' Coy and 'Z' Coy were in IBEX Reserve Trench, 'W' Coy held both ICE Trench and ICE Support Trench and 'X' Coy, containing Pte Frank Fogg, held both IBEX Trench and IBEX Support Trench, battalion HQ was positioned in IBERIA Trench. At 7:23am 'Y' Coy moved forward towards the position known as Douglas Villa and the trench system around it in order to cover units of the 2nd Royal Dublin Fusiliers. At 9:23am 'Y' Coy moved east of Douglas Villa and the vacated position was occupied by 'Z' Coy. Those men attached to both 'W' Coy and 'X' Coy spent much of the day in their original positions however at 5:00pm they received orders to move forward in close support and take up positions in IBEX Reserve Trench. Pte Frank Fogg and the rest of his company remained in IBEX Reserve Trench for the rest of the day however due to German counter attacks all positions held by the 1st RMF were severely shelled by the enemy. According to their battalion war diary during the period 16th – 17th August the casualties for the 1st RMF were as follows:

Officers = 1 Missing + 2 Wounded
Other Ranks = 4 KIA + 1 Missing + 22 Wounded

In their supporting roll the 1st RMF suffered very few casualties in comparison to those units of 48th Brigade and 49th Brigade however as a result of the shellfire experienced by the battalion Pte Frank Fogg was unfortunately among the four men reported as having been killed; he was 22 years old. During the day and night of the 17th August owing to the fact that 16th Division had failed to achieve its objectives and suffered heavily in the process its troops were withdrawn and replaced by units from the 15th Division. As for the 1st RMF on completion of relief the battalion proceeded to camp at Vlamertinge where it remained for two days before being moved back down south to the Somme.

Tyne Cot CWGC Cemetery stands on the top of Passchendaele Ridge looking out over the Flanders fields below; it's the largest British war cemetery in the world. At the eastern end of the cemetery stands the Tyne Cot Memorial to the Missing which lists the names of more than 35,000 officers and men who were killed in the Ypres Salient after 16th August 1917 and have no known grave. In the case of Pte Frank Fogg his body - along with the three other Munster's killed during the same period - was never found therefore his name appears on Panel 143 of the Tyne Cot Memorial to the Missing. No mention of Frank's death appeared in either the Woodford Times or the Chigwell Parish Magazine, after the war his wife Kathleen Fogg moved to Wexford on the southeast coast of Ireland.

* * *

The Battle of Langemarck had not been a total failure for the British; after all in the north ground had been gained with Langemarck captured however to the south the vital ground of the Gheluvelt Plateau still remained in enemy hands. It had temporarily stopped raining but by now the damage had been done, the ground was a mess, a swamp of mud; it was no place to fight a battle and expect to win convincingly. In most places the British frontline no longer consisted of trench lines as such but of ditches and shell holes loosely connected to each other by poorly constructed communication trenches. The rear areas were connected to the front by makeshift roads and tracks most of which the enemy guns had a fix on. At night the engineers and infantry would find themselves laying paths made up of all sorts; wooden duckboards were preferred but not always at hand. As Third Ypres continued the conditions of the battlefield would become just as dangerous to the troops as any enemy shell or bullet, if a man slipped off a track into the mud there was a good chance he would sink beneath the slime and once in it was virtually impossible to haul yourself out again unaided. As the Langemarck action came to a close it was in these muddy ditches and shell holes that the men found themselves. They needed supplies and their wounded needed attention, without it they stood little hope. With the enemy positioned a few hundred yards away the situation was bad and moral amongst the weary troops reached an all time low. However in spite of the conditions once again the British soldiers proved their resilience, they struggled through the mud and eventually the wounded were evacuated, supplies were brought up and relief's were made with fresh divisions replacing those that had suffered heavy losses. Over the next week further attempts to advance were made but again as the troops attacked little was achieved in terms of ground gained, more casualties were incurred and sent back to the already overstretched aid stations and hospitals. The British did manage however to make small insertions into the remains of Glencorse Wood and Inverness Copse. Due to these small scale attacks up and down the line the German troops were also suffering; it should not be forgotten that they too were stuck in the miserable conditions surrounding the Ypres Salient and although holding the better positions they still had to defend them. During the early hours of 24th August the Germans launched an artillery barrage followed by a counter attack in an attempt to capture the ground they had lost at Glencorse Wood and Inverness Copse. The British put up a stiff defence but in both areas their line was pushed back however the situation was eventually stabilized. That same day on seeing the situation of the troops under his control Gough requested another meeting with Haig. The army commander expressed his feelings that no tactical advantage could possibly be achieved without his forces acquiring huge losses; as before his conclusion was that the Flanders offensive should be abandoned. Haig listened to Gough but spurred on by shaky intelligence reports - supplied by his {Haig's} staff officers - that the Germans were weakening the CIC decided the fight should continue. It was however at this time that Haig realised a change of command may be necessary in order for success to be achieved. That same day he extended 2nd Army's front northwards to include the area that covered the Gheluvelt Plateau. As a result of this change it now meant that overall control for Third Ypres passed from Sir Hubert Gough and 5th Army to Sir Herbert Plumer and 2nd Army.

The depth of the German defensive system at Ypres had been responsible for most of the casualties incurred by the British especially in those areas around Gheluvelt. General Plumer along with his staff officers were well aware of this and realised a change of tactics had to be adopted if success was to be achieved. In the run up to the Battle of Messines careful planning and training by those involved had assured a successful outcome, Plumer knew the same amount of preparation would have to be carried out if Third Ypres was to prove a success. Not wishing to be rushed into fruitless attacks that carried no clear objectives Plumer requested and got a three week delay in which to prepare his strategy. Every man would be trained and briefed on his role prior to the attack. Plumer aimed to use the artillery and infantry together like never before, advances would only be made if a clear victory was in sight. Known as a bite and hold technique his strategy was designed to capture ground with a minimal amount of casualties, it also aimed at disrupting all threats of German counter attacks by way of a standing barrage. The British heavy artillery would pound enemy positions then the infantry would advance under the protection of a creeping barrage laid on by lighter guns, on reaching their objectives the troops would then consolidate the ground they had gained. The British guns would then shell the rear areas of the German lines to disrupt any units that may be forming up there for a counter attack, should any Germans breakthrough British troops would be dug in and waiting for them. Once this process was completed the heavy guns would be moved forward and their sights then set on the next target, fresh infantry units would also move up and at the same time any wounded would be evacuated. The large guns would then open up on these new positions as the whole process was repeated. In this way Plumer hoped he could achieve success on a sector previously clouded in failure however as good as his plan seemed it would not be easy to move his guns, men and munitions forward across the dreadful conditions that covered the Ypres battlefield.

As the three week lull started temporarily it stopped raining allowing the rear areas to be cleared up and sorted out, supplies were brought in and men were trained, fresh units were also brought up in readiness. On the frontline however it was business as usual, forward positions still had to be defended despite the conditions. Although preparations were underway for a large scale attack by 2nd Army the British still carried out line straightening operations along the frontline. It was during this period on one of these line straightening operations that Chigwell suffered its next casualty.

PATRICK FITZGERALD
Tulla is a small village situated in County Clare in western Ireland and its here that Patrick Fitzgerald was born to parents Charles and Margaret. The exact year that Patrick was born is unknown and unfortunately his family background regarding brothers and sisters also remains somewhat of a mystery as does his education. What is known is that Patrick left Ireland and moved to England, probably sometime around 1910, and soon after found

work as a stores porter at Claybury Hospital. Patrick met and married a young lady called Gladys and together the couple set up home at 1 Brunel Terrace, Brunel Road, Woodford Bridge, they were to have two children. As war broke out Patrick did not enlist right away and it was not until May 1916 that he was conscripted into the army having attended a recruiting office in Woodford. Although Patrick's army service record no longer exists we know from his MIC and the Medal Rolls at the NA that after passing a medical he was posted as Private 32108 to the reserve battalions of the Norfolk Regiment. After completing a period of basic training Patrick was scheduled to join the 8th Norfolk's in France but before this happened for reasons unknown he was transferred to the Territorial Force. At this point Patrick's army service number changed to 41313 however instead of staying with the Norfolk Regiment he was posted to the territorial reserves of the Worcestershire Regiment. The 7th Worcester's to which Patrick was sent consisted of three lines. The 1/7th had crossed to France in March 1915; the 2/7th was also in France having been sent there in May 1916 whilst the 3/7th Battalion was their reserve unit based by mid 1916 on Salisbury Plain. The 8th Battalion Worcester Regiment was much the same as the 7th Battalion in so much as it consisted of three lines of which two were in France with the third based in England. In September 1916 the 3/7th and 3/8th Worcester's were amalgamated to form one battalion known as the 7th Reserve Battalion. This battalion like most reserve battalions was designed to send out reinforcements to its first and second lines in France. Initially Pte Patrick Fitzgerald found himself attached to the 7th Reserve Battalion and involved in training on Salisbury Plain but in May 1917 he received orders to head overseas and was sent to France arriving that same month. Patrick as part of a draft of reinforcements joined the 1/7th Worcester's in positions on the Somme and remained there until the battalion moved northwards to Ypres during the third week of July. The 48th (South Midland) Division was commanded by Major General R Fanshawe and consisted of the 143rd (Warwickshire) Brigade, the 144th (Gloucester and Worcester) Brigade and the 145th (South Midland) Brigade. It was the 144th Brigade that contained 1/7th Battalion, the Worcestershire Regiment along with the 1/4th (City of Bristol) Battalion, the Gloucestershire Regiment, 1/6th Battalion, the Gloucestershire Regiment and the 1/8th Battalion, the Worcestershire Regiment.

The 48th Division was attached to XVIII Corps and during the Battle of Langemarck its 145th Brigade was responsible for capturing St Julien, once consolidated the division occupied positions east of the village. On 19th August the division saw action again when supporting a tank attack it managed to capture no fewer than four enemy pillboxes immediately east of its position. The division was deployed with its 143rd Brigade on the right flank east of St Julien to the left of 61st Division, the 144th Brigade – in positions just east of the Steenbeek River – held the left flank next to 11th Division whilst the 145th Brigade was held in reserve.

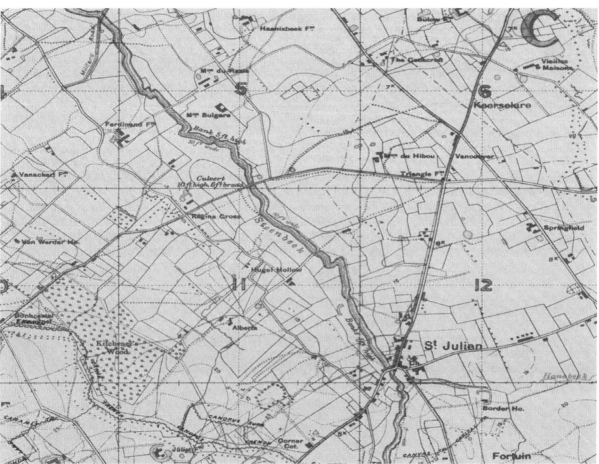

Map 36, The 1/7th Worcester's position near St Julien (26th August to 28th August 1917)

Three days later the forward brigades were in action again when they attacked towards two farm buildings in front of their positions known as Springfield Farm and Winnipeg Farm however on this day none of these buildings were captured. Tanks were supposed to provide support but could not leave the roads due to their fear of getting bogged down in the muddy conditions. In front of the farms minimal ground was captured as enemy positions were won and lost however by nightfall small improvements had been made. During these operations the 1/7th Worcester's were not directly involved although when not in camp they provided somewhat of a supporting role. The next few days saw minimal rainfall as the brigades of 48th Division held their positions and periodically dealt with any German counter attacks that materialised. On the morning of Saturday 25th August the 1/7th Worcester's, under the command of Lieutenant Colonel J M Tomkinson, were ordered to relieve the 1/4th Gloucester's in reserve positions known as the Canal Bank situated west of the Steenbeek River to the north of St Julien. This relief was carried out by men of 'C' Coy along with a company attached from the 1/8th Worcester's. As they moved forward Germans flares lit up the night sky and hostile shelling hampered the relief, 'C' Coy found it particularly hard going as they were carrying extra rations of food and rum for rest of the battalion. Although aware that something was in the offing the next morning the 1/7th Worcester's received orders that they were to be part of a line straitening operation scheduled for 1:55pm the following afternoon that involved several divisions stretching southwards from Langemarck to Gheluvelt. On the night of 26th August both 'A' Coy and 'D' Coy who were to lead the 1/7th Worcester's assault moved to assembly trenches in front of the position known as Mon du Hibou.

Although we can not be certain it is most likely that Pte Patrick Fitzgerald was attached to one of these two companies. Both 'A' Coy and 'D' Coy reported that their ability to reach their assembly positions was made extremely difficult due to intense darkness, heavy rain, congested trenches and enemy shellfire however by 3:00am on the morning of 27th August they managed to be in position. The right flank was held by 'A' Coy with two platoons of 'B' Coy attached under the command of Captain Geoffrey Robert Wallace MC; on his right were men of the 1/8th Worcester's. The left flank was held by 'D' Coy, also with two platoons of 'B' Coy attached, under the command of Captain A O Lloyd MC; on his left stood units of 32nd Brigade, 11th Division; 'C' Coy was in battalion reserve. The position known as Mon du Hibou was a large concrete building with many rooms and it was here that the 1/7th Worcester's set up their battalion HQ, the battalion aid post was situated to the southwest of Mon du Hibou at the point marked Alberta. The objectives set for the battalion were Vancouver Farm, the boundary line Langemarck - Gheluvelt plus a line of concrete machine gun bunkers positioned 150 yards further east.

As Pte Patrick Fitzgerald and the men of the 1/7th Worcester's waited nervously in their assembly positions the enemy had no idea they were there thanks to the men of the Royal Engineers who had effectively camouflaged the area. The morning was quiet but at noon it started to rain making the already muddy conditions even worse, at zero hour a creeping barrage commenced - that was due to move forward at a rate of 100 yards in 8 minutes - whilst whistles blew and troops began to advance. The barrage was described as heavy and accurate as the infantry initially pushed on in good order however it didn't take long for the awful conditions of no mans land to slow the attackers down. The terrain was a series of muddy shell holes and men found that having covered a distance of only 50 yards they were up to their waists in water. A large number of Germans occupied shell holes opposite the Worcester's and on seeing the attackers they almost surrendered but when it became apparent the British were in trouble they changed their mind and instead opened up with what the battalion war diary describes as heavy rifle fire. On the right the men of 'A' Coy under Captain Wallace did manage to overcome difficulties to advance beyond Vancouver Farm and moved to within 100 yards of the concrete bunkers. As Wallace lead his men forward clearing occupied shell holes as they went he was shot in the stomach by a sniper, several NCO's rushed to his assistance but they too came under fire and some became casualties (29). As the battle continued the men came under fire from Springfield Farm which hampered their advance, this position was an objective of the 1/8th Worcester's and they were having a hard time capturing it. The men of 'A' Coy had no choice but to take cover and a rifle fight with the enemy ensued, some Germans fled towards the concrete bunkers and many were shot and killed. On the left 'D' Coy under Captain Lloyd had advanced from their assembly positions and started to make good progress but conditions on the ground meant they couldn't keep up with the barrage. The leading waves managed to reach a point 60 yards in front of the Langemarck – Gheluvelt line where they took heavy machine gun fire on their right flank, at this point they took cover and shot at any targets that presented themselves. German troops positioned behind hedge rows opened with rifle fire but enemy machine guns housed in bunkers caused Captain Lloyd's men the most problems.

To the left 11th Division were having trouble taking Vieilles-Maisons and fire from there also took its toll on 'D' Coy. As the British artillery barrage lifted the Worcester's found they were pinned down by both rifle and machine gun fire. As evening approached the situation seemed hopeless and those who could withdrew their position slightly and dug in, as Captain Lloyd moved back he was shot through the shoulder. At this point it started to rain heavily and consolidating positions became impossible. 'D' Coy withdrew again and dug in on a line in touch with 11th Division on its left but by 7:00pm a space had developed between 'A' Coy and 'D' Coy and a platoon of 'C' Coy was brought forward to fill the gap. In the forward areas the 1/7th Worcester's were not really hampered by hostile shelling however in order to prevent reinforcements being brought forward German guns shelled the rear areas especially between Mon du Hibou and St Julien. Units of 145th Brigade had crossed the Steenbeek at 5:00pm having had orders to pass through the 1/7th Worcester's and 1/8th Worcester's and consolidate objectives further east however due to the awful conditions and shellfire the leading battalions could not get near the front line. Later that evening these troops eventually managed to reach a point roughly 100 yards east of Mon du Hibou but communications became strained, these difficulties were eventually overcome and at 11:00pm they received orders to relieve the Worcester's in the front line. Shortly after midnight groups of the 1/7th Worcester's were relieved, firstly 'C' Coy then members of 'A' Coy 'B' Coy and 'D' Coy, the men moved back to a bridge on the Steenbeek where they were collected by lorries and taken back to camp west of Ypres. Captain Lloyd and nearly eighty other ranks were not relieved right away and had to spend another night and day in the front line; it was not until late the following evening that they were finally relieved by troops from the 58th Division.

It is frustrating not knowing exactly which company Pte Patrick Fitzgerald was attached to during the 1/7th Worcester's attack on the afternoon of 27th August 1917 but thanks to an article that appeared in the Woodford Times on Friday 14th December 1917 we do know what happened to him. It appears that whilst going forward Patrick was badly wounded in the arm by a shell, stretcher bearers came to his aid and placed him in a dug out with other wounded men whilst they took the more serious cases back to the aid post. The stretcher bearers had an awful time crossing the muddy battlefield with wounded men and several were mentioned by their commanding officers for gallantry but when those who had helped Patrick returned to the dug out there was no trace of him or the other wounded men. This being the case Pte Patrick Fitzgerald was initially classified as wounded and missing but as time passed on he was later reported as having been killed. The CWGC as well as SDGW lists the day he was killed as the 26th August however the 1/7th Worcester's war diary states this was a quiet day and reports no casualties. It is clear from the events that took place on the 27th August that it was almost certainly on this day that Patrick was wounded and later died. During the period 26th August to 28th August 1917 the 1/7th Worcester's according to their war diary suffered the following number of casualties:

Officers = 1 KIA + 4 Wounded (SDGW lists 4 KIA)
Other Ranks = 21 KIA + 68 Wounded + 7 Missing (SDGW lists 31 KIA + 2 DOW)

Many of those men killed including Pte Patrick Fitzgerald have no known grave and their names appear on Panels 75 to 77 of the Tyne Cot Memorial to the Missing. As well as the Woodford Times article Patrick's death was also mentioned in the December 1917 edition of the Chigwell Parish Magazine, after the war it appears that Gladys remarried and remained in the Woodford Bridge area.

During the operations carried out by the British between the 26th August and 28th August virtually every division that took part failed to achieve its objectives. Only the 11th Division managed minimal gains and the biggest prize of the day for 48th Division came on the evening of 27th August when Springfield Farm was outflanked from the north and captured by the 1/8th Worcester's, on the whole though the division gained little.

* * *

Back behind the lines Plumer's 2nd Army continued to prepare itself for the coming attack and as men and munitions kept piling into the rear areas at their respective headquarters those in command were optimistic success could be achieved. As August came to an end the wet weather didn't and for those people in and around Ypres they must have felt it would never stop raining. On 31st August a preliminary bombardment started that would lead to the next phase of British action, it was to last the best part of three weeks. During this period as British guns pounded the German lines night and day Chigwell suffered another casualty.

GEORGE CHARLES BELCHER

George Belcher was born and grew up in the East End of London, whilst nothing is known of his mother it seems his father died quite young. George's grandparents were Charles and Esther Belcher and they owned a house at 67 Upper North Street in Poplar, it was here with them that George spent his childhood. Charles worked as a boot repairer whilst Esther stayed at home; their grandson was educated in Poplar and on leaving school had various jobs before becoming a Cutler dealing in knives and utensils. As a young man George met an Electricians daughter called Edith Alice Warren who was born on 3rd January 1892, the couple married at St Gabriel's Church in South Bromley on 21st December 1912. Initially George and Edith lived at 177 Chrisp Street in Poplar however soon after they moved to the Chigwell area and set up home at 6 Mount Pleasant Cottages, Grange Hill. On 20th May 1914 their only child Albert was born. When war was declared the popular belief was that it would be over by Christmas, when it became clear this wouldn't be the case George decided to enlist in the army. Being an East End boy on 3rd March 1915 he attended the offices of the 17th Battalion London Regiment which at that time were based at 66 Tredegar Road in Bow, this territorial unit was also known as the Poplar and Stepney Rifles or 'The Poplars' for short (30). George underwent a medical examination and once successful enlisted for a period of four years or the duration of the war, as a result he was given army service number 3628. The 17th London's initially had two lines and that day George was posted to the 2/17th Battalion. This unit was formed in August 1914 and by March 1915 was in training up at St Albans in Hertfordshire with the 1/17th Battalion. On 16th March the first line battalion was sent to France however George continued training up at St Albans with the second line battalion where he remained for the next four months. The 1/17th London's or the Poplars as we will now call them had their baptism of fire in trenches at Festubert in early April 1915, this was followed by a brief spell out the line but in May they held positions in and around the La Bassée Canal. During the early part of July the Poplars were in reserve positions around Mazingarbe to the south of Béthune and having suffered their fair share of casualties whilst in the line reinforcements were required. On 10th July 1915 Pte George Belcher was sent to France with a draft of replacements joining the Poplars in the field two days later, on the 14th July the battalion went back to the trenches and George got his first taste of life in the frontline. The 47th Division to which George's battalion was attached has already been mentioned in the story of Pte Charles Bailey; its 141st Brigade contained the following battalions: 1/17th (County of London) Battalion, the London Regiment, 1/18th (County of London) Battalion, the London Regiment, 1/19th (County of London) Battalion, the London Regiment and the 1/20th (County of London) Battalion, the London Regiment.

Towards the end of September the 47th Division took part in the Battle of Loos and by early November it found itself still in position. The Poplars found themselves holding positions to the north of the battlefield still covered with the dead bodies of those who'd fallen in late September, their sector saw them cover the German strongpoint known as the Hohenzollern Redoubt. Throughout the war this notorious position was constantly the scene of bitter and heavy fighting and most British soldiers who were unlucky enough to serve there truly hated the place. Later that month the Poplars were relieved and moved back to camp and billets at Burbure to the west of Béthune. During this period, sometime around the 20th November, it appears that Pte George Belcher was wounded however what injury he sustained is unclear, the Poplars battalion war diary records no incident of any man being wounded. On the 24th November George was sent back to a hospital in England for treatment, he recovered quickly and was probably discharged sometime in mid December to spend Christmas and New Year at home with Edith and Albert. Having recovered and passed fit for service on 15th January 1916 George was sent to Winchester with orders to report to the 3/17th London's stationed there, he remained here training and refitting for the next two months (31).

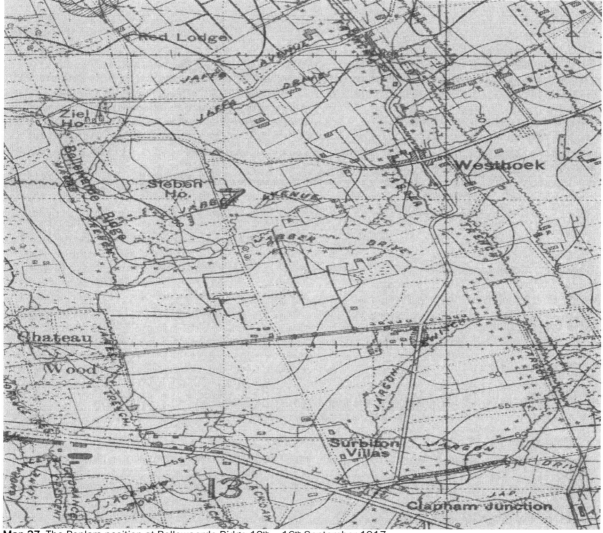

Map 37, The Poplars position at Bellewaerde Ridge 12th – 16th September 1917

On 10th March having been passed fit for frontline service George was transferred back to the 1/17th London's, he crossed the Channel and joined the Poplars 'A' Coy in billets near the village of Camblain-Chatelain southwest of Béthune two days later. As already explained in the story of Charles Bailey during the autumn of 1916 the 47th Division took part in various actions in and around the Somme and moved north to the Ypres Salient during October 1916. In March 1917 as part of the reorganisation of Territorial Force numbers George saw his service number change from 3628 to 571386 and soon after on 1st May 1917 he was promoted to the rank of Acting Lance Corporal. As previously mentioned on 7th June the 47th Division took part in the Battle of Messines and following this action three days later George was made Lance Corporal. By the start of Third Ypres the 47th Division was in reserve positions west of Ypres and although it played no major part in the opening actions it did provide various supporting roles in and around Westhoek Ridge and the Menin Road towards the end of August.

By the beginning of September the 47th Division found itself still in positions north of the Menin Road around Bellewaerde Ridge its movements closely watched by the enemy from positions in Polygon Wood as well as high ground west of Zonnebeke. As for L/Cpl George Belcher and the rest of the Poplars after a spell at the front they found themselves relieved on the 2nd September by units of 74th Brigade, 25th Division and preceded to billets near Ypres. During the early hours of the following morning the battalion climbed aboard busses and moved to Ottawa Camp west of Ypres where they remained for the next four days. Whilst in camp the Poplars, under the command of Lieutenant Colonel WW Hughes MC, cleaned up and refitted and indulged in some much needed rest. Various training exercises were also carried out which included company drill, physical training, bayonet fighting, bombing instruction and Lewis Gun practice. The Poplars war diary mentions that during this period the skies above Ottawa Camp and the surrounding areas were full of enemy aircraft constantly keeping a watchful eye on British movements. Around this time the Poplars and other units of 47th Division temporarily came under the command of the 1st Anzac Corps who were due to play a leading part in the next phase of action being prepared by 2nd Army. At 2:30pm on Saturday 8th September the Poplars paraded and left Ottawa Camp for billets at Ypres where they were closer to the frontline in order to assist Anzac units prepare for action. The following three days saw the battalion provide a draft of 5 officers and 150 other ranks to form carrying parties to work alongside the 1st Australian Tunnelling Coy. It was their job to improve forward areas by laying tracks and roads as well as helping construct a trench railway system running up towards positions on Bellewaerde Ridge.

On the 10th September whilst assisting the Anzacs gas shells fell where the carrying party was positioned and several casualties were sustained, around this time those Poplars who remained at Ypres were detailed to clean up areas around their billets and rebuild paths and roads nearby that had been destroyed by shellfire. During the early morning of 12th September one officer from each company under the command of another officer called Major Beresford reconnoitred areas on the right sector of Bellewaerde Ridge as the Poplars were due to take up positions there later that evening. Whilst in the frontline it would be the Poplars job to prepare the area for the Anzacs to take over prior to their attack with of 2nd Army. At 7:30pm dressed in full fighting gear the poplars left their billets at Ypres and moved out along the ramparts, out through the Menin Gate and headed eastward down the Menin Road towards the front line. As they moved enemy artillery was extremely active along the route and a gap of 200 yards was left between each platoon with a ten minute interval between each company. As the poplars moved down the Menin Road Very Lights lit up the night sky and enemy shells fell continuously, more than once the men were forced to disperse and take cover as shrapnel rained down and smoke filled the air. The Menin Road really was the key to the southern sector of the Ypres Salient and after three years of war the German gunners could hit every inch of it with extreme accuracy often making the lives of those allied troops using it a misery. The most dangerous spot on the road it was widely agreed was Hell Fire Corner where an intersection saw roads lead northwards to Potijze and St Jan and southwards towards Zillebeke. The next intersection along was known as Birr Cross Roads and this too was regarded as somewhat of a hotspot. A few yards east of this point the Poplars turned left heading northeast along a single lane duckboard track towards their allotted positions on Bellewaerde Ridge. The track was heavily congested and it was tough going for the Poplars laden down with supplies for their spell at the front. Luckily during their journey the battalion suffered no casualties and they relieved the 1/18th London's (Irish Rifles) in positions around Jacob and Jabber Trenches during the early hours on 13th September. As previously mentioned by this stage of Third Ypres the frontlines in and around the salient no longer consisted of trench lines as such but of fortified shell holes and strong points. This said the disposition of the battalion was 'D' Coy on the right, 'B' Coy centre and 'A' Coy containing L/Cpl George Belcher on the left; 'C' Coy was in reserve.

At daybreak as the Poplars settled down once again to life in the frontline German aircraft where seen patrolling the skies overhead as the artillery of both sides constantly fired shells across no mans land. The enemy guns, clearly directed by the planes, paid particular attention to positions in and around Jabber Trenches making the Poplars life a difficult one. That evening the battalion sent out patrols in order to attain the exact whereabouts of the enemy frontline and determine where strong points were and whether or not they were manned. Several positions were located and some thought to be held by the enemy were found to be held by British troops. Not surprisingly given the condition of the battlefield at times it was difficult for staff at battalion and brigade HQ's to know exactly where the British front ended and the German front started, as will be seen the consequences concerning this lack of knowledge could sometimes prove disastrous. On the 14th September once again the artillery of both sides was in action. The guns of 47th Division having been engaged in practice barrages several days earlier carried out an organised bombardment on enemy positions opposite however the German gunners, not wishing to be out done, returned fire. That evening the Poplars sent out one platoon, commanded by Second Lieutenant H J Chappell, to attack an enemy machine gun post that had been spotted by the patrol sent out the previous evening. The platoon under the cover of darkness advanced in pairs and when in range rushed the post successfully capturing it and killing its occupants, unfortunately in the process the Poplars themselves had five men killed and nine men wounded. This attack by the Poplars would have certainly upset the German defence on this section of front as enemy posts relied on each other to cover the frontline. The loss of one post created a gap in the line which in turn left the posts either side vulnerable to attack. The morning of Saturday 15th September was overcast however rainfall that day would prove to be minimal as once again the Poplars settled down to another day in the frontline. Again the artillery of both sides was constantly in action with the Germans firing a mixture of 77cm and 4.9inch shells whilst the British, in addition to shellfire, launched mortar rockets at enemy strong points from projectors situated on Westhoek Ridge. Meanwhile L/Cpl Charles Belcher along with other men from 'A' Coy occupied a fortified shell hole in an advanced position to the left of the Poplars line. Throughout the morning both hostile and friendly artillery fire became extremely heavy and shells whizzed back and forth. Following the capture of posts and the nature of the battlefield at times it was difficult to update the British gunners on which positions where in British hands and which ones were still held by the enemy and as a result sometimes mistakes occurred. As 'A' Coy held its position heavy guns of the Royal Artillery aiming for German targets saw some of their shells fall short and land amongst the Poplars causing severe casualties, eleven men including L/Cpl Charles Belcher were killed whilst a further twenty were wounded. This mistake was due entirely to a breakdown in communication between artillery observers and signallers based in the frontline. The incident highlights just how important it was for the infantry to constantly update artillery units and what could happen when messages weren't passed on quickly enough. The following day saw artillery barrages by both sides continue however luckily for the Poplars no further mistakes by the British guns were reported. That evening the battalion was relieved by units of the 22nd Australian Infantry Battalion and headed back down the Menin Road to billets at Ypres. The five days spent in the frontline by the Poplars had been extremely tough and Lieutenant Colonel Hughes described it as their worst ever. On the 18th September the Poplars moved to the village of Eecke about five miles northeast of Hazebrouck where in the days that followed the battalion regrouped. Around this time 47th Division was transferred from the command of the 1st Anzac Corps and moved southwards to join XIII Corps northeast of Arras, with that their war in the Ypres Salient was over.

L/Cpl George Charles Belcher along with the ten other Poplars killed on the 15th September 1917 has no known grave therefore their names appear on Panel 52 of the Menin Gate Memorial to the Missing (32). No mention of George Belcher's death appeared in either the Chigwell Parish Magazine or the Woodford Times Newspaper. Edith Belcher was entitled to her late husband's medals and on the 9th October 1917 she attended Thames Police Court in East London and signed a declaration to receive a widow's pension. It can only be assumed that at the time both her and Albert were staying with relatives as instead of 6 Mount Pleasant Cottages she gave her address as 144 Upper North Street Poplar.

* * *

After meticulous planning 2nd Army resumed the Flanders offensive on 20th September with a third phase of action that lasted five days and became known as 'The Battle of the Menin Road Ridge'. Compared to the previous actions of Third Ypres this battle was an overwhelming success for the British on those sections of front previously dogged with failure. With divisions of Gough's 5th Army providing a supporting role to the north ground was gained along the southern end of the front facing the Gheluvelt Plateau and the ridges beyond. At 5:40am six divisions of 2nd Army - supported by a creeping barrage laid down by the Royal Artillery - advanced on German positions along a frontline stretching from the Ypres-Lille railway line - east of Battle Wood north of Hollebeke - to positions astride the Menin Road. The artillery support saw that just over half hour after zero most divisional first objectives were reached and captured. As the ground gained was consolidated further units pushed on and by noon most of the days planned objectives were taken, amongst others these included the bitterly fought over position of Inverness Copse. North of the Menin Road two Australian divisions from the 1st Anzac Corps (attached to 2nd Army) were instrumental in capturing not only Glencorse Wood but another enemy strong point, a wooded area known as Nonne Bosschen, by the end of the day they found themselves on the western edge of Polygon Wood. That afternoon and over the days that followed whilst consolidation continued enemy counter attacks were successfully dealt with by a well prepared 2nd Army; as a result the Germans suffered heavy losses. Once again Plumer had demonstrated that thought and planning was the key to success; as a result not only was ground gained with a minimal amount of casualties but British moral was given a much needed boost. Luckily for the British the weather remained dry for the rest of the month, it was just as well as their fourth phase of action occurred on 26th September; it officially lasted for seven days and was known as 'The Battle of Polygon Wood'. Again realistic objectives were fought for and wrestled from the enemy by well prepared troops covered by well thought out and directed artillery fire. That day although hampered by stiff resistance south of the Menin Road enemy positions – west of Gheluvelt - around an area known as Tower Hamlets were captured, further north yet again Australian divisions excelled by taking Polygon Wood and units of Gough's 5th Army captured Zonnebeke. The Germans could not believe that the tide of success was turning against them, as counter attacks were launched again British artillery and machine gun fire saw they were broken up. Over the following days as the British consolidated their gains and worn out divisions were replaced by fresh ones more enemy counter attacks were attempted, the worst of these occurred on 1st October and although some ground was lost it was minimal. The next day it started raining again which saw conditions on the battlefield take a turn for the worst, the fifth phase of British action came on 4th October and was known as 'The Battle of Broodseinde'.

WILLIAM ALBERT KERRY

William Albert Kerry was born at Leyton in East London sometime during 1885. His father Lorenzo worked as a foreman in a factory making cardboard whilst his mother Susan looked after the family and home. William had an older sister called Lillian as well as an older brother called Harry, after William was born his parents had two further children, a son called Edward and a daughter called Agnes. At the turn of the century the Kerry family were living at 16 Farmers Road in Leyton, after leaving school William worked as a boot maker's apprentice. Prior to the outbreak of war we know William married however unfortunately we don't know his wife's name, its also unknown if the couple had children. By 1914 William and his wife had moved to Grange Hill occupying a small house in Oak Terrace, when war was declared William decided to leave his job and join the army. William enlisted at a recruiting office in Hackney and after successfully passing a medical was given army service number 4105, he was then posted to the (City of London Regiment) Royal Fusiliers.

The (City of London Regiment) Royal Fusiliers was an entirely separate formation and should not be confused with the London Regiment which was purely territorial but whose first four battalions (as well as their second lines) were also known as Royal Fusiliers. The various battalions – and there were many - that made up the (City of London Regiment) Royal Fusiliers consisted entirely of regular, reserve, and (after Lord Kitchener's call for volunteers) service battalions, in addition Labour battalions were also created (33). As has been explained in the chapter entitled '1914' some battalions of the London Regiment were given name or area affiliations, this was also the case with some battalions of the (City of London Regiment) Royal Fusiliers. Two examples of this were the 22nd Battalion which was raised in Kensington and was known as the Kensington Battalion and the 26th Battalion which was raised from bank staff and was known as the Bankers Battalion. Although its title suggests it was purely a London based regiment throughout the war the (City of London Regiment) Royal Fusiliers cast its net in areas right across the south of England in order to recruit men into its battalions.

Soon after volunteering Pte William Albert Kerry found himself posted to the 13th (Service) Battalion Royal Fusiliers, this unit was formed at Hounslow in West London during September 1914 as part of K3 and began training at various camps on the south coast soon after. The battalion initially was attached to 24th Division however instead of forming part of an infantry brigade it found itself assigned as one of three battalions detailed to serve as Divisional Troops. All army divisions kept several battalions to act as Divisional Troops, they took their orders direct from divisional HQ and their role quite simply was to help the division operate efficiently. Their duties included amongst other things the loading and unloading of supplies as well as providing men for guard duties etc, they were also expected to lend assistance to other units within the division as and when it was required. Pte William Kerry and his battalion moved with the rest of 24th Division to Worthing during December 1914, in March 1915 however the 13th Royal Fusiliers were transferred along with a number of other battalions that had served as Divisional Troops in other divisions to an infantry brigade within the 44th Division. At the time this division was stationed at Ludgershall on Salisbury Plain however two months later it was renumbered the 37th Division; it consisted of the 110th Brigade, 111th Brigade and the 112th Brigade. The 13th (Service) Battalion, the Royal Fusiliers was attached to 111th Brigade along with the 10th (Service) Battalion, the Royal Fusiliers, 13th (Service) Battalion, the Kings Royal Rifle Corps and the 13th (Service) Battalion, the Rifle Brigade. The 37th Division was sent to France towards the end of July 1915 and over the next year it held positions on various sectors up and down the frontline. On 1st July 1916 the division found itself on the Somme taking part in 3rd Army's diversionary attack at Gommecourt, several months later it went on to participate in the Battle of the Ancre. Soon after the Somme battles started 37th Division saw its 110th Brigade transferred to the 21st Division and replaced in a straight swap by 63rd Brigade (34). During the spring of 1917 the 37th Division took part in the Battle of Arras and soon after was moved northwards to participate in the Flanders offensive. Having played various parts in both the third and fourth phases of Third Ypres by the start of October the division was once again ready for action.

As October began the 13th Royal Fusiliers commanded by Lieutenant Colonel R A Smith MC found themselves in support positions around Bodmin Copse and Dumbarton Lakes to the south of the Menin Road about two miles west of Gheluvelt. Instead of being lettered 'A' to 'D' or 'W' to 'Z' the infantry companies of the 13th Royal Fusiliers were numbered from 1 to 4. Pte William Kerry found himself attached to No.1 Coy as part of its signalling section. Not only during a battle but also when holding the line unsurprisingly the job of the signaller was an extremely important one. We have seen in the story of L/Cpl George Belcher just what can happen when messages were not passed on quickly enough or communications were allowed to break down. As part of a signal section it would have been William's job to help relay messages to battalion HQ regarding his company's position, depending on the situation this could be done in a number ways including by telephone, the firing of flares, flag waving, by runners or even by carrier pigeon. Whilst in support the 13th Royal Fusiliers found itself providing men for work parties however on the last day of September No.2 Coy had been sent forward to help fend off a German counter attack near the frontline and as a result the company now found itself under strength. In spite of this the following day orders were received that on the morning of 4th October the battalion, along with the rest of 37th Division, would provide a supporting role in the next phase of British action.

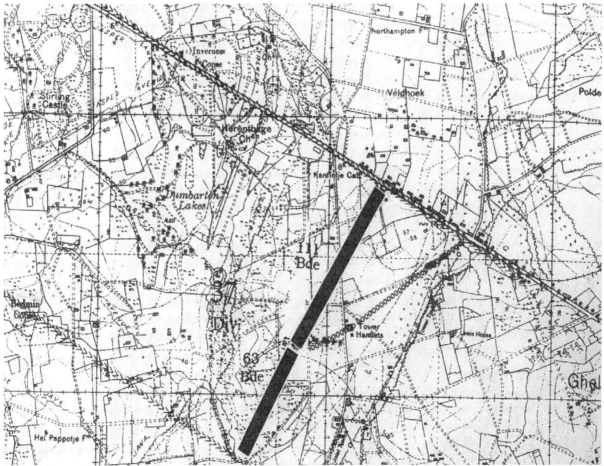

Map 38, The position of 37th Division on 4th October 1917

The Battle of Broodseinde was to be carried out on an eight mile front by a total of twelve divisions; eight were British three were Australian and one was from New Zealand. The proposed attack front stretched from positions northeast of Langemarck southwards to a point just east of Polygon Wood, from here the front swung round southwards crossing the Menin Road to a point just west of Tower Hamlets. The action was unique as for once there was to be no preliminary barrage prior to zero. As the British prepared to advance their creeping barrage started and caught the enemy completely by surprise. On that morning the Germans were also preparing to attack in an attempt to regain lost ground, troops positioned in forward trenches and behind the lines found they were subjected to terrible shellfire as the Royal Artillery covered the British assault; as a result the Germans suffered huge casualties. At 6:00am the British attacked and in pouring rain - that was worse than ever – the troops advanced towards the enemy lines, despite the awful conditions it was to be another successful day. In the north both the 29th Division and 4th Division (XIV Corps, 5th Army) managed to maintain a successful defensive flank northeast of Langemarck as further south divisions of 2nd Army took the fight to the enemy. Assisted by ten tanks those brigades attached to 11th Division managed to enter the village of Poelcapelle and after successfully fending off enemy counter attacks they stayed there. In the area east of Zonnebeke the Anzac divisions managed to move up the Broodseinde Ridge to penetrate deep into the German defences of Flandern 1 and at last it seemed as if the enemy was about to crumble however, as bad as things were, this was not yet the case. In the centre of the attack front the British line was successfully extended eastward to secure the high ground beyond Polygon Wood down towards the Menin Road. South of the road on the extreme right of the attack front the 37th Division, commanded by Major General H Bruce-Williams, found itself to the right of 5th Division in positions west of Tower Hamlets, 111th Brigade held the left flank, 63rd Brigade held the right flank whilst the 112th Brigade were in support.

Pte William Kerry and the 13th Royal Fusiliers moved up towards the frontline from their support positions in Bodmin Copse and Dumbarton Lakes about 11:00pm on the night of 3rd October, the journey was made in pouring rain and extreme darkness saw some groups lose their way however eventually the battalion found its intended positions. Over the next few hours the 13th Royal Fusiliers relieved men of the 13th Rifle Brigade in areas north of Tower Hamlets and south of the Menin Road, according to their battalion war diary the relief was completed at 5:15am only 45 minutes before zero. To the left of the battalion - north of the Menin Road - stood the 1st Royal West Kent Regiment (13th Brigade, 5th Division) whilst to the right stood two machine guns of the 111th MGC and the 13th KRRC, in support stood the 10th Royal Fusiliers. After various discussions between battalion and company commanders it had been decided that No.1 and No.3 Coy would lead the 13th Royal Fusiliers assault with No.4 Coy in support, No.2 Coy following its recent exploits would be divided amongst the leading two companies whilst in reserve would be one company of the 13th Rifle Brigade. Pte William Kerry's company consisted of 3 officers and 78 other ranks, the total strength of the 13th Royal Fusiliers numbered 13 officers and 233 other ranks. The battalion was to attack in four waves on a frontage of one platoon with a gap of 15 yards left between each wave. No. 1 Coy on the left flank would make up the first and second wave whilst No. 3 Coy on the right made up waves three and four. Battalion objectives were to provide a defensive flank for 5th Division and the capture of several concrete block houses and strong points which lay strung out in Gheluvelt Wood - situated northwest of Gheluvelt itself. The 13th KRRC on the right however had a much tougher task. Their objective was to raid and capture an enemy strongpoint known as Lewis House, this position was heavily defended and the key to 37th Division's attack, failure to take it would certainly upset the apple cart.

At 5:30am as Pte William Kerry and his battalion waited to go over the top they found themselves subjected to hostile shellfire as enemy gunners laid down a preliminary barrage ahead of the proposed German attack. Most of these shells however fell north of the Menin Road and luckily for the leading companies of the 13th Royal Fusiliers they escaped relatively unscathed. As the rain poured down at 6:00am the whistles blew and the first wave of No.1 Coy, led by a Second Lieutenant Allen, fixed bayonets and advanced to the assault. The creeping barrage laid down by the Royal Artillery assisted the men as they crossed the ploughed up battlefield although it wasn't long before they ran into difficulty. Heavy machine gun and rifle fire from the dug outs and blockhouses in Gheluvelt Wood hampered their advance and fire from Lewis House also caused problems. The second wave of No.1 Coy led by 19 year old Second Lieutenant Eric Holdcroft tried to mop up positions left by the first wave but also ran into problems. Whilst leading his men Holdcroft was killed and very few of those not wounded managed to move forward effectively, Second Lieutenant Allen eventually rallied men from both waves and dug in under fire. Pinned down and wounded Allen, along with his men, had no choice but to remain where he was for the rest of the day. Due to the weather and conditions on the ground it was very difficult to get messages back to battalion HQ regarding the leading waves progress, a phone line was run out but broken within a few minutes and flares and flag waving was useless. The only way to communicate therefore was by using runners and unsurprisingly this was a hazardous task for those men concerned. This being the case every 200 yards a relay post was established which minimised the distance each man had to cover, as part of No.1 Coy's signalling section it is quite possible Pte William Kerry was employed as a runner and subsequently killed whilst relaying a message. Meanwhile No.3 Coy managed to advance under fire and established a line of posts to cover No.1 Coy; unfortunately they suffered quite heavily from British guns whose shells persistently fell short of their targets. Around the same time No. 4 Coy left their positions and moved up in support eventually occupying the starting positions vacated by the leading waves, the reserve company from the 13th Rifle Brigade then moved forward to fill their position. On the right the 13th KRRC advanced and briefly occupied Tower Trench but found it impossible to take Lewis House, shellfire and trench mortar rockets aimed at the target fell behind leaving the enemy in position there free to man their trenches. These troops were chiefly responsible for holding up 37th Division's attack as they also assisted the German units positioned in Gheluvelt Wood. Having successfully put up a defensive flank for 5th Division the 13th Royal Fusiliers initially had problems linking up with the 1st Royal West Kent's on the Menin Road, the latter were having problems of their own regarding their attack and it wasn't until nightfall that contact was suitably established. Throughout the day enemy shellfire continuously fell around Tower Hamlets where battalions of 63rd Brigade, having made some progress, were dealing with enemy counter attacks. Shelling occurred right along 37th Division's frontline as well its rear areas around Bodmin Copse and Dumbarton Lakes however although they'd gained some ground no enemy counter attacks were attempted on the 13th Royal Fusiliers front. Throughout the evening various units were moved forward in support of 111th Brigade however the 13th Royal Fusiliers received no real reinforcements until early the following morning. According to their war diary the 5th October passed without incident for the battalion as they consolidated their positions. The 13th Royal Fusiliers were eventually relieved later that evening and early next morning by men of the 8th East Lancashire Regiment (112th Brigade), luckily no further casualties were reported as the battalion, exhausted and few in number, evacuated their wounded and moved out of the line.

Over the days that followed the 13th Royal Fusiliers were congratulated by both their divisional and brigade commanders for the part they had played on 4th October. The exact number of casualties sustained by the battalion during the actual attack is quite confusing, many men were wounded and several were reported missing, but according to their war diary the number of men killed was 2 officers and 18 other ranks (35). Most of those killed including Pte William Albert Kerry have no known grave therefore their names appear on the Tyne Cot Memorial to the Missing. It is not known exactly what happened to Mrs Kerry after the war or when she first learnt that her husband had been killed however a small article reporting the incident appeared in the January 1918 edition of the Chigwell Parish Magazine. Pte William Kerry was entitled to the 1915 Star, the BWM and the VM. In

Central London at the junction of Holborn and Grays Inn Road stands the (City of London Regiment) Royal Fusiliers Memorial in commemoration of the 22,000 men of the regiment who fell in the Great War. Half a mile east of the memorial on the north side of Holborn Viaduct between Snow Hill and Giltspur Street stands the Royal Fusiliers Church and Remembrance Garden.

* * *

As the Battle of Broodseinde came to a close the situation within the Ypres Salient was truly appalling. Stuck in the mud were rotting corpses, dead horses and wagons, unexploded shells and abandoned guns also lay in amongst the splintered tree stumps and ruined buildings that once had been the woods and orchards and farms and houses of Belgium. The men as well as the wounded lay out in amongst the ditches and shell holes, as the rain continued the water levels rose and conditions simply became worse than they'd ever been. Just to bring up relief and supplies was near on impossible, the shortest of journeys took hours to complete as the men stumbled back and forwards along the shell torn wooden tracks between the rear areas and frontlines. As a result of the conditions and despite their recent successes both Plumer and Gough realised a tactical victory was nigh on impossible, whatever happened from here on in it was obvious the Flanders offensive would not provide the breakthrough that was hoped for. In the eyes of most people enough was enough; on the evening of 5th October a conference was held where both Plumer and Gough met with Haig to discuss their views on the situation. As always the CIC listened to his army commanders but once again - spurred on by incorrect intelligence reports regarding the state of the enemy - he decided to continue the offensive in a last ditch attempt at a breakthrough.

The sixth phase of the Flanders offensive began at 5:20am on 9th October and became known as the 'Battle of Poelcapelle'. Involved in the battle along an eight mile front were eight divisions of Plumer's 2nd Army, four British and four Anzac, at the north eastern edge of the salient Gough's 5th Army was to participate with five divisions. The Battle of Poelcapelle was doomed to failure right from the start; an important factor in this was the weather; it hadn't stopped raining since the Battle of Broodseinde on 4th October. Another factor was the preliminary barrage laid down by the Royal Artillery before the attack; it proved ineffective in destroying the German defences. The British guns were caked with mud having been pulled forward with great difficulty through appalling conditions. As the guns were fired they started to sink in the mud and as a result the chances they had of hitting their targets became very remote indeed (36). The troops themselves found moving forward just as tough and reaching their objectives proved an arduous task. Having suffered tremendous losses due to Plumer's tactics the Germans decided to strengthen their frontlines where before they were lightly protected, barbed wire was deployed in depth and machine gun posts were positioned to cover all approaches. At the southern end of 2nd Army's front - just north of the Menin Road – the troops of 5th Division attacked but virtually no lasting gains were made, northwest of the village of Becelaere however minimal ground was captured by troops of 7th Division. In positions east of Broodseinde the Australian Division managed to clear various strong points and dug outs however having suffered huge casualties by the time they reached their final objective further up Broodseinde Ridge they had no choice but to fall back. The 66th Division was attached to II Anzac Corps and was responsible for attacking directly up Passchendaele Ridge towards Passchendaele itself. Unfortunately their efforts were hampered by both shell and machine gun fire, some troops reached the outskirts of the village but those that were not killed or wounded were forced to fall back. On 2nd Army's northern boundary stood the 49th Division, its troops also struggled up the slopes of Passchendaele Ridge but for their trouble no real advance was made. On 5th Army's sector south of Poelcapelle British troops tried desperately to clear enemy positions in front of them but met with little success. In front of Poelcapelle itself the 11th Division did manage to clear various strong points only to be pushed backwards by counter attacks; they ended the day virtually were they began. The only real British success during the battle came on 5th Army's left flank where troops of the 4th Division, the 29th Division and the Guards Division managed to advance in areas northwest of Poelcapelle and north of Langemarck (37). Having captured enemy pillboxes and strong points these divisions then adopted defensive positions, as a result when enemy counter attacks materialised they were dealt with most effectively. With the outcome of the Poelcapelle action still debatable further attacks were made over the days that followed however it soon became clear that the game was up for Third Ypres, even Haig recognised this however he was determined to get to Passchendaele. The original idea of an amphibious landing on the Belgian Coast had been shelved a month or so previously and the thinking now was if no breakthrough could be achieved at least the top of Passchendaele Ridge would be a good place for the British Army to spend the winter. On 12th October the seventh phase of Third Ypres commenced with the action known as 'The First Battle of Passchendaele'. Yet again the wet weather and muddy conditions hampered any hopes of a decisive advance by British troops and with little ground gained it was almost as if the Battle of Poelcapelle was repeated. The Germans had once again switched their policy of a heavily manned frontline to one held primarily by machine guns and strong points, again masses of barbed wire also stood in the way. As allied troops tried to advance across the mud they found themselves easy targets for German gunners, enemy shells also rained down some of which contained Mustard Gas. Over the days that followed the weather remained miserable however Haig in his determination to reach Passchendaele ordered the Canadian Corps forward to capture the village. At this point however we must break briefly from events in Flanders and turn our attention southwards to cover the story of Chigwell's tenth casualty of 1917.

ERNEST HANDY HERRING

Ernest Herring was a well known figure around Chigwell and Woodford Bridge as his parents owned the Three Jolly Wheelers Public House, a business that still exists today. Situated at the Woodford Bridge end of Chigwell Road the original pub building was built during the first half of the eighteenth century, as well as being publicans Ernest's parents Edward and Mary Herring also ran a wagon repair business from the premises. Ernest was born in Woodford Bridge in 1893 and was the third youngest of ten children; having such a large family Edward and Mary worked hard to raise their children and run their business. In all they had five daughters and five sons and at one time or another they all helped out with the business, despite the pressures of day to day life the Herrings always found time to laugh and joke with their customers and were known locally for being jolly hence the pub name. Like his brothers and sisters Ernest was educated locally and on leaving school worked at the Wheelers, eventually however he met and married a local girl called Mabel. Shortly before the war the couple moved to Maybank Cottage on Maybank Road in South Woodford, around the same time Mabel gave birth to a baby boy. Despite his family commitments when war was declared Ernest seized the chance to do his bit for king and country, in October 1914, having virtually wasted no time at all, he joined Kitchener's 'New Army'. Ernest enlisted at a recruiting office at Stratford in East London and having successfully passed a medical was posted to the ranks of the Royal Field Artillery. This was a suitable posting for Ernest, although he held the rank of gunner, in this unit his experience in wagon repair would no doubt come in handy, after all that was his middle name.

The Royal Field Artillery as a unit is quite a complicated arrangement and as this book is not the place to explore it in depth a brief summary of its make up and purpose follows. Chiefly responsible for the lighter guns the men of the RFA operated primarily close to the frontline, it was their job to destroy enemy defences and pave the way prior to assaults by the infantry (38). The RFA was attached to the Infantry Division and was split into brigades. Known as Artillery Brigades it must be stressed these were totally different from Infantry Brigades. Each division contained three numbered Artillery Brigades and to avoid confusion they were not only numbered but also used roman numerals to define themselves (e.g. 21st Brigade RFA or XXI Brigade RFA). Each Artillery Brigade had its own HQ and was split into three or four smaller units known as a 'Battery'. Containing in the region of four to six guns these Battery's, like Infantry Companies, were usually lettered 'A', 'B', 'C' and 'D' however it should be pointed out that in some cases they were numbered. Each Battery generally consisted of a Major in charge of several officers commanding approximately two hundred men. During the first two years of the war all Artillery Brigades had an Ammunition Column attached whose job it was to bring up shells and supplies to each Battery, shortly before the 1916 Somme offensive however these units were replaced by Divisional Ammunition Columns who then took care of this role.

Unfortunately Ernest Herring's army service record has not survived therefore tracing his movements during the early part of the war is quite difficult. Although we don't know with which unit he initially served Ernest first went to France on 18th September 1915, he remained there for five months before being sent to Salonika (now Thessalonika) in northern Greece. During the First World War Greece was split in its support for both sides of the warring factions, whilst the Greek Prime Minister supported allied actions King Constantine's sympathies were pro German. In October 1915 allied troops landed at Salonika initially to look after Greek interests in the area and to provide the Serbs with support against Austrian and Bulgarian attacks. On their arrival however the allies found the Serbs already beaten and the enemy occupying the heights to their north, if this was not enough soon after the Greek Prime Minister was dismissed and King Constantine declared his country neutral (39). Despite these events the Gallipoli campaign was in progress therefore it was decided that allied troops should remain at Salonika to protect shipping in the area. As the allies dug in over the next two years various actions occurred, in 1917 King Constantine abdicated and the Greek Prime Minister was reinstalled, as a result Greece re-entered the war on the allied side. Over the following year further battles were fought in the areas north of the city however the allies remained at Salonika right up until the Bulgarians surrendered in late September early October 1918. Day to day life for the troops at Salonika was extremely tough and just like at Gallipoli the conditions the men endured saw that death and disease inevitably played its part. Gunner Ernest Herring was not immune to such conditions and having served just under a year in Greece he found himself invalided back to England suffering from both malaria and dysentery. Having been treated in hospital Ernest eventually made a full recovery; given the all clear for active service in May 1917 aged just 24 he was sent once again to the Western Front.

On arrival Ernest found himself posted to 'D' Battery, 70th Brigade RFA; this unit was attached to the 15th (Scottish) Division in positions around Arras. Soon after Ernest arrived his division moved north to the Ypres Salient in readiness for the Flanders offensive. At the end of July it took part in the Battle of Pilckem Ridge and two weeks later participated in the Battle of Langemarck however by September the unit moved southwards once again to take up positions east of Arras. As October started the 70th Brigade RFA under the command of Lieutenant Colonel G B Daubeny DSO found itself behind the frontlines in positions around Athies, a village situated on the north bank of the River Scarpe. During this period with events being played out in Flanders the lines around Arras were relatively quiet however artillery units were called on daily to carry out a general bombardment of enemy positions. This being the case the first week of October saw Gunner Ernest Herring and the 70th Brigade RFA employed in such tasks as shelling enemy machine gun emplacements and strong points. At night they were also expected to prevent the enemy from operating in no mans land and improving or digging new trenches, all German troop movements such as the carrying out of relief's or the bringing up of supplies were also to be disrupted. On the night of the 7th October the infantry of the 45th Brigade (15th Division) carried out a raid on German positions near the village of Plouvain and 70th Brigade RFA were called on to assist, the following few days however were uneventful for Ernest Herring's unit. When not in action the men would generally be kept busy maintaining the guns as well as cleaning all gun pits and dugouts, under normal circumstances a Battery officer was required to check the guns in his section twice a day. Inspection took place once in the morning and once in the evening, it was imperative that all weapons were not only kept clean but inspected close up for signs of damage as that would undoubtedly affect their performance. On the 11th October it was noted that German units opposite 15th Division were constructing new trenches and 70th Brigade RFA were ordered to engage, 'D' Battery was given the task of carrying out the bombardment which it did effectively. During the course of the next week 70th Brigade RFA continued to make its presence felt shelling German positions daily, raids carried out by neighbouring divisions were covered and enemy tracks and strong points were constantly targeted.

I'm sure the reader will agree that up until this point the story of Gunner Ernest Herring has been quite interesting however it ends somewhat confusingly leaving several important questions unanswered. Around the second to third week of October Ernest was wounded in some way, the war diary of 70th Brigade RFA records no such incident to explain how this happened and leaves no clues to lead us in some sort of direction. Being positioned behind the frontlines its extremely unlikely Ernest received bullet wounds therefore its reasonable to suggest he was injured by either enemy or friendly shellfire. German gunners aided by observation aircraft would constantly try to silence British guns and were chiefly responsible for the large number of casualties sustained by the men of the RFA during the course of the war, on the other hand however it was not unusual for British guns to misfire and cause serious harm to those men operating them. It would appear that Ernest was initially taken to a CCS where his wounds were assessed before being transferred one would suppose to hospital; at this point yet again confusion surrounds his movements but one thing remains certain, on the 20th October 1917 he died of wounds. The main problem I have with Ernest's story is where exactly was he when he died as his place of burial just doesn't make sense. Gunner Ernest Herring is buried northwest of Ypres at Solferino Farm CWGC Cemetery; he is the only man from his unit buried there. Most soldiers killed in action were buried close to where they served however with those that died of wounds they were buried far and wide depending on where they were sent whilst wounded, what I find strange however is why would a wounded man be sent from a relatively quiet sector towards an area were heavy fighting was taking place. Several explanations present themselves and the main one has to be did Ernest ever serve with 70th Brigade RFA or was he part of another unit, the original records of the CWGC show no mistakes so we have to believe that he did. This being the case was he wounded back in August when 15th Division was in the Ypres Salient, this is possible but during the two month period since then he would surely have been sent back to England to recover or at least to a hospital away from the fighting. The most probable explanation is that he was wounded whilst serving with 70th Brigade RFA in positions east of Arras and was being transferred by ambulance to a hospital near the coast, on the way however he died of wounds and was buried in due course near Ypres. Although this explanation does appear to be the most logical I still find it frustrating that we'll never really know what actually happened. On Friday 16th November 1917 an article appeared in the Woodford Times reporting that Ernest had been killed in France, it stated he left behind a widow and young son and went on to say his parents thanked all those people who had sent messages of sympathy on hearing the news of their loss. The December 1917 edition of the Chigwell Parish Magazine also carried the story, it remarked that Ernest was a loyal soldier who had done his duty and in doing so had made the supreme sacrifice. Almost a year later another article appeared in the Woodford Times placed there by Ernest's parents, brothers and sisters.

HERRING - *In Loving Memory of our dear son, Gunner Ernest Handy Herring who was killed in action October 20th 1917, third son of Mr and Mrs Herring, The Three Jolly Wheelers, Woodford Bridge.*

"One year has passed since that sad day
When one we loved was called away
A son so true a brother brave
Lies buried in a soldier's grave".

From his sorrowing parents, brothers and sisters.

Ernest had two brothers called Edward and George who also served as soldiers in the Great War; although we don't know to which units they belonged it appears they both survived the conflict. Ernest's mother died in March 1932 aged 73 whilst his father died in June 1935 aged 80; both are buried in the graveyard of All Saints Church at Chigwell Row along with two of their daughters (40). Nothing is known of what happened to Mabel and her son after the war although it's possible she remarried. On the west side of Hyde Park Corner in Central London stands a memorial dedicated to the 49,076 officers and men of the Royal Artillery who died in the Great War, the memorial was designed by architect Lionel Pearson and sculpted by Charles Sargeant Jagger, it was unveiled in 1925.

* * *

With the fate of Third Ypres already sealed but with British troops in position for a final push on Passchendaele village the last phase of the Flanders Offensive began on 26th October. This action became known as the 'Second Battle of Passchendaele' and lasted for just over two weeks. On the first day in those areas north and south of the Menin Road little if any advance was made, further north however the men of the Canadian Corps managed under extreme conditions to inch ever closer up the ridge to Passchendaele. At the northern end of the front as always units of 5th Army managed to gain ground whilst supporting the main advance. Over the days that followed tired divisions were replaced by fresh ones as further attempts to reach the village were made. By this time with no hope of attacks in Flanders providing any decisive victory Lloyd George had lost interest in events on the Western Front. The Prime Minister it should be remembered favoured sending troops to Italy; it was around this time that he did so following the Italian defeat at Caporetto. Much to his annoyance Haig was ordered to send five divisions from the Western Front to Italy, as if this was not enough he also lost Plumer who was sent out to command them (41). On 6th November another push for Passchendaele was made and at last men of the Canadian Corps entered the village, over the next few days all ground gained was consolidated. The Third Battle of Ypres finally came to an end on 10th November with both sides having lost in the region of 260,000 men either killed, wounded or missing; it was on this day that Chigwell suffered its last casualty of 1917.

JOHN ARTHUR WITHAM

In most cases we know a little regarding the backgrounds of the men covered in this book however with the story of John Witham although this is also the case concrete evidence has been hard to come by. This said after a fair amount of research I have pieced together the story I believe to be the truth; any inaccuracies in John's story are the fault of me as the author. John Arthur Witham was born John Arthur Judd on the 15th July 1897, nothing is known of his biological father however his mother, Florence Amelia Judd, was born at Ongar in 1876. Nothing is known of John's early life; on the 1901 census it appears he may have attended boarding school at Brentwood in Essex. Florence worked as a dressmaker and during the early 1900's met a young farmer from Woodford Bridge called George but commonly referred to as James Witham. On 2nd June 1906 James and Florence were married at St Paul's Church, Woodford Bridge, as his wife's son James adopted John and brought him up as his own. The Witham's lived in a small house at 2 Smeaton Road and in September 1906 James and Florence had their first child together, a son they called George. Over the next few years James and Florence had four further children, two boys and two girls. Meanwhile as the eldest child John continued his education locally before finding work, shortly before the outbreak of war he left home and moved to Westcliff-on-Sea in Essex, unfortunately his profession around this time is unknown. The next part of the story is pretty vague but John most likely attested under the terms of the Derby Scheme during late 1915 or early 1916. According to SDGW John enlisted at a recruiting office in Colchester, after successfully passing a medical it seems he was then posted to the 3rd (Reserve) Battalion Essex Regiment based at Felixstowe. Unfortunately John's army service record no longer exists making his movements mainly guess work however his father James also joined the army around the same time; his service record has survived.

James Witham enlisted, probably at Warley, under the terms of the Derby Scheme on 2nd December 1915 aged 36; he was 5ft 7˝ tall. Like his son James was initially posted to the 3rd Essex at Felixstowe; he remained there for just over six months before being posted to the 12th (Reserve) Battalion Essex Regiment based a few miles away at Harwich. Soon after James received treatment at a military hospital in Dovercourt for reasons unknown, he rejoined his battalion at the beginning of September 1916. Six weeks later on 12th October James, on the authority of the War Office, was transferred to the Norfolk Regiment and drafted for service overseas, he crossed the Channel to France arriving at Etaples on 18th October. James found himself posted as a replacement to the 1st Norfolk's; this battalion was badly in need of reinforcements having played its part in the Somme battles. The 1st Norfolk's formed part of 15th Brigade, 5th Division; James was to serve with them for the next two years. Although two divisions had been despatched the previous month in December 1917 the 5th Division (along with the 7th Division and 48th Division) was sent to Italy; the unit stayed there for four months before returning to France in April 1918. Shortly before the end of the war and after another brief period in hospital - this time for headaches and pains - James left the 1st Norfolk's and transferred to the Labour Corps, he survived the war and was demobilised on 27th March 1919.

Although the exact dates are unknown Pte John Witham eventually finished training and was drafted for service overseas. He was sent to the Western Front where he joined the 10th Battalion Essex Regiment. This New Army battalion was attached to the 18th (Eastern) Division as part of 53rd Brigade (42) along with the 8th (Service) Battalion Norfolk Regiment, 8th (Service) Battalion Suffolk Regiment and the 6th (Service) Battalion Royal Berkshire Regiment. The 10th Essex had arrived in France in July 1915 along with the rest of 18th Division, the following year the battalion took part in the Battle of the Somme and in May 1917 served at the Battle of Arras, a few months later the unit moved northwards to participate in the early phases of Third Ypres. That October the 18th Division found itself holding the British lines just east of Poelcapelle and on 22nd October its 53rd Brigade was in action. That morning the 8th Norfolk's attacked and captured an enemy position northeast of Poelcapelle known as the Brewery, a short time later the 10th Essex passed through the Norfolk's and took three strong points known as Nobles Farm, Meunier House and Tracas Farm. During the afternoon German troops attempted a counter attack but were driven off by Lewis Gun fire, the day was an overwhelming success for the Essex men although casualties were quite heavy (43). Having had a rough time of things the 10th Essex needed to rest and refit and on 31st October, having been relieved by men of the 11th Royal Fusiliers (54th Brigade), they moved to Poll Hill Camp near Houtkerque on the border between Belgium and France. At this time the battalion, under the command of Lieutenant Colonel C W Frizell DSO MC, had a fighting strength of just 22 officers and 685 other ranks. Around this time as various units were being sent to Italy the men of the 10th Essex hoped they might strike lucky and wave goodbye to the Ypres Salient, unfortunately however it wasn't to be. After several days spent resting and training on 4th November Pte John Witham and the 10th Essex left Poll Hill Camp and moved into brigade support at Coldstream Camp arriving there around 8:00pm. Situated on an open hillside north of Boezinge Coldstream Camp consisted mainly of Nissen Huts and tents, being quite close to the frontline the site provided little protection from enemy shellfire. Having spent the 5th November improving the camp that evening hostile shelling became a problem but the 10th Essex continued their duties, at the same time officers from the battalion were sent out to reconnoitre the forward areas ahead of a move back up the line. The following morning as work continued things got so bad at Coldstream Camp that the battalion was forced to evacuate, by 5:00pm that evening the 10th Essex had two companies as well as its HQ in position at Baboon Camp on the banks of the Ypres Canal west of Pilckem. Around this time the battalion CO went on leave having served at the front in one form or another almost continuously since the war started, his place was temporarily filled by Major T M Banks (44). Orders had been received to take up positions at the southern edge of the Houthulst Forest north of Poelcapelle, both 'A' Coy and 'D' Coy had moved off ahead of the others to establish support positions near both the Steenbeek and Broembeek Canals. Unfortunately without the help of his service record it has not proved possible to determine which company Pte John Witham served with.

The sector of front in and around the Houthulst Forest was truly unpleasant and no one unfortunate enough to serve there had a good word to say about the place. The area was basically a muddy swamp strung out in the middle of nowhere and miles from help should it be needed, small streams brought on by incessant rainfall covered the region as splintered tree stumps littered the ground, mustard gas filled shell holes and rotting corpses also provided an additional feature. The only way to enter the area was at night along a series duckboard tracks that were smashed and broken every few yards, carrying supplies and munitions in pitch darkness under shellfire meant that men moving up to the line had a really tough time. It was not uncommon to lose your way, as you stepped from one track to the next you could find yourself literally going round in circles, the sheer patience and endurance needed to reach the frontline was a battle in itself and tested the toughest of men.

Map 39, The position of the 10th Essex (November 1917)

As expected no trenches could exist here, yet again the forward line consisted of fortified shell holes with raised breastworks protected by minimal barbed wire. Although under constant shellfire captured enemy pill boxes, feet deep in water and filled with rotting corpses, served as battalion and company HQ's, this was pure luxury compared to the shell holes where the men had no warmth, no shelter, nowhere dry to sit or lie and couldn't move by day for fear of being shot at. As always the Germans held the high ground to the east only sending down an outpost line at night to guard against attack, any movement in the British line was answered swiftly by both machine gun and rifle fire. Due to the nature of the ground in this sector it proved virtually impossible to mount serious attacks, small scale raids were carried out however night time patrols into no mans land were frequently undertaken to determine the strength and identity of the enemy.

Early on 7th November the remaining companies of the 10th Essex left Baboon Camp and made for the Houthulst Forest where the entire battalion had orders to relieve the 6th Royal Berkshires. A distance of six miles separated the Ypres Canal from the edge of the Forest and the battalion moved along three lines of track known as Clarges Street, Hunter Street and Railway Street completing the last few miles only once it got dark. After an unpleasant and tiring journey the 10th Essex reached Louvois Farm where they met guides who led them the remaining distance towards the frontline. The relief was reported complete by 8:30pm and company HQ's were established at Panama House, Colombo House and les 5 Chemins whilst battalion HQ was established at Ajax House. To the left of the Essex stood French troops whilst to their right stood the 8th Norfolk's who themselves had just relieved men of the 8th Suffolk's. In front of the battalions on the other side of no mans land stood the enemy who held such positions as Renard Farm and Marechal Farm. That night the 10th Essex worked on improving their positions and no doubt Pte John Witham was employed in this task, communications were also worked on and the first of several patrols, led by two junior officers, ventured out into no man's land. As nothing could happen during the hours of daylight the following morning and afternoon were uneventful for the Essex men and many rested as best they could, only as darkness descended on the Houthulst Forest did once again the frontline become a hive of activity. The 10th Essex continued to improve their positions and whilst carrying out work on forward observation and listening posts the battalion was assisted by men of the 79th Field Coy RE (45). Night time patrols into no man's land continued and supplies, chiefly food and munitions, were brought up to the frontline from the rear areas. It would appear that at this time Pte John Witham was one of several men given the ominous task of occupying an isolated post in the region of Owls Wood, it was difficult to supply those men in advanced positions and at times they had no choice but to look after themselves. The next day passed without incident for the 10th Essex except for the odd enemy shell that came their way, that evening however things turned out to be quite different. During the night of the 9th/10th November the acting CO - Major Banks - accompanied by a runner felt it his duty to venture out and inspect the various posts dotted along the Essex front including those situated in Owls Wood. Having by all accounts found everything to be quite satisfactory he turned and headed back towards battalion HQ but merely ten minutes later a series of explosions occurred that signalled an enemy raid was in progress. It was not just the British who patrolled no man's land, German troops also felt it their duty to raid enemy positions and on this occasion two separate posts were attacked by a combined force of about 20 men. Unfortunately details are sketchy as to exactly what happened however it appears that the 10th Essex lost four men that night with 20 year old Pte John Witham being one of those killed. No sooner had the Germans attacked they withdrew leaving the Essex stunned by what had happened, later that night in order to make sure no further raids were attempted Major Banks ordered an advance of 200 yards on a frontage 500 yards long which it appears was carried out without incident. The following morning the 10th Essex remained in position and that night were relieved by men of the 11th Royal Fusiliers, the battalion moved back to De Wippe Camp near Boezinge for a brief spot of rest and recuperation. Towards the end of November the 10th Essex once again served a spell in the frontline but early December saw them turn their backs on the Houthulst Forest for the last time, they spent Christmas behind the lines and were moved south towards the Somme early in the New Year.

Several sources have been used to piece together the story of Pte John Witham and the 10th Essex but all contradict themselves as regards to the date that the enemy raid occurred. The most reliable source of information has to be the battalion war diary, written at the time this states the German's attacked on the night of the 9th/10th November. The Essex Regiment (10th Battalion) by J W Burrows was written in 1935 and refers to the incident but states the raid occurred on the night of the 8th/9th November, in order to compile this book the battalion war diary would have to of been consulted therefore I believe somewhere along the line the wrong date has been used. Another source of information used is the book entitled 'With the 10th Essex in France'. Written in 1924, by the then Lieutenant Colonel T M Banks as co author, the book states that the raid took place on the 8th November, of course as the writer was actually there it's hard to dispute this claim. Both the CWGC and SDGW state that the casualties sustained by the 10th Essex occurred on 10th November and give no figures for the previous two days; this said however the amount of men that were actually killed is contradicted by all sources.

Like many of those killed during 1917 Pte John Arthur Witham has no known grave, he is commemorated on Panels 98 to 99 of the Tyne Cot Memorial to the Missing. It did not take long for the War Office telegram reporting John's death to reach his family back in England and soon after a small article appeared in the December 1917 edition of the Chigwell Parish Magazine:

Mrs Witham of 2 Smeaton Road whose husband is with the forces in Salonika (46) has just received sad news of the death of her son, 10th Battalion Essex Regiment, killed in action France 10th November 1917.

Like many families who lost a loved one during the Great War a few years after the conflict John's parents received a memorial plaque as well as the medals their son was entitled to, James Witham received his own medals including the BWM and VM in March 1920. According to the records of the CWGC after the war the Witham family remained in Smeaton Road but lived at 31 Hawksworth Terrace.

* * *

Although the British had spent much of 1917 pouring their resources into the Flanders Offensive before the year was out they had one last trick up their sleeve; it was to take the Germans completely by surprise and almost provide the breakthrough the allies had longed for since the war began. Since its early beginnings those involved in the development of the Tank had envisioned that at some point a large scale attack could take place whereby hundreds of machines could be used to turn the tide against the enemy. As yet this was still to materialise and some people at GHQ were still sceptical that the Tank could be used as an effective weapon even though it had first been used with some success on the Somme in September 1916. At the beginning of the year those who commanded the Tank Corps had devised a plan to attack one of the strongest German positions on the whole of the Western Front, the Hindenburg Line defences in front of the French town of Cambrai. Their reasoning for this was that the ground in this area, much like the Somme, was hard and made up of rolling fields which made it ideal terrain for a Tank attack. The proposed area to be attacked stood on the sector controlled by 3rd Army therefore its commander Sir Julian Byng was approached by Tank Corps commanders with the idea (47). Initially the plan was to attack the German positions, score a quick victory by way of destroying his defences and then retire however Byng had other ideas. He favoured not only destroying the defences of the Hindenburg Line but also severely disrupting German communications by capturing Cambrai itself, in addition if successful he also had visions of an all out attempt at a breakthrough. The two parties took their plan to GHQ, after some consideration Haig and his staff officers decided that first being committed to supporting the French at Arras and then putting their efforts into an attack in Flanders was stretching their resources a little too far and the Cambrai idea was rejected. As Arras closed and the Flanders offensive stuck in the mud the Tank Corps and 3rd Army were quick to revive their plan. To most by now the possibility of an attack at Cambrai looked like a good alternative considering the poor show of events further north, even though Tanks had been used at Ypres the muddy conditions there saw they were ineffective with good men and machines lost for little gain. The Cambrai plan was once again looked at by staff at GHQ and finally during the middle of October it was given the green light with a date set for 20th November. As good as the Cambrai plan was its downfall was to lay with events further north. Even when it was clear the Flanders Offensive would not provide a decisive breakthrough its continuation meant that vital reserves were used up that would have been better served exploiting any success created by the Cambrai action. Although no men listed on the Chigwell Village War Memorial were killed in what became known as 'The Battle of Cambrai' undoubtedly men from Chigwell and its surrounding areas fought in the action (48). In terms of First World War battles events at Cambrai were quite important as the tactics used would go a long way to winning the war for the allies the following year, these events are briefly covered in the following two paragraphs.

As mentioned the ground in front of Cambrai was ideal for a large scale Tank attack, the battlefront was roughly six miles long and bounded by two canals. To the east stood the St Quentin Canal and to the west stood the newly constructed but unfinished dry banked Canal du Nord, both formed part of the German defences. The plan was to push up between these two boundaries capturing the various villages that lined the path to Cambrai. The area had two dominating features, they were a stretch of high ground known as the Flesquières–Havrincourt Ridge and further north the mass that was Bourlon Wood, both would have to be captured if success was to be achieved. The German defences in the area consisted of an outpost line situated some 1,000 yards in front of their main first line, beyond that lay support lines with their main second line positioned some two miles further back. The German trenches in front of Cambrai were quite wide making them virtually impossible for Tanks to cross unaided; the British however had devised a plan to overcome this problem. Each of the leading Tanks would carry large fascines made of Brushwood; these would be dropped into the German trenches allowing the forward Tanks to cross as well as creating a path for those Tanks that followed. There were to be 378 fighting Tanks in all dispersed along the whole front, in addition 1,000 guns would also be used employing a recently developed firing technique of surveying and mapping targets without first having to fire registering shots (49). The infantry units on the ground consisted of two corps of 3rd Army, once the tanks had cleared a path through the enemy wire and destroyed his machine gun posts it was their job to move up close behind and consolidate the ground gained as well as mop up those defenders still holding out. In addition to all the above units the Cavalry Corps was also made available to exploit any gaps that might appear in the German lines, thus creating a breakthrough. In order for everyone to know what was expected of him behind the lines prior to the battle a mock exercise was staged giving all involved a chance to prepare for the coming action. One problem however stood in the way, the commanders of 3rd Army were to throw all their resources into the opening action and they had no reserves!

The Germans defending the Hindenburg Line considered their position impregnable; as a result any action that came their way they figured would surely be signalled by a preliminary bombardment, this however was not the case. The mist had not settled at 6:20am on the morning of 20th November when hundreds of Tanks followed by infantry attacked the enemy positions in front of Cambrai, the Germans holding defences there were taken completely by surprise. On most of the front the British were successful in overrunning the enemy positions, guns and prisoners were captured as the attackers managed in some places a penetration of up to five miles deep. Most of the villages that stood on the path to Cambrai fell to the British. These included Havrincourt, Ribecourt, Marcoing and Flesquières however the latter had caused the division assigned to take it some problems, on the eastside of the St Quentin Canal the village of Masnières was also reached in the hope of securing a clear route to Cambrai. As night fell the British forces were on the point of a decisive breakthrough however both Tank crews and infantry were exhausted. Although large gaps existed in the German lines the bulk of the Cavalry Corps failed to exploit them whilst the infantry with virtually no reserves at hand found it difficult to continue the advance. Despite their strength over the days that followed the British made further gains, to the north both the villages of Moeuvres and Anneux were captured along with the all important position of Bourlon Wood. Prior to the battle being given the green light it was decided by GHQ that if events were not successful after 48 hours the action would be stopped, this however was unnecessary given the situation and on the evening of 21st November Haig gave permission for the battle to continue. As news filtered back to England of the successes at Cambrai for the first time since the start of the war church bells were rung in celebration; these celebrations however would turn out to be somewhat premature (50). The Germans now desperately aware of the seriousness of their situation began to rush troops to the front in order to plug the gaps in their line whilst the British, desperately in need of fresh troops, failed to capitalise on their gains. Over the week that followed many of the same troops that had attacked on the opening day of the battle were still in position, on the 30th November as was expected the Germans launched a counter attack to regain their losses. Specially trained battalions made up of the fittest and strongest men were brought in to penetrate deep into the British lines. These units were known as stormtrooper battalions, supported by new artillery techniques, it was their job to move forward dealing with strong points and key positions whilst regular units followed up behind and mopped up. Over the days that followed ground gained in the north was lost and in the south the British found themselves pushed backwards beyond their original start line. It had not taken long for success to turn to defeat and those in high command were quick to blame those below them for the turn of events. The Battle of Cambrai came to a close on the morning of 5th December; both sides had suffered in the region of 40,000 casualties. The action was important as it proved that given the right tactics the allies were capable of defeating their enemy as they would prove the following year. The simple reason for their failure to do so on this occasion it is widely agreed was the sheer lack of reserves available to secure the breakthrough once it was created.

As 1917 drew to a close events on the Eastern Front took a dramatic turn. Ever since Tsar Nicolas II had abdicated and a provisional government installed in his place the situation in Russia had been fragile however despite this the country had remained committed to the war. This all changed in late November when revolution erupted and the Bolsheviks seized power, that December an Armistice was sought which saw Russia withdraw from the war. This inevitably had a significant effect on the allied forces fighting in France and Flanders when the Germans, no longer threatened by Russia, began transferring large numbers of men and munitions from the east. Despite their efforts throughout the year both sides had failed to achieve the victory they'd hoped for and as a result the war on the Western Front was to continue into a fourth year. Those people who had been sure when the war started that it would be a long one were being proved right, one such person was Winston Churchill who after the failure of the Gallipoli Campaign was convinced that both sides were in for a long fight. An article had appeared in the Woodford Times back in April 1917 that quoted Churchill when asked for his feelings regarding allied intentions for the coming months; his reply was such: *'In any case it seems to me it would be very foolish not to make our preparations now for the campaign of 1918'*.

56, The memorial to the officers and men of the Machine Gun Corps on the north side of Hyde Park Corner in Central London

58, The Arras Memorial to the Missing

60, The gravestone of Pte Daniel James Trevett at Fins CWGC Cemetery Somme, France

57, The grave of an unknown soldier attached to the Machine Gun Corps

59, The name of Pte Harry Mark Brown as it appears on the Arras Memorial to the Missing

61, The gravestone of Pte George Pleasance at Bray CWGC Cemetery Somme, France

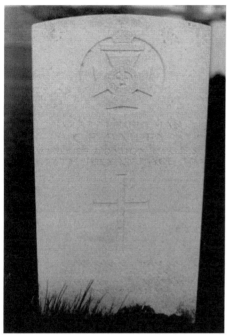

62, Pte Charles Ernest Bailey's gravestone at Oak Dump CWGC Cemetery, Ypres, Belgium

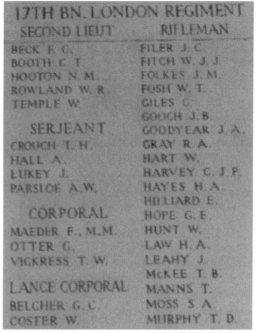

63, The name of L/Cpl George Charles Belcher as it appears on the Menin Gate Memorial to the Missing at Ypres

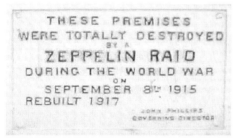

64, The plaque outside 59-61 Farringdon Road commemorating the Zeppelin Raid in September 1915

65, The name of Pte Frank Fogg as it appears on the Tyne Cot Memorial to the Missing

66, The Royal Artillery Memorial at Hyde Park Corner in Central London

67, Solferino Farm CWGC Cemetery Ypres, Belgium

69, The names of Pte Patrick Fitzgerald, Pte William Albert Kerry and Pte John Arthur Witham as they appear on the Tyne Cot Memorial to the Missing

70, The Third Battle of Ypres 1917. (Photograph courtesy of the Imperial War Museum. Ref E Aus 1220)

68, The gravestone of Gunner Ernest Handy Herring at Solferino Farm CWGC Cemetery

71, Muddy shell holes at Ypres (Photograph courtesy of the Imperial War Museum Ref CO 2241)

72, The Mud of Passchendaele 1917. (Photograph courtesy of the Imperial War Museum Ref CO 2246)

PALESTINE -
THE WAR IN THE MIDDLE EAST

For thousands of years the Middle East has found itself at the forefront of world events, its countries and cities are home to some of the mankind's oldest cultures and religions. Over the centuries the people of the region have successfully developed a vibrant trading ground that has provided the background for many stories, as the point where east meets west the area has never failed to capture the world's imagination. Despite all of this the Middle East has not been without its problems and remains even today one of the most disputed regions on the planet. As previously mentioned in the chapter on Gallipoli prior to the Great War much of the area that made up the Middle East was controlled by the Turkish Ottoman Empire and had been for some four hundred years. The Arab tribes that inhabited the region, and there were many, longed for a change in the way things were run however prior to the war they had stood alone, not only did they lack organisation but they lacked leadership, without these qualities gaining independence was impossible. As the First World War developed with the help of the allies the Arabs would not only unite but eventually rise up against the Turks, as a result before the war was over four centuries of Ottoman rule in the Middle East would be brought to an end. The term Palestine is widespread and used to cover allied operations - between the period 1914 to 1919 - in not only Palestine itself but a number of other places including the Sinai Peninsular, Arabia and what is now Jordan and Syria. As far as the fighting in the Middle East goes the other main theatre of war that saw allied action was Mesopotamia or Iraq as it is now called. As the war started its fair to say the allies never intended to occupy lands in the Middle East, they did however have plans for the region if and when Turkey was defeated. As far as Great Britain was concerned her main priority was the defence of two key points vital to her war effort and vital to the survival of the British Empire; the Suez Canal and the Persian oil fields. The latter was primarily the reason for British operations in Mesopotamia, these events will briefly be covered towards the end of this chapter; the former however is chiefly responsible for what would lead the British Army into Palestine.

The Suez Canal dates back thousands of years however its present form was constructed between 1859 and 1867 by Egyptian labourers under the guidance of a French engineer called Ferdinand de Lesseps. Situated between mainland Egypt and the Sinai Peninsular the canal is just over 100 miles long and via a series of lakes links the Mediterranean with the Red Sea, it provides a vital link between Europe and Asia alleviating the need to sail around the coast of Africa. In the days before air travel the route through the Suez Canal saved weeks off journey times between the two continents, eventually Great Britain acquired the canal and it became the lifeline of the British Empire. The British used the canal as a vital trade route with Asia but during the Great War it became the fastest way to transport soldiers and munitions from the far reaches of the Empire to the battlefields of Europe. Long before the outbreak of war the importance of the canal was realised and a garrison was permanently based in Egypt to make sure the canal remained open and British interests in the region were protected. Although Egypt was technically part of the Ottoman Empire it operated with a certain degree of independence, a nominal ruler existed that remained faithful to Turkish interests. In the early months of the war however various political transformations occurred, the British made sure that the Turkish sympathiser was deposed and replaced by another more sympathetic to their interests. The new man – a cousin of the his predecessor - was Prince Hussein and although he was given the title of Sultan he was to act as a puppet for Sir Henry McMahon, the British High Commissioner based in Cairo who took on the role of running the country. As the war intensified more and more empire troops passed through the Suez Canal on their way to France, the original garrison based in Egypt had also left for the Western Front; their position was quickly filled by Indian, Anzac, Territorial and Yeomanry units. During the early part of the war the CIC of all British units based in Egypt was Major General Sir John Maxwell; his main task at the time was to protect the canal at all costs. Turkey also realised how vital the Suez Canal was to Britain's war effort, with this in mind it came as no surprise when - soon after her declaration of war against Britain - she drew up plans to attack the canal. Apart from a few scattered troops on the Sinai Peninsular most of Turkey's forces in the immediate area were concentrated across to border in Palestine, attached to the Turkish Fourth Army and trained by German officers their CIC was Djemal Pasha who also held the title 'Governor of the Ottoman Empire in Palestine'. Based at camps in and around the town of Beersheba any attack on the Suez Canal would involve Pasha's troops crossing 100 miles of desert to reach their objective; the Sinai Desert had very few roads on which to travel, no rail links to transport supplies and most importantly very few wells in which to find clean water. Despite all of this the Turks did cross the desert and in late January 1915 they attacked British positions on the east bank of the canal, spotted almost at once by Indian troops holding the area their attack was quickly brought to a halt (1). Not being ones to give up easily the Turks tried again to capture the canal over the days that followed but again they failed, although some troops crossed the canal in small boats they were soon stopped by well concentrated machine gun fire, with that the Turks retreated back across the desert. Turkey had hoped that if she attacked British interests in Egypt those Egyptians opposed to British rule would rally to help her, a misjudgement on Turkey's part this failed to happen.

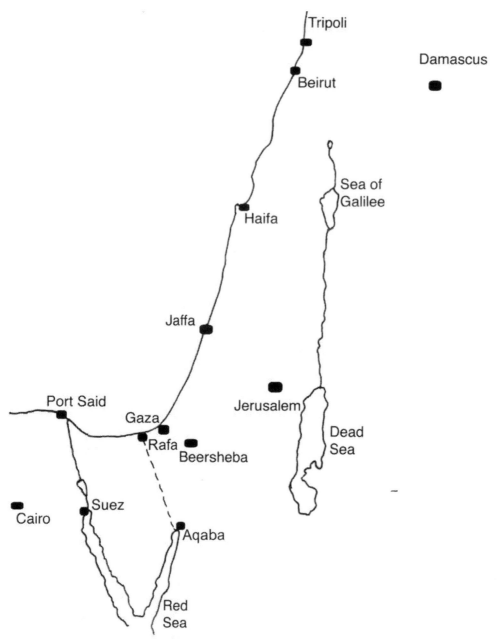

Map 40, Palestine (Map taken from 'A Village Goes to War' by David Tattersfield)

In addition to attacks by the Turks from the east, Egypt's western frontier also gave the allies something to worry about. Between late 1915 and early 1917 a tribe known as the Senussi launched sporadic attacks - from base camps situated in the Western Desert - against allied targets in western Egypt. Although these attacks could not be ignored in the grand scheme of things they did little to disrupt allied movements in Egypt during the course of the war. During the early months of the war Turkish commanders based in Constantinople had tried to persuade the world's Muslim population to rise up and turn on Turkey's enemies, they called for a Jihad (Muslim Holy War), fortunately for the allies the call went unanswered. The Arabs of the Middle East were many in number and to have them on side was in everybody's interest. The Turks wanted them but the allies did too, lured by the offer of land and independence after the war - although somewhat mislead by the British and French governments as to what they would be entitled to – the Arabs were eventually won over and entered the conflict on the allied side.

Following the failed Turkish attack on the Suez Canal the British set about improving their defences in the area, trenches and strong points were erected on the canal's east bank and more troops were moved across to man them. Around this time the Gallipoli Campaign started and most of the troops based in Egypt were sent to the Dardanelles. With the influx of Anzac troops heading for the fighting the defence of the Suez Canal was now as important as ever, it must not be forgotten however that events at Gallipoli also involved the Turks and they too found themselves sending troops to the Dardanelles. It was agreed that the best way for the British to protect the Suez Canal was for them to advance into Sinai, cross the desert and head towards the border with Palestine. The hostile terrain the desert afforded meant that as they moved eastward the British would have to establish permanent lines of communication, this would include amongst other things constructing a rail line to ferry supplies and more importantly a pipe line to carry water. Towards the end of 1915 and well into 1916 the British went to work on their plan of action, eventually – after the Gallipoli Campaign was brought to an end – the MEF was merged to become the EEF, in the shake up Sir John Maxwell was replaced as CIC in Egypt by Sir Archibald Murray (2). Slowly the British constructed a railway across the desert, choosing to stay north they followed the Sinai coastline the start point being Qantara, a town on the east bank of the Suez Canal. As for the water pipeline that too was constructed, its source was a sweet water canal situated near Ismailia; this canal was virtually the only place to obtain fresh water on the whole of the Sinai Peninsular. As was expected British operations in Sinai did not go unnoticed by the Turks, once again they planned an advance into Sinai from their bases in Palestine with the sole purpose being to disrupt British work on the peninsular and disrupt allied traffic passing through the Suez Canal. By mid April the rail line the British were constructing was well underway; it had reached a point just west of the village of Romani with advanced parties of British troops holding Qatiya further east. Turkish attacks during the course of April managed to capture both of these villages temporarily disrupting work on the rail line, before the month was out however both had been reoccupied by British and Anzac forces. Due to the summer heat the next couple of months saw a suspension in Turkish action, as they waited for reinforcements to arrive the British continued constructing the railway, they also set about improving their defences as a safeguard against future attacks. The next major clash between the two armies came in August when Turkish forces clashed with British units east of Romani, in the fighting that ensued the Turks scored early successes however the British managed to hold on to a strong defensive line, eventually the Turks, tired and low on supplies retreated eastwards. Over the days that followed the British counter attacked however due to a lack of reconnaissance aircraft, reliable intelligence, training in desert warfare and water supply problems the Turkish Army was allowed to escape back across the desert. This Turkish withdrawal not only signalled the beginning of the end to their occupation of Sinai but also extinguished any hopes they had of sparking unrest in Egypt and capturing the Suez Canal. In late December further clashes developed between British and Turkish troops around El Arish and Magdhaba, the final engagements to take place on the peninsular centred on the border town of Rafa and at El Magruntein in early January 1917. Following these final engagements the Turks withdrew across the border to Palestine; as a result the British now found their path clear to continue pushing their lines of communication eastwards. It was agreed by those in command that any delay might give the Turks time to plan and carry out further attacks; this said however the British still had no immediate plans to follow their enemy and advance into Palestine.

With the Turkish Army now situated across the border in Palestine the Sinai Peninsular lay firmly in British hands. Whilst the War Office in London made it clear to Murray they had no real objection to him pursuing the Turkish Army across the border they made it clear he could expect no extra troops for such a purpose, in fact due to events unfolding in France Murray found some of his troops sent to the Western Front. Around this time the EEF produced two new formations; the first was known as the Eastern Force, it consisted mainly of infantry units such as the 52nd Division, 53rd Division, 54th Division and 74th Division (3). The second formation was known as the Desert Column and was made up of both British and Anzac mounted troops. As the EEF followed the Sinai coast towards the border with Palestine that February saw the railway and water pipeline reach El Arish, work continued over the following weeks and by early March they'd reached the border at Rafa. At a conference held in Calais in late February allied leaders were itching for some kind of success in order to maintain public support for the war. Lloyd George, always the Easterner, on seeing Murray's troops nearing the border put his weight behind a British advance into Palestine. The Prime Minister's idea gained support, the nod was given and as a result Murray's forces geared up to cross the border. Unlike the yellow sand of the Sinai Desert the countryside of Palestine was green, fruit trees could be found as well as fields containing hops such as wheat and barley, for soldiers on both sides it was certainly a better place to be than the Sinai Peninsular. It was around this time that revolution broke out in Russia, since Turkey's entry into the war her troops had faced the Russians on their common border. Early 1917 also saw events unfold in Mesopotamia, as already mentioned a brief explanation of these can be found at the end of this chapter. Turkish attention needed to be drawn away from both of these areas; a British advance into Palestine could achieve this. In order for success to be achieved British troops crossing the border needed to capture the southern towns of Beersheba and Gaza as quickly as possible. As the first main settlements north of the border these towns not only boasted clean water, essential to both men and animals, but also offered vital road links to other towns throughout Palestine such as Jaffa - a port on the Mediterranean seaboard - and the holy city of Jerusalem. An attack on Beersheba was ruled out as British lines of communication would stretch from the coast; they would be long and therefore vulnerable to Turkish attack. The British decided to concentrate on Gaza; an attempt to take the town was scheduled for late March. This action came to be known as the 'First Battle of Gaza'; it claimed the life of the only man listed on the Chigwell Village War Memorial to be killed during the Palestine Campaign.

WILLIAM HAROLD HYDE
William Hyde was born in Chigwell in 1896, his parents Luke and Ellen Hyde had lived in the village their whole life. Luke worked as a postman whilst Ellen remained at home to look after their six children. William had three older brothers, one older sister and a younger brother; they all lived together in a small house on Hainault Road. Whilst little is known of William's life we do know he attended the council school in the village. Another piece of

information we have is that on a sunny afternoon in June 1911 aged 15 William attended an event held at St Mary's Church to celebrate the coronation of King George V. The celebrations comprised of a fete and sports day, that afternoon William participated in several events and won various prizes, a Tug of War competition was also held and William found himself on the winning team. Nothing is known of William's profession after he left school, his elder brother worked as a Butcher, maybe William did too but there's no evidence to back this up.

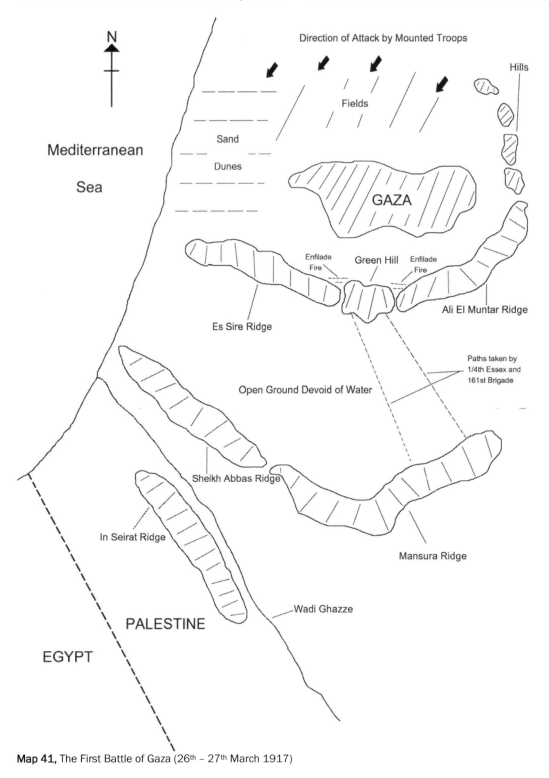

Map 41, The First Battle of Gaza (26th – 27th March 1917)

Regarding his time spent in the army William's service record no longer exists, this said however having consulted the Medal Rolls at the NA it appears he didn't join up until late 1915 early 1916, most likely under the terms of the Derby Scheme. William attended the offices and main HQ at Gordon Road, Ilford of the 4th Battalion Essex Regiment; this was the same place where Denham George King had enlisted back in 1914. It should be remembered that this battalion was a territorial unit, by the time William joined its ranks all territorial reserves of the Essex Regiment were based at Halton Park Camp in Buckinghamshire. William held the rank of Private and was given army service no 200837, on arrival at Halton Park he underwent the standard period of basic training. Having spent several months preparing for combat eventually Pte William Hyde found himself detailed for service overseas; he was kitted out and sent off to join the 1/4th Essex in Egypt. After the evacuation of Gallipoli the 1/4th Essex had been sent back to Egypt where they remained as part of 161st (Essex) Brigade, 54th (East Anglian) Division. After a period spent refitting and resting the battalion was used briefly for defence against the Senussi, after that it was moved eastwards to defend the Suez Canal, eventually in January 1917 the battalion as part of Eastern Force received orders to move eastwards across Sinai. Although it's not clear exactly when Pte William Hyde first landed in Egypt he probably joined the battalion as part of a draft of reinforcements sometime towards the end of 1916. On Christmas Eve of that year the effective strength of the 1/4th Essex was put at 32 officers and 869 other ranks. The sand that made up the Sinai Desert was extremely difficult for troops to march on; no roads existed so one was constructed out of wire mesh. Staked at regular intervals the wire was laid on top of the sand, maintained by companies of Royal Engineers it provided the perfect surface for soldiers to march on whilst crossing the desert. With the help of this wire road by February Pte William Hyde, the 1/4th Essex and the other battalions that made up 161st Brigade reached El Arish, on 20th March they set off for Palestine reaching Rafa four days later, upon their arrival 161st Brigade awaited further orders concerning the Gaza action (4).

Roughly five miles south of Gaza in Palestine lies the Wadi Ghazze River, during the winter it flows from the Judean Hills in the east out westwards to the Mediterranean Sea. During the summer the river bed is dry however small springs still exist that provide an essential source of water for those who inhabit the area. The Wadi Ghazze forms a natural barrier for anyone entering Palestine from Egypt via the coastal route, any troops wishing to advance on Gaza would have to cross the river, not exactly an easy task for a large army. Gaza itself sits on a small hill two miles inland from the coast; in 1917 to its north were rolling fields used mainly as farmland. To the west of Gaza a series of sand dunes stretch out to the sea, in the east a range of high ground spreads eastwards towards Beersheba some thirty miles away. This high ground is made up of hills that in turn form ridges; these ridges run southeast and south of Gaza and provide yet another barrier for anyone wishing to capture the town. The main ridge southeast of Gaza is known as Ali el Muntar Ridge, it dominates all southern approaches to the town, the ridge runs westward eventually forming another position known as Es Sire. South of these ridges is a stretch of open ground that for the most part provides very little in the way of cover, most importantly for men and animals this area is devoid of water. South of this area and parallel to Ali el Muntar is another ridge known as Mansura Ridge, it too stretches westwards becoming the Sheikh Abbas Ridge, the area south of here leads down to the Wadi Ghazze River. Fearing a British attack was imminent the Turkish troops had fallen back to a defensive line on Ali el Muntar Ridge and Es Sire Ridge, at the same time a small garrison was stationed in Gaza itself in order to protect the town. The ridges were used to great effect by the Turks, gun batteries were erected and trenches were dug, machine gun posts were also constructed in positions that gave them a clear field of fire. The nature of the ground in and around the ridges saw cactus hedges growing at every turn; these not only afforded the Turkish troops cover but also provided a formidable barrier as hazardous as any barbed wire. The plan of attack drawn up by British command was for mounted troops to surround the northern outskirts of Gaza from east to west, this was to prevent Turkish troops withdrawing and reinforcements arriving from bases north and east of town. In the south a full scale infantry assault would go in, protected by an artillery barrage the idea was to seize the ridges south of Gaza most importantly Ali el Muntar. Due to the conditions of the region it was agreed the attacking force would last only 24 hours before supplies and water ran short, if Gaza was not captured by nightfall on the first day the attack would be cancelled and all troops withdrawn. The infantry divisions used in the battle would be the 53rd Division and 54th Division whilst in general reserve would be the 52nd Division.

The First Battle of Gaza commenced on the morning of 26th March, during the early hours mounted troops crossed the Wadi Ghazze and by mid morning had virtually surrounded the town to the east and north having met very little in the way of resistance. Just before dawn the 54th Division crossed the river and headed for the Sheikh Abbas Ridge to await further orders. The 53rd Division, commanded by Major General A G Dallas, set off from positions west of the Wadi Ghazze however their approach was clouded in fog; this caused a delay of roughly two hours the knock on effect of which would have major consequences later on. By 9:00am that morning the Turks sensed something was up, reports were arriving that British forces were heading their way, Turkish commanders issued orders that troops from bases in the surrounding area were to make for Gaza immediately. At midday covered by an artillery barrage two brigades of 53rd Division - the 158th Brigade and 160th Brigade - advanced from positions on Mansura Ridge across open ground towards the Turkish positions on Es Sire and Ali el Muntar Ridge. Despite stiff opposition from enemy rifle, machine gun and shellfire they managed to advance up the ridges towards the Turkish lines. Whilst 158th Brigade held the right flank 160th Brigade took care of the left, 159th Brigade - also of 53rd Division - moved up in support also on the right. As they pushed on the two leading brigades soon came across cactus hedges which slowed down their advance, entrenched on top of the ridge in well hidden positions the Turks continued to rain down fire on the advancing troops. As the attack intensified the leading brigades, with little in the way of cover, fell victim to enfilade fire from enemy troops on a position known as Green Hill, this seriously hampered their attempts to take Ali el Muntar Ridge. Green Hill was situated southwest of Ali el Muntar and east of Es Sire, it lay directly in the gap between 158th Brigade and 160th Brigade. Around 1:30pm the GOC 53rd Division called up 161st Brigade, although attached to 54th Division the brigade was temporarily assigned to him for the duration of the battle. His instructions to the brigade commander was take Green Hill, his exact words were *"Put the lid on it"* (5). It was hoped if this was achieved the enemy would abandon its positions on Ali el Muntar Ridge and as a result leave attacking infantry units a clear path to take Gaza. By this time further north mounted troops were ordered to close in on Gaza from the north and east, the enemy were slow to react their main concern still being the infantry assault by 53rd Division to the south.

The troops of 161st Brigade didn't formally enter Palestine until the morning of 25th March; they proceeded to the town of In Seirat west of the Wadi Ghazze arriving there at 7:30am. The 1/4th Essex were ordered to form an outpost line on the edge of town where they remained, after a cold night without blankets, until the following morning whilst the remainder of the brigade was ordered to rest up as best it could. Early on the 26th March the brigade was on the move once again, it crossed the Wadi Ghazze with orders to head for Mansura Ridge; it arrived there about 10:00am. Whilst the battalions assembled at Mansura Ridge they came under fire from Turkish artillery, enemy aircraft were also in action overhead, some casualties were sustained from shellfire and due to the heat the troops were already running low on water. As the day drew on the exploits of 53rd Division could be heard in the distance, finally come mid afternoon 161st Brigade were ordered forward to take Green Hill. The 1/4th and 1/5th Essex were to lead the attack supported by two companies of the 1/6th Essex, the remainder of the battalion was held in reserve along with the 1/7th Essex. The enemy strength on Green Hill at the time was unknown however machine guns positioned there had a clear field of fire, fortified trenches protected by wire also existed making the Essex battalions task a difficult one. The 1/5th Essex was to advance on the left flank whilst the 1/4th Essex took care of the right. The 1/4th was deployed with 'A' Coy and 'B' Coy up front on the right and left respectively, 'D' Coy was in support with 'C' Coy most likely containing Pte William Hyde in reserve (6).

The battalion, along with the 1/5th Essex attacked Green Hill just after 4:00pm, the leading companies advanced in extended lines equal to roughly platoon strength without support from artillery. Wave after wave went forward making for the Turkish trenches, all was good but when roughly a mile from their objective the Essex men came under fire as the enemy opened up with machine guns. As the troops pushed on bullets whizzed everywhere, casualties were heavy but determined to reach their objective the Essex pushed forward. As the attackers neared Green Hill they fixed bayonets and charged however the enemy gun fire intensified, shrapnel also rained down as Turkish shells burst all around. The 1/4th Essex had no fixed battalion HQ, the commanding officer Lieutenant Colonel Edmund Jameson DSO, also carrying a rifle and bayonet found himself moving between both the firing and support line urging his troops on. Horses ran alongside the men carrying supplies and ammunition, many however fell victim to gun and shellfire and in the midst of the fighting their cargos were unloaded and brought forward by hand. Captain Jack Bell, the company commander with 'B' Coy, was killed as he went forward then, just 200 yards from the Turkish lines, Jameson fell mortally wounded. The colonel realising the seriousness of his injuries refused medical help, instead he insisted those wounded around him were looked after (7). Having crossed ground devoid of cover just in front of the enemy trenches a slight rise existed; it afforded the leading companies a little protection and allowed them to regroup before mounting a final charge on the Turkish line. Meanwhile 'C' Coy commanded by Captain L F Bittles had followed up in support, as he moved forward Bittles was wounded but Pte William Hyde and the rest of the company found themselves nearing the enemy front line. Finally with a large cheer and reinforced by the arrival of supporting troops the leading companies broke cover and mounted the enemy wire before taking the Turkish trenches on Green Hill. Those Turks that remained in position were bayoneted whilst those that fled were shot as they ran away, by 5:30pm the whole of Green Hill was in British hands. The infantry of 161st Brigade set about consolidating their gains; due to senior officers in both battalions being killed or wounded the 1/4th and 1/5th Essex found themselves temporarily commanded by the CO of the 1/6th Essex (8). The troops were low on water and due to congestion on the battlefield supplies were slow in coming forward, for the same reason the men also found it hard to evacuate their wounded.

In capturing Green Hill the troops of 161st Brigade had been instrumental in helping 53rd Division achieve its objective, by nightfall the whole of Ali el Muntar Ridge lay in British hands leaving the path to Gaza now clear. The mounted troops to the north had entered the northern outskirts of town and the Turkish garrison in Gaza itself was close to surrender. Unfortunately due to communication problems commanders at GHQ directing the attack had no idea they were on the brink of victory, unsubstantiated reports had been received that Turkish reinforcements were arriving from bases north and east of Gaza. It was feared if these reinforcements were engaged the mounted troops operating north and east of town would be cut off, a decision on what to do next had to be made. As for 53rd Division their delayed start earlier that morning had cost them two vital hours of daylight, as it got dark they too lost communication with GHQ which meant that commanders there didn't realise the extent of ground the division had gained. As previously mentioned it had been agreed that if Gaza wasn't captured by nightfall on the first day all troops would be withdrawn, with little knowledge of how close they were to victory GHQ had no choice but to order the mounted troops north and east of Gaza to fall back to the Wadi Ghazze. The 54th Division, waiting patiently on Sheikh Abbas Ridge, was ordered up to Mansura Ridge to cover their withdrawal; Major General Dallas commanding 53rd Division was not informed of this order. With the mounted troops falling back the right flank of 53rd Division would be left in the air, as a precautionary measure GHQ ordered Dallas to withdraw his right flank to meet up with 54th Division. Dallas was not pleased with this order believing 54th Division to still be at Sheikh Abbas Ridge, instead he asked GHQ for more troops to come forward and plug the gap. Dallas found his request denied, as a result he began to withdraw the whole of 53rd Division - including 161st Brigade - from Ali el

Muntar Ridge. The battalions of 161st Brigade received orders to fall back from Green Hill at 10:00pm, the 1/7th Essex provided an outpost line as the other battalions headed back to Mansura Ridge. It was not until the early hours of the 27th March that Dallas realised 54th Division was also arriving at Mansura Ridge, at 5:00am the commanders at GHQ realised that 53rd Division had abandoned the whole of Ali el Muntar Ridge and issued immediate orders for the position to be retaken.

At this point the troops were exhausted, they had little water and hadn't rested for a day and a half, they were being asked to retake a position they had already captured at huge expense a few hours earlier. Once again 53rd Division headed for Ali el Muntar Ridge and 161st Brigade headed back to Green Hill, briefly both positions were reoccupied. The 1/4th Essex, well under strength found itself for the duration commanded by an officer called Captain Lee, he organised the battalion into two companies. Unfortunately what followed next is not exactly clear, the battalion war diary of the 1/4th Essex is extremely vague concerning events at the First Battle of Gaza and this isn't surprising as the unit suffered huge losses amongst officers especially on the first day. As expected it wasn't long before large numbers of Turkish reinforcements arrived, Green Hill was once again the scene of heavy fighting. The Essex battalions fought gallantly but they were few in number, strong enemy counter attacks developed which saw them relinquish their hold on Green Hill. As the 1/4th Essex fell back under the weight of Turkish pressure once again the battalion incurred heavy losses, amongst those men who fell during this withdrawal was 20 year old Pte William Harold Hyde. As for 53rd Division enemy pressure saw it too was ejected from Ali el Muntar Ridge, eventually GHQ realised their position was hopeless and cancelled all further attacks. The British withdrew to a defensive line west of the Wadi Ghazze; it was thought the Turks might go on the offensive however they decided to remain in position on the ridges south of Gaza, with this the action known as the First Battle of Gaza was over.

The 161st (Essex) Brigade headed back to Mansura Ridge, at 11:00pm that evening it was withdrawn beyond the Wadi Ghazze to bivouacs at In Seirat. The 1/4th Essex had gone into action on the 26th March and lost their commanding officer, his second in command was wounded and out of the battalion's four company commanders one was killed and three were wounded, in total the battalion had nine officers killed (9). According to SDGW over the two day period the battle lasted the battalion had 169 men killed in action and a further 11 died of wounds, many more were wounded and some were taken prisoner. At first William was reported missing and it was hoped he might be alive but in Turkish hands as a prisoner, a small article appeared in the June 1917 edition of the Chigwell Parish Magazine stating just this. Unfortunately this was not the case; eventually the War Office listed William as having been killed in action on 27th March 1917. Pte William Harold Hyde has no known grave is commemorated on Panels 33 to 39 of the Jerusalem Memorial to the Missing. The memorial stands in Jerusalem CWGC Cemetery and commemorates almost 3,300 servicemen who were killed in operations throughout Egypt and Palestine during the First World War and who have no known grave.

* * *

The main failure for the First Battle of Gaza was quite simply a breakdown of communication between GHQ and the units in the field, the fact that messages were not relayed concerning progress as well as the loss of daylight meant commanders had no overall picture of how the battle was going. As darkness fell a decision had to be made, even though the British were on the brink of victory GHQ didn't know this, instead a policy of safety first had to be adopted which saw the troops were withdrawn.

In the wake of defeat it wasn't long before the British government urged the CIC of the EEF Sir Archibald Murray to try once again to take Gaza. Just less than three weeks after the first attempt had failed on the 17th April the action known as the 'Second Battle of Gaza' commenced. In the period between the two battles the Turks had strengthened defences in the areas around the town and eastwards towards Beersheba, when the British attack went in it found itself up against a strong Turkish line and almost at once it started to falter. Having suffered such a defeat three weeks earlier moral amongst the British troops was at an all time low, the battle went on for two days and although Tanks were used and gas shells were fired they failed to have the desired effect. It was soon evident to those in command that the situation was hopeless; on the evening of the 19th April the 'Second Battle of Gaza' was abandoned however unlike the first battle any ground that was gained was held onto. It didn't take long for questions to be asked, a general reshuffle of commanders within the EEF took place before the finger was pointed at Murray himself. The War Cabinet back in London discussed the possibility of replacing him and soon a successor was found in General Sir Edmund Allenby. At the time Allenby was commanding the British 3rd Army on the Western Front, the Battle of Arras had just come to an end and results had been considered as poor. The army commander on hearing he was being posted to take command of the EEF felt he was being transferred because of the poor showing at Arras, after meetings with the War Cabinet however he soon changed his mind.

General Allenby arrived in Egypt on 27th June 1917, the following day he replaced Sir Archibald Murray as CIC of the EEF, he was told by the British Prime Minister to ask for whatever he needed in order to defeat the Turkish Army in Palestine. As far as Lloyd George was concerned he thought that if Jerusalem was captured it would provide a massive moral boost for the English people, support for the war had to be maintained and his plan was

– Jerusalem by Christmas. As for Allenby the new CIC was quick to restore moral amongst his troops and strengthen relations between the officers and men, after Murray's failures to most Allenby was seen as a breath of fresh air. GHQ was moved from Cairo closer to the frontline and once again a reshuffle of those in command and the units they commanded took place, then attention was turned to defeating the enemy. Plans were drawn up for another attempt to take Gaza however a third direct attack on the town was ruled out due to the strength of the enemy's defences. Instead it was decided to outflank the Turks as their left flank was lightly defended in positions just west of Beersheba. The plan was to strike a blow and secure water supplies at Beersheba itself, if successful Allenby's troops would then move westwards to encircle the enemy. The British hoped to approach Gaza from the north and northwest however diversionary attacks south of Gaza would also be carried out to convince the enemy a third direct attack on the town was being made. The action came to be known as the 'Third Battle of Gaza', it commenced during the last week of October and was a resounding success; the Turks were finally ejected from their positions in and around Gaza allowing the British at last to move up into Palestine. Over the weeks that followed further actions took place, the British captured several towns and villages as well as the railway that connected Jerusalem to the Mediterranean; as a result the city was literally cut off. Despite Turkish counter attacks it wasn't long before Jerusalem finally fell and on 11th December 1917 Allenby's troops entered the city bringing with them an end to nearly 400 years of Turkish rule.

At the same time that the British were clashing with Turkish forces in Sinai those Arab tribes based in the Hejaz - a province of Arabia - started a rebellion against Turkish rule. With the help of the British and inspired and led by Major T E Lawrence - later known as Lawrence of Arabia - they were successful in attacking various outposts of the Turkish Army in towns and villages throughout the province. The first blow came in June 1916 when Arab tribesmen attempted to capture the town of Medina; unfortunately their attempt failed but further south they were successful in defeating the small Turkish garrison holding the holy city of Mecca. The Arabs were led by Sherif Hussein; he had four sons and each one lead a force of local tribesmen. Although intent on disrupting Turkish interests throughout the region the Arabs were undisciplined, added to this they lacked modern weapons which made their task more difficult. Despite these shortcomings having captured Mecca the Arabs set off up the Red Sea coast and with help from the Royal Navy they soon captured the port town of Jeddah, from here they continued northwards, further clashes ensued and further gains were made. That July another attempt by Arab tribesmen to take Medina failed, with that they took up positions west of the town well out of range of the Turkish guns. The Turkish lines of communication throughout the Hejaz were very long and therefore venerable to attack; the Turkish troops based in the region relied heavily on reinforcements and supplies being sent down a railway that ran southwards from Turkey into Syria and down through the northern Hejaz to Medina. In September a force of Turkish troops based in Medina set out to recapture Mecca, their route took them south westerly through mountainous terrain in the direction of the Red Sea port of Rabegh. It was in this area that further clashes developed between both sides, the Turkish soldiers were better trained and soon had the Arabs on the run however supplies sent to the region by the allies helped stabilise the situation. Redeploying themselves in the areas north and northwest of Rabegh the Arabs managed to block Turkish troops moving southwards, over the months that followed the fighting continued as the two sides moved northwards up the coast firstly fighting for Yenboo and then Wejh. At this point the Turks moved eastward and the Arabs at Wejh found it a perfect base from which to launch attacks on the Hejaz Railway. These attacks were successful in cutting the Turkish forces in two, half found themselves guarding Medina whilst the other half were forced to forget regaining interests further south and fall back to protect the railway. Those Turks holding Medina were eventually cut off however Arab tribesmen never took the city; the Turkish troops based there held out and didn't surrender until January 1919. As for those troops protecting the railway continued Arab attacks saw Turkish communications severely disrupted, as a result the Turks were pushed northwards. Allied commanders based in Cairo now saw the Arab revolt tying down enemy soldiers that could have been used against its forces in Sinai and later Palestine. Although the allies welcomed the Arab contribution it was feared they may occupy parts of the Middle East required by Britain and France after the war. In 1916 an agreement was reached by the two nations, known as the Sykes-Picot Agreement it divided parts of the Middle East into zones for occupation by both countries after the war, little regard was included for Arab interests. At this point Major T E Lawrence, aware of this agreement and fearful the Arabs might be cheated out of initial promises made by the allies, urged Sherif Hussein to consider a move northwards, his intention being that Arab forces should occupy areas east of the River Jordan as well as Syria ahead of the allies.

It wasn't long before the Arabs captured the Red Sea port of Aqaba and from here they moved northwards pursuing the Turks in areas east of the River Jordan and Syria. After the fall of Jerusalem in late December the British took Jaffa, the first half of 1918 however saw little activity. Due to events on the Western Front Allenby saw some of his troops sent to France, eventually replacements arrived and he continued to push northwards. The main British advance followed the Mediterranean Coast before moving eastwards through northern Palestine. The Turkish Army still managed to mount counter attacks however these were repulsed, demoralised they retreated knowing full well the end was in sight. A joint effort in late September by both Arab and British forces brought them to the gates of Damascus in just over a week; eventually the Turks were pushed northwards to Aleppo in northern Syria where during the last week of October they finally sought peace terms.

British operations in Mesopotamia during World War One were originally designed to protect oil pipelines that ran from the Persian oil fields down through the region to the Persian Gulf at Basra. The Royal Navy relied on this oil to keep its ships at sea and maintain its presence in and around Middle Eastern waters. In November 1914 both British and Indian troops were sent to the region and without difficulty captured Basra in southern Mesopotamia, with this the oil pipelines were secure and the job of the troops accomplished. Those in command however seeing how easy Basra had fallen set their sights on the capital Baghdad, their was no real justification to advance on the city and no real plan set aside in order to do so. The British forces in Mesopotamia were commanded by General Sir John Nixon, between late 1914 and spring 1915 he prepared his troops to move northwards. That April Turkish troops tried to take Basra but were pushed back by the British, a few weeks later Nixon's troops began their advance on Baghdad. The attacking forces were split into two columns and each followed the path of one of two rivers that ran through the country. To the west troops commanded by Major General Sir George Gorringe set off up the Euphrates whilst to the east troops commanded by Major General Sir Charles Townsend followed the Tigris towards Baghdad. Initial progress by both parties was good however the further the troops advanced the harder it was to keep them supplied, death and disease took its toll and eventually Townsend found himself in trouble. After pushing the enemy northwards to Ctesiphon - a few miles south of Baghdad - he was pushed back to Kut el Amara by a large enemy force; eventually he was surrounded by Turkish troops. The siege at Kut lasted from December 1915 until Townsend surrendered in April 1916 however several unsuccessful attempts by the British during that time had failed to relieve Townsend and his troops. Due to ill health Nixon stepped down in August 1916 and was replaced by Major General Sir Stanley Maude, British forces in Mesopotamia were eventually re-supplied before further attempts to move on Baghdad were made. Turkish troops were eventually defeated at Kut in February 1917 and on 11th March the British captured Baghdad giving the public back home at last something to celebrate. Over the following months further clashes developed, Maude contracted cholera and died in November 1917 his replacement being Sir William Marshall. During the final year of the war not much happened on the Mesopotamian front however Marshall's troops did occupy the oil fields in the northern city of Mosul. During October 1918 operations in Mesopotamia finally drew to a close, many had died in battle, thousands had died of disease, overall the campaign had produced very little to shout about.

The Turkish Army formally surrendered on 30th October 1918 (10), in the years following the Great War with the fall of the Ottoman Empire the map of the Middle East changed dramatically. Following the events of the Second World War in 1948 Palestine became a Jewish state and was renamed Israel, this fact is still viewed controversial and sees continued unrest in the region today. As the First World War unfolded many saw events in the Middle East as a side show to events in France, once Russia pulled out of the war in late 1917 the need to keep her supplied and divert Turkish attention was gone. Even if Turkey had been defeated it would not have changed events in France and Flanders, as thought by many the war could only be won on the Western Front.

73, *Advance of the 1/4th Essex at the First Battle of Gaza 26th–27th March 1917 (Photograph courtesy of the Imperial War Museum)*

74, *The Jerusalem CWGC Cemetery and Memorial to the Missing*

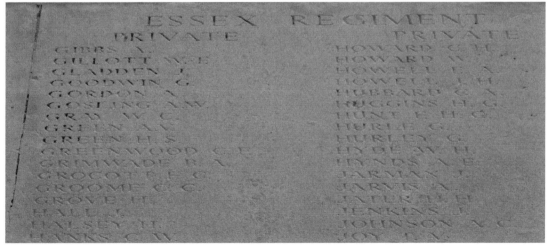

75, *The name of Pte William Harold Hyde as it appears along with other Essex men on the Jerusalem Memorial to the Missing*

1918

As the war entered what was to be its final year the British people, although having to deal with setback after setback on the battlefield, remained committed to the conflict and still remained hopeful of an allied victory. For the people of Chigwell daily life in the Essex village continued however the war was never far from their thoughts, even though the fighting was taking place on foreign fields the village still did what it could for the war effort and did what it could for the soldiers. The Parish Council was always coming up with ideas to raise money for bereaved families, local hospitals or organisations such as the Red Cross. Local exhibitions and concert parties were held regularly which not only generated funds but also provided the villagers with an opportunity to forget world events, if only for an afternoon or an evening.

On the Western Front the stalemate continued, the New Year began as the old one had ended and despite all their attempts of the previous year both sides were still locked in trench warfare. Since the start of the war with each New Year the Germans had made certain moves that persuaded the allies that 1918 would be no exception. April 1915 had seen them launch the Second Battle of Ypres, February 1916 had seen them attack the French at Verdun and early 1917 had seen them strengthen their positions with their withdrawal to the Hindenburg Line. This said however for the most part the Germans had spent much of the war on the defensive quite happy for the allies to bring the fight to them however 1918 would prove to be different. The German commander Erich Von Ludendorff knew that now they were under pressure, although in the east hostilities against Russia were virtually at an end in the west they had to take the fight to the allies and win the war before the Americans arrived. The sheer manpower and munitions the United States promised to bring with her would make any hopes of a German victory extremely difficult; Ludendorff knew this and concluded the war had to be won before the Americans arrived in force (1). On the 11th November 1917 a meeting took place at Mons in Belgium and several plans to defeat the allies were discussed. Ludendorff played with the idea of first defeating the French but was quick to realise should Britain remain in the war she could be a greater threat. Not only did Britain have vast resources amongst its empire to call on but the Royal Navy, whose blockade against Germany saw conditions within the country deteriorating rapidly, would be free to continue. Eventually it was agreed on that firstly the British must be beaten, it was then hoped that a French Army devoid of British support could be defeated soon after.

By the beginning of 1918 the strain put on the British Army after four years of war was beginning to show, the Somme and Passchendaele battles had taken their toll and the numbers of fit men enlisting began to fall. This said however men were continually being called up to the colours; those who had been boys when the war started now found themselves old enough to be conscripted. Those men who at one time were considered too old or medically unfit also found themselves now eligible for service (2). Whilst some men remained in England and saw service on the home front others were trained up and sent overseas to join battle hardened veterans in those battalions and units that needed replacements. The War Cabinet however, desperate not to see fresh troops squandered in fruitless attacks were slow to provide Haig with large numbers of reinforcements. After the lack of success caused by the Third Battle of Ypres and the disappointments following initial successes at Cambrai Lloyd George, along with the War Cabinet, had lost faith in Haig. But, after much discussion, it was realised there was no one on the immediate horizon who could replace him and do the job better. As a result Haig remained as CIC however various figures including the CIGS Sir William Robertson were replaced, his successor being Sir Henry Wilson. During the first quarter of 1918 the British Army on the Western Front saw several changes, firstly to deal with the shortage of manpower a reorganisation of units occurred. This reorganisation amongst other things saw some battalions merged with others; in addition some service and territorial battalions raised on the outbreak of war in 1914 were disbanded altogether. At the same time to cope with these changes the number of British infantry battalions within an infantry brigade was reduced from four battalions to three, in the case of Anzac, Canadian and other empire units however their numbers remained unchanged. After various heated discussions between British and French commanders in January 1918 Haig reluctantly agreed to take over a further 40 miles of frontline previously held by the French Army. This development now saw the British responsible for some 125 miles of front stretching from Ypres in the north to just west of La Fère on the River Oise in the south - the latter position being roughly 13 miles south of St Quentin (3). This new stretch of line fell to 5th Army to defend and General Sir Hubert Gough, finding himself already short of manpower, was not best pleased when he discovered the poor quality of the positions he'd inherited. Over the following two months 5th Army went to work improving their positions however around this time GHQ implemented a change in the way the BEF defended its frontline. As a result, and modelled on German tactics, the British were to create three zones each with its own level of defence. The 'Forward Zone' was to provide a degree of resistance against enemy attack and manned by enough infantry to cope with initial assaults, at strategic positions within the zone strong points existed protected by barbed wire and machine guns. Roughly 3,000 yards behind the Forward Zone and about the same distance in depth stood the 'Battle Zone'. Designed to be the main line of defence it was here that enemy attacks would be dealt with more vigorously. It was hoped that after initial attacks troops in the Forward Zone would fall back here where the bulk of the infantry was situated. Within the Battle Zone a greater number of strong points existed in addition to Tanks and artillery pieces of various calibres, at the rear of the Battle Zone would be further troops ready to be called on if necessary. Behind the Battle Zone was to be the 'Corps Line' or 'Rear Zone, here was to be more Tanks, artillery and infantry as well as supply dumps etc. In theory these defences were to seem fool proof however due to the shortage of manpower within the BEF, by the time the Germans launched their attack, on sections of both 3rd Army and 5th Army's front these areas were incomplete. In addition to these shortcomings, due to the amount of work needed to bring these areas up to full strength, the troops occupying the zones found they had insufficient training regarding defensive tactics. By far the worst parts of the line fell on 5th Army's front and, due to intelligence reports received at GHQ, it was realised a large scale enemy attack was on its way.

Map 42, The 1918 German Offensives (Map taken from 'THE WESTERN FRONT' (BBC Books) by Richard Holmes. Reprinted by permission of The Random House Group Ltd)

Having toured the frontlines Ludendorff and his commanders looked at various areas where a possible breakthrough could be achieved; as a result they came up with several options each designed to cut deep into the allied lines (see map 42). To the north attacks aimed towards Ypres, Hazebrouck, St Omer and eventually the Channel Ports were codenamed 'George I' and 'George II' respectively. Further south pushes towards Arras and Vimy would be called 'Mars' and 'Valkyrie' whilst a large scale assault between Bapaume and St Quentin would be called 'Operation Michael'. In addition to these assaults plans to attack French positions on the Aisne and either side of Rheims were also agreed on. Owing to the fact that an attack in Flanders needed good weather to succeed and given the time of year 'George' was ruled out as a first choice. The British hold on Vimy Ridge and the nature of the ground before it also made 'Mars' a tough first option. In late January a final decision was made that 'Operation Michael' would provide the first blow, it was decided that once successful other plans like 'George', 'Mars' and 'Valkyrie' could then be swung into action. Although not the most strategic place to attack a breakthrough between Bapaume and St Quentin it was hoped could cut the British and French armies in two, if successful the former would find itself pushed back across the wasteland of the old Somme battlefield. Split into three attacks 'Michael I' would be aimed north of St Quentin towards Peronne and Ham, 'Michael II' would go in towards Albert whilst 'Michael III' would be aimed at Bapaume. On forcing a British retreat Ludendorff hoped to drive deep into enemy lines before turning his forces northwards and pushing the British up towards the sea. German high command decided the start date for their spring offensive would be the 21st March. As preparations began Ludendorff instilled in his troops the belief that the forthcoming series of actions would defeat the enemy and win them the war, it was to be known to the Germans as the 'Kaiserschlacht' – 'The Kaisers Battle', after the war the British would refer to the opening phase as the March Offensive (4).

As spring approached the allies knew an attack was imminent however it was still unclear exactly where that attack would come. In the build up to their offensive the Germans were masters of deception striking diversionary blows, including artillery bombardments and infantry assaults, along various sections of the Western Front. Haig decided to concentrate most of his reserves in the north in case the Germans made a drive for the Channel Ports, the CIC thought it possible an attack may also take place on 1st Army's front around Lens. This said however up until a few days before, when various reports were received that proved otherwise, Haig was quite convinced the main assault would fall in the south on sectors held by the French Army. Due to a lack of troops holding the British frontline around this time Haig managed to obtain from Pétain, the French CIC, a guarantee that if his forces were attacked French units would be brought in to assist them. Meanwhile the British improved their defences but progress was painfully slow. Due to the weakness of 5th Army's front Gough was given permission to fall back to rearward defences along the line Ham - Peronne if heavily attacked, it was stressed however that every effort should be made to hold onto ground when and where possible. On 3rd March 1918 peace between Germany and Russia was formally agreed, the treaty of Brest-Litovsk was signed, and as a result German troops from the east continued to arrive in the west in readiness for the offensive. During the Cambrai counter attack of 30th November 1917 the Germans had used stormtrooper battalions supported by concentrated artillery fire to breakthrough the British lines, Ludendorff planned to use the same tactics during the Michael Offensive but on a much bigger scale. The Germans assembled their largest ever concentration of guns along a 70 mile front, they would fire a mixture of shrapnel and gas shells hitting the same targets time and time again in order to demoralise the enemy. For the Germans failure to create a decisive breakthrough would surely mean eventual defeat, Ludendorff knew success would depend on just how well the British fought and defended.

At 4:40am on the 21 March 1918 the British line just west of Cambrai southwards to La Fère found itself on the receiving end of the greatest artillery bombardment the world had ever known. The ground shook as the Germans unleashed what they hoped would be the decisive action of the war; diversionary bombardments were also carried out in Flanders, Champagne and Verdun. During the course of the day over 3 million shells were fired hitting command posts, trench systems, artillery positions, supply dumps, strong points, road junctions, railway lines, telephone exchanges and any other target considered vital to the enemy. Although an attack had been expected for those men of 3rd Army and 5th Army the bombardment seemed to come straight out of the blue, this said however GHQ had received intelligence reports up to two days before that something was afoot. That morning a mist covered the battlefield which afforded the enemy complete surprise. At 9:40am the infantry attack started and German stormtroopers rushed forward supported by their artillery. The British machine gunners positioned to resist such an action stood no chance their vision clouded by mist, gas and smoke, these conditions also saw British artillery observers and gunners made virtually redundant although some managed to fire back. On 5th Army's front for the majority of troops positioned in the Forward Zones by the time they saw the enemy it was too late, many were killed or wounded and thousands surrendered when they found themselves surrounded. In some cases the British resisted and heavy fighting ensued, the Germans however thanks to the mist had succeeded in taking their enemy totally by surprise, but in the process they also lost heavily. Throughout the day the fighting continued as German troops entered the battle zone held by 5th Army, further north Byng's 3rd Army also found its frontlines breached in areas west of Cambrai. The Germans had attacked that morning with a total of sixty two divisions, facing them had been just fourteen divisions of 3rd Army and fifteen divisions, including three cavalry divisions, of 5th Army. As well as having guns captured the British suffered in the region of 40,000 casualties, of this number half were taken prisoner, 7,000 were killed and the remainder were either wounded or missing. Although they had broken through 5th Army's front to a depth of roughly four miles surprisingly throughout the day the Germans suffered the same amount of losses, hardly any men were captured but thousands were wounded and many of Ludendorff's best men were killed. The furthest advance made by the Germans on the opening day came at the southern end of 5th Army's front where they penetrated beyond the Battle Zone in the area of the Crozat Canal (5). On the morning of 22nd March the German advance continued and Gough's army, suffering severe communication difficulties thanks to enemy artillery, was forced into retreat, it's on this day in this southern sector that Chigwell suffered its first casualty of 1918.

MATTHEW AMOS WESSON MASON

Matthew Mason was the eldest child of Amos Josiah Mason and his wife Emma Mary Ann and was born in Chigwell in 1888. Amos had been born in Barkingside whilst his wife came from the East End of London, once married the couple moved to Manor Road, Grange Hill where they ran the Prince of Wales Public House. The Mason family lived at the pub and when Matthew was two Mary gave birth to a daughter called Florence, nine years later the Mason's second daughter Elsie was born making three children in all. All the children were educated locally at Chigwell Council School and when old enough helped out in the pub, eventually Matthew met and married a lady called Esther and the couple went on to have several children. Their eldest child, called Florence after her aunt, was baptised at St Mary's Church on 2nd July 1911. The following year Matthew and Esther had a son they called Henry James, he was baptised on 1st December 1912 but died 6 months later and is buried in St Mary's Churchyard. It has not proved possible to determine what Matthew Mason did for a living prior to joining the army, it is reasonable to suggest he continued to work with his parents at the Prince of Wales Public House (6). On the outbreak of war it seems unlikely that Matthew enlisted right away, unfortunately his army service record no longer exists which makes it virtually impossible to know for sure. In early 1915 Esther gave birth to another child. James Mason was baptised at St Mary's Church on 7th February, it would appear that Matthew was present at the ceremony. According to SDGW Matthew Mason enlisted at a recruiting office in Ilford, having been passed fit he was initially posted as private 6950 to the 25th Battalion Middlesex Regiment. This unit was quite unique as it was a reserve battalion that went on to become a garrison battalion. The initial battalion was raised in October 1915 and made up of men from reserve companies of the 18th Battalion, 19th Battalion and 26th Battalion of the Middlesex Regiment; it is possible Matthew Mason initially joined one of these. The 25th Middlesex became a Garrison Battalion in September 1916 and as a result soon after some men were posted to other units. Pte Matthew Mason was one of those transferred and on 2nd December 1916 he joined the reserves of the 20th Battalion (City of London Regiment) Royal Fusiliers, around this time his army service number changed to G/51782. Less than a week later Matthew found himself, and several other men, headed for France and on 11th December 1916 they joined the 11th Battalion (City of London Regiment) Royal Fusiliers in training near Abbeville. This battalion had first been sent to France in July 1915 and along with the 7th Battalion Bedfordshire Regiment and 6th Battalion Northamptonshire Regiment (7) was attached to 54th Brigade, 18th (Eastern) Division. It should be remembered that this division also contained the 53rd Brigade and 55th Brigade that both Pte John Witham and Pte Frederick Dunkley had served in.

Having participated in the Somme battles of 1916 early 1917 saw the 11th Royal Fusiliers remain in the Picardy area. On 3rd February whilst holding the lines near the Ancre Pte Matthew Mason was wounded, although his injuries are unknown it would appear they were sufficient enough for him to be sent back to Blighty. Having spent time recovering on 7th June Pte Matthew Mason was passed fit for duty and sent back to France temporarily joining the 1st Battalion (City of London) Royal Fusiliers, just over two weeks later on 26th June he rejoined the 11th Royal Fusiliers in billets near Doullens. A few days later the units of 18th Division moved north to the Ypres Salient.

By March 1918 the units of 18th Division found themselves attached to III Corps of Gough's 5th Army. The division was responsible for some 4.5 miles of front along the banks of the River Oise stretching from the village of Travecy in the south to Alaincourt in the north. On their left stood 14th Division whilst their right flank was covered by 58th Division who had the distinction of holding the extreme right of the British line where it joined the French Army. Throughout the morning of 21st March the forward zone on 18th Division's front had been held by units of both the 53rd Brigade and 55th Brigade, during the day these units managed a strong defence of their positions however the weight of the German advance proved too strong and eventually they were forced to yield ground. When the German bombardment started that morning the units of 54th Brigade, commanded by Brigadier General Sadleir-Jackson DSO, were in corps reserve and concentrated roughly eight miles south of Ham around the village of Caillouel, the brigade had spent the previous two weeks training in counter attack drill and by night had provided men for work parties and reconnaissance duties. At 8:00am that morning the brigade received orders to move and the various units boarded army trucks and headed northeast about seven miles towards the frontline and the Crozat Canal. At midday the battalions of 54th Brigade arrived in positions just west of the canal, they occupied a wooded area just north of Faillouel village where brigade HQ was established. In the meantime German troops in this area had penetrated the British lines, having crossed the River Oise they were headed between the villages of Essigny and Benay in the direction of the Crozat Canal and 54th Brigade. At 1:00pm brigade HQ received orders to counter attack the enemy and retake a defensive line that had just been lost known as the Camisole Switch (See Map 43). This line lay east of the canal between the villages of Montescourt and Ly Fontaine however the Germans occupied in force the village of Gibercourt situated between the two. As 54th Brigade crossed the Crozat Canal it posted both flank and advanced guards to cover the movement. Its battalions passed through woodland as Pte Matthew Mason and the 11th Royal Fusiliers, commanded by Lieutenant Colonel A E Sulman MC, held the left flank around Montescourt, the 6th Northampton's held the right flank at Remigny and the bulk of the 7th Bedford's moved up in reserve.

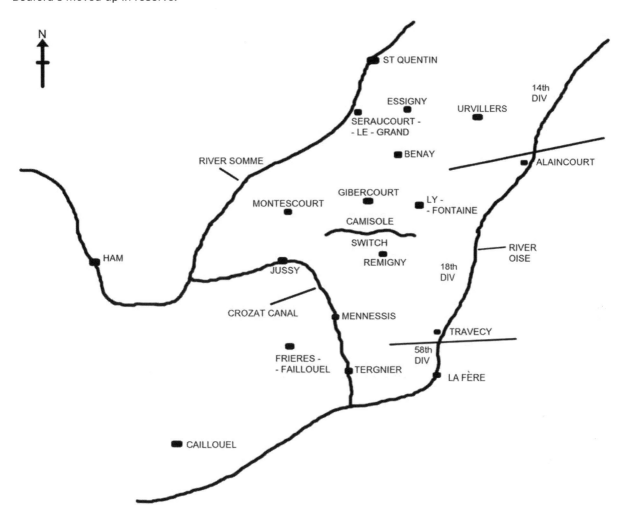

Map 43, Area held by 18th Division 21st March 1918

At sunset the battalions advanced on the Camisole Switch defences and occupied the area meeting little resistance in the process, by 7:00pm the whole line had been taken and the job of consolidating the position began. Meanwhile a few miles to the south the Germans had broken through and crossed the Crozat Canal north of Tergnier, it soon became clear to those in command that all British troops positioned east of the canal now risked being cut off and would have to be withdrawn immediately. As a result no sooner had consolidation began that orders were received for the battalions of 54th Brigade to abandon the Camisole Switch and fall back across the canal. Throughout the day units attached to 14th Division had also had a rough time and found themselves falling back from the direction of Urvillers, 54th Brigade was ordered to cover their withdrawal across the canal before retiring themselves. Just after midnight, with 14th Division clear, the whole of 54th Brigade had crossed the canal and taken up positions on its west bank, as for the 11th Royal Fusiliers they received orders to march to Jussy where they were to take up defensive positions in the village. The battalion arrived near Jussy around 11:00pm and having been on the move all day the men including Pte Matthew Mason were immediately served with a hot meal.

By the early hours of 22nd March the Fusiliers, along with the Bedford's and Northampton's were deployed between Jussy and Mennessis sandwiched between the canal and a railway embankment that ran through the area (See Map 44). In the foggy conditions the men of the 11th Royal Fusiliers formed up on the canal bank at Jussy with their left flank resting on a quarry situated between a canal bridge and the village itself. The left was held by a mixture of units including machine gunners whilst the bulk of the battalion dug in throughout and behind the village one company behind the other A Coy, B Coy, C Coy and D Coy. Unfortunately it has not proved possible to determine which company Pte Matthew Mason was attached to however cross checking other casualties suggests that it could have been 'C' Coy. The Fusiliers right flank covered a railway bridge and right of that stood the Bedford's, the Northampton's were in support chiefly positioned along the railway embankment. At midday

German troops were spotted close to the village and fighting erupted, due to the bend in the canal at Jussy hostile machine gun fire from the far side of the canal enfiladed the Fusiliers positions which made movement extremely difficult. At the same time hostile shellfire fell behind the village and enemy troops made a determined effort to cross the canal across bridges that 54th Brigade had been ordered to but failed to destroy. Unfortunately due to a lack of supplies several crossings at Jussy and Mennessis were not prepared correctly for demolition and remained intact despite several failed attempts by British units to destroy them with trench-mortar shells.

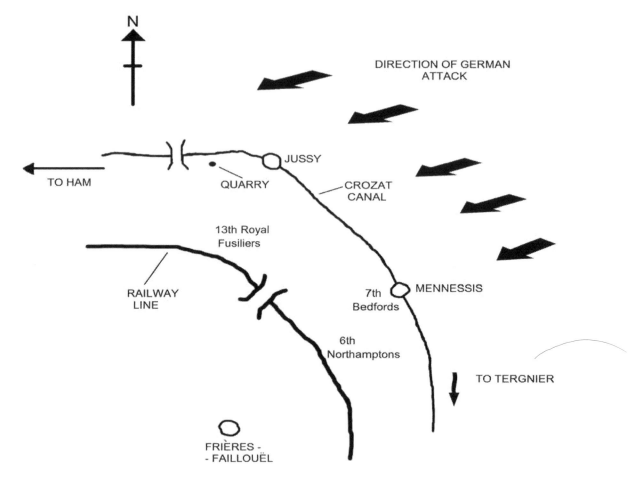

Map 44, Position of 54th Brigade (22nd – 23rd March 1918)

By mid afternoon the 11th Royal Fusiliers reported the whole of its line under attack as German pressure continued, the battalion was feeling the full force of the enemy assault however although men were killed and many were wounded the Fusiliers managed to hold firm. At 6:00pm German troops created a breakthrough in places held by the Bedford's, the Northampton's quickly moved forward to counter attack and the brigade line was soon re-established however by now the enemy had a foothold on the west bank of the canal. Due to the weight of the onslaught gaps were starting to appear on the Fusiliers left flank, their battalion CO immediately ordered men from 'B' Coy and 'C' Coy to move up and assist 'A' Coy who'd been in forward positions near the canal bank, 'D' Coy however remained in support. It's most likely around this time that Pte Matthew Mason was killed in action, heavy fighting continued throughout the night as more German troops crossed the canal and skirmishes took place along the towpaths. Despite heroic attempts by all concerned to save the situation at dawn the following morning, again assisted by fog, the Germans took Jussy. By daybreak the 11th Royal Fusiliers, due to flank fire from the village, were forced off the canal bank and dug in about 200 yards further south, patrols sent back out towards the village ascertained that the Fusiliers left flank was in the air and further withdrawals were necessary. Meanwhile the Bedford's and Northampton's were also being pushed backwards by the force of the German assault, by 9:00am the whole of 54th Brigade was ordered to withdraw towards Frières-Faillouel. During the days that followed the retreat continued, enemy aircraft shadowed the brigades every move however despite heavy losses small attempts were still made to stand and fight. On 24th March the 11th Royal Fusiliers regrouped at Caillouel, before reinforcements they numbered just 2 officers plus 25 other ranks (8).

In the fighting at Jussy on 22nd March 1918 the 11th Royal Fusiliers had 3 officers and 39 other ranks killed in action whilst many more were either wounded or taken prisoner. Matthew who was 31 years old when he died is one of just three men killed that day who have a known grave. Pte Matthew Amos Wesson Mason and the two other identified casualties are buried at Grand-Seraucourt CWGC Cemetery, Aisne, France. Originally buried elsewhere their graves were moved here sometime between 1920 and 1926 when burials from the surrounding battlefields and other cemeteries in the area were concentrated on this site. It was not until August 1918 that the death of Pte Matthew Mason was recorded in the Chigwell Parish Magazine, the small article extended sincere sympathies to the Mason family on behalf of the parish and went on to say that Pte Mason had done his bit and done it well. Inside St Mary's Churchyard stands a small gravestone that over time has become harder and harder to read. It lists the names of several members of the Mason family who have passed away; amongst them are Matthew's son Henry, Matthew himself and tragically his eldest child Florence who was to die in 1920 aged only 9. Nothing is known of what happened to Esther and James Mason after the war, as for Matthew's parents according to the records of the CWGC they moved to 13 Digby Road, Corringham Essex. Amos Josiah Mason died on the 29th November 1934 aged 73 whilst his wife Emma died in June 1946 aged 83.

* * *

At the southern end of the British front in two days 5th Army had been pushed back roughly twelve miles. As the Germans progressed they occupied towns and villages on route, Ham fell and then on the 23rd March Peronne was captured, the following day Bapaume was also lost as British troops found themselves falling back across the old 1916 Somme battlefields. Although success had been achieved on the right of the British line instead of reinforcing this area Ludendorff decided to push on in places where his troops had met resistance. In areas north and west of Cambrai Byng's 3rd Army had stood fast only giving ground where it had to and in accordance with 5th Army's retreat, as a result over the next few days heavy fighting continued and on 25th March Chigwell lost another man.

JAMES SIMPSON

Tracing the family background of James Simpson has proved quite difficult as no concrete evidence can be found via the 1901 census; fortunately however sections of his army service record still exist at the NA which provides some valuable information. James was born at Poplar in East London sometime during May 1886, whilst nothing is known of his father his mother was called Rebecca and she too was born at Poplar in 1857. James had three sisters called Jane, Rebecca (after her mother) and Francis; although his name is unknown it appears a younger brother also existed. Whilst nothing is known of James early life or where he was educated we know the Simpson family moved to Woodford Bridge a few years before the war setting up home at 2 Fern Cottages, Brunel Road. Before joining the army James worked as a Carpenter and Painter, as far as is known he never married and remained at home with his family. On the outbreak of war James didn't join up right away, called upon as part of the Derby Scheme he enlisted at a recruiting office in Woodford on the 11th December 1915. James like all new recruits underwent a medical examination. The results state he was 5ft 9˝ tall weighing 165lbs, he had a 36˝chest that when fully expanded measured 38½˝, he had perfect vision and listed distinguishing marks as a scar on the back of his left elbow and a scar over his left eyebrow. Having been passed fit James was posted as Private 37459 to a reserve battalion of the Essex Regiment based at Harwich; he remained here until March 1916 when the unit was transferred to Felixstowe. Pte James Simpson was destined to spend the next year in the reserves training for eventual service overseas, he was mobilised on the 18th April 1917 but before he could leave for the front he caught an infection that saw him hospitalised. James spent five weeks at Felixstowe Military Hospital from the 20th May until the 23rd June, it is not known if during this period Rebecca Simpson visited her son. Having recovered James left hospital and rejoined the Essex reserves; finally having been given the all clear on 23rd September 1917 he embarked at Folkestone for France arriving at Calais the same day. Upon his arrival in France Pte James Simpson found himself posted to the 2nd Battalion Essex Regiment who at the time found themselves resting behind the lines at Swindon Camp roughly a mile north of Poperinghe. James joined the battalion on the 25th September but two days later the unit left for service on the frontline, it appears however that James wasn't with them and instead was posted to another battalion. On the 2nd October Pte James Simpson was renumbered 44860 and transferred to the 20th Battalion Durham Light Infantry, he joined the unit in billets at Middlesex Camp, situated close to St Idesbald and Bray Dunes on the French-Belgian coast between Nieuport and Dunkirk ten days later.

The 20th DLI was formed at Sunderland in Wearside in July 1915; it crossed the Channel to France just under a year later as part of 123rd Brigade, 41st Division. Amongst other units this division comprised of the 122nd Brigade, 123rd Brigade and 124th Brigade and saw action on the Somme during 1916. As part of Plumer's 2nd Army the division was present at the Battle of Messines in June 1917 and also participated in the early stages of Third Ypres. When James Simpson joined the 20th DLI the 41st Division was out of the line refitting as it was one of the five divisions destined for Italy to help the Italians after their near defeat at the Battle of Caporetto (9). The 41st Division arrived in Italy during the third week of November and took up positions on the River Piave facing the Austrians, the situation on the Italian front soon improved and in early March 1918 the division was one of two sent back to France (10). On the 7th March Pte James Simpson and the units of 41st Division, commanded by Major General S Lawford, found themselves attached to IV Corps of Byng's 3rd Army and concentrated near Doullens southwest of Arras. Following its return from Italy a general reorganisation of 41st Division took place and as a result on 17th March the 20th DLI, commanded by Lieutenant Colonel P W North DSO, found itself transferred to 124th Brigade.

The units of 124th Brigade were concentrated at Warluzel northeast of Doullens and as the Durham's marched into the village they found themselves welcomed by the band of the 10th QRWS and 26th Royal Fusiliers - the two other infantry battalions within 124th Brigade. Pte James Simpson and the men of the 20th DLI spent the following morning settling into their new surroundings as well as reorganising, that afternoon however orders were received that the battalion should be ready to move at short notice. The men were due to move off with their fellow battalions in the direction of the frontline and quickly set about preparing themselves, each man was given an extra 50 rounds of ammunition as well as their next days ration. As the men moved off towards the brigade starting point, a field just outside of Warluzel, word came through that the whole exercise had been a practice run and instead the men were treated to a lecture on various subjects by a senior officer. The following day James and the 20th DLI were inspected by the GOC 124th Brigade, he expressed his complete satisfaction with the battalion and welcomed them to his brigade. On 21st March as the Germans launched Operation Michael the Durham's were still near Warluzel, at 1:20pm that afternoon the battalion marched to the neighbouring village of Saulty before boarding a train to Albert. On arrival at Albert the men received further orders to proceed by train to Achiet-Le-Grand northwest of Bapaume; they arrived at 2:00am and then marched eastwards to Favreuil entering a camp in the village at 5:00am.

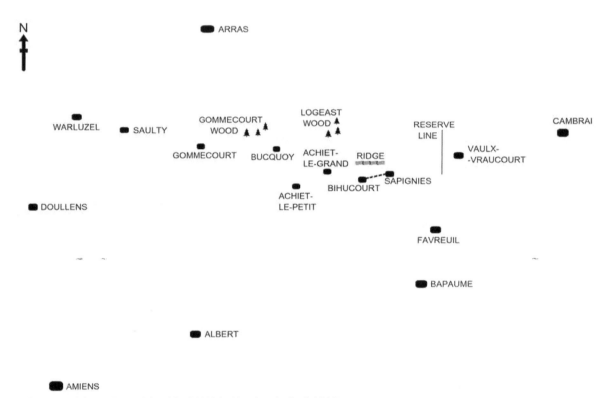

Map 45, Area of Operations of the 20th DLI (21st March – 1st April 1918)

At 8:00am on the 22nd March the Durham's were ordered to stand by, two hours later James and his battalion moved up to hold the reserve line situated behind the village of Vaulx-Vraucourt. The men arrived at 12:30pm and immediately set about improving the trenches along their stretch of line, the enemy had been pressing British troops in forward areas all day and at 5:00pm British units in front of the Durham's fell back whilst German troops occupied Vaulx-Vraucourt. That night proved quiet for James and his battalion however active patrolling was carried out to warn against German attacks. The Durham's didn't have to wait long for the enemy to make an appearance, the following morning at 8:00am German troops attacked the right flank of the battalion but, owing to good positions and well aimed machine gun and rifle fire, the attack was withheld. Throughout the day further assaults were made by the enemy and although carried out well with vigour and determination they failed to penetrate the Durham's wire. The night once again proved quiet but as before active patrols were carried out, the next morning however the Durham's were informed that British units to their right had fallen back and that afternoon having received orders to do so James's battalion followed suit. The Durham's withdrew in an orderly manner to a line through Favreuil and dug in, all the time as the men fell back continuous machine gun and rifle fire was kept up on the advancing enemy. Since leaving Favreuil two days earlier the battalion had had 2 officers and 27 other ranks killed along with many more men wounded and missing, up until now however Pte James Simpson had been lucky and come through unscathed. Shortly after their arrival at Favreuil at 1:00am on the morning of 25th March the Durham's received fresh orders to fall back towards Sapignies, this withdrawal commenced at 3:30am and just before dawn the men arrived and dug in to the right of the village. What happened next is best described by the Durham's battalion war diary.

'About 8:00am the enemy attacked Sapignies from our left and obtained the village. About 9:00am owing to the left being "in the air" the battalion withdrew to the ridge along the Bihucourt–Sapignies Road and dug in. Fire was kept up against the enemy during the withdrawal. At 1:15pm the enemy captured the village of Bihucourt and as the left flank of the battalion was also threatened at the same time the battalion withdrew to a line on the reverse slope of the ridge northwest of the Bihucourt–Sapignies Road. The battalion withdrew from this line about 2:00pm and took up a position in support to the 42nd (East Lancashire) Division east of Logeast Wood. About 7:00pm the troops in front withdrew and on orders this battalion withdrew to the village of Gommecourt where it reorganised.'

There's no doubt the 25th March was a tough day for the Durham's and having spent much of it in retreat moral was at an all time low, to make things worse the battalion suffered casualties and unfortunately 32 year old Pte James Simpson was one of several men killed. Although we don't know quite how he died its possible he was among those men who kept fire upon the enemy whilst the bulk of the battalion withdrew. The following day the Durham's, tired and depleted, found themselves south of Gommecourt Wood holding what had been a German frontline trench on the morning of 1st July 1916, by the night of 28th March however the situation along their stretch of front had stabilised. Having rested and reorganised sufficiently the 29th March saw the Durham's move eastwards once more, they relieved men of the 1/5th Lancashire Fusiliers (125th Brigade, 42nd East Lancashire Division) in front of Bucquoy and remained in position here until early April.

On the day Pte James Simpson died casualty figures according to the war diary of the 20th DLI were:

Officers = 2 wounded + 1 missing (later confirmed killed)
Other ranks = 8 killed (11) + 48 wounded + 20 missing.

All of the Durham's killed that day including Pte James Simpson have no known grave and are commemorated on Bay 8 of the Arras Memorial to the Missing. The Chigwell Parish Magazine for reasons unknown never reported the death of Pte James Simpson however Rebecca Simpson received word that her son had been killed as early as April 1918. Later that month pension forms were processed and by the following October she received a small allowance to compensate for her loss, personal items were also returned on completion in 1919 of a next of kin form. On 24th September 1919 the officer in charge of DLI infantry records at York wrote to Rebecca informing her she was entitled to a memorial scroll and plaque, these were received on the 29th May 1920. In 1919 Rebecca had received the BWM on behalf of her son and on 24th August 1921 she also received the VM.

* * *

On the 26th March as 5th Army retreated westward the town Albert, which had been so important for the British back in July 1916, fell into German hands, seeing the situation as desperate Petain, the French CIC, honoured an earlier agreement with Haig and sent French units northwards to help out. That day however things looked bleak and a conference between allied leaders was held in the town hall at Doullens. If the Germans reached Amiens and severed its rail links without doubt they'd split the British and French armies, if both had to fight on alone it would be only a matter of time before both were defeated. Everyone present knew that if an allied victory was to be realised Amiens had to be held at all costs. After heated discussions Haig suggested that someone should be responsible for overall command of the allied forces in France and Flanders, British and French delegates agreed and French commander General Ferdinand Foch was appointed to the role.

By this time however as bad as things were, and unbeknown to the allies, the German advance was losing momentum. Lines of supply were stretched and owing to casualty rates and fatigue it was hard for attacking troops to cross ground that had virtually been made impassable. On their retreat to the Hindenburg Line back in early 1917 the Germans had employed a scorched earth policy leaving devastation in their wake, now they were expected to cross this ground and found that they'd made life hard for themselves. In addition the Somme battlefields had seen almost three years of war the effects of which had taken their toll on the landscape. Another reason for the slowdown was that German troops who'd been led to believe that their country's naval blockade was starving Britain out of the war came across stockpiles of food and wine that had been left behind by retreating soldiers, tired and hungry unsurprisingly they over indulged themselves. Although a breakthrough had been created south of the Somme and east of Amiens up until now the area gained held no strategic importance, instead of letting his forces in the south turn northwards to roll up the British line Ludendorff kept a tight lead on them as they continued westwards. The German commander, as earlier explained, had instead decided to push on in places where he'd met resistance gaining only short term advantage whilst crucially deviating from his original plan, as a result by the time he realised his mistake it was too late. As the Michael Offensive continued on 28th March Ludendorff launched another set of attacks across the Douai plain aimed at Arras and Vimy. This fresh assault, codenamed 'Mars', didn't last long and did little as it went in against well prepared and well trained units of Byng's 3rd Army. That same day Gough was relieved of his command and on 2nd April General Sir Henry Rawlingson, who'd presided over the Somme offensives of 1916, took over what remained of 5th Army renaming it 4th Army in the process (12). Although the British appeared to be coping, for those units in the thick of it the situation seemed bad. Back home Lloyd George made fresh troops just out of training available for France and pressure was put on America to send troops across the Atlantic as British ships lined up to transport them. The 3rd April saw another allied conference take place, this time held at Beauvais some 40 miles south of Arras, American representatives were present and Foch was given formal permission to take control of the allied armies, the title however of Allied Commander-in-Chief was not bestowed on him for a further two weeks. On 5th April the Michael Offensive came to a halt however German units to the south would continue to gain minimal ground for the next few weeks finally reaching the village of Villers-Bretonneux, some 10 miles southeast of Amiens on 24th April. Within that time however Ludendorff had turned his attention northwards to launch a second main phase of action that started on 9th April was codenamed 'Operation Georgette' and later referred to by the allies as the 'Lys Offensive'.

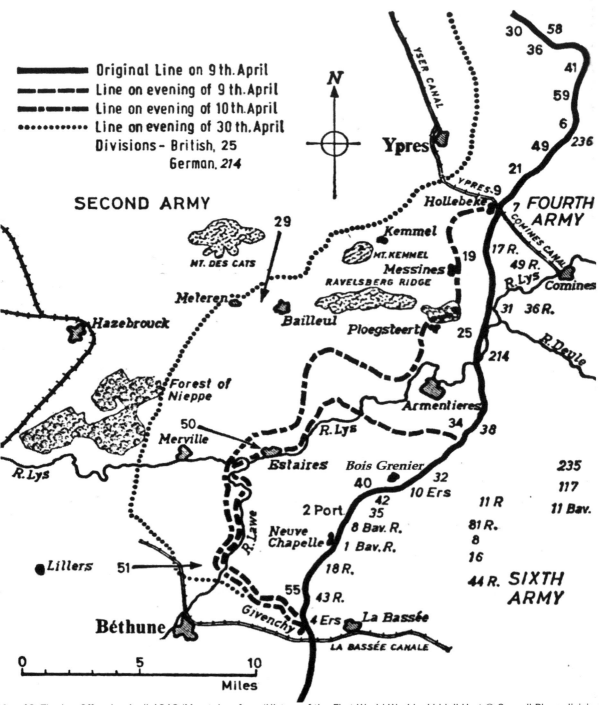

Map 46, The Lys Offensive April 1918 (Map taken from 'History of the First World War' by Liddell Hart © Cassell Plc, a division of The Orion Publishing Group London).

A scaled down version of his original George I and George II attacks Georgette was initially aimed at attacking the British lines - held by 1st Army under Sir Henry Horne - between Givenchy on the La Bassée Canal and the area of the River Lys south of Armentières with the distant objectives being Estaires, Merville and Hazebrouck along with its rail network. Although wishing to strike his blow several days earlier Ludendorff needed time to prepare, heavy artillery, men and munitions where sent northwards in full view of allied aircraft who wasted no time in reporting their findings to GHQ. Armed with this vital information Haig, along with his staff and army commanders, felt the movements were some sort of diversionary tactic and expected the Germans to once again strike a blow towards Arras and Vimy. So it was that on Tuesday 9th April at 8:45am following an artillery bombardment lasting some 4½ hours, and exactly a year to the day that British troops had attacked enemy lines opposite Arras, men of the German Sixth Army advanced on an 11 mile front hoping their actions would create a breakthrough substantial enough to win them the war. The main thrusts fell either side of Neuve Chapelle where an unprepared and over stretched Portuguese division held the frontline (13). The Portuguese who were under trained, low on munitions and in the process of being relieved were completely surprised as the enemy approached and the scale of the attack was such that they upped and fled leaving the British units on either side with their flanks in the air and plenty to do. To the right at Givenchy British troops attached to the 55th (West Lancashire) Division held firm managing to turn their left flank enough to stop the Germans breaking their line, as a result virtually no ground was lost. To the left however the battle weary 40th Division, who'd only just been moved northwards having been caught up in the allied retreat following the March Offensive, were not so lucky. This division, under the command of Major General John Ponsonby, had taken over the frontline to the left of the Portuguese on the night of the 7th - 8th April having relieved units of 29th Division. As its battalions entered the line they'd heard and saw shellfire as German guns fired registering shots in preparation for their attack. Positioned with its 119th Brigade on the right flank, next to the Portuguese and its 121st Brigade on the left flank, in front of Bois Grenier, its 120th (Highland) Brigade stood in reserve near Laventie (14).

FREDERICK ELLIOT NOBLE

Frederick Elliot Noble is the oldest man to appear on the Chigwell Village War Memorial having been born in Chigwell in 1876/7. Whilst nothing is known of his father who died relatively young his mother, a Laundress called Mary, was born in Chigwell in 1834. Fredrick had a sister some five years older called Ellen who was disabled from childhood however despite this she followed her mother's profession. At the turn of the century the family lived on Hainault Road and having been educated locally Frederick initially found work as an insurance salesman and newsagent assistant. There were many Nobles in and around Chigwell during this period and to piece together their family history would be a huge undertaking. A local historian and author called Nina Hansen, herself once a Noble, describes several members of the family in a book she wrote in 1985 entitled 'Memories of Chigwell'. On 12th October 1911 Frederick married a lady called Eleanor Mary Whitbread at St Mary's Church and soon after the couple set up home at 9 Saville Cottages on Hainault Road (15). There first child, a boy named Eric Henry, was born the following year and baptised at St Mary's Church on 1st December 1912, the same day as Henry James Mason. A little over a year later Eleanor gave birth to a baby girl called Olive May, she was baptised at St Mary's Church on 3rd May 1914. On the outbreak of war it seems unlikely that Frederick enlisted right away, given his age and his status of being married with children its probable he attested under the terms of the Derby Scheme and was conscripted in late 1916 early 1917, unfortunately his army service record no longer exists. One clue does exist however in the fact that during the spring of 1916 Eleanor gave birth to a third child, Frederick William as he was called was baptised at St Mary's on 7th May, we must assume his father was present at the ceremony. According to the Medal Rolls at the NA in Kew on passing a medical Frederick was originally posted as Private 4328 to the 11th Battalion Essex Regiment, again this most certainly was well after Lieutenant Maurice Austin Murray, who'd also served in this battalion, had been killed at the Battle of Loos in September 1915. Whilst still with the Essex Regiment Frederick saw his service number change to 35899, this probably occurred in early 1917 but soon after he was transferred as Private 54902 to the 16th Battalion (Cardiff City) Welsh Regiment. Unfortunately Frederick's geographical movements around this time are unknown, its reasonable to suggest he was training in England as both the aforementioned battalions were already in France and had been since 1915 (16). It's not known when Frederick first crossed the Channel to France or if he saw action with either the Essex or Welsh Regiment, to hazard a guess I'd say he landed in early 1918, saw action with neither and within days of arriving was transferred once again for a third and final time. What is known is that by April 1918 Pte Frederick Elliot Noble was Private 34956 (17) and attached to the 13th Battalion Yorkshire Regiment (18) which in turn, along with the 12th Suffolk's, 18th Sherwood Foresters (Nott's & Derby Regiment) and 20th Middlesex, formed part of 121st Brigade, 40th Division.

As the Portuguese fell back in disarray the units of 40th Division had their work cut out, shells fell everywhere and gas filled the air as men were forced into retreat wearing respirators. The battalions of 119th Brigade had the toughest time and although some resistance was tried advancing Germans broke through the flanks forcing various units northwest towards Estaires, Fleurbaix, Bac-St Maur and across the River Lys. Those units of 121st Brigade were caught up in events however the 13th Yorkshire's, along with Pte Frederick Noble, found themselves positioned on the extreme left of the brigade front where the German assault had not been concentrated. As a result working closely with units of the neighbouring 34th Division and aided by artillery fire, rifle grenades and trench mortars they maintained a stiff defence in front and to the left of Bois Grenier holding positions such as

Shaftsbury House and Red House Post. During the opening day of the Georgette offensive German troops managed to penetrate the allied line north of Givenchy to a depth of some 3½ miles on a frontage almost 11 miles wide, their spoils included Richebourg, Neuve Chapelle and Laventie and the following day more gains were made.

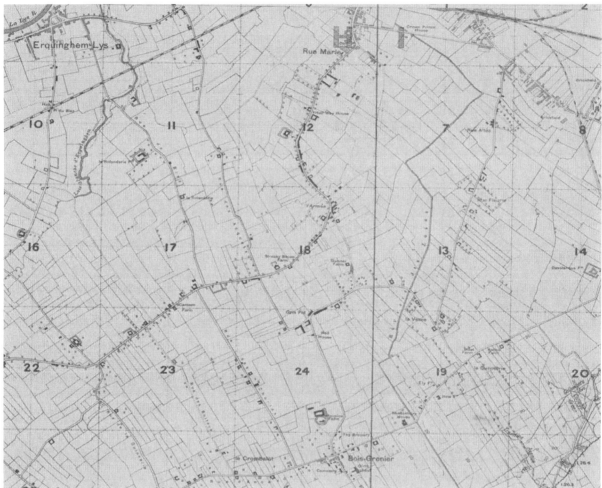

Map 47, Bois Grenier

On the morning of 10th April, following the success of his troops the previous day, Ludendorff extended the right of his attack front northwards to include positions in front of Armentières and the area south of Ypres. This move saw units of the German Fourth Army launch attacks on both units of 1st Army, under Horne, and 2nd Army under Plumer. That day Armentières, which had been in allied hands since October 1914, fell to the Germans as those troops holding it reluctantly gave ground. Further north Ploegsteert was lost as well as large sections of Messines Ridge that had been captured so dramatically by 2nd Army the year before. To the south Germans troops crossed the River Lawe and Estaires was captured, two British divisions were thrown forward but pushed back again as the enemy advanced. Meanwhile Pte Frederick Noble and the 13th Yorkshire's had started the day defending their section of front near Bois Grenier, throughout the morning skirmishes took place as enemy troops tried to push their way forward. The battalion, still assisted by units of 34th Division in addition to troops from their own brigade, held on remarkably as Germans massed only yards away, by mid afternoon however the strain was too much and at 3:25pm orders were received to withdraw. Although a possible counter attack was mentioned it was soon cancelled and that evening the battalion withdrew north and then westward towards Erquinghem through Rue Fleurie Post, Gunner Farm and Streaky Bacon Farm. Their movement was aided by mist that descended over the Flanders plain, as they fell back shells constantly rained down and buildings on route were ablaze. About 6:30pm the 13th Yorkshire's crossed the Pont de Nieppe and having received orders to do so by midnight found themselves, along with battalions of 121st Brigade and 34th Division, holding positions near the Armentières to Bailleul rail line west of the Lys.

By now panic was starting to set in from the men at the top to the men on the ground, after four years of war ground was being lost on an unprecedented scale and it looked to all like the allies could lose the war. By the evening of 10th April Ludendorff's troops had penetrated the allied line on a front almost 30 miles wide to a depth at its widest point of roughly 6 miles. The area between the British Army and the sea was getting smaller and smaller and it was almost as if they had their backs to the wall. On Thursday 11th April 1918 Field Marshal Sir

Douglas Haig issued what was to become his most famous 'Order of the Day', it was addressed to all ranks of the British Army in France and Flanders and included the following statement:

"There is no other course open to us but to fight it out! Every position must be held to the last man: there must be no retirement. With our backs to the wall, and believing in the justice of our cause, each one of us must fight on to the end. The safety of our homes and the freedom of mankind alike depend on the conduct of each one of us at this critical moment".

That day there's no doubt the overall situation seemed serious for the officers and men of the 13th Yorkshire's as having withdrawn the previous night they hastily set about defending their current position near the railway west of the Lys.

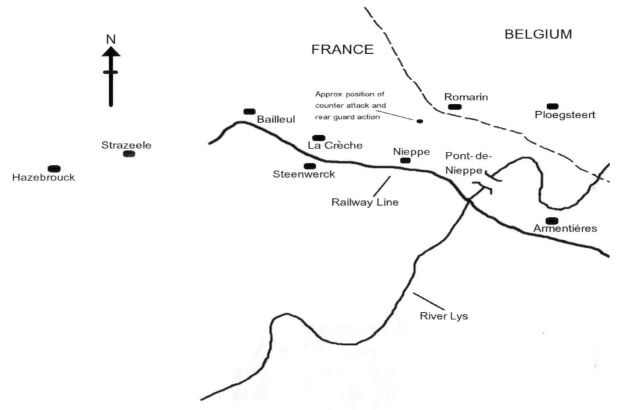

Map 48, Position of 13th Battalion Yorkshire Regiment (April 11th-12th 1918)

The area was crowded with troops when at 5:30am the CO of the 13th Yorkshire's met with battalion commanders of 101st Brigade, 34th Division. After some discussion it was decided that the 13th Yorkshire's would move into support whilst a new frontline was held by men of the 10th Lincoln's and 11th Suffolk's (101st Brigade). At 6:30am the 13th Yorkshire's contacted 121st Brigade HQ for further orders and 1½ hours later they dug in having established support lines at Pont D'Achelles between Nieppe and Steenwerck. Around 1:00pm men who'd become detached from the battalion during their withdrawal from Bois Grenier started to come in armed with information regarding enemy movements. These men were rounded up and returned to their units, it's possible of course that Pte Frederick Noble was amongst them but if not it's most likely he was employed either moving supplies or helping improve the Yorkshire's position. At this point, as has been the case throughout Frederick's story, confusion exists that surrounds the events of the next 48 hours. Having carefully pieced together and studied the story of Frederick Noble I can't help but think that his date of death has been incorrectly recorded by both the CWGC and SDGW. According to both these sources Frederick was killed in action on 13th April 1918 but as will be explained I disagree and think it more likely he was killed on the evening of 11th April 1918.

During the afternoon of 11th April a counter attack was launched against enemy units near Romarin as they prepared to push westward toward Steenwerck and Bailleul, the 12th Suffolk's of 121st Brigade were in front with the 13th Yorkshire's in close support. Details of this attack are sketchy however faced by a determined enemy both battalions managed an advance of some 200 yards; despite this at 2:30pm the attackers received orders not to pursue the assault as further withdrawals would be made that evening. At 5:00pm the 13th Yorkshire's were handed orders to provide a rear guard whilst the 12th Suffolk's passed through, I believe its either during the assault or this rear guard action that Pte Frederick Noble was killed. Having successfully covered the Suffolk's withdrawal at 9:30pm the 13th Yorkshire's withdrew to a point on the Bailleul Road north of La Crèche where they took up support positions. At 5:00am on the morning of 12th April the battalion moved off once again this time headed for Strazeele east of Hazebrouck. They marched via the villages of Bailleul, Outtersteene and Merris arriving at 3:30pm, their war diary reports that even though patrols were sent out they found no sign of the enemy. The following day, the day Pte Frederick Noble is recorded as having been killed, was a quiet day for the men of the 13th Yorkshire's as they set about improving positions, further patrols were sent out but again no contact was made with the enemy. That night they moved again and by morning on 14th April the battalion found itself in billets at St Martin-au-Laeurt to the north of St Omer, here they reorganised and a tally of losses was recorded for the period 9th – 13th April 1918.

Although their battalion war diary records no casualty figures for the month of April according to SDGW the 13th Yorkshire's lost 1 officer and 55 other ranks between the 9th – 13th April, of the latter figure 47 men are recorded as having been killed in action on 13th April. It's highly unlikely that 47 men were killed on a day when no contact was made with the enemy and if they were its unlikely that such a high number of losses would go unmentioned in the battalion war diary. From the figure of 55 some 44 have no known grave and are commemorated on the Ploegsteert Memorial to the Missing. Fortunately the body of Pte Frederick Elliot Noble was recovered and is buried in Plot II, Row G, Grave 16 of Le Grand Beaumart CWGC Cemetery, Steenwerck, France. The fact that Frederick is buried at Steenwerck only supports my theory that he was killed on 11th April given that the counter attack and subsequent rear guard action took place in this area. The only mention of Frederick in the Chigwell Parish Magazine came in July 1918 when an article appeared stating he'd been reported missing and that his family had no news of him. Whilst it's not known what happened to his wife and children after the war it's also unknown when they received confirmation that he'd actually been killed in action (19). As mentioned in this books introduction some stories regarding the men of Chigwell are more conclusive than others, the story of Pte Frederick Noble is one where the absolute truth has been hard to come by and given the passage of time unfortunately may never be known.

* * *

It was a determined Ludendorff that continued to push his troops westward into the third week of April however over the days that followed the Georgette Offensive slowed down due to a combination of allied air attacks (20), fatigue and lack of discipline by troops on the ground. In the case of the allies British and French units were moved northwards to help stem the advance and out on the Passchendaele Ridge General Plumer reluctantly ordered a well timed withdrawal adopting a sharper defensive position for 2nd Army just east of Ypres. On 14th April the allied CIC General Foch sensed German pressure was easing however the enemy continued to gain ground. As allied counter attacks proved costly on 15th April German troops captured Bailleul along with positions out on the Ravelsberg Ridge, it was during this advance that Chigwell's next casualty was sustained.

CHARLES WILLIAM DAY

Barkingside is situated roughly two miles south of Chigwell and it was here in February 1883 that Charles William Day was born. His father called John Day worked as a coach builder and originally came from Elsenham in Essex whilst his mother Esther - maiden name Phillips - came from Barkingside. Once married John and Esther remained in Barkingside and went on to have ten children in total, Charles was the fifth of seven sons. Along with his brothers and sisters Charles was educated locally and on leaving school started work as a Groom before becoming a full time gardener. Eventually he met a young mother from Chigwell called Mary Jane Dodkins whom he married in a ceremony at St Mary's Church Chigwell on 23rd April 1908. Along with a daughter called Charlotte that Mary had from a previous relationship the couple set up home at Mount Pleasant Cottages, Grange Hill, soon after Charles adopted Charlotte, aged 6 at the time, and brought her up as his own. On 30th January 1909 Mary gave birth to a baby boy, named after his father, Charles John Day was baptised at St Mary's Church two months later. In late 1910 Mary gave birth to another boy, Edward George Day was baptised on 5th February 1911. A third boy called Robert Walter Day was born on 5th April 1913 and baptised at St Mary's Church on 1st June the same year, four months later however tragedy struck as 2 year old Edward George Day died suddenly, he was buried in the churchyard at St Mary's on 16th October 1913. Around this time Charles started work as a gardener in the grounds of Chigwell Hall, owned by Walter Waugh his story is told in the chapter entitled '1916'. Although somewhat confusing and possibly part of an additional caretaker's role Charles at times occupied Chigwell Hall Cottage, situated on Church Lane in Chigwell it was this address that he gave when joining the army some two years later. When war was declared in August 1914 Charles didn't enlist right away, being in his early thirties with a wife and small children he continued with duties at Chigwell Hall and on 3rd December 1914 Mary gave birth to another son. Albert Edward Day was baptised at St Mary's Church on 7th February 1915 in a joint ceremony that saw Matthew and Esther Mason's son James also baptised. As the war continued and the number of volunteers slowed down conscription appeared on the horizon and the Derby Scheme was introduced, being a married man but eligible for duty on 6th December 1915 Charles Day walked in to a recruiting office in Epping to join the army. As with all new recruits he underwent a medical examination and fortunately sections of his army service record survive at the NA. Charles was 5ft 6½" tall weighing 128lbs, he had a 36" chest that measured 39" when fully expanded and had perfect vision. Giving his religion as Church of England as required he enlisted for the duration of the war, Charles naturally listed Mary as his next of kin. Having enlisted under the terms of the Derby Scheme

Charles wasn't mobilised right away, the following day his name was transferred to the lists of the army reserve and for the time being he was free to go about his business. It should be remembered how Charles had several older and younger brothers. Like Charles many of these were old enough to enlist and we know for sure at least one of them joined the army.

William Day was barely a year older than Charles having been born in Barkingside in early 1882. After leaving school he worked as a general labourer and whilst it's not known if he married and had children in August 1914 he answered Kitcheners call for volunteers enlisting at a recruiting office at Stratford in East London. Although his service record no longer exists on passing a medical William was posted to the RFA where he held the rank of Driver. Attached to 'A' Battery, 104th Brigade RFA part of 23rd Division he trained along with other artillery units at Mytchett Camp near Frensham in Hampshire before moving to Ewshott near Aldershot. Having moved to Shorncliffe barracks in Kent in February 1915 then back to Hampshire the following May that August saw units of 23rd Division sent to France. William arrived at Boulogne on 27th August 1915 and took up positions near Tilques northwest of St Omer. As Christmas approached, having experienced several months of life in the frontline, the 23rd Division found itself in position south of Armentières. Although the exact circumstances are unknown according to SDGW William died on 26th December 1915, the fact that his entry doesn't say killed in action or died of wounds suggests he possibly contracted some kind of disease or even pneumonia. Driver William Day is buried in Plot I, Row G, Grave 3 of Erquinghem-Lys Churchyard Extension, Nord, France.

As 1916 started Charles found himself working at Chigwell Hall and as news of William's death reached the family deep down inside he must have felt a call from the army wasn't too far away. On 4th April 1916 Mary gave birth to another boy, Arthur Thomas Day was her fifth son and was baptised at St Mary's Church on 7th May 1916, barely a month later the wait was over as Charles received word from the army. On 9th June a letter arrived stating that Charles would be drafted and two days later he was mobilised and posted as Private 30533 to the ranks of the 12th Battalion Essex Regiment. Based at Harwich and mentioned elsewhere in this book the 12th Essex was a reserve battalion, Charles remained with this unit a little under three months during which time he underwent a period of basic training. On 1st September 1916 due to conscription a reorganisation of army reserve units took place that saw some battalions disbanded whilst others were renamed and absorbed into new units of numbered training reserve battalions attached to numbered training reserve brigades. The details of this reorganisation are quite complex and this book is not the place to go into detail however the 12th Essex was absorbed into a unit known as the 25th Training Reserve Battalion attached to the 6th Training Reserve Brigade. Charles continued training with this unit in areas in and around Harwich until the 12th October 1916 when, on the authority of the War Office, he was posted as Private 30009 to the ranks of the Norfolk Regiment. Leaving for France the same day Charles sailed from Folkestone and arrived at Boulogne, six days later he was in camp at Etaples where he was detailed to join the 9th Battalion Norfolk Regiment.

Having arrived in France in 1915 by October 1916 the 9th Norfolk's were involved in operations on the Somme as part of 71st Brigade, 6th Division, when Charles joined the battalion on 24th October 1916 they were out of the line refitting in camp at Montauban. In early 1917 the units of 6th Division moved north to the Lens - Béthune sector where they remained for most of the year. On the night of 21st – 22nd September the 9th Norfolk's headed into the trenches on line holding duties, whilst relieving existing troops Charles was injured. Although we don't know the extent of his wounds or the details surrounding his injury its also unclear if he required hospital treatment of any kind. According to his service record the army launched an inquiry into the incident however Charles was relieved of any blame, self inflicted wounds were seen as a sign of cowardice and if found guilty a man could expect the harshest of punishments and sometimes a firing squad. During November the 6th Division, under the command of Major General T Marden, took part in the Battle of Cambrai. In early March 1918 the 9th Norfolk's were in trenches at Lagnicourt northeast of Bapaume. When Operation Michael started on 21st March the battalion was still in the line and as a result experienced the preliminary bombardment laid down by the Germans. As part of Byng's 3rd Army over the days that followed the unit was withdrawn and moved northwards towards Ypres where they concentrated in and around Winnezeele. Having spent time refitting and regrouping the units of 6th Division joined 2nd Army and some battalions including the 9th Norfolk's found themselves inspected by General Plumer. As April started Pte Charles Day and the 9th Norfolk's left Winnezeele for a spell in the trenches, the battalion relieved men of the 6th Duke of Wellington (West Riding) Regiment in frontline positions near the remains of Polygon Wood. As expected with the Ypres Salient the conditions the men endured during this time were awful with mud everywhere, poor defences and shell holes full of water due to incessant rainfall. During the tour however the Norfolk's fortunately reported no casualties and described enemy activity as very quiet causing no trouble at all. The Norfolk's left frontline positions on 7th April and moved into reserve trenches near Westhoek, over the next two days men of various companies were detailed for salvage collecting and work parties however it's unclear if Charles was amongst them. Unfortunately although part of his service record exists it doesn't record which company of the 9th Norfolk's Charles served in. During the early hours of 10th April senior officers received word from captured prisoners that an enemy attack was due to commence on frontline areas at 6:30am, along with other units the 9th Norfolk's were ordered forward as a precautionary measure but when no attack materialised on their stretch of line they returned once again to original positions. Pte Charles Day and the 9th Norfolk's were relieved on the 13th April by men of the 11th Essex and marched back to barracks at Ypres, the following morning they boarded buses and made for Dranoutre where they joined up with other units of 71st Brigade (21). Having barely arrived the 9th Norfolk's were ordered to take up defensive positions west of Dranoutre but soon after they moved again this time adopting positions east and southeast of the village.

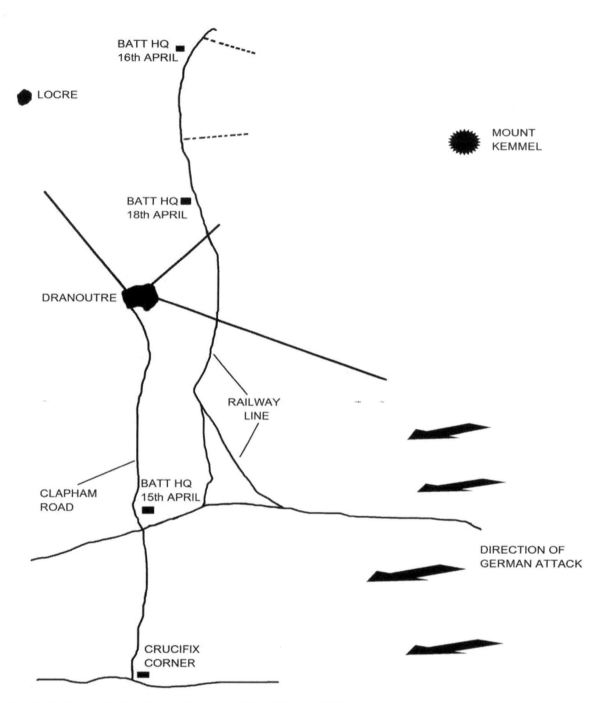

Map 49, Position of 9th Norfolk's near Dranoutre (15th – 18th April 1918)

Although German troops were known to be advancing weight of numbers were unknown, the situation on the ground for British commanders was at best confusing. During this period several divisions were caught up in the fighting however 71st Brigade was the only brigade involved from 6th Division, to its left stood units of the 59th (2nd North Midland) Division whilst to the right stood troops of the 49th (West Riding) Division. Late evening on 14th April saw the men of the 9th Norfolk's dug in awaiting developments, to their right stood troops of the 1st Leicestershire Regiment. Fighting nearby saw the Norfolk's 'D' Coy placed temporarily under the command of the Leicester's whilst the remaining companies were placed on standby. The men were informed they might be needed to reinforce units in neighbouring areas should the fighting reach crisis point, luckily however this wasn't the case. On the morning of 15th April Pte Charles Day and the 9th Norfolk's remained in position defending

Dranoutre, 'D' Coy was returned to the battalion and all companies were reorganised. The men of 'D' Coy were ordered to hold the right front whilst 'A' Coy held the left front next to units of 59th Division, the men of 'C' Coy took up positions near Crucifix Corner and Clapham Road ready to counter attack should the frontline be broken whilst 'B' Coy were held in reserve. As the battalion waited conditions must have been awful for men like Charles Day, they knew an attack was imminent and from midday onwards enemy artillery pounded their positions in readiness for a German assault. The men of 'C' Coy suffered terribly during this bombardment and as a result the company became ineffective, because of this 'B' Coy were ordered up to launch when required any counter attack. At 2:30pm German troops advanced on the Norfolk's position, heavy fighting ensued but despite this by 3:00pm they'd gained a foothold in the battalion frontline. Almost immediately 'B' Coy moved forward to counter attack and successfully, by will and determination, drove the enemy out however things were far from done and dusted. The men of 'B' Coy put up a stiff resistance and managed to hold on forming a defensive flank to their right, the line in that direction had all but gone as neighbouring units, overwhelmed by the advance, were forced to withdraw. German troops continued to attack and when reinforcements were moved forward with heavy machine guns the men of 'B' Coy, having sustained heavy losses, had no option but to follow neighbouring troops and retire. The Norfolk's having had quite a time of it formed up by the railway with their left boundary being Clapham Road, here they made contact with men of the 1st Leicestershire Regiment however the situation to the right was extremely obscure. During the fighting it appears Pte Charles Day was mortally wounded, possibly in defence of the Norfolk's position or part of 'B' Coy's counter attack, its reasonable to suggest he may even have been injured by shellfire along with large numbers of 'C' Coy. The Norfolk's continued to adopt defensive positions throughout the evening fully expecting further attacks, fortunately these didn't materialise. At 10:30pm orders were received that at midnight a force of various details, some 1500 strong, would hold the frontline allowing hard pressed units and 71st Brigade to withdraw. The Norfolk's moved northwards taking up fresh positions west of Mount Kemmel, this withdrawal was carried out without casualty and on arrival the battalion, severely weakened, reorganised as best as it could. Over the days that followed units of 71st Brigade were moved into divisional reserve however they remained on standby in positions west of Mount Kemmel. The surviving men of the 9th Norfolk's were finally relieved by French troops on the night of 19th – 20th April and moved into camps west of Ypres, on arrival they rested, regrouped and received a much needed draft of reinforcements (22).

Back in Chigwell it wasn't until 14th May 1918 that Mary received word from the war office that her husband was missing, at that time nothing further was known. In July 1918 an article appeared in the Chigwell Parish Magazine stating that Charles was listed as missing and reports that he was injured and recovering in hospital had turned out to be incorrect. As time went on and the war ended with no further news regarding her husband Mary looked to the future for her and the children. She filled out forms for an army pension and asked that Charlotte should be included stating although adopted by Charles he'd cared for her since a baby. On the pension form Mary lists Charles parents as deceased; she also lists the names and addresses of Charles brothers. Albert aged 47 living in Uphall Road Ilford, John 41 living in Ilford, Henry 34 living in Stanley Road Ilford, Arthur 29 living in High Street Barkingside and Bert 29 living in St Mary's Road Barking. Although not named on the form Charles sisters are recorded as living in Ilford, Woodford and Basingstoke. On 29th April 1919 the army confirmed that Charles had died on or since 15th April 1918, as brief as this was Charles exact fate was still unknown. With no real answers on 16th September 1919 the War Office wrote to the officer in charge of the Norfolk Regiment requesting that any personal items belonging to Charles should be returned to Mary at Mount Pleasant Cottage. On 3rd February 1920 Mary received a memorial scroll in memory of her husband; Charles was also entitled to both the BWM and VM. A month later a report was sent to the officer in charge of infantry records at Warley in reference to Pte Charles William Day, it turned out his name was on a list of German burials of prisoners of war, on 4th March 1920 Mary finally found out the fate of her husband. As German troops attacked on 15th April 1918 and captured the Norfolk's frontline Charles was wounded, unable to move as his battalion withdrew, along with other men he was rounded up and taken prisoner. Charles was held for two days and moved southwards towards Armentières however his wounds were such that he died as a prisoner of war on 18th April 1918. His body was buried by German soldiers and lies in a communal grave at Pont-De-Nieppe Communal Cemetery at Nieppe northwest of Armentières (23). Charles headstone lies in a row of four, each stone stands shoulder to shoulder with its neighbour, this practice carried out by the CWGC indicates the fact that a soldier lies buried in a shared grave. Another point worth mentioning is that when the Chigwell Village War Memorial was constructed Charles initials were incorrectly inscribed as GW instead of CW. In addition several members of the Dodkins family were killed in the mine explosion at the Prince of Wales Pub on 19th April 1941 whilst another died serving king and country in July 1941; his name appears on the Chigwell Memorial under Second World War casualties.

* * *

As Ludendorff's influence on the Georgette Offensive waned allied troops were able to regroup and offer resistance, Australian troops had stopped the enemy reaching Hazebrouck and as a result the German commander once again saw the chances of victory slipping away. A lull in the fighting on 18th April saw actions around Ypres scaled down temporarily however on this day near Béthune fighting continued. During the morning German troops launched a half hearted attack from Givenchy in the south across the River Lawe aimed at areas west of Merville, this action after the war became known as the 'Battle of Béthune' and occurred on sections of frontline held by units of 1st Army under Sir Henry Horne. Four British divisions were involved in the battle including the 4th Division which contained the next soldier from Chigwell to be killed in the fighting of 1918.

SYDNEY JAMES BODGER

Unfortunately Sydney James Bodger is one of those men we know little about, nothing concrete can be found via the 1901 census and sadly his army service record no longer exists. What we do know is that he was born at Epping in 1895 the son of James Mears Bodger and wife Sarah, early movements regarding whereabouts and education are unclear however when war was declared the family lived at 12 Smeaton Road, Woodford Bridge. In September 1914 when Kitchener requested volunteers Sydney wasted no time in answering the call, aged 19 at the time, he walked into a recruiting office at Stratford in East London and joined the army. Sydney underwent a medical examination and on being passed fit was made Private 16983 and sent to the reserves of the Essex Regiment, he completed nearly nine months of basic training before, according to information stored on his MIC, being sent to France on 1st June 1915. On arrival Sydney was posted to the ranks of the 2nd Battalion Essex Regiment, this unit has already been explained in the stories of William Frank Gapes, George Pleasance and briefly James Simpson however Sydney joined the battalion before all the aforementioned men. Briefly to recap on the unit's movements the 2nd Essex was a regular army battalion and arrived in France with the BEF in August 1914 as part of 12th Brigade, 4th Division (24). It took part at Le Cateau and in April 1915 served at the Second Battle of Ypres, when Sydney joined as a reinforcement two months later the battalion was in billets at Elverdinge northwest of Ypres. As explained in the story of William Frank Gapes on 1st July 1916 the 2nd Essex was involved on the first day of the Somme, it appears that Sydney was present that day but given the lack of progress made by the battalion was most likely attached to one of those companies that never left the trenches to go over the top. As explained in the story of George Pleasance early 1917 found the 2nd Essex still on the Somme, that April however the battalion served at the Battle of Arras and later that year played significant parts in several actions of Third Ypres. As 1918 started Pte Sydney Bodger and the 2nd Essex found themselves back near Arras in positions east of the town, they remained in this area for several months and were in support lines here during March when the German spring offensives began. The 2nd Essex like many battalions had a tough time of it during this period and suffered terrible casualties, by this stage of the war however Pte Sydney Bodger would have been regarded as an experienced soldier and compared to most a battalion veteran. It appears Sydney came through unscathed and by the beginning of April the 2nd Essex, commanded by Lieutenant Colonel R N Thompson, found itself based at Haute-Avesnes some eight miles northwest of Arras. Having reorganised sufficiently by 8th April the battalion moved once again this time marching southwest a few miles to Fosseux. On 12th April given the fact that Ludendorff had launched his Georgette Offensive units of 4th Division were moved northwards to help stem the advance, as a result the 2nd Essex and Pte Sydney Bodger boarded trucks bound for Busnes near Lillers.

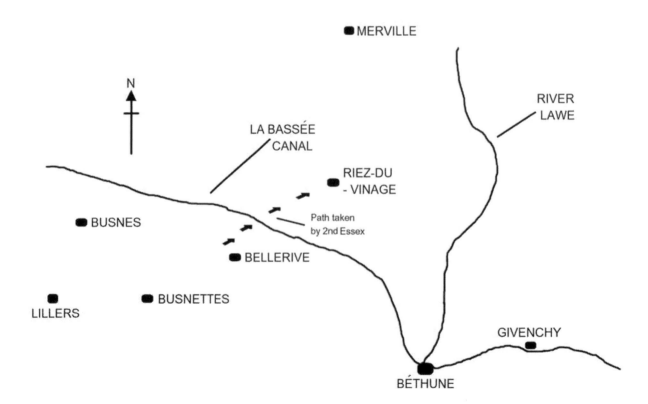

Map 50, Area of Operation of 2nd Essex (16th – 24th April 1918)

According to a piece that appears in the book entitled 'The Essex Regiment 2nd Battalion by J W Burrows & Son a soldier present wrote that during the journey they witnessed the roads crowded with refugees each one carrying a few belongings they'd scrambled together. He went on to describe women pushing prams and old men pushing wheelbarrows in addition to carts laden with furniture owned by farmers fleeing the frontline. On arrival at Busnes Sydney's battalion equipped and prepared itself ready for action, the men weren't immediately ordered towards the frontline but some companies were detailed for outpost duty. At 6:00pm on 13th April the battalion moved to Busnettes, south of Busnes east of Lillers, here the battalion again stood in readiness and again provided companies for outpost duty. On 16th April the 2nd Essex relieved men of the 1st Battalion Rifle Brigade (11th Brigade, 4th Division) in support line areas near Bellerive on the banks of the La Bassée Canal, in the process unfortunately the battalion suffered casualties however they maintained this position throughout the following day. At 1:00am on the morning of 18th April enemy guns opened fire on British positions including those held by men of the 2nd Essex. This preliminary barrage, designed to pave the way ahead of the German attack, although not heavy managed to cause the battalion further casualties and this time amongst their number was 23 year old Pte Sydney James Bodger (25). Unfortunately the problem with shell fire was such that most of the time you couldn't tell where they'd land, in most cases you ducked and hoped for the best and with a direct hit regardless of protection nine times out of ten you stood no chance. It seems unbelievable that a soldier like Sydney Bodger who'd seen and been through so much was killed in this way but being exposed to such conditions on a daily basis over a period of three years suggests that given the law of averages your luck can last only so long. At 3:00am German units attacked frontline positions held by 4th Division however due to good defences and determined effort their advance, somewhat frustrated, made little progress. That evening the 1st Battalion Kings Own (Royal Lancashire) Regiment attacked the eastern side of Riez-Du-Vinage but despite holding its ground lost heavily, the 2nd Essex were ordered forward in relief and occupied the perimeter whilst awaiting events. The next morning the village was found to be still full of Germans and heavy fighting at close quarters continued amongst the ruins all day, on the evening of 21st April the men of the 2nd Essex were relieved by men of the 2nd Lancashire Fusiliers and took up positions north of the village. Over the days that followed fighting continued in the region and the 2nd Essex, not actively engaged, remained in support. It wasn't until 24th April that the battalion finally moved back to billets near Busnes in order to refit and reorganise. According to their war diary casualty figures for the 2nd Essex during the period 16th – 24th April 1918 were as follows:

Officers: 4 killed in action + 6 wounded + 2 missing + 2 to hospital
Other Ranks: 43 killed in action + 115 wounded + 36 missing + 42 to hospital + 2 died of wounds (26)

No mention of Pte Sydney Bodger's death appeared in either the Chigwell Parish Magazine or Woodford Times Newspaper, like many men killed by shellfire he has no known grave and is commemorated along with other Essex men - including Lieutenant Maurice Austin Murray - on panels 85 to 87 of the Loos Memorial to the Missing. When the Chigwell Village War Memorial was inscribed a spelling mistake saw Sydney's name spelt Booger instead of Bodger. It's not known when Sydney's parents first received word that their son had been killed, his medal entitlement included the 1915 Star, BWM and VM. After the war it appears Sarah Bodger remained in Woodford Bridge however by time the IWGC compiled its records in the mid 1920's her husband James had passed away.

* * *

Whilst Ludendorff still harboured hopes of a breakthrough in Flanders his next significant action occurred back on the Somme. Although the Michael Offensive had ended on 5th April as previously mentioned German troops in the area continued to gain minimal ground over the following weeks reaching Villers-Bretonneux southeast of Amiens on 24th April. That day assisted by tanks German forces captured the village inflicting heavy casualties in the process, British tanks however were soon on hand resulting in the worlds first ever tank-versus-tank battle. Whilst machines from both sides suffered heavy losses British tanks managed to gain the upper hand. The following morning General Rawlingson ordered British and Australian units to counter attack and by dawn on 25th April Villers-Bretonneux was back in allied hands, with that any further ambitions the Germans had of reaching Amiens were over. Back in Flanders Ludendorff resumed his Georgette Offensive on a limited front on 25th April. French troops who'd relieved British units holding Mount Kemmel found themselves in the firing line and that day despite heavy fighting they lost control of this large hill that dominated the generally flat landscape of southern Belgium. Although Mount Kemmel was a vital position Ludendorff failed to capitalise on his gain, short of reserves he launched another more costly attack on 29th April that did little to improve the overall situation. Having failed to achieve the breakthrough he'd hoped and fearing his current positions were open to counter attack Ludendorff decided to pull the plug on Georgette, the Lys Offensive was over. Since the first German offensive back in March the allies had suffered substantial casualties, the British especially had been hit hardest and it was months before they'd recover sufficiently (27). Having tried three times to break the allied lines Ludendorff felt the sands of time running out, now however far from finished he turned his attention south to where the French held the line. His plan was to attack the French Army on the Chemin des Dames attracting British reserves from the north in the process, if successful he then hoped to resume his attack on a weakened British line in Flanders and push on to the Channel Ports. As May started the Germans prepared for their next attempt, at this point however to tell the story of Chigwell's next casualty our attention is turned back to the Somme which in the grand scheme of things had become a relatively quiet sector.

FREDERICK ARTHUR BAILEY

When war was declared in August 1914 Frederick Arthur Bailey was barely 16 years old, it didn't take long for its effects to reach home as that November his older brother, Able Seaman Harry Norman Bailey, died tragically whilst serving with the Royal Navy aboard HMS Kestrel. Educated locally Frederick initially lived with his parents Harry and Charlotte in a small house on Turpins Lane Woodford Bridge. On leaving school like his father Frederick worked for the Post Office however losing his older brother made him determined to volunteer. By mid 1915 Frederick had left Turpins Lane to live at 59 Francis Avenue Ilford, that August however and possibly against his parents wishes he lied about his age and joined the army. On 13th August Frederick attended a recruiting office at Stratford in East London telling the recruiting officer, Major Raphael Jackson, he was 19 years old, having been born in Chigwell in 1898 in fact he was just 17. As mentioned at the beginning of this book in the piece entitled 'Authors Explanations' most army service records from the First World War were destroyed by fire caused by an air raid in 1941. Fortunately the service records of those men who served with guard regiments were kept separately and many survive at the archive department of the Guards Museum in Birdcage Walk, London, SW1. Frederick Bailey was destined to join the corps of the Household Cavalry (28) and subsequently the reserve regiment of the 1st Life Guards, his service record survives and provides the following information. On enlistment like all new recruits Frederick underwent a medical examination, he was 6ft 2¼˝ tall with a 36˝ chest; distinguishing marks were listed as a mole in the middle of his back and a mole on his left breast. Having had his application approved on 16th August 1915 Trooper 3891 Frederick Arthur Bailey was sent for training at Hyde Park Barracks in London, for over a year he continued training in and around England during which time he took part and completed a course in bomb throwing. On 1st September 1916 a new unit known as the Household Battalion was created at Knightsbridge Barracks in London, designed as an infantry battalion it took its personnel from reserve regiments of the Household Cavalry which included the 1st Life Guards Reserve Regiment. Frederick found himself along with many others transferred to the ranks of the Household Battalion, he was renumbered Trooper 22 and subsequently drafted for service overseas.

Destined for France the newly formed Household Battalion including Trooper Frederick Bailey sailed from Southampton on 8th November 1916 and arrived at Le Havre the following day. On 17th November 1916 the Household Battalion found itself attached to 10th Brigade, 4th Division in positions on the Somme. Frederick settled down quickly to life in the front line however just over a month later he was wounded. Unfortunately the circumstances surrounding his injuries are unknown but on 18th December 1916 he was treated at the 2/2nd London CCS at Grovetown near Bray-sur-Somme (29). His wounds were such that soon after Frederick was admitted to No.6 General Hospital at Rouen where he spent Christmas and New Year. On 4th January 1917 he was transferred back to England and the following day was posted to the reserves of the Household Battalion stationed at Windsor. Frederick's exact movements over the following year are unclear, he probably spent some time convalescing however we know he remained in England most likely at Windsor. It's reasonable to suggest that at some point during 1917 Frederick returned home to Ilford and Woodford Bridge in order to visit his friends and family. In July his eldest brother, Pte Charles Ernest Bailey, was killed whilst serving with the 1/6th Battalion London Regiment in positions south of Ypres, with two boys killed and Frederick having been wounded the war was certainly taking its toll on the Bailey family. On 29th January 1918 Frederick was transferred once again, this time to the reserve ranks of the Grenadier Guards based at Caterham in Surrey, given the rank of Guardsman his service number changed to 30360 (30). Having remained with the reserves a little over two months Frederick again found himself drafted for service overseas, on 31st March 1918 he sailed from Southampton arriving in France the following day. Upon arrival things must have looked bleak for men like Frederick as British units struggled to cope in the wake of the German Spring Offensives, regardless he found himself moved southwards to areas southwest of Arras where troops of the Guards Division held the line.

The Guards Division has already been touched upon several times in this book and was created in France in September 1915. A regular army formation its infantry units were made up entirely of guard battalions and regarded as elite units, the best of the best. The division had no New Army or Territorial Force battalions however the guard battalions did accept conscripts and volunteers such as Frederick Bailey. Having participated at Loos, the Somme, Third Ypres and Cambrai in early 1918 the division commanded by Major General G Fielding found itself attached to Byng's 3rd Army and subsequently involved in the Spring Offensives. In addition to other units that made up a regular army division its infantry battalions comprised the 1st Guards Brigade, 2nd Guards Brigade and 3rd Guards Brigade, by early 1918 each brigade consisted of three battalions as well as Machine Gun Companies and Trench Mortar Batteries (31). Most divisions including the Guards Division had a base depot behind the lines where new recruits were sent prior to joining a tactical unit such as an infantry battalion.

Late evening on 1st April saw Frederick Bailey arrive at the Guards Division base depot where he remained for two days; on 3rd April he was detailed to join the 2nd Battalion Grenadier Guards who, along with the 1st Battalion Irish Guards and 2nd Battalion Coldstream Guards, formed part of the 1st Guards Brigade. On 6th April Frederick arrived in the village of Pommier, east of Doullens southwest of Arras, where the 2nd Grenadier Guards reinforcement battalion was situated, at this time the mainstay of the battalion was in the line whilst some of its number as well as reinforcements remained in reserve. Frederick remained at Pommier for several days accustoming himself once again to life in France, around this time nice weather prevailed and on 13th April the 2nd Grenadier Guards, commanded by Lieutenant Colonel G E C Rasch DSO, came out the line.

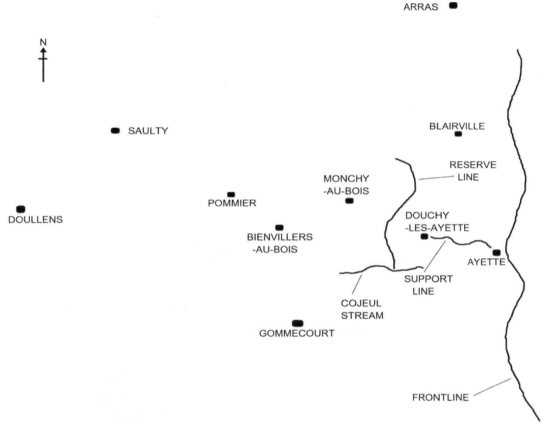

Map 51, Area held by units of the Guards Division (April – June 1918)

The battalion had been in position near Ayette and relieved by units of 2nd Division, on relief they marched north to Blairville then boarded busses to Saulty northwest of Pommier where they arrived at 4:00am the following morning. This particular tour had been relatively quiet for the battalion and on arrival at Saulty half its companies went into tents whilst the other half rested in billets. Like with the 13th Royal Fusiliers as described in the story of Pte William Albert Kerry instead of lettered A through D or W through Z the companies of the 2nd Grenadier Guards were numbered from 1 to 4. Allowed to rest until early afternoon at 2:00pm on 14th April the battalion gathered to spend the rest of the day reorganising and cleaning up, that morning however a draft of 2 officers and 128 other ranks arrived in Saulty to join the battalion, amongst them was Guardsman Frederick Bailey. Many of this draft had come via the same route as Frederick joining the Grenadier Guards via the Household Battalion, a mixed bunch some had and some hadn't already seen action in France. Frederick found himself detailed to join No 1 Coy and over the following few days along with other new arrivals was paraded before senior officers, the battalion remained at Saulty resting and training and participating in sports such as football until 24th April. The weather was fair and thanks to fresh drafts the battalion was up to strength, at 2:00pm that afternoon Frederick Bailey and the men of the 2nd Grenadier Guards boarded busses and proceeded to Bienvillers-au-Bois to relieve units of 32nd Division in reserve positions west of Douchy-lès-Ayette. The 32nd Division had captured the village of Ayette on the night of 3rd April easing the pressure on troops of the Guards Division positioned in the area, since then this sector of the British front line had become relatively quiet as the Germans concentrated their efforts elsewhere. Most days saw little happen except for the odd shell or mortar round come over however this said casualties still occurred, regular night time patrols were sent out into no mans land and although they caused little trouble the enemy was kept an eye on. On arrival at Douchy-lès-Ayette tea and cigarettes were provided by the field kitchens of 32nd Division, the divisional band even played for the guardsmen as they marched into the village. Two companies proceeded to billets west of Monchy-au-Bois in what had once been the old German frontline whilst the remaining two occupied trenches between Douchy-lès-Ayette and Monchy-au-Bois. Frederick and his battalion spent two days improving their accommodation and then on the night of 26th April they moved off to relieve companies of the 1st Irish Guards (32) in frontline positions on the eastern outskirts of Ayette. In this sector the Guards Division was positioned with its 2nd Brigade on the left and 3rd Brigade on the right, the centre was held by units of 1st Brigade and the 2nd Grenadier Guards found themselves holding a 900 yard front. From left to right No 4 and No 2 Coy held the frontline with No 3 Coy in support and No 1 Coy and Frederick Bailey in reserve.

The support lines ran between Douchy-lès-Ayette and Ayette itself whilst the reserve line was a trench running north to south some 1,000 yards west of Douchy-lès-Ayette with its right resting on the dry bed of the Cojeul Stream. Very little activity occurred for the men of the 2nd Grenadier Guards over the following two days, general line duties were carried out but the fact that Ayette was out of observational range of the enemy meant that men were able to move about quite freely and hot meals could be cooked and served relatively safely. As always night time patrols were carried out and on 29th April a company relief saw No 1 and No 3 Coy relieve No 2 and No 4 Coy in the frontline. As Frederick's company remained in the frontline throughout the 30th April the battalion was involved in improving trenches, joining up advanced observational posts, cleaning its area, and salvaging equipment left lying about. Since taking the line the battalion had suffered a small amount of casualties however on 1st May they were relieved by men of the 2nd Coldstream Guards and marched into camp at Monchy-au-Bois where they remained in brigade reserve. Two days were spent in reserve and on the evening of 4th May the battalion once again relieved men of the 1st Irish Guards in frontline positions east of Ayette. An American company commander and three NCO's were attached to the battalion for a spot of instruction however as the Grenadiers took the line it was a quiet relief, No 4 Coy held the right sector whilst No 2 Coy held the left, No 3 Coy was in support and Frederick Bailey and No 1 Coy were positioned in reserve. Since their last spell at the front the battalion had found that the 1st Irish Guards had advanced the line slightly therefore barbed wire entanglements needed to be erected in order to protect the new position, this work was to be carried out at night by way of a wiring party. No 1 Coy being in reserve was detailed to provide men for the task and along with several others Frederick Bailey was selected for the role, hazardous to say the least it meant working in exposed conditions out in no mans land. That evening Frederick and other members of the wiring party gathered supplies and struggled forward towards the frontline, on instruction they ventured out of the trenches and set about the task in hand. In order not to alert the enemy the men had to work as quietly as possible, at intervals Very Lights lit up the sky and the men were forced to remain perfectly still. At the best of times erecting barbed wire entanglements was no easy feat, in darkness and silence it seemed impossible and that night whilst working the enemy was alerted that something was up. Faced with such circumstances the common response for both sides was to spray no mans land with machine gun fire, you didn't necessarily have to see a target but it was the most effective way of preventing whoever was out there from going about their business. As the party of Grenadiers worked out front German gunners on hearing something unexpectedly opened fire, as they did so unfortunately Frederick was unable to take cover quickly enough and as a result he was hit in both legs by a hail of bullets. Its not known if work continued however being dark it was possible to move Frederick back to the frontline, from there he was carried by stretcher to an Aid Post before being admitted that night to the 9th Field Ambulance, one of three such units attached to the Guards Division. It appears that Frederick remained with the medical unit for several hours however during that time his situation deteriorated, his injuries were serious and unfortunately the following day he died of wounds. The men of the 2nd Grenadier Guards remained in the frontline at Ayette until the 10th May before returning briefly to Monchy-au-Bois, the remainder of the month into early June was spent with five days at the front followed by two days in reserve (33). On 6th June the battalion moved back to Saulty where they rested and reorganised, the unit along with the rest of the Guards Division would continue to be heavily involved in various actions right up until the end of the war (34).

Harry and Charlotte Bailey were notified by the War Office on 16th May 1918 that their youngest son had died from wounds received in action, as the telegram arrived one can only imagine how tough this news must have been for the Bailey family. In June 1918 the Chigwell Parish Magazine ran the following article:

"Mr and Mrs Bailey of Turpins Lane have been informed their youngest son Frederick, well known to many of us in the parish, who was in the Grenadier Guards, has been killed. This is a particularly hard case as Mr and Mrs Bailey had already given two sons who had laid down their life for their country. By the death of this, their last remaining son, they have given their all and may god comfort and support them in their irreparable bereavement".

Many brothers were lost in the Great War, contained within this book we record at least five sets that Chigwell lost however for one family to lose three boys so close together was especially harsh. It's almost a certainty that life in the Bailey household never truly recovered and Harry and Charlotte as well as their daughters must have felt the effects of their loss for the rest of their lives. Guardsman Frederick Arthur Bailey spent a total of 59 days in France during his first tour followed by just 35 days in his second, entitled to both the BWM and VM he is buried in Plot XVII, Row C, Grave 6 at Bienvillers CWGC Cemetery, Pas de Calais France.

* * *

Having had a rough time of it up in Flanders at the end of April five British divisions were replaced by French ones and sent down to rest on the Chemin des Dames, given the level of fighting to the north in contrast this sector of front was considered to be relatively peaceful. On the morning of 27th May however that all changed as Ludendorff, having had the best part of a month to prepare, launched his next phase of attack. Known as 'Operation Blucher' as previously mentioned its aim was to attack the French in the south whilst attracting British reserves from the north in the process. If successful the German commander then hoped to launch a fresh assault against a somewhat weakened allied line back in Flanders with the intention of pushing on to the Channel Ports. The Chemin des Dames Ridge lies north of the River Aisne and runs between Soissons and Reims, held by troops of the French Sixth Army the recently arrived British divisions, far from having the quiet time they'd hoped for, found themselves holding its eastern side under French command. Although some suggested an attack might fall in the region these warnings were ignored until it was too late, the preliminary bombardment laid down by the Germans inflicted serious casualties on the defenders and when Ludendorff's troops attacked they swept over allied positions with relative ease. Heavily outnumbered the allies gave ground however in some cases not without a fight, where they'd failed to destroy bridges by nightfall the enemy had advanced over ten miles and crossed the River Aisne. Over the following few days the Germans took Soissons and continued to gain ground reaching the banks of the River Marne on 30th May, then as had happened before the weight of their attack slowed down and allied resistance began to harden. Realising yet another chance slipping away Ludendorff, surprised by his gains, pressed his attack too hard and too long, he tried to push westward toward Paris but French reserves stood in the way, finally his troops took Château-Thierry on 1st June. By now American units had arrived on the scene having been sent to France in great numbers for several months, on 3rd June they were involved in their first significant action stopping German troops crossing the Marne at Château-Thierry. Fighting would continue in the region throughout June but the enemy gained no further ground. The Germans now found they'd created two great bulges in the allied line and Ludendorff's next attempt was to link them together, his next attack codenamed 'Gneisenau' came on 9th June. Designed to join the gains made by both 'Michael' and 'Blucher' it fell on the line held by French units, despite warning the Germans advanced some six miles taking Montdidier in the process, two days later however the French counter attacked pushing the Germans back to their start line. It would be over a month before Ludendorff tried anything further, a delay that allowed the British and French armies to regroup and American presence to grow stronger, for Germany it proved fatal and the next significant action in France came from the allies.

When General Sir Henry Rawlingson took over the remains of 5th Army at the beginning of April 1918 as previously mentioned along with units already under his command he renamed it 4th Army. Having been pushed westward in the wake of the Michael Offensive the sector of front now held by his troops in front of Amiens was in poor shape and offered little protection. Convinced the Germans would try once again to take Amiens Rawlingson studied German tactics and battle plans and set about improving defences to deal with the threat. Hard work followed however as we know Ludendorff turned his attention elsewhere, chiefly to areas in and around Flanders and the Chemin des Dames. A series of small scale raids carried out by units of 4th Army throughout May and June also determined that German troops opposite were themselves ill prepared and of poor quality, given these two factors it soon became apparent that Rawlingson's new defences wouldn't be tested. This said Rawlingson planned for an attack of his own but due to a lack of troops at his disposal he decided that machine guns, tanks, armoured cars and aircraft would make up for the shortage in manpower. A small scale attack using such methods was carried out at Hamel, northeast of Villers-Bretonneux and south of the River Somme, on the morning of 4th July. Involved were troops of the Australian Corps, attached to 4th Army, under the command of Lieutenant General Sir John Monash as well as several companies of American troops. Having trained sufficiently for the attack in areas behind the lines careful attention was paid to how tanks supported the infantry, the Australians had been let down by tanks during the Battle of Arras in April 1917 and were somewhat sceptical of their ability. Since that time however vast improvements had been made and by July 1918 a new more reliable model known as the Mark V was on the scene, not only was it faster than earlier models but it was also easier to drive and offered more protection. The objective at Hamel was to straighten out a small salient that existed in the German frontline; the attack was to be carried out on a frontage some 7,000 yards wide. In order to achieve maximum surprise there was no preliminary bombardment and at 3:10am the Australians and Americans supported by tanks attacked, whilst allied guns bombarded German batteries further guns laid down a creeping barrage ahead of the infantry, the RAF was also on hand dropping supplies as the troops advanced. The assault lasted only an hour and a half and was hugely successful, the salient was eradicated and the Germans lost heavily in comparison to the allies who suffered just short of 1,000 casualties. The tactics used by the allies at Hamel would be a template for the way they operated for the rest of the war.

Still hoping for victory on 15th July 1918 Ludendorff launched what was to be the last offensive action carried out by the German Army during the Great War, officially known as the Reims-Marneschutz Offensive it later became known by the allies as the 'Second Battle of the Marne' (35). The attack was once again directed towards the French Army either side of Reims however for them it's coming was no surprise. German prisoners captured in the days leading up to the attack spilled the beans regarding dates and times, east of Reims well prepared troops of the French Fifth and Fourth Army managed to stop the Germans by mid morning on the first day. To the west of the city however it was a slightly different story as allied troops, still recovering and struggling to rebuild their lines since the Blucher assault in late May, found it hard to stop the Germans crossing the Marne and advancing some four miles. As the enemy continued however their position became vulnerable, lines of supply were threatened by allied aircraft and what they hoped would provide a significant victory descended into small scale battles that first slowed down and then halted their overall advance. Aided by tanks on 18th July the French Army counter attacked from the direction of Villers Cotterets (southwest of Soissons) intending to cut off German units in the salient between Soissons and Reims. Over the days that followed allied units including British and American divisions launched further attacks from the south that pushed the Germans back northwards towards their start line. The fighting would continue into August with both sides suffering appalling casualties, instead of being cut off however the Germans managed to resist attacks long enough to withdraw their troops and straighten their line to a defensive position along the River Vesle (36). Given his situation on 20th July Ludendorff had no option but to postpone his proposed attack in Flanders, a few days later he was forced to cancel it. Since March the Germans had launched six all out attacks aimed at defeating the allies, despite having advanced many miles none had broken through strategically enough to do any lasting damage. Whilst many of Ludendorff's best men were killed many more were wounded or taken prisoner, the Germans had lost their advantage and the ball now laid firmly with the allies.

For the allies although they weren't to know that the enemy would launch no further offensives the time felt right to organise an offensive of their own, this had been impossible over the previous few months as they'd struggled to deal with successive German attacks. Although allied troops were still engaged in the Second Battle of the Marne their CIC was determined to maintain pressure on German forces. On 24th July General Foch gathered allied commanders at his HQ near Melun, some 25 miles southeast of Paris, to discuss a series of operations aimed at straightening out frontline areas and improving communications. Following his success at Hamel on 4th July however the British commander of 4th Army, General Rawlinson had outlined plans for a large scale surprise attack some 10 miles east of Amiens. Having carried out raids that revealed a weakened enemy details were submitted to Haig on 17th July who having studied them carefully agreed in principle. A week later at his meeting with Foch the British CIC discussed the idea, whilst Foch proposed a British attack further north on the Lys he was soon persuaded by Haig that the Somme was more suitable. After deliberations Foch agreed but suggested the proposed attack front be extended southwards to include troops of the French First Army. As Rawlinson's plan was tweaked here and there the overall idea was to attack units of the German Second Army along a 14 mile front from the River Ancre in the north to the village of Moreuil in the south. The proposed battlefield spanned such features as the River Somme and Amiens to Villers-Bretonneux Road, further south it also included the Amiens toward Chaulnes rail line as well as a small stream known as the River Luce. Rawlinson's 4th Army was rather limited consisting of just III Corps made up of four British divisions with one American division attached and the Australian Corps containing five divisions.

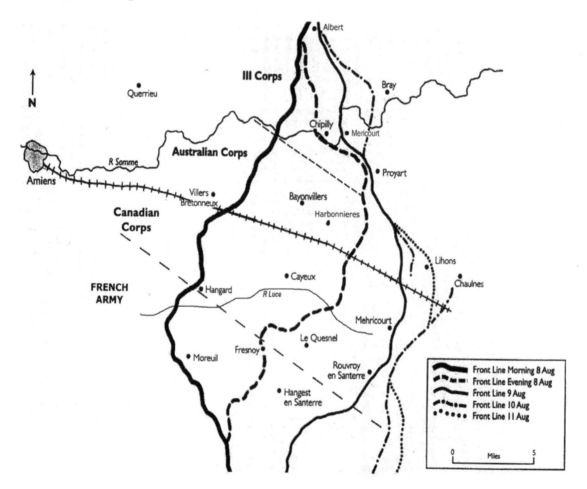

Map 52, The Battle of Amiens (Map taken from Amiens to the Armistice by J P Harris, courtesy and copyright of Brassey's Publishing)

In order for his attack to succeed Rawlingson knew that the amount of troops and equipment under his command would have to be doubled, for this purpose he considered a vital component to be the Canadian Corps. Both the Australian Corps and Canadian Corps were considered by many to be the best that the BEF had to offer, at that time fully rested and fighting fit both had virtually been untouched in the wake of the German offensives although the Australians had played a small but vital part in the Lys Offensive. On balance stronger than British divisions during the reorganisation of the British Army in early 1918 Australian and Canadian divisions remained exempt from cutbacks and their infantry brigades continued to adopt the four battalion structure instead of three (37). Another feature that made them unique was the way that Australian and Canadian divisions were permanently attached to their respective corps unlike British divisions which regularly rotated from one corps to another. It wasn't just the British that realised the value of Australian and Canadian units, the Germans appreciated their status and whenever they arrived on the scene they knew it meant trouble. The proposed attack as laid out by Rawlingson was to be a three phase assault with each corps involved having its own area of operation.

In order to minimise confusion a system of leapfrogging was to be adopted whereby once an objective was taken by say Australian units they would consolidate as second wave Australian units passed through and pushed on. As the infantry attacked, as was the case at Hamel, it was to be supported not only by artillery but by large numbers of aircraft, armoured cars and tanks, in addition once relative success had been achieved cavalry units would be on hand to secure the final objective ahead of the infantry. As a three phase attack the first objective was to be the German frontline (Green Line) which lay roughly 3,000 to 4,000 yards east of the allied frontline whilst the second objective (Red Line) was situated a further 2,000 to 5,000 yards distant. The final objective (Blue Line) was a position known as the Outer Amiens Defence Line, constructed by the French in 1916 and captured by the Germans during the Michael Offensive its location was roughly Hangest - Harbonnières - Mericourt, a distance of somewhere between 10,000 and 14,000 yards from 4th Army's intended start line. III Corps constituting the 12th Division, 18th Division, 47th Division and 58th Division along with the 33rd American Division was to attack in the north from the Ancre west of Albert to the Somme over what was considered to be difficult terrain. Whilst in places the landscape was smooth it soon gave way to steep slopes and gullies, in addition high ground to the east near Chipilly favoured the enemy. Further south the Canadians were to attack between the Amiens toward Chaulnes rail line and regions south of the village of Hangard along the Amiens to Roye Road, this sector although mainly flat and open did contain areas of high ground as well as marshland bordering a small stream known as the River Luce. Whilst on the Canadians right stood units of the French First Army to their left and in the centre of the attack front were to be the Australians. Their front stretched from the River Somme in the north to the Amiens towards Chaulnes rail line in the south and was considered to be the most favourable ground over which to attack, mainly flat consisting of scattered woods and villages it was ideally suited for the deployment of tanks. In order for his plan to succeed the most important factor outlined by Rawlingson was the element of surprise, during the first week of August as preparations got underway extreme measures were taken to ensure that this was achieved. With a great deal of deception the Canadian Corps were transferred southwards from Flanders, regarded as shock troops by the Germans it was imperative their presence on 4th Army's front wasn't revealed. The RAF cleared the skies overhead as over 2,000 guns of various calibres were moved into position, munitions were stockpiled as 342 Mark V tanks were also assembled in addition to smaller but faster Whippet tanks and supply vehicles. As various units arrived in the area their commanders were briefed on a need to know basis, the troops themselves were only informed at the last possible minute. On 6th August as divisions of III Corps were preparing themselves German troops opposite carried out a surprise raid along their frontline that bagged 200 prisoners, preparations were severely disrupted and last minute changes were rapidly introduced. With everything in place the action was scheduled for Thursday 8th August, known as 'The Battle of Amiens' two men listed on the Chigwell Village War Memorial were involved and one was certainly killed on the opening day.

FREDERICK WILLIAM BARTON

Frederick William Barton had joined the army before the war having enlisted at a recruiting office in Bedford along with his good friend Harold Henry Shuttle, when war broke out both men were stationed in Ireland whilst serving with the 1st Battalion Bedfordshire Regiment. They crossed the Channel to France with the BEF during the third week of August and ten days later took part in the Battle of Le Cateau, unfortunately Harold was killed in this action and his story was told in the opening chapter. Although Frederick survived this battle its possible he was wounded, regrettably his army service record no longer exists making it impossible to know for sure. Frederick was born at Mapleton near Ashbourne in Derbyshire in 1893 to parents William George and Alice Barton, originally from Woodford his father worked as a General Labourer whilst his mother, a housewife, had been born at Chiddingstone in Kent. The family moved around quite a lot and two years before Frederick was born his mother gave birth to her eldest child, born at Rotherfield in Sussex Stanley Barton went on to serve in and survive the Great War. Towards the end of the 19th Century William Barton moved back to Essex taking his family with him, they set up home in a small house on Cross Road in Woodford Bridge. In 1898 Alice gave birth to a daughter called Gertrude, two years later her youngest child Edith was born. Frederick attended the council school in Chigwell however his profession between leaving and joining the army is unknown, prior to the outbreak of war the Barton family moved from their house in Cross Road around the corner to 1 Birchwood Villas, Brunel Road. Unfortunately without his service record it proves difficult to trace Frederick's movements during the early years of the war, according to his MIC at the NA however we know he achieved the rank of corporal before being transferred somewhat confusingly with the lower rank of Lance Corporal to the Army Cyclist Corps. The ACC was formed in 1915 grouping together many pre war cyclist battalions, mostly territorial units due to the nature of the First World War many remained in England and found themselves disbanded prior to and just after the Armistice (38). On transfer Frederick saw his army service number change from 9762 as it had been with the Bedfordshire Regiment to 1166. It's not known how long Frederick served with the ACC however it's almost certain that during this period he was based in England, it's also possible that during this time he managed to visit friends and family in Chigwell. Another transfer soon beckoned and somewhat confusingly again Frederick was posted with the lower rank of private to the ranks of the MGC, once again his army service number changed this time to 76048. As previously explained in the story of Charles Alfred Flack the MGC was formed in October 1915 therefore we can only assume that Frederick remained firstly with the Bedfordshire Regiment and then the ACC either on active service or in the reserves until at least this time. Whilst it's possible that Frederick never saw action with the MGC prior to the Battle of Amiens he was transferred again, this time promoted to corporal his service number remained unchanged as he was posted to the ranks of the 2nd Battalion Tank Corps.

As previously explained elsewhere in this book tanks were first designed in 1915 and after successful trials in England were shipped to France where they first saw action during the Battle of the Somme in September 1916. Initially operated by sections attached to the MGC towards the end of that year a new unit known as the Heavy Branch MGC took control. As more machines were built and designs improved tanks took part at the Battle of Arras in April and May 1917, shortly after expansion was needed and on 27th July 1917 the Tank Corps was formed. Over the months that followed although tanks proved rather useless at the Third Battle of Ypres they proved themselves greatly at the Battle of Cambrai in November 1917. As with infantry units numbered brigades and battalions existed within the Tank Corps (e.g. 5th Tank Brigade and 5th Battalion Tank Corps). Whilst various units supplied men Tank Corps personnel came chiefly from units attached to the MGC and ASC. In most cases men never actually officially transferred, this could explain why Cpl Frederick Barton retained the army service number he'd held with the MGC.

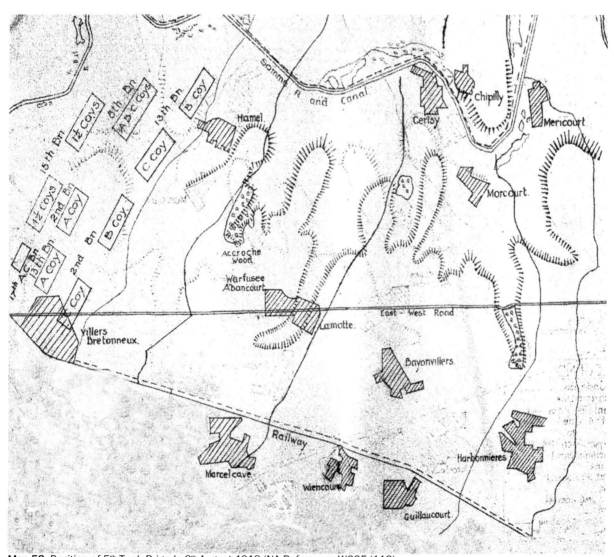

Map 53, Position of 5th Tank Brigade 8th August 1918 (NA Reference: WO95/112)

The number of models and machines within each unit varied however at full strength a tank brigade contained up to five battalions. Each battalion contained in the region of 30 officers and 370 men and was divided into three companies lettered 'A', 'B' and 'C', each company had roughly twelve tanks usually split into four sections of three. No fewer than ten tank battalions were assembled for the Battle of Amiens. These chiefly contained Mark V tanks as well as an extended version used for crossing wide trenches and carrying supplies known as the Mark V*, further supply vehicles were also included and some battalions contained armoured cars. Conditions inside tanks were cramped and nauseating to say the least, the number of men required to operate each vehicle varied depending on make and model however an officer or senior NCO was usually in charge. At Amiens Tank Corps HQ was responsible for deploying tank battalions however at various times throughout the battle two battalions of faster Whippet tanks came under the command of the Australian, Canadian and Cavalry Corps. The 2nd Battalion Tank Corps along with the 8th Battalion, 13th Battalion, 15th Battalion and 17th Armoured Car Battalion formed part of 5th Tank Brigade. During the Battle of Amiens 5th Tank Brigade was detailed to support the Australian Corps therefore towards the end of July its battalions completed a series of training exercises together with Australian units. The Australian Corps were due to attack eastward from Hamel and Villers-Bretonneux with four divisions. To the north on the left stood the 3rd and 4th Australian Divisions supported by tanks of the 13th, 8th and 15th Battalion Tank Corps. To the south on the right with objectives such as Warfusée-Abancourt, Bayonvillers and ultimately ground east of Harbonnières stood the 2nd and 5th Australian Divisions supported by tanks of the 2nd, 13th and 15th Battalion Tank Corps as well as the 17th Armoured Car Battalion.

The beginning of August saw Cpl Frederick Barton and the men of 2nd Battalion Tank Corps in positions at Querrieu Wood some six miles northeast of Amiens, whilst there they not only worked on tanks but carried out last minute adjustments, cleaned guns and checked equipment. On the night of 4th August the battalion left Querrieu Wood for assembly positions at Fouilloy situated south of the River Somme some two miles north of Villers-Bretonneux. During the journey congested roads meant progress was slow but crucially as not to alert the enemy the sound made by tanks moving was covered by planes of the RAF. The battalion remained at Fouilloy for two days making sure that during that time all vehicles were camouflaged and kept out of sight from enemy aircraft patrolling the skies above. Tanks belonging to 'B' Coy on the left and 'C' Coy on the right were due to lead the attack closely supported by tanks from 'A' Coy on the left and 'A' Coy of 13th Battalion Tank Corps on the right. Unfortunately and rather frustratingly with no army service record to turn to it's proved impossible to determine with which company Cpl Frederick Barton served and also his precise role within that unit. At midnight on 7th/8th August tanks belonging to 2nd Battalion Tank Corps left their positions at Fouilloy and moved south towards Villers-Bretonneux again the sound of their engines being covered by planes from the RAF. One hour before zero they moved again this time taking up final positions just north of the village in front of the waiting infantry.

At 4:20am on the morning of 8th August some 2,000 guns concentrated at intervals along 4th Army's front sprang to life and began pounding German trench and artillery positions opposite. Whilst special attention was paid to silencing hostile guns a creeping barrage was laid down as British, Australian and Canadian infantry units supported by tanks advanced eastwards across no mans land. That morning a thick mist covered the battlefield enhancing the element of surprise, this aided the allies in much the same way it had the Germans on the opening day of the Michael Offensive. Enemy forward positions were quickly overrun sending German troops into disarray, overwhelmed by the pace of advance many were left with no other choice but to surrender. North of the Somme III Corps went forward whilst further south the Canadians advanced followed soon after by French troops, in the centre the Australians wasted no time in taking the fight to the enemy. On the left flank 3rd Australian Division lead the charge whilst to their right Cpl Frederick Barton and the 2nd Battalion Tank Corps, under the command of Lieutenant Colonel E D Bryce DSO, supported infantry brigades of the 2nd Australian Division. At zero men and machines from both 'B' Coy and 'C' Coy went forward followed close behind by attacking troops, the mist that covered the battlefield put visibility down to only a few yards however despite this initial progress was good. To the west of Warfusée-Abancourt one tank belonging to 'B' Coy hit a land mine and in the process one of its tracks was blown off, as units moved closer towards the village hostile shelling intensified. The first objective, known as the Green Line, was reached by 7:15am at which point a brief pause ensued whilst ground gained was consolidated. At this point infantry brigades from 5th Australian Division supported by 'A' Coy 2nd Battalion Tank Corps and 'A' Coy 13th Battalion Tank Corps leapfrogged infantry brigades of 2nd Australian Division. In the meantime surviving tanks of both 'B' Coy and 'C' Coy 2nd Battalion Tank Corps rallied north and south of Warfusée-Abancourt (39). As artillery units moved forward the creeping barrage closed down and the mist that covered the battlefield started to lift, at 8:20am the assault continued as men and machines of 2nd Battalion Tank Corps made off towards their second objective. To their surprise enemy resistance was relatively weak however as the mist cleared hostile guns found their targets a lot clearer, on the ground in places German machine guns held up Australian troops and tanks were brought in to help overcome difficulties. Three tanks from 'B' Coy and three tanks from 'C' Coy were detailed to attack Bayonvillers but all three from 'B' Coy received direct hits before reaching the village with two of their three officers killed. In the case of 'C' Coy a fourth tank from that company was brought in to help and all four were instrumental in clearing the village. In the area around Bayonvillers enemy shells fell at an alarming rate although the attackers still gained ground. 'A' Coy of 13th Battalion Tank Corps lost no fewer than nine tanks to direct hits whilst both 'A' Coy and 'B' Coy from 2nd Battalion lost a total of four each with one tank receiving as many as six direct hits. During the attack along with units of infantry Lieutenant Colonel Bryce followed his battalion on foot; at times he found himself slightly off course however as machine guns temporarily held up the advance he managed to direct nearby tanks to deal with them. In some places so little opposition was met that by 9:00am units of 5th Australian Division had reached their second objective, roughly an hour and a half later the whole of the Red Line was in Australian hands along with large numbers of German artillery and prisoners. As consolidation began cavalry units appeared on the scene, as they moved forward vehicles of the 17th Armoured Car Battalion raced on to do damage behind German lines. After another brief pause the Australians and tanks pushed on towards the Blue Line their final objective. As hostile shelling died down surviving tanks of 2nd Battalion led troops on towards Harbonnières, ahead of their arrival allied guns shelled the village and planes from the RAF dropped supplies. At first glance it appeared Harbonnières was empty and on entering the village both the Australian and Tank Corps flag were raised in the upstairs window of a ruined building. As troops dug in and machines moved deeper into the village a few German machine guns opened fire, as several tanks moved off to engage their presence alone was enough to send the enemy packing. At this stage cavalry units followed by Whippet and Mark V* tanks passed through Harbonnières headed for the Blue Line objective, to the south of the village a German ammunition train pulled into the station as if nothing was happening and found itself immediately shelled and destroyed. By mid morning having reached Harbonnières the 2nd Battalion Tank Corps had fulfilled its objectives, south of the village near the railway however some machines helped deal with stubborn pockets of resistance in addition to small scale counter attacks. During the afternoon the surviving tanks of 2nd Battalion Tank Corps were released by Australian infantry units and relieved by vehicles of 8th Battalion Tank Corps, they then rallied in positions north of Warfusée-Abancourt in order to reorganise and refuel. The battalion had started the day with 35 tanks but only a handful reached their final objective, eventually a total of 13 tanks rallied but casualty figures according to the battalion war diary numbered:

Officers: 4 killed in action + 9 wounded
Other Ranks: 17 killed in action + 67 wounded

Although we have a detailed account of 2nd Battalion Tank Corps exploits on 8th August 1918 we have no way of knowing the individual part played by Cpl Frederick William Barton. As initial opposition was relatively weak its possible he made it through the first objective but was killed in fighting near Bayonvillers. Conditions inside the tanks must have been truly appalling for men like Fredrick as the battalion went forward, receiving direct hits from both shell and machine gun fire whilst working in such cramped surroundings would test both the toughest and bravest of men. Frederick's death was reported in the September 1918 edition of the Chigwell Parish Magazine, the small article expressed sincere sympathy towards his family and stated his loss along with others is the price paid for each victory. Cpl Frederick William Barton is buried in Plot II, Row D, Grave 1 at Heath CWGC Cemetery, Harbonnières, France. Initially buried elsewhere his grave was concentrated on this site after the Armistice and his headstone includes the words 'Father in thy gracious keeping, leave we now thy servant sleeping'. In addition it stands in a row of five alongside four other graves of men who served with the Tank Corps and were killed on the first day of the Battle of Amiens (40). When the Chigwell Village War Memorial was inscribed a mistake saw Frederick's rank given as sergeant instead of corporal, having checked all available sources none record him as having held the higher rank. Having served with the BEF in August 1914 Frederick's medal entitlement was the 1914 Star, BWM and VM. Although the whereabouts of his medals is unknown at time of writing relatives of Cpl Frederick William Barton still live in Woodford Bridge and as far away as New Zealand.

* * *

On the opening day of the Battle of Amiens the Australians by far had the most straightforward task covering undoubtedly the easiest ground. Whilst on the right flank where 2nd Battalion Tank Corps and both the 2nd and 5th Australian Divisions had been the Blue Line was reached and consolidated further north the 3rd and 4th Australian Divisions achieved all their objectives except for a small stretch of Blue Line immediately south of the Somme. Overall the Australian Corps advanced up to six miles capturing some 170 pieces of artillery in addition to almost 8,000 German prisoners. North of the Somme on III Corps front the going was tough which ultimately affected progress on the Australian left flank. Whilst leading divisions made initial gains once the mist lifted experienced German machine gun teams entrenched in woodland made it hard for troops to advance. At times the enemy counter attacked which made things especially difficult for men of the 18th Division and 58th Division, by nightfall III Corps held little ground beyond their first objective although they'd managed an overall advance of 2 miles and bagged 2,000 prisoners along with various enemy artillery pieces. Whilst the 33rd American Division attached to III Corps didn't attack that day the German raid on 6th August had seriously disrupted things for 18th Division, overall many units that did attack were tired, under trained and largely inexperienced. To the south in order to maintain security the Canadians had taken over their sector of front at the last possible minute from a skeleton force of Australian troops, at zero they moved forward managing successfully to overcome initial resistance and gain ground. To their right the French didn't attack immediately, instead they laid down a preliminary bombardment lasting some 45 minutes. As the Canadians pressed on their guns done good work as supporting tanks dealt with hostile machine guns and infantry, just after 6:00am the mist cleared in their sector affording visibility on behalf of the Germans. The River Luce proved a formidable obstacle however by early afternoon the Canadians had achieved their first two objectives; cavalry units passed through and by late evening 8 miles had been covered with most of the Canadians third and final objective secure. The French attacked 45 minutes after zero greatly assisting the Canadians to their left, whilst they inflicted heavy lost on the enemy during the course of the day they advanced up to five miles captured numerous prisoners and guns but failed to achieve all their objectives.

Despite the relative failure of III Corps attack north of the Somme the gains achieved by the allies on 8th August 1918 made it their most successful day of the war so far. Although no major breakthrough was realised the enemy was severely rumbled soaring moral amongst allied troops to an all time high. Whilst allied casualties that day were put at roughly 9,000 men killed and wounded German losses in killed and wounded were virtually equal. As for German commanders undoubtedly their greatest loss was the number of prisoners the allies had captured, the figure totalled some 18,500 men many of whom had surrendered in large groups without much of a fight. In addition the German Army lost almost 400 artillery pieces, a loss at this stage of the war it could ill afford. In his memoirs Ludendorff referred to the 8th August 1918 as "the black day of the German Army in the history of the war". It was on this day he was forced to realise Germany would not win a decisive military victory on the battlefield, instead her only hope now was to fight a good defensive battle and hold some of her gains whilst favourable peace terms were negotiated.

On 9th August the battle continued with allied troops in action again, once more aircraft and tanks supported infantry units however due to losses the previous day less machines were available. Determined to maintain pressure on German forces the allies pushed eastwards beyond the Outer Amiens Defence Line, with no real timeframe the overall pace of advance proved difficult, in addition lack of communication rendered artillery support on much of the front poor and ineffective. Despite extreme exhaustion amongst rank and file fierce fighting developed as German reinforcements were rushed to the scene. To the south the French went forward whilst further north the Canadians, somewhat beset by a last minute change of plan gained ground in the morning before pausing and continuing their advance around noon. The Australians were by far the strongest corps in action on the second day, they continued to gain ground advancing several miles; in addition they also managed the capture of several hundred prisoners. North of the Somme, given their lack of success the previous day, units of III Corps still faced tough opposition, it was possibly here in heavy fighting between 9th - 10th August that Chigwell sustained what turned out to be its penultimate casualty of the Great War.

HAROLD HULL MOSELEY

Harold Hull Moseley was a well known figure in and around Chigwell and whilst his story is rather interesting gaps unfortunately appear from time to time, in addition some confusion exists regarding the date he was killed however all is explained in due course. One of the older men listed on the Chigwell Memorial Harold was born at Thaxted in Essex on 18th June 1882 to parents John and Sarah Jenny Moseley. John had been born in Shelly in Yorkshire in 1857 and worked as a school teacher whilst Sarah was born in Leicester the same year. After the couple met and married they moved to Essex settling for some time in Thaxted, whilst there Sarah gave birth to three children. Harold was her eldest child followed on 12th August 1883 by another son called Edgar, the following year a daughter called Winifred was born. Sometime around 1890 John Moseley was offered the job of headmaster at Chigwell Council School for Boys, he readily accepted the post and the Moseley family moved from Thaxted to Chigwell occupying a small house within the school grounds. Harold done well at primary school and in 1893 he attended Chigwell Grammar School where he won prizes in English Essay and Modern Language; he left in 1895 to continue his education at Christ's Hospital based at that time at Newgate in the City of London. At 18 years old Harold found work as an office clerk and dealt with insurance, over the following years he rose steadily through the ranks to achieve an assured position in business. During his spare time Harold helped out at the Mission Room in Grange Hill, at weekends he also helped teach children at Sunday school and on alternate Sundays was responsible for taking services. Whilst working at the Mission Room Harold met a young lady called Elizabeth (Lizzie) Smith and shortly before the war the couple were married, soon after they set up home together in a small house called North View near Grange Hill. When war was declared in August 1914 Harold scaled down his activities in Grange Hill and Chigwell, determined to serve both king and country that December whilst working in London he joined the army. Like many of those men whose story we've covered the army service record belonging to Harold no longer exists, despite this we know he enlisted at offices in Bunhill Row that were HQ to the 5th Battalion London Regiment.

As previously explained on several occasions elsewhere in this book the London Regiment was purely territorial, as also explained the regiment contained many battalions some with names such as Royal Fusiliers and some with area affiliations such as the Poplar and Stepney Rifles. The 5th Battalion was no different and whilst it wasn't area affiliated it was simply referred to as the London Rifle Brigade. The outbreak of war saw the London Rifle Brigade create a second and third line formation. The 1/5th Battalion went to France in November 1914 leaving Harold on enlistment to join the 2/5th Battalion in training at various camps in and around South London, Sussex and Surrey. Harold obtained the rank of corporal and was given army service number 1384, by the spring of 1915 his battalion had moved to Norwich and by early summer was based near Ipswich. In March of that year a small article appeared in the Chigwell Parish Magazine confirming that Harold was in the territorial's and in training, it went on to say that his work at both the Mission Room and Sunday school was sorely missed. Whilst Harold continued training by mid 1916 his brother had joined the army; Edgar Moseley enlisted and served in the ranks of the RFA but unlike Harold went on to survive the war. On Friday 4th August 1916 having suffered for several months with heart trouble Sarah Jenny Moseley died aged 59, she was buried the following Tuesday at St Mary's Church in Chigwell. Both Harold and Edgar were present at the service having been given special leave to attend by the army, standing alongside their father and sister they joined in as prayers were recited and hymns were sung in memory of their mother (41). Harold continued training with his battalion for several more months and in late November was drafted for service overseas. On 4th December 1916 he crossed the Channel to France as part of a group of reinforcements; his move was reported in the January 1917 edition of the Chigwell Parish Magazine. On arrival Cpl Harold Moseley was posted to the 1/5th Battalion London Regiment (London Rifle Brigade) at that time out of the line and in billets at Lestrem on the River Lawe a few miles due north of Béthune.

The London Rifle Brigade as it shall now be called was commanded by Lieutenant Colonel R H Husey and attached to 169th Brigade, 56th (London) Division. The battalion remained in billets for several days and undertook both training exercises and route marches then on 6th December the men were inspected by their corps commander. On 9th December the London Rifle Brigade went into the trenches and Harold got his first taste of life in the frontline, holding positions near Neuve Chapelle and Aubers the tour lasted five days with enemy artillery extremely active. On relief the battalion moved back to billets however the men soon found themselves used for work parties. On 21st December the London Rifle Brigade again entered the line near Neuve Chapelle but Harold was left behind, instead on 24th December he was temporarily transferred to 193rd Machine Gun Company. This unit was attached to the 56th (London) Division and served as divisional troops, a brief description of the role played by divisional troops has previously been explained and can be found in the story of William Albert Kerry. When Harold joined 193rd MGC on 24th December he found them at Laventie north of Neuve Chapelle, the weather that day was cold, wet and windy. In order to stop fraternisation over the Christmas period as was the case in December 1914 artillery belonging to 56th Division incessantly bombarded the German lines opposite, as a result no Germans dared show themselves. Cpl Harold Moseley remained with 193rd MGC at Laventie until the first week of March 1917; at that point they moved southwest to Le Cauroy in preparation for the Battle of Arras. The beginning of April saw 193rd MGC at Achicourt and on the opening day of the Arras Offensive the unit saw action, two days later on 11th April Harold was renumbered 300852 and transferred back to 1/5th Battalion London Regiment (London Rifle Brigade). Upon his return Cpl Harold Moseley was posted to 'B' Coy and that day the battalion were positioned at Agny, just south of Arras and Achicourt, in support of both 167th Brigade and 168th Brigade of 56th (London) Division. That night there was no rest for Harold as the men of the London Rifle Brigade were involved in a bombing raid close to the frontline. On 3rd May as part of the Arras Offensive the battalion was involved in a large scale attack west of Guemappe and Cpl Harold Moseley and 'B' Coy took part. During this action several company commanders in Harold's patrol were rendered *'hors de combat'* leaving Harold himself to handle the troops, for his bravery and leadership he was later awarded the Gallant Conduct Certificate. In August 1917 a report congratulating Harold on this achievement appeared in the Chigwell Parish Magazine. By July however elements of 56th Division had moved north to Ypres and the men of the London Rifle Brigade in early August found themselves positioned northwest of the Belgian town. Around this time a change of command occurred within the battalion and it wasn't long before orders were issued to head south to the Somme, for Harold however another move beckoned and on 27th August he was transferred to the ranks of 169th Trench Mortar Battery (42). Harold joined his new unit the following day however it hasn't proved possible to trace his precise movements, unfortunately at time of writing the war diary belonging to 169th TMB has been misplaced at the NA in Kew. What we do know however is that whilst serving time with this unit Harold was diagnosed as suffering with Shell Shock, as a result he was returned to the London Rifle Brigade and on 8th December 1917 was sent back to England for treatment. Whilst in recovery Harold returned to Chigwell to visit friends and family and it wasn't until 15th July 1918 that he eventually returned to France. According to information found on the Medal Rolls at Kew although still technically attached to the London Rifle Brigade upon arrival Harold was posted to the ranks of the 8th Battalion London Regiment, a unit also known as the 'Post Office Rifles'. As its name would suggest and previously touched on elsewhere in this book on the outbreak of war this battalion was assembled from postal workers, by July 1918 however when Harold joined its ranks its make up had changed quite dramatically. By this stage of the war many original members had either been killed or wounded, whilst some remained the battalion now consisted mainly of recuperated but generally unfit veterans and inexperienced young conscripts hurried out from England with little or no training. The 8th Battalion London Regiment or the Post Office Rifles as we shall now call them, along with the 6th Battalion and 7th Battalion London Regiment formed part of 174th Brigade. This brigade along with 173rd Brigade and 175th Brigade formed part of the 58th (London) Division; by July 1918 as previously mentioned this division was one of four attached to III Corps and Rawlinson's 4th Army.

The middle of July saw brigades belonging to 58th (London) Division holding various positions east of Amiens, for those men of the Post Office Rifles they found themselves under the command of Lieutenant Colonel R N Johnson and in training near Baizieux some two miles north of the Amiens to Albert Road. On 18th July the battalion moved up to support lines east of Bresle however despite having been in France for several days it wasn't until the 19th July or 21st July that Harold joined the battalion along with other reinforcements. On 22nd July the battalion, including Harold, was relieved in support lines and moved back to tents at Round Wood, a small copse situated north of the Béhencourt to Franvillers Road. Whilst here the men rested however three days later they took part in a large scale raid on enemy positions. This attack was delivered in daylight and whilst relatively successful the

Post Office Rifles lost heavily sustaining just over a hundred casualties. It appears Harold took part in the raid and came through unscathed although once again, with no service record to turn to, the company to which he belonged is unknown. On 28th July having returned to tents at Round Wood to reorganise and refit the battalion was moved to St Lawrence Farm Camp near Baizieux, the weather was bright and hot as men including Harold equipped and engaged in various training exercises.

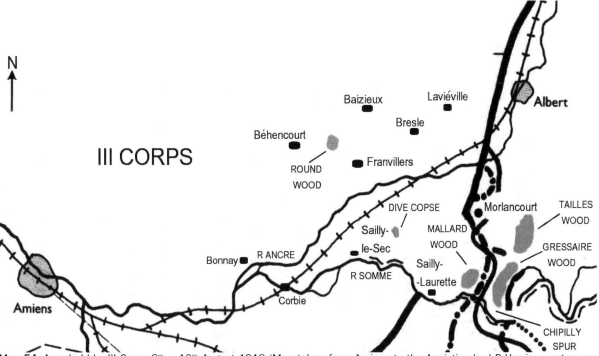

Map 54, Area held by III Corps 8th – 10th August 1918 (Map taken from Amiens to the Armistice by J P Harris, courtesy and copyright of Brassey's Publishing)

The last day of July saw Lieutenant Colonel Derviche-Jones DSO MC take command of the Post Office Rifles, whilst half of the battalion occupied billets at Baizieux the remainder held support lines near Laviéville, its total fighting strength numbered 21 officers plus 655 other ranks. The first day of August was bright and hot for men of the Post Office Rifles, whilst half the battalion remained in billets at Baizieux those men in support lines near Laviéville were finally relieved the following morning. As battalions attached to 174th Brigade were placed in divisional reserve late afternoon on 2nd August saw the Post Office Rifles move westward by route march and bus to Wargnies some 8 miles north of Amiens. On arrival the battalion rested, reorganised and cleaned up, over the following two days the weather was changeable seeing a mixture of sunshine and showers. On 4th August a church parade was held commemorating the fourth anniversary of the outbreak of war, it's reasonable to suggest that being a religious man Cpl Harold Moseley attended. That afternoon the men of the Post Office Rifles received orders to head back to the frontline, that evening they climbed aboard buses and travelled throughout the night. During the early hours of 5th August the men debussed just west of Franvillers on the Amiens to Albert Road, from there they marched via Bonnay to a small wood known as Dive Copse on the Bray to Corbie Road. That morning bad weather prevailed and as the day went on what started as slight drizzle turned to heavy showers. Amongst the ranks conditions proved tough however men like Harold tried resting as best they could, early evening saw officers and senior NCO's move forward to reconnoitre the frontline. At 8:30pm the order was given to relieve men of the 2nd Battalion Bedfordshire Regiment (54th Brigade, 18th Division) in frontline positions near Sailly-Laurette, this signalled the start of a long and difficult relief. In heavy rain Cpl Harold Moseley and the men of the Post Office Rifles marched forward towards the frontline, whilst moving up they found conditions within communication and frontline trenches appalling. By dawn on 6th August the relief was still not complete when German troops attacked units of 18th Division to the Post Office Rifles left. As previously explained this raid by the enemy caused major problems for 18th Division and hampered preparations for the Amiens Offensive, caught up in the melee the Post Office Rifles quickly formed a defensive flank that German troops failed to penetrate. Whilst the battalion was instrumental in driving the enemy off to their left damage was done and ground was lost, hostile shells and trench mortars pounded positions throughout the following day and by the morning of 8th August the men of the Post Office Rifles were caked in mud and extremely tired.

Whilst writing this book I've always tried to be meticulous in the way stories are covered, in order to do this on most occasions I've relied heavily on content contained within battalion war diaries. Unfortunately events surrounding the Battle of Amiens as far as the Post Office Rifles are concerned are sketchy to say the least, for the period 8th – 10th August 1918 the diary refers to various reports within separate appendixes. Whilst some of these reports exist many are copies of copies outlined on black paper and impossible to read, this said detailed events concerning battalion exploits during the first day of battle are largely unknown whilst events covering the 9th – 10th August are somewhat inconclusive. In 1919 a book was published entitled 'History of the Post Office Rifles' however again events concerning battalion exploits during the Amiens period are vague to say the least. Whilst I've tried hard to keep day to day events in context as previously mentioned there's also confusion regarding the date that Cpl Harold Moseley was killed. As shall be explained several local sources say 8th August 1918 whilst somewhat official sources say 10th August 1918, in addition an article from the Woodford Times newspaper dated 6th September 1918 states he was killed sometime between the 8th and 10th August 1918. On this occasion the truth has been hard to come by and if I'm totally honest having studied available evidence I'm still unsure. This being the case we must return to the first day of battle and follow the Post Office Rifles journey as best we can. The following information as brief as it is mainly comes courtesy of the book entitled 'History of the Post Office Rifles' as well as a special report compiled by Lieutenant Colonel Derviche-Jones DSO MC dated 9th August 1918.

On the morning of 8th August Cpl Harold Moseley and the men of the Post Office Rifles found themselves in brigade reserve to the west of Mallard Wood however due to the mist that covered the battlefield just a few minutes after zero they were thrown into the fighting. Having been in position for almost two days when it came to direction their general prospective was better than most, this said battalion progress still wasn't easy. By 9:30am units of 58th Division had captured Sailly-Laurette, as for the Post Office Rifles their primary role was to clear and hold the western edge of Mallard Wood. Enemy resistance proved tough and despite being badly behind schedule this was achieved; in addition the battalion also managed the capture of prisoners, trench mortars and machine guns. As previously explained the first day of the Amiens Offensive proved difficult for divisions of III Corps with little progress made beyond first objectives, enemy units positioned on high ground surrounding the Chipilly Spur proved to be a formidable obstacle that caused most of the problems. The morning of 9th August saw the men of the Post Office Rifles dispersed all over the place, many were helping out other units whilst some had been detailed for carrying and work parties. Eventually the battalion regrouped and on doing so its fighting strength numbered somewhere in the region of 11 officers and 234 other ranks. As steps were taken to clean rifles and other equipment late afternoon saw 174th Brigade HQ order its battalions to resume the attack. Soon after fresh orders were issued and the Post Office Rifles were temporarily attached to 175th Brigade, instructions were then received for the battalion to move up on the brigade left flank to a barrage line some two miles north of their current position at Mallard Wood. By the time they set off it was 5:20pm however they had just ten minutes to arrive as British guns were due to provide artillery support at 5:30pm. Although the battalion had no chance of making it on time Lieutenant Colonel Derviche-Jones DSO MC had no time to discuss things such as direction or objectives with company commanders, whilst on the move companies were rapidly organised into platoons and sections. As they pushed on at various times direction was lost, conditions were severe as men came under both hostile machine gun and shellfire. Also known as 'The Rangers' the 12th Battalion London Regiment (175th Brigade, 58th Division) were due to participate on the Post Office Rifles right flank, in order they shouldn't lose touch from the start the two battalions marched towards their proposed start line side by side (43). Eventually both arrived however on the way up Lieutenant Colonel Derviche-Jones DSO MC was struck in the leg by shrapnel, this said soon after his battalion moved off to attack. Advancing astride the Bray-Corbie Road open warfare ensued and by 6:30pm both the Post Office Rifles and Rangers had made steady progress in the direction of Morlancourt. Following exploits the previous day to the left of the Post Office Rifles units of 18th Division had been relieved and replaced by units of 12th (Eastern) Division, this said a large gap existed between the two. With German troops holding positions east of Morlancourt and fearing an enemy counter attack Lieutenant Colonel Derviche-Jones DSO MC requested a support battalion be brought forward to fill the void. Whilst this was dealt with a temporary measure saw artillery and machine gun teams cover the area. At 8:45pm men of the 5th Royal Berkshire Regiment (36th Brigade, 12th Division) arrived on the scene, they filled the void as steady fighting continued. With several officers killed and many wounded the Post Office Rifles ended the day some 150 men strong holding lines in and around Morlancourt, with them stood men of the Rangers as well as troops attached to the 33rd American Division initially brought in to operate on the Rangers right flank. Overall units of III Corps fought hard on 9th August making good disappointments the previous day; by nightfall they'd taken Morlancourt, Tailles Wood and Gressaire Wood whilst American troops had captured the all important Chipilly Spur.

Like many battalions involved at the Battle of Amiens the Post Office Rifles had a tough time of things, they fought hard and lost heavily and whilst events for 10th August are unclear the following day saw men relieved and moved back to positions near Dive Copse on the Bray to Corbie Road. Many of those men killed whilst serving as part of the Post Office Rifles lie in small cemeteries in and around the Somme, Cpl Harold Hull Moseley lies buried in Plot III, Row J, Grave 18 at Dive Copse CWGC Cemetery close to the village of Sailly-le-Sec. In regards to casualty figures the battalion war diary proves inconclusive whilst SDGW records such a low number of men killed it has to be deemed unrealistic. Whilst we know Cpl Harold Moseley was involved in fighting on 8th August 1918 we don't know to what extent, did he survive that day only to be killed between 9th – 10th August, its almost certain we'll never know for sure. Whilst sources such as the Medal Rolls in Kew, the CWGC and SDGW all state he was killed on 10th August some crucial evidence exists that appears to suggest otherwise. For many years a small marble plaque in the form of a private memorial stood in the grounds of St Mary's Churchyard in Chigwell, dedicated in memory of Harold Hull Moseley it said he was killed in France on 8th August 1918. If we assume this memorial was commissioned by members of Harold's family how did they know the date he was killed, I think it's reasonable to suggest that either a soldier or officer who'd served alongside Harold told them. To support this theory further evidence exists. In September 1918 the Chigwell Parish Magazine ran an article reporting that Harold had been killed in action whilst serving in France, it states that his death although tragic had been mercifully instantaneous. Designed not to cause additional upset this was the standard reply given to relatives by officers and comrades of soldiers killed, this said it suggests at some point the Moseley family had communication with someone who'd served alongside Harold. If this is true it's guaranteed they were told the date he was killed and if that date was 8th August 1918 then surely, as was the case, this would appear on his private memorial. Over the years the memorial deteriorated to such an extent that sadly today it no longer exists, this said thanks to a local man called Bill Oliver who luckily had the foresight to take photos a picture appears in this book. The article in the September 1918 edition of the Chigwell Parish Magazine went on to say that having seen much fighting Harold was about to receive his commission, given his background and education it's seems strange he hadn't been commissioned before (44). Having attended Chigwell Grammar School the name of Harold Hull Moseley also appears on a plaque in the school memorial chapel, whilst the motto that follows his name as chosen by Headmaster Ernest Stuart Walde is *'Faithful unto Death'*, the date he died is also given as 8th August 1918. As previously mentioned September 1918 saw Harold's death reported in the Woodford Times Newspaper, a short obituary followed and being headmaster of Chigwell Council School deepest sympathy was expressed to John Moseley regarding the loss of his son. Having served overseas since late 1916 Harold was entitled to both the BWM and VM, these were sent out to next of kin in late 1920 along with a memorial plaque and scroll. After the war Elizabeth Moseley left Chigwell and by the mid 1920's was living at 106 Chesterfield Road, Bristol, its not known if she later remarried. Given the lack of details regarding battalion exploits and the confusion surrounding the date he was killed the story of Cpl Harold Hull Moseley proved a tough one to cover; this said I hope that in doing so I've served a brave man justice.

* * *

On 10th August Sir Douglas Haig visited the Amiens front and found German resistance beginning to harden, that day however allied units still gained ground although their overall advance had begun to slow down. Over the next two days on much of the front the fighting diminished as troops of 4th Army approached the wilderness of the old Somme battlefields, the Battle of Amiens finally ended on 12th August. In four days of fighting the Germans had suffered substantial losses. Although the British had captured some 21,000 prisoners - most of those on the first day - all in all they themselves had sustained only 20,000 casualties 4,000 of which proved fatal. The period spanning the end of the Battle of Amiens to the Armistice is generally referred to as the 'Hundred Days' and whilst the German Army wasn't defeated fierce fighting developed as her troops were pushed eastward. During the second and third weeks of August the French armies extended their lines to the south and moved forward to hustle German forces. Determined to maintain maximum pressure General Foch demanded that 4th Army resume its attack east of Amiens however Haig fearing a waste of reserves for no real gain persuaded him otherwise. Instead 3rd Army commanded by General Sir Julian Byng positioned north of Albert was ordered to prepare to move in the direction of Bapaume and Péronne. At the same time 1st Army under Horne in front of Arras, 5th Army under Birdwood on the Lys and 2nd Army under Plumer holding the Ypres Salient were all instructed to mount operations to assess the strength of German troops opposite (45). Although the fighting in France was far from over it was during one of these operations carried out by units of 2nd Army between 18th – 19th August that the last man named on the Chigwell Village War Memorial to die in the Great War was mortally wounded.

JOHN GREEN

John Green was born in Chigwell in 1899 to parents Walter and Amelia Lydia Green and was barely 15 years old when war broke out in August 1914. Walter Green had been born in Worksop in Nottinghamshire in 1872 and during his twenties he moved south towards London where he started a Laundry business. Amelia was a year younger having been born at Paddington in West London in 1873; whilst it's not known when or where the couple met once married they settled in Chigwell. At the turn of the century they occupied a house on Chigwell High Road where they employed a young lady from Islington in North London to serve as domestic help. When John was just over a year old Amelia gave birth to twins, Ben and Rose Green were born in Chigwell in 1901. Unfortunately being so young little is known about John's life other than that he was educated locally, whilst his profession on leaving school is unclear sometime during 1917 he found himself conscripted into the army. John underwent a medical but sadly no details survive as his army service record like many no longer exists, this said we know he enlisted at Romford and on being passed fit was posted as Private 71168 to the ranks of the 106th Training Reserve Battalion. Originally the 30th (Reserve) Battalion Royal Fusiliers this unit had been formed at Romford in August 1915. As previously touched on during the story of Charles William Day on 1st September 1916 following the onset of conscription a reorganisation of army reserve units took place that saw some battalions disbanded whilst others were renamed and absorbed into new units of numbered training reserve battalions attached to numbered training reserve brigades. Again the details of this reorganisation are rather complex and as this book isn't the place to go into detail quite simply the 30th (Reserve) Battalion Royal Fusiliers was renamed the 106th Training Reserve Battalion and one of five attached to the 24th Training Reserve Brigade. Whilst with the training reserve Pte John Green underwent a period of basic training lasting several months, its likely this occurred up in Scotland as 24th Training Reserve Brigade was based in and around Edinburgh. John continued his training into the summer of 1918, eventually he was drafted for service overseas and his army service number changed to 87071, on 14th July he landed in France along with other reinforcements and was posted to the ranks of the 2nd Battalion Royal Fusiliers. Attached to 86th Brigade, 29th Division this unit initially saw action at Gallipoli; it then served on the Somme, at Ypres and Cambrai and was also involved in the 1918 Spring Offensives (46).

By the summer of 1918 the 29th Division formed part of 2nd Army and was stationed both in and out of the line around Hazebrouck. The beginning of July 1918 saw the men of the 2nd Royal Fusiliers commanded by Lieutenant Colonel E M Baker out of the line and in camp at Sablonniere some 8km southeast of St Omer. A few days before John arrived being part of 2nd Army the battalion was inspected by General Sir Herbert Plumer himself, he presented ribbons to recipients of recent awards and expressed satisfaction with regards to the steadiness of drill and movement of troops. Like most fusilier battalions the companies belonging to 2nd Royal Fusiliers were lettered X through Z, with no service record to turn to however it hasn't proved possible to determine with which company Pte John Green served. The day John arrived the weather was a mixture of sunshine and showers, being a Sunday a voluntary church service was held in the morning. Whilst out of the line when not in training the 2nd Royal Fusiliers entertained themselves by attending concert parties and sporting events, Monday 15th July saw the battalion involved in a football match to determine the brigade cup and drew 1-1 with the 1st Royal Dublin Fusiliers. The following day the game was replayed and the 2nd Royal Fusiliers won 3 – 1, later that afternoon however they lost a brigade Boxing competition. Over the days that followed as Pte John Green became accustomed to life in France his battalion was involved in mock battle and training exercises, in addition whilst some companies practiced on rifle ranges other units practiced the art of both sending signals and relaying messages. Sunday 21st July saw the battalion receive orders 'be ready to move' and at 8:00am the following morning having equipped and paraded the men marched out of Sablonniere some 20km northeast to Noordpeene. On arrival that same afternoon the battalion found billets were favourable and men such as Pte John Green settled down to rest and clean up after their long march. On 24th July the battalion was back training and whilst some men were given time off to take baths both officers and senior NCO's moved forward to reconnoitre areas of front line, the rest of the month saw the 2nd Royal Fusiliers remain at Noordpeene partaking in sporting events and various training exercises.

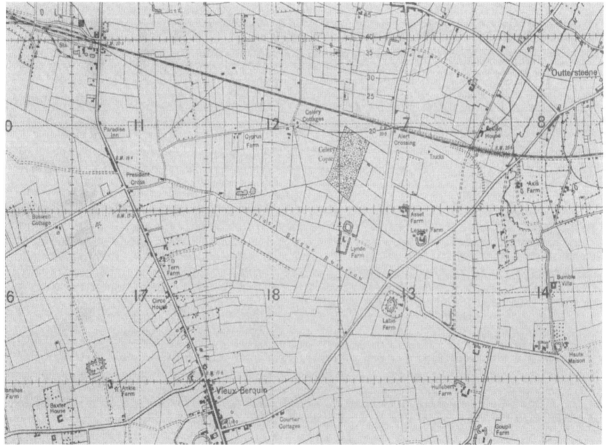

Map 55, Vieux-Berquin

As August started Pte John Green and his battalion moved southeast from Noordpeene to billets at La Kreule some 4km north of Hazebrouck. That first week saw all companies in training close to billets however at night there was little rest as men were used to form work parties for various duties including wiring up near the front line. On the evening of 10th August the 2nd Royal Fusiliers moved eastward from La Kreule and relieved men of the 1st Lancashire Fusiliers in support lines near Strazeele, that night the battalion continued to provide men for work parties. Battalion HQ was established close by in a building known as Curfew House, the following day it was shelled however luckily no casualties were reported. During the course of the next few days the men of each company took it in turns to head back to transport lines for baths and supplies, inspections were carried out and box respirators, or gas masks, belonging to all units were checked by specially trained officers. On the evening of Friday 16th August the 2nd Royal Fusiliers were relieved in support lines by men of the 1st Royal Dublin Fusiliers, in turn they moved forward to relieve men of the 1st Lancashire Fusiliers in front line positions north of Vieux-Berquin. The battalion was positioned to the right of both 9th Division and 87th Brigade with 'Y' Coy on the left and 'Z' Coy on the right holding the front line, 'X' Coy in front line support near Strazeele Station and 'W' Coy in front line reserve. For many men including Pte John Green this was the first time they'd held an advanced position. The following day was fairly quiet for the battalion and the men got on with making positions their own, at night however several patrols were sent out into no mans land. To the north stood a railway running east out of Strazeele Station which straddled the frontline, 'Y' Coy held this area whilst 'Z' Coy held positions east of Cyprus Farm, on night time patrols opposition was encountered from a line of Trucks parked close to the railway as well as from areas in and around Lynde Farm.

As part of a probing exercise the morning of Sunday 18th August saw troops from both 9th Division and 87th Brigade attack and successfully capture German positions out on the Outtersteene Ridge, in conjunction the 2nd Royal Fusiliers sent out patrols to capture the line of Trucks and Lynde Farm. Despite having encountered opposition on night time patrols battalion HQ hoped to achieve its objectives relatively easily, unfortunately this wasn't the case. Rather frustratingly not knowing with which company Pte John Green served means it's impossible to track his precise movements, what follows however is a battalion account describing the day's action.

At 11:00am a barrage started allowing attacking troops to move forward within storming distance of their objectives. Two platoons of 'Y' Coy held the left with two further platoons in support, 'Z' Coy held the right with similar dispositions. Scouts from both companies moved on ahead to assess the strength of the enemy, whilst they found them to be sufficient in number around the Trucks and Lynde Farm it was also their job to liaise with British units operating on each flank. The left platoon from 'Y' Coy led by a second lieutenant moved quickly along the north side of the railway to Alert Crossing, which was reached with relative ease, on arrival several Germans were encountered and killed whilst others were taken prisoner. Pushing on towards a line of low trees it wasn't long before men were held up by machine gun fire from Asset and Lesage Farms, suffering casualties they withdrew back to Alert Crossing. The right platoon from 'Y' Coy lost an officer early on as it advanced over fields towards Celery Copse, on reaching the western edge it continued its movement through the copse only to be held up by machine guns positioned in and around Lynde Farm. The left and right platoons of 'Z' Coy only managed to advance some 70 yards before they too took fire from enemy positions in and around Lynde Farm, despite this they continued to push forward covered by trench mortar rockets and Lewis Guns fired from British lines. Around this time two white Very Lights went up, this was the signal for "Lynde Farm Taken" however it caused confusion as Lynde Farm remained firmly in enemy hands. Eventually units of 'Z' Coy were pinned down, trench mortar fire now proved inadequate as few rounds hit their targets, fearing a direct assault would involve heavy casualties two attempts were made to outflank Lynde Farm however heavy machine gun fire prevented this. Meanwhile near the railway men of the 2nd Battalion South Wales Borderers (87th Brigade), operating to the left and in support of 'Y' Coy put up a blue smoke signal to indicate their arrival at Alert Crossing. Unfortunately this signal was confused by 'Y' Coy's CO with his own units signal for "Trucks Taken". Thinking therefore that both Lynde Farm and the Trucks had fallen 'Y' Coy's right platoon pushed eastward through Celery Copse and attempted a frontal advance on the Trucks. When barely 50 yards clear of the copse some Germans appeared with their hands up and these were shot, the advance continued when suddenly machine guns opened up from the vicinity of the Trucks and Lynde Farm. The attackers suffered casualties and those who were able had no choice but to obey pre arranged orders and return to Celery Copse. It was deemed unfortunate that identical signals were used for different objectives on the left flank and undoubtedly it contributed to casualties sustained, in addition it was never discovered who fired the two white Very Lights signalling "Lynde Farm Taken". Overall the two attacking companies ended the day back on their original line with the exception of retaining Alert Crossing. That evening 'X' Coy moved up and relieved units of 'Y' Coy in frontline positions near the railway and 'W' Coy came forward to relieve units of 'Z' Coy in areas of frontline west of Celery Copse. According to the battalion war diary casualty figures for the 2nd Royal Fusiliers on 18th August were put at:

Officers: 1 killed + 1 wounded
Other Ranks: 5 killed + 14 wounded

At this point I have to ask myself was Pte John Green amongst the men wounded that day, although I have no concrete evidence to back it up my gut feeling tells me he wasn't, I believe he was injured in action the following day. Unfortunately the full report detailing the exploits of the 2nd Royal Fusiliers on 19th August 1918 has disappeared from the NA in Kew, as a result the following account, as brief as it is, comes mainly from the battalion war diary.

At 5:00pm the battalion attacked under a covering barrage, 'X' Coy on the left and 'W' Coy on the right along with two platoons of 'Z' Coy in support. They captured the line of Trucks, Lynde Farm, Asset Farm and Lesage Farm; they also assisted in the capture of Labis Farm which formed part of the objective of the 12th Norfolk's (94th Brigade, 31st Division) who attacked in conjunction on the right. The operation was completely successful and a line was established along the road running northeast out of Vieux-Berquin just east of Lesage Farm. A total of 1 officer and 110 prisoners were captured along with machine guns and trench mortars, in addition several casualties were inflicted on the enemy as he fled in confusion. Whilst no counter attack was delivered the 2nd Royal Fusiliers sustained substantial casualties, according to the war diary casualty figures for 19th August were:

Officers: 2 killed + 2 wounded
Other Ranks: 18 killed + 63 wounded

Whilst it appears that heavy fighting took place during the course of 19th August its frustrating a full report isn't to hand, the question has to be asked how come the battalion achieved so much on this day when the previous day it met heavy resistance. Over the days that followed the 2nd Royal Fusiliers not only consolidated their gains but in conjunction with units on either side managed a further advance. Whilst no serious opposition was encountered abandoned weapons and supplies were discovered, the troops however were shelled heavily at regular intervals by the enemy. Eventually on 21st August the battalion moved into reserve positions before moving to transport lines the following day, although for now their spell at the front was over the men of the 2nd Royal Fusiliers would see plenty more action before the end of the war.

The 2nd Royal Fusiliers reported no casualties in the days prior to 18th August and no casualties in the days immediately after 19th August therefore we know Pte John Green was wounded in fighting on one of these two dates. Although the exact part he played is unknown we know from a report in the September 1918 edition of the Chigwell Parish Magazine that his wounds were serious and he was evacuated to a Base Hospital at St Omer (47). It appears that from there John, almost certainly aware he wouldn't recover, was able to send his last thoughts and words to family and friends back in Chigwell. Pte John Green died of wounds in hospital on Thursday 22nd August 1918 aged only 19; he is buried in a communal grave with a touching headstone – like that of Pte Charles William Day - at Longuenesse (St Omer) Souvenir Cemetery, Pas de Calais, France. Sometime after the war John's parents received a plaque and scroll as well as the BWM and VM in memory of their son, when the IWGC compiled its records the couple were living at 3 Forest View Cottages, Chigwell, Essex.

* * *

After several weeks preparation the morning of 21st August saw divisions of Byng's 3rd Army push eastward attacking enemy positions on a front north of Albert south of Arras in an action known as the 'Battle of Albert'. Despite German units already beginning to give ground in places advancement proved tough however British units gained the advantage and resistance encountered was dealt with. By nightfall most of the day's objectives were secure, amongst them the villages of Ablainzeville and Moyenneville, however easing on the side of caution Byng paused momentarily to consolidate gains, move forward artillery and regroup. This decision nevertheless annoyed Sir Douglas Haig who realising the Germans were on the run felt that maximum pressure should be placed on the enemy. The following day German troops counter attacked however their effort was wasted as units of 3rd Army, dug in and waiting, were ready for them. That morning further south units of Rawlinson's 4th Army attacked and captured what remained of Albert, by this stage of the war this small but important town had been reduced to little more than a pile of rubble. That evening given that German forces no longer posed the threat they once did Haig issued orders to army commanders relaxing the policy of how troops attacked. Instead of advancing step by step in line with ones neighbour units were urged to push on in areas of progress and reach their objectives even if it meant that at times they were temporarily exposed. This method Haig hoped would help him secure victory in 1918 whilst many including some leading politicians were sure it would take well into 1919. On 23rd August following Haig's insistence 3rd Army resumed its attack between Albert and Arras, Byng made it a larger affair than that of two days previous and whilst troops made impressive gains they met with a mixture of light and heavy German defence. With sights firmly set on ground lost the previous spring early on the village of Gomiecourt was captured by infantry units supported by heavy guns, field artillery, tanks and planes of the RAF. Later that day northeast of Gomiecourt the village of Ervillers was taken whilst to the south both Achiet-le-Grand and Bihucourt fell, on 4th Army's boundary the Tara-Usna Line east of Albert west of La Boisselle was reached whilst patrols were pushed out into Thiepval Wood. As units of 3rd and 4th Army hustled German forces back over the wilderness of the old 1916 Somme battlefields on 26th August further north Sir Henry Horne's 1st Army attacked German positions east of Arras. The Canadian Corps, recently transferred from 4th Army following the Battle of Amiens, despite bad weather and heavy resistance started well and were instrumental over the following few days in capturing several miles of enemy held territory including the village of Monchy-le-Preux where Pte Harry Mark Brown had been killed back in April 1917.

By this stage things were looking desperate for Ludendorff who was hoping to withdraw his troops to a safe line of defence for the winter somewhere west of the Hindenburg Line, as units of 3rd Army and 4th Army pushed eastward this move was hampered however German machine gunners knowingly sacrificed themselves in order to buy comrades more time. Throughout August British units suffered some 80,000 casualties whilst German losses were also severe; many of Ludendorff's men became prisoners whilst the worldwide flu epidemic of 1918 begun taking its toll affecting armies of all nations. On 29th August the town of Bapaume was captured by men of the New Zealand Division and the following day Australian units launched an attack to capture Péronne on the banks of the River Somme. As previously explained in the chapter entitled 1917 the Germans had created an extension to the Hindenburg Line defences some 5 miles east of Arras known as the Drocourt–Quéant Switch. With things as they were, opposite 1st Army's front at least, Ludendorff had no option but to order a withdrawal of troops in the area back to this position. The end of August early September saw British and Canadian units of 1st Army fight hard and gain sufficient ground from which to attack the Drocourt–Quéant Switch whilst to the south Australian units of 4th Army captured high ground north of Péronne known as Mont St Quentin before taking Péronne itself on 2nd September. It soon became clear that if allied pressure could just be maintained then an end to the war on the Western Front shouldn't be too far away, as a result the allied ClC General Foch along with allied commanders drew up plans for a general offensive involving all allied armies. The day Péronne fell Canadian units east of Arras broke through the Drocourt–Quéant Switch on a frontage some 7,000 yards wide, success hadn't proved easy and losses were high both on the ground and in the air despite the capture of several thousand prisoners. The effects of this breakthrough sent shockwaves from Ypres in the north to the River Oise in the south as German units had no choice but to fall back even further. To the north they were forced to give up ground gained in the Georgette Offensive by withdrawing from the Lys Salient between Ypres and Lens consequently allowing units of both Plumer's 2nd Army and Birdwood's 5th Army to advance. To the south they had little option but to fall back onto the main Hindenburg Line defence system whilst in the centre they adopted a position along the newly constructed but unfinished dry banked Canal du Nord as well as the Sensee Canal roughly 10 miles west of Cambrai. At this point Haig wished briefly to conserve resources whilst following up the German retreat however it was imperative not to give the enemy time to regroup and strengthen defences.

On the morning of 12th September divisions of Byng's 3rd Army attacked the outer defences of the Hindenburg Line at Havrincourt and whilst the village itself was secured and German moral was shaken overall resistance proved tough making further advancement difficult. That same day further south, as part of the plans laid out by General Foch, troops of the American First Army commanded by General Pershing along with troops of the French Fourth Army attacked and eradicated the St Mihiel Salient southeast of Verdun, this stretch of line was formidable having been a thorn in the side of French forces since 1915. Despite German units expecting attack and withdrawing troop's accordingly American successes at St Mihiel proved their strength as a fighting army; the battle however was smaller than had been originally intended. With no major breakthrough actually achieved once lines were straightened little else was gained and attention was turned towards plans for a later action known as Meuse – Argonne. The next assault by British forces came on 18th September as corps within 4th Army attacked German defences in front of the Hindenburg Line south of the village of Epehy. When the Germans withdrew to the Hindenburg Line back in February 1917 and British forces advanced eastwards to meet them in turn they created two fresh lines of defence. During the Michael Offensives however the British were swept out of these positions which then lay unused for several months. Now as the Germans withdrew to the Hindenburg Line they occupied the old British front lines and turned them into defensive positions in advance of the main Hindenburg system. Rawlingson knew that before any attempt on the main line was made these advanced positions would have to be captured; the action was known as the 'Battle of Epehy'. The Australian Corps occupying the centre ground managed the furthest advance and despite heavy fighting in bad weather captured all outpost lines bringing them up to the main Hindenburg Line defences, British divisions on either side however had a tougher time and whilst gains were made they weren't sufficient. Over the days that followed fresh attempts were made and after a reorganisation of sorts enough ground was eventually gained to the south with which to launch an attack on the main system. The third week of September saw planning step up a gear as allied armies in France and Flanders made final arrangements for a general offensive, their ClC General Foch spurred on by Haig's belief that an end was in sight ordered *'Everybody to battle'*. Following a preliminary bombardment the battle known as Meuse – Argonne began on the morning of 26th September and was carried out on a front some 44 miles long by troops of the American First Army and French Fourth Army. Designed to draw enemy units away from the Hindenburg Line near St Quentin ahead of an attack by British forces after a small and somewhat difficult advance it soon lost momentum due to logistical problems caused by inexperienced American staff officers. Whilst it failed to have the desired effect the fighting still remained heavy at times resulting in heavy losses for both sides. After a period of reorganisation and enlargement within the American forces the battle continued into October and fresh assaults were made. Ultimately by early November the allied line was advanced in this region mainly northwards along the banks of the Meuse to the small town of Sedan, the main breakthrough however responsible for turning the tide on the Western Front would come in the British sector.

On the morning of 27th September the Canadian Corps from Horne's 1st Army covered by a creeping barrage advanced eastward and captured German defences on the Canal du Nord, having crossed this obstacle before noon surrounding villages were taken including Bourlon and Bourlon Wood. As British units north and south of the

Canadians joined the hunt they met with some degree of success and failure. Over the days that followed however with help from tanks and the RAF further villages and fortifications, defence systems and vital rail lines were captured bringing units of 1st Army and elements of Byng's 3rd Army to the outskirts of Cambrai. Having been relatively quiet since mid August the 28th September saw Plumer's 2nd Army as well as the Belgian Army with French troops in reserve attack German positions up in Flanders. Following four years of war the battlefield was little more than a mass of craters virtually devoid of plant life, as previously explained with the Third Battle of Ypres the weather was always atrocious making movement impossible most of the time. Despite this that day Belgian forces, led by King Albert of Belgium, attacked in areas north of Ypres to Dixmude and supported by British artillery and aircraft made surprisingly good ground. Plumer held lines just north of Ypres south to the Lys at Armentières however that day his troops only attacked from Ypres down to St Eloi. Fortunately the rains held long enough for 2nd Army to achieve a decent advance, in fact also supported by aircraft and artillery that day they achieved all pre set objectives and a total advance of some six miles. This distance was virtually the same that was covered by British forces during the whole of the Third Battle of Ypres however by this stage of the war their enemy although expectant was somewhat demoralised. Over the days that followed further ground was gained expunging the Ypres Salient once and for all but as always the weather broke making movement and supply fairly difficult, with no point in continuing and with enemy reinforcements arriving, early October saw the battle abandoned.

If things weren't bad enough for Ludendorff in mid September the Bulgarian Army holding his strategic flank in Macedonia was attacked and split by Serbian, French and British forces based in Salonika (48). Whilst the Bulgarians put up a fight this soon turned to disorderly retreat and having had enough of the war they sought peace terms agreeing an Armistice on 29th September. Having been told of their plight the evening before Ludendorff now knew that Austrian forces at home and abroad were vulnerable to attack, none more so than those troops fighting in Northern Italy, in his mind it was only a matter of time before Germany's closest ally was threatened. With things as they were in France and Flanders it was now that he knew that peace terms had to be negotiated, if his army could just hold out long enough it was hoped that those peace terms may be favourable. Along with the Chief of Staff of the German Army, Field Marshal Paul Von Hindenburg, a meeting with the Kaiser was booked for the following morning however a few hours before this meeting took place the British delivered a knock out blow.

Following several weeks planning the morning of 29th September saw units of Rawlinson's 4th Army attack and breakthrough the Hindenburg Line defences in areas north of St Quentin finally sealing the fate of the German Army so far as the war on the Western Front was concerned. In planning their attack 4th Army were fortunate as detailed plans of the Hindenburg Line defences along this sector of front had been captured by the 17th Armoured Car Battalion during the Battle of Amiens on 8th August. Having studied the plans carefully Rawlingson, along with his corps commanders, discovered that despite its unquestionable strength the defence line north of St Quentin suffered a potential weakness. As previously mentioned during the chapter entitled '1917' where the Hindenburg Line met the St Quentin Canal at Bellicourt a tunnel existed some 3 miles long. The tunnel itself was modified to house troops and incorporated into the main defence system however because of this German frontlines in the area were positioned in front of the canal rather than behind it. The frontline trenches were heavily wired and housed dug outs along with machine gun posts connected by communication trenches, in addition further wire entanglements existed between the frontline and the canal. At each end of the tunnel sector the canal banks in places stood 50 feet high whilst the canal itself was 35 feet wide and 6 feet deep, filled with water and mud it didn't take much to work out crossing it wouldn't be easy. With this in mind Rawlingson decided to concentrate his main attack on the 3 mile wide section of tunnel in the hope that once the frontline was broken the tunnel itself could then act as a bridge across the canal. Beyond the main front line and east of the tunnel stood the Hindenburg Support Line defences whilst beyond that stood the Hindenburg Reserve Line position known as the Beaurevoir Line, if these could be breached then beyond stood nothing but open countryside with no other lines of defence. As well as attacking the tunnel sector a plan was also devised, by one of Rawlinson's corps commanders, to cross the canal itself. Lieutenant General Sir Walter Braithwaite, the man in question and commander of IX Corps, was sure that south of the tunnel he could get a division across using light portable boats and lifebelts from cross Channel steamers as well as ropes and ladders, it was an ambitious plan but one that worked well. The troops responsible for attacking the tunnel sector were American divisions under the temporary command of the Australian Corps, whilst closely supported by artillery, tanks and armoured car battalions to their left stood British units of III Corps whilst to their right stood units of Braithwaite's IX Corps.

Two days prior to zero British artillery units bombarded German defences along the canal ahead of the main attack, then at 5:50am on the 29th September supported by creeping barrage the infantry, tanks and armoured cars advanced. The weather that morning was favourable despite slight drizzle and ground fog covering the battlefield, in the centre the American troops had an arduous task however despite inexperience they fought hard advancing with Australian support north and south of the village of Hargicourt. North of the village little was achieved and heavy casualties sustained, to the south however despite tough opposition the Hindenburg Line was breached on a narrow front over the tunnel sector at Bellicourt. Whilst heavy fighting ensued the breach remained small however the breakthrough served to undermine German moral, on III Corps front minimal gains were made however south of the tunnel was a different story. Against all odds men of the 46th (North Midland) Division attached to IX Corps crossed the canal with minimal casualties, whilst British artillery had flattened canal bank defences and destroyed barbed wire entanglements enemy troops in position here hadn't expected such an attack and were taken somewhat by surprise. As advancing troops overran trench positions east of the canal tanks crossed over the breach in the tunnel sector and swung south to help out the infantry, as a result by mid afternoon the whole of the main Hindenburg Line defence system on 46th (North Midland) Divisions front was in British hands. By nightfall an advance of 2½ to 3 miles had been made on IX Corps front which included the Hindenburg Support Line defences, in addition several villages on route were captured as well as enemy guns and some several thousand prisoners. Whilst north of the tunnel results had been disappointing where they broke through to the south the American and Australian divisions achieved an advance of some 1½ to 2 miles, by nightfall they too reached the Hindenburg Support Line however in doing so their casualties were much higher. Despite 4th Army's success Rawlingson remained somewhat disappointed by overall results, this said once the Germans were driven out of the Hindenburg Line defences it was clear to all that now they had no chance of winning the war. At 10:00am on Sunday 29th September fresh with the news of the latest allied attack both Ludendorff and Von Hindenburg met the Kaiser to call for an immediate Armistice, he listened and agreed and somewhat secretly over the following few days - after a change of Chancellor - the German government made contact with American President Woodrow Wilson (49).

Whilst peace terms were negotiated Ludendorff still hoped to save his army from all out defeat, as a result some six weeks of fighting still lay ahead that would turn out to be some of the heaviest and most costly in terms of casualties sustained of the entire war. As far as the allied armies on the Western Front were concerned by the start of October to the south both American and French endeavours had run out of steam in the Meuse – Argonne region whilst to the north bad weather had stopped Belgian and British operations in Flanders. In the centre Birdwood's 5th Army was positioned facing German formations west of Lille whilst Horne's 1st Army and Byng's 3rd Army were positioned north and west of Cambrai respectively. Whilst the end of September early October saw the Canadian Corps active for little gain in areas just north of Cambrai little else was happening, just as it looked like the allied advance was about to slow down once more units of 4th Army went on the offensive.

Having broken the Hindenburg Line as well as the Hindenburg Support Line the gap created on 29th September had to be exploited; as a result Rawlingson resumed operations on 30th September - 1st October with the aim of taking the Hindenburg Reserve Line position known as the Beaurevoir Line. As previously mentioned this was the Germans last prepared line of defence and once broken 4th Army would be in open countryside that showed few signs of war. Despite opposition in places and enemy counter attacks over the following few days Rawlingson's troops improved their line greatly, American and Australian units broke through at the northern end of the Bellicourt Tunnel whilst further south British troops wasted no time in reaching the Beaurevoir Line. On 3rd October a major effort was made to move the whole front forward and after heavy fighting that saw some of the same villages change hands on several occasions by 6th October the Beaurevoir Line and ground beyond was in allied hands. Whilst several thousand prisoners were captured along with guns and munitions further south troops of the French First Army had entered St Quentin. Rawlingson, pleased this time with overall results, congratulated his army, as for the Australian Corps having fought like lions since the end of July they were relieved for a well deserved rest west of Amiens, although not known at the time they had fought their last battle of the First World War.

By Sunday 6th October both Foch and Haig were aware that the Germans had asked for an Armistice but both men were also aware that pressure on the battlefield should be maintained. Next it was the turn of Byng's 3rd Army to rejoin the attack and preparations were made to advance on Cambrai. To bring Byng's troops in line with 4th Army close co-operation was needed, on 8th October both armies attacked once again in places meeting a mixture of light and heavy German defence. The day however turned out to be one of heavy defeat for the Germans with thousands more prisoners captured, that evening German high command gave the order to abandon Cambrai and retreat to a line immediately behind the River Selle, as a result Canadian troops entered the town on 9th October. The River Selle stands roughly 10 miles east of Cambrai and towards its southern end sits the small town of La Cateau; it was just south of here back in August 1914 that Chigwell suffered its first casualty when Cpl Harold Henry Shuttle was killed whilst retreating from Mons with the 1st Battalion Bedfordshire Regiment. As the Germans dug in on the east bank of the river units of Byng's 3rd Army and Rawlingson's 4th Army moved forward to meet them hampered only by enemy rearguards consisting mainly of field artillery and machine gun units. To Byng's left Horne's 1st Army advanced whilst on Rawlingson's right the French First Army moved forward thus by the second week of October all allied armies to the centre were once more facing the Germans. Up in Flanders Plumer's 2nd Army renewed its offensive on 14th October with Belgian and French support to its left, the attackers made surprisingly good ground with little support from artillery however the majority of German troops facing them put up little resistance. As enemy forces pulled back from the River Lys near Menin Plumer's troops moved forward liberating Courtrai on 16th October, soon after Belgian troops having fought famously were temporarily relieved by French ones and ground was made in the direction of Roulers towards Ghent. Meanwhile further south elements of Birdwood's 5th Army moving eastward entered and liberated the city of Lille on 17th October, that same day Byng's 3rd Army and Rawlingson's 4th Army attacked German forces dug in east of the River Selle. Having been delayed slightly due to logistical problems the battle, preceded by a two day artillery bombardment, once underway lasted for three days. Having broken the Hindenburg Line defences it was hoped that crossing the River Selle would prove easy in comparison however German divisions dug in there defended positions most vigorously. British troops had a difficult time and whilst heavy fighting occurred, especially in and around Le Cateau, by 20th October both armies had crossed the river in pursuit of the enemy once more.

Meanwhile away from the battlefield peace terms were being negotiated, as previously mentioned Ludendorff hoped that the longer his armies held out the better those terms may be. Despite still wanting an Armistice he was convinced his army could regroup to a defensive line on the German border and offer resistance over the winter should terms prove unfavourable, on the home front however the will of the German government and will of the German people was beginning to crumble. The allies were demanding Germany's unconditional surrender and military commanders were called in to give their view on what terms should be imposed, Sir Douglas Haig was summoned to London to meet with the War Cabinet and Prime Minister David Lloyd George at 10 Downing Street. During the meeting Haig warned that although the German Army was in full retreat she was still capable of providing adequate defence should peace terms not prove acceptable, this he said could prolong the war into 1919 at the expense of many more lives, also and somewhat more importantly he warned that politicians should not try to humiliate Germany to such an extent that she'd be intent on revenge in years to come! By the last week of October following the passage of notes between the two sides Woodrow Wilson was stuck to his guns demanding the German government accept nothing short of unconditional surrender, in addition he let it be known his unhappiness with regards to the Kaiser remaining in place. Whilst not entirely happy the government in Berlin was prepared to agree to such terms however Ludendorff, adamant his army was still not beaten and therefore capable of further defence, was not. On 26th October after heated discussions between him and the Kaiser both he and Von Hindenburg offered their resignations, whilst Ludendorff's was accepted Von Hindenburg's wasn't. On the streets of Germany widespread unrest aimed at those in power was beginning to break out, people were starving due to the blockade imposed by the Royal Navy and the flu epidemic was sweeping the country, spurred on by successive bad news from the Western Front the German people had had enough. To make matters worse on 23rd October allied armies successfully attacked Austrian forces in Northern Italy in an action known as the 'Battle of Vittorio Veneto'. Attempting to make a stand Austrian resistance didn't last long and although the battle itself lasted for several days by 30th October not only was the Austrian Army in retreat it was split in two. Having had enough that same day the Austrian government requested an Armistice which was formally signed on 4th November. At the same time both Hungary and Bosnia declared independence and with Bulgaria already out of the war Serbian forces marched north from Salonika to retake their capital Belgrade on 1st November. The same day that Austria surrendered Turkey capitulated following allied successes in Palestine; with her allies defeated Germany now stood alone. Vulnerable to attack from all directions Ludendorff's successor General Wilhelm Groener had no easy answers; as a result within days of his appointment he too was demanding an Armistice in order to save the German Army.

Despite the fact they were losing the war German troops on the Western Front continued to offer in places substantial resistance in the last minute hope that some kind of negotiated peace could be reached. During the last week of October however whilst their lines of supply got shorter their opponents got longer, despite roads and railways used to feed and supply troops being in a desperate state intent on ending the war in 1918 the allied advance showed no signs of slowing down. Up in Flanders King Albert of Belgium moved eastwards along the Belgian Coast reaching and liberating Bruges on 25th October, to his right Plumer's 2nd Army, having overcome difficulties moving forward artillery, also made progress despite some opposition reaching the banks of the River Schelde roughly 10 miles south - southeast of Courtrai by the start of November. On the front of Birdwood's 5th Army and Horne's 1st Army progress was too being made as troops followed up the German withdrawal, towards the end of October beginning of November both armies had reached the River Schelde with Birdwood positioned just west of Tournai and Horne positioned west and southwest of Valenciennes. Having pushed German forces out of defensive positions east of the Selle both Byng's 3rd Army and Rawlingson's 4th Army mounted small operations to improve their positions. Whilst Byng's troops had fought hard and captured some several thousand prisoners whilst crossing the Selle they now made for Le Quesnoy and the Forest of Mormal with eyes on Maubeuge. Whilst 4th Army found itself slightly under strength due to depleted and tired divisions it continued its move eastward, by the end of October beginning of November it found the Forest of Mormal to its left and the Sambre and Oise Canal to its right. Despite all their gains the month of October proved costly for the British, in terms of casualties sustained the figure topped 100,000 however as the war entered what was its final phase further fighting was still to come.

Valenciennes was identified as a key area of German defence and the last week of October saw Horne's 1st Army suffer quite heavily whilst clearing enemy positions west and southwest of the city. On 1st November however sufficient troops and artillery were in place for an attack on an area of high ground south of Valenciennes known as Mont Houy, once this was captured an attempt could be made for the city itself. With support from elements of Byng's 3rd Army on the right the 'Battle of Valenciennes' as it came to be known was to last for approximately three days, during that time artillery cover in support of attacking troops would be stronger than ever. As British and Canadian units crossed the Schelde moving east to north on the city heavy fighting ensued, as enemy positions were reached upon no mercy was shown to the occupants. Canadian units managed without delay to eject German units from Mont Houy however whilst many soldiers surrendered many more were killed. As attacking troops approached Valenciennes care had to be taken not injure civilians, at this stage of the war the city was full of refugees who had fled from surrounding villages. Whilst fighting occurred in the southern suburbs from house to house and street to street German positions within Valenciennes soon became hopeless, as a result by the early morning of 2nd November the order had been given to evacuate the city. The following day saw Valenciennes pass into allied hands however whilst Horne's troops had fought in their last real action they continued pursuing the enemy, in the meantime the main focus of British attention turned southwards.

The final battle of the First World War involving British forces began early on Monday 4th November as units of Byng's 3rd Army and Rawlinson's 4th Army - with the French First Army in support - attacked German positions on a frontage some 20 miles long. The area in question began north and west of Le Quesnoy and stretched southwards and west of the Forest of Mormal and Sambre and Oise Canal before ending just west of the village of Fesmy. Later known as the 'Battle of the Sambre' the weather that morning saw conditions begin somewhat misty before clearing revealing a cloudy but fine day. Whilst enemy guns remained active across much of the front attacking troops met with a varying degree of light and heavy German defence. Supported by massed artillery, various tanks and planes of the RAF to the north of the battlefront British units of 3rd Army attacked over open ground whilst to their right the New Zealand Division outflanked the fortified town of Le Quesnoy, eventually the enemy there was forced to surrender and units pushed onto and into the Forest of Mormal. Despite not being as densely populated as it had been prior to the war the forest in places, with thick undergrowth, still proved a formidable obstacle. Whilst in some cases German troops dug in there put up a bit of a fight many were found not to be positioned in strength, as a result overall progress was easily made in places. Further south on 3rd Army's right troops attacked over hedgerows and orchards towards fortified villages beyond, in some cases intense fighting at close quarters developed. Those units to the north on 4th Army's front found the forest jutted back westward and close to their start line, as a result troops in position here attacked virtually straight into woodland. Further south open ground developed, devoid of trench lines machine gunners existed to try and slow down the British advance. Whilst initial resistance in this area proved tough attacking troops made for and entered the town of Landrecies as it crossed over the Sambre and Oise Canal, it was here back in August 1914 that elements of I Corps under the then command of Sir Douglas Haig were attacked by a small German force. Further south on the banks of the Sambre and Oise Canal near the village of Ors heavy fighting developed, enemy machine gunners had a field day as troops tried to cross the canal and it was here that the poet Wilfred Owen was killed (50). Towards the southern end of the battlefront whilst enemy artillery and machine guns remained active British troops pushed on, units crossing the canal on 4th Army's southern boundary however met with stiff opposition and sustained heavy casualties before a bridge was erected that allowed men to advance. In general across the whole of the battlefront progress was made and by 6th November the Forest of Mormal and towns like Landrecies were firmly in allied hands, whilst in places an advance of up to 10 miles was made overall casualties remained light as enemy guns and prisoners were captured. Over the days that followed whilst their enemy withdrew British troops kept pace where possible, in places German machine gun teams and artillery units stayed on to cover withdrawals however as units fell back in disarray at no stage were German front lines ever broken.

During that first week of November right across the Western Front allied armies pushed eastward, with no hope of stemming their continued advance Germany was forced to agree peace terms. On the night of 7th – 8th November, having received word from Woodrow Wilson, a German delegation in great secrecy left Berlin and crossed allied lines to discuss Armistice terms with allied commander General Foch. The meeting took place in Foch's railway carriage situated on a siding within the Forest of Compiègne, the allied terms being offered stopped not far short of unconditional surrender. The delegation returned to Germany however the situation there had deteriorated, the country was gripped in civil war and the navy, ordered to sea on one last mission, had mutinied. The Kaiser was blamed by the German people for Germany's problems and his refusal to abdicate swelled further unrest. Without his knowledge, in order to calm down the situation, the German Chancellor Prince Max of Baden announced the Kaiser's abdication on 9th November which led to the collapse of the government (51). Overnight Germany became a republic and the new men in charge had no choice but to accept allied terms. The delegation returned to France on 11th November and at 5:00am in Foch's railway carriage an Armistice was signed, it was agreed it would come into effect later that morning. Meanwhile Canadian troops advancing eastward arrived at the Belgian town of Mons; it was here back in August 1914 that the BEF fired their first shots of the war. At 11:00am on the 11th November 1918 from the Belgian Coast to the borders of Switzerland the guns fell silent and after four years of conflict the First World War finally came to an end.

76, *The gravestone of Pte Matthew Amos Wesson Mason at Grand-Seraucourt Cemetery, Somme, France*

78, *An unidentified soldier from the First World War whose picture hangs in the Dining Room of the Kings Head Public House in Chigwell (Picture produced by Reeds Ltd)*

77, *The Mason family gravestone situated inside St Mary's Churchyard in Chigwell*

79, *An unidentified corporal from the First World War whose picture hangs in the Dining Room of the Kings Head Public House in Chigwell (Picture produced by Reeds Ltd)*

80, The gravestone of Pte Frederick Elliot Noble at Le Grand Beaumart CWGC Cemetery, Steenwerck, France

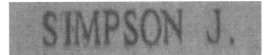

81, The name of Pte James Simpson as it appears on the Arras Memorial to the Missing

82, The gravestone of Pte Charles William Day (Far left) along with three other soldiers buried at Pont-De-Nieppe Communal Cemetery northwest of Armentières, France

83, The name of Pte Sydney James Bodger as it appears on the Loos Memorial to the Missing

84, The gravestone of Guardsman Frederick Arthur Bailey at Bienvillers CWGC Cemetery, Somme, France

85, The Guards Division Memorial on Horse Guards Road in Central London

86, The Tank Corps Memorial at Pozières on the Somme

87, The gravestone of Cpl Frederick William Barton at Heath CWGC Cemetery, Harbonnières, Somme, France

88, The gravestone of Cpl Harold Hull Moseley at Dive Copse CWGC Cemetery Somme, France

89, The private memorial to Harold Hull Moseley that used to exist in the grounds of St Mary's Churchyard in Chigwell

90, The Mission Room and Chapel at Grange Hill - Chigwell Row

91, The gravestone of Pte John Green at Longuenesse (St Omer) Souvenir Cemetery, Pas de Calais, France

AFTER THE ARMISTICE

Despite having started in Europe the First World War was a conflict that involved armies of many nations. Away from the battlefields of France and Flanders as we have seen fighting also occurred in Italy, Greece, the Balkan States, Russia, Turkey, the Middle East and North Africa. In fact fighting also occurred in East Africa, West Africa and Southwest Africa as allied troops protecting their colonies also invaded those colonies under German control. Taking the war at sea into account amongst other places action occurred off the coast of China, in Far Eastern waters and the Indian Ocean, out in the Atlantic, down near the Falkland Islands and off the coast of South America. Following hostilities however the map of Europe changed dramatically as Germany and Russia became Republics and the Austrian Empire was broken up as Balkan states declared independence, in addition as previously mentioned the fall of the Ottoman Empire also ended 400 years of Turkish rule in the Middle East. Whilst precise casualty figures will never been known it is estimated in terms of those killed that Britain and her Empire lost just short of a million men whilst France lost 1.4 million and Germany lost 1.8 million. Whilst many more men were injured total allied casualties for those killed and wounded stand somewhere close to 9 million whilst those suffered by Germany stand somewhere over 6 million. It is impossible to know how many people suffered premature deaths as a result of injuries sustained in the war however in 1918 as already touched on a flu epidemic spread worldwide affecting those of all nations. Known as Spanish Flu as brief as it was it claimed many more lives than the war ever did, it is estimated that somewhere between 20 and 40 million people died as a result with entire populations of small towns and villages wiped out. After the Armistice was signed in November 1918 with the fighting over terms in regards to peace settlements had to be arranged, in January 1919 allied leaders met in Paris to discuss such matters. Whilst France demanded severe punishment for Germany the Americans decided it was probably better to act more reasonably, in the event following six months of detailed negotiations agreement was finally reached. Whilst all losing nations were ordered to sign treaties and make concessions none were so harsh than the treaty dished out to Germany. On 28th June 1919 the Treaty of Versailles was signed at the Palace of Versailles to the west of Paris, signed under protest Germany was ordered to hand back the two French provinces of Alsace and Lorraine whilst limits were placed on the size of her army and restrictions were placed in regard to her navy. In addition German colonies in the Near East and Africa were handed over to the League of Nations, set up by Woodrow Wilson this organization served as forerunner to the United Nations we know of today. Another term of the treaty saw Germany ordered to pay substantial compensation to those allied nations directly affected by the war, the effects of this would be felt right through the depression years of the late 1920's leading to much bitterness and suffering amongst the German people. Allied troops were to occupy areas of the Rhineland along the frontiers of both Belgium and France for some 15 years to serve as a precaution against further invasion; whilst this was needed to maintain control it caused further upset amongst German citizens. As it turned out the harsh terms imposed on Germany were to have huge repercussions, as suffering continued into the 1930's a right wing organization known as the Nazi Party grew in stature whilst promising stability. Whilst initially as far as the German people were concerned the future looked brighter it didn't take long before certain groups and religions were persecuted. Over the years that followed Germany rearmed quite significantly somewhat ignored by the allies for fear of more conflict, in August 1939 however under the leadership of Adolf Hitler, who'd been made Chancellor some six years previous, the German Army invaded Poland which ultimately led to another world war.

EPILOGUE

'We shall remember the 11th November all our lives as the day when this hideous warfare ceased, this parish has suffered in common with all, and the victory has only been won at terrible cost in gallant, splendid lives'.

Chigwell Parish Magazine December 1918

In the week following the Armistice all over the country people celebrated the fact that the war was over and victory had been won, Chigwell was no exception and church bells were rung out in triumph with a thanksgiving service held at St Mary's Church on Sunday 17th November 1918. However despite the celebrations the month of November saw the Chigwell Parish Magazine record six fatal cases of Spanish Flu within the village, in fact most schools in Chigwell were closed for a month to stop the virus spreading. It's possible that down the road in Woodford Bridge the only casualty from the Great War buried inside St Paul's Churchyard succumbed to the flu epidemic. Pte Percy Green was attached to the Labour Corps and lived in Woodford Bridge, whilst some sources say that he died of wounds its possible, like many wounded soldiers who had survived the war, his injuries left him vulnerable to the effects of the disease, buried close to the vestry door he died on 29th November 1918. Over the weeks and months that followed as soldiers and sailors returned home victory parades and parties were held in their honour, whilst some families were joyful however those who'd lost loved ones couldn't help but reflect sadness. As previously mentioned elsewhere in this book in late 1915 the Reverend Fredrick Auriol Murray had established a Roll of Honour within St Mary's Church that altered month on month to record the names of those parishioners killed whilst on active service for king and country. In early 1919 however, like most towns and villages throughout the land, it was decided that Chigwell should have its own permanent memorial to honour its war dead (1). Having lost his own son in the fighting Reverend Murray wasted no time in starting a fund for such a purpose. With him as chairman on the evening of 8th May 1919 a public meeting of all parishioners was held at the Girls and Infants School on Chigwell High Road. It was announced that the memorial should be both adequate and fitting and that Chigwell should be proud in making it so, it was requested that those parishioners who'd lost loved ones attend so as to list names and have a say in proceedings. It was eventually decided that two memorials would be unveiled to honour those men killed, one inside St Mary's Church and one outside in what was considered by all to be the most suitable and poignant place in Chigwell. By August the memorial fund had raised £500 and by January 1920 some £700 had been collected, in total £1,000 was collected to pay for the two memorials. In the case of the outside memorial it was decided that a cross bearing the names of those men killed would stand as a fitting tribute, in March 1920 a 20ft memorial cross of grey granite was approved and ordered. Whilst the outside memorial was prepared work started without delay on the memorial to be placed inside St Mary's Church which it was hoped would be completed ahead of the second anniversary of the end of the war. In order to keep things in context however we must leave Chigwell temporarily to cover two significant post war events that took place in Central London on Armistice Day 1920.

Despite the fighting finishing several months earlier the signing of the Treaty of Versailles on 28th June 1919 officially marked the end of the war and to celebrate, after much preparation, a victory parade was held in London on 19th July 1919. The focal point of the parade involved thousands of veterans marching first past King George V at Buckingham Palace and then past a temporary structure erected in Whitehall designed by Sir Edwin Lutyens. Initially made from wood and plaster the structure was intended to represent both the missing and fallen however due to public demand it was soon made permanent. A white column made from Portland stone with an empty tomb depicted on top and engraved with the words "The Glorious Dead" the Cenotaph was officially unveiled at 11:00am on 11th November 1920 (2). Shortly after the Cenotaph was unveiled the same morning the tomb of the Unknown Warrior was laid to rest in Westminster Abbey. It had been mentioned in the British press some months before that with many of the fallen buried overseas and many having no grave at all their families should have somewhere in Britain that they could go to mourn the loss of their loved ones. Firstly it was suggested that an unknown soldier should be buried beneath the Cenotaph in Whitehall however after much discussion it was decided that a serviceman buried amongst the great and the good inside Westminster Abbey was much more appropriate. As it was six unidentifiable British corpses from each of the armed services were lifted from six different areas of battle in France and Flanders and placed in identical coffins draped with the Union Jack. The coffins were then moved to a small town in France and placed inside a makeshift chapel, in due course a high ranking officer was blindfolded and led into the chapel where he reached out and touched one of coffins thus selecting the Unknown Warrior. The chosen coffin was then transported back to England finally arriving at Victoria Station (3) in London; from there the Unknown Warrior was placed on a gun carriage and moved through crowd lined streets to proceedings in Whitehall. After the Cenotaph was officially unveiled two minutes silence ensued before the Last Post was sounded and the gun carriage moved off towards Westminster Abbey. In front of King George V, the Prime Minister and other notable dignitaries a funeral service with full military honours was conducted, the coffin was then lifted and the Unknown Warrior was laid to rest.

Back in Chigwell the first of two memorials to honour the war dead was unveiled by Lieutenant General Sir Francis Lloyd G.C.V.O., K.C.B., DSO (4) inside St Mary's Church on the evening of Sunday 14th November 1920. The memorial consists of an oak screen chancel which stands in the south aisle of the church and covers the entrance to the Lady Chapel (5). On top of the screen to the centre sits a beautifully carved cross under which are the words in old English lettering 'Greater love hath no man than this'. On either side of its central archway are two panels listing the thirty nine names of those men killed, above the panels in gold relief sit the words 'In honoured memory of Chigwell men who gave their lives in the Great War'. A large congregation was present at the service with pews directly in front of the memorial screen reserved for the families of those men killed. Prayers were read by the Reverend Fredrick Auriol Murray whilst James Pleasance, a minister with the Congressional Church and father of Pte George Pleasance, also gave a short address. During the hymn 'Stand Up, Stand Up for Jesus' the church choir, clergy and churchwardens accompanied Sir Francis Lloyd to the oak screen where he unveiled the memorial before reading through the list of names of those men killed. After the unveiling Sir Francis Lloyd gave a short speech from the chancel steps praising not just those from Chigwell but all those who'd served king and country during the Great War. After the speech the Right Reverend Thomas Stevens (1841 - 1920) the Bishop of Barking dedicated the memorial and floral tributes were laid at the foot of the screen before the Last Post was played on the church organ by organist Mr Henry Riding. To close the service Land of Hope and Glory, written by Edward Elgar in 1901, was played once again by way of the church organ. With an internal memorial to be proud of the people of Chigwell still required one outdoors for all to see as they passed through the village, almost a year later this memorial was ready.

On the afternoon of Sunday 6th November 1921 a large crowd of people assembled in bright but chilly conditions on the road outside St Mary's Church to witness the unveiling of the Chigwell Village War Memorial. Those attending included families of the fallen and local people of all ages, also in attendance were army personnel and other uniformed organisations along with parish councillors and church members. The initial service was conducted by Reverend Frederick Auriol Murray with the actual unveiling performed once again by Lieutenant General Sir Francis Lloyd G.C.V.O., K.C.B., DSO. The memorial stands roughly 20ft high and takes the form of a Celtic cross. Made from grey Aberdeen granite it was erected in a prominent position close to the road on land adjoining the churchyard donated at the time by a local man called Sir Guy Garnet. The middle of the memorial is hexagonal in shape and back in 1921 just listed the thirty nine names of those men killed in the Great War, towards the base of the memorial the words 'In sacred memory of the men of Chigwell who died for freedom and mankind' are inscribed (6). The memorial can be reached direct from the roadway or through a gap in the wall down some steps from the churchyard; back when the memorial was first erected fields made up the view behind. The service took place around the cross and began with hymns sung by combined choirs from St Mary's Church and Chigwell School; following on Congressional Minister James Pleasance once more addressed those present. At the close of the address the combined choirs sang the hymn 'How bright these glorious spirits shine' before Reverend Murray formally asked Sir Francis Lloyd to unveil the memorial. Members of the OTC from Chigwell School formed a guard of honour as Sir Francis unveiled the large grey cross, he then turned to address the crowd. He began by saying he had heard it said that towns and villages were spending too much on erecting memorials, he went on to say that he disagreed and no price was too high for the sacrifice made by those who fell. Like at the service the year before Sir Francis reiterated his praise not just for the men of Chigwell but for all those who fought and died in the Great War, he went on to speak of Commander Francis Goodhart who's story is told elsewhere in this book. Once his speech was over the Last Post and the Reveille were sounded by buglers from Sir Francis's former regiment the Grenadier Guards, following on as before the hymn 'Stand Up, Stand Up for Jesus' was sung. Reverend Murray then read the dedicatory prayer which was followed by two minutes silence, the service then continued with more hymns, a blessing and the National Anthem. It was then that wreaths were laid at the foot of the memorial; many by family members of those who were killed including the mother of Captain Edward Daniels killed on the Somme in 1916. Further wreaths were laid by groups such as the church choir and members of Chigwell Council School where, to name just a few, Sgt Sidney Hayter MM and L/Cpl Edward Stephen Scott had sung and Pte Matthew Amos Wesson Mason and Pte Harry Mark Brown had attended in those years before the war. As the service concluded and the people went home did they ever imagine wreaths would still be laid to honour the fallen over ninety years later, its possible but they probably never imagined another world war.

Between the wars Chigwell prospered as London's suburbs moved ever closer however its hard to know how many villagers who went to war returned for a better life, I'm sure many did but how many like Harry Cecil Dunkley died prematurely due to the wounds they'd received or the horrors they'd witnessed. The village of Chigwell played a prominent part in the Second World War however sadly another generation of men were to lose their lives, maybe one day a book will tell their story. In August 1938 Balloon Command controlled by the Auxiliary Air Force established a base close to Roding Lane in Chigwell, once war was declared the following year it done much to protect skies over London. In April 1943 the base became RAF Chigwell, whilst no aircraft were stationed there during the war it survived until 1962, following the closure however buildings and items were auctioned off and today a David Lloyd Fitness Club stands on the site. Although I've tried hard to tell each mans story there's still many unanswered questions, hopefully when the census for 1911 is made public in 2011 some of these will be answered. If I had to pick one thing about writing this book that frustrated me most it would have to be the lack of pictures available, having written about and researched the men of Chigwell killed in the Great War for the best part of eight years it would be nice to know what they looked like (7). Every year on Remembrance Sunday I look at the names on the Chigwell Village War Memorial and during the two minutes silence I go over the stories in my head of those men killed, on reading this book if you didn't already know you can now do the same. The people of Chigwell erected a memorial in the hope it would stand as a silent witness for years to come of the brave boys who left Chigwell and died for their country in the Great War. With those people too now departed they can rest safe in the knowledge that the Chigwell Village War Memorial still stands strong and that the names of ALL those inscribed upon it who fought for our freedom will live for evermore.

92, The gravestone of Pte Percy Green of the Labour Corps at St Paul's Church, Woodford Bridge who died of wounds on 29th November 1918

93, The gravestone of Harry Cecil Dunkley who was gassed during the Great War and died in February 1939 aged 44

94, The Oak Screen Memorial unveiled inside St Mary's Church, Chigwell on 14th November 1920

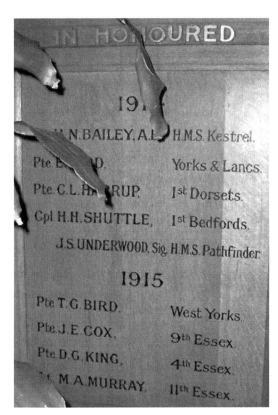

95, The names of the men of Chigwell killed between 1914 - 1916 as they appear on the Oak Screen Memorial

96, The names of the men of Chigwell killed between 1917 - 1918 as they appear on the Oak Screen Memorial

1914

H.N. BAILEY, A.B.	H.M.S. KESTREL.
PTE. E. BIRD,	YORKS & LANCS.
PTE. C.L. HARRUP,	1ST DORSETS.
CPL. H.H. SHUTTLE,	1ST BEDFORDS.
J.S. UNDERWOOD, SIG.	H.M.S. PATHFINDER.

1915

PTE. T.G. BIRD,	WEST YORKS.
PTE. J.E. COX,	9TH ESSEX.
PTE. D.G. KING,	4TH ESSEX.
LT. M.A. MURRAY,	11TH ESSEX.

1916

PTE. H.J. CLARK,	6TH Q. WEST SURREYS.
L/C. A.G. COX,	1ST NORFOLK.
CAPT. E.A. DANIELS,	8TH SOUTH LANCS.
PTE. F.W. DUNKLEY,	7TH BUFFS.
LT. J.L. FISH,	7TH SUFFOLKS.
PTE. G.A. FLACK,	M.G. CORPS.
PTE. W.F. GAPES,	2ND ESSEX.
SGT. S. HAYTER,	12TH RIF. BRIGADE.
L/C. E.S. SCOTT,	11TH RIF. BRIGADE.
PTE. A.G. VINCE,	11TH RIF. BRIGADE.
CAPT. A.J. WAUGH,	R.A.M.C.

1917

PTE. G.E. BAILEY,	CITY OF LONDON RGT.
L/C. G.C. BELCHER,	17TH LONDON.
PTE. H.M. BROWN,	1ST ESSEX.
PTE. P. FITZGERALD,	7TH WORCESTERS.
PTE. F.M. FOGG,	R. MUNSTER F.
GNR. E.H. HERRING,	R.F.A.
PTE. W.H. HYDE,	4TH ESSEX.
PTE. W.A. KERRY,	13TH R. FUSILIERS.
PTE. G. PLEASANCE,	2ND ESSEX.
PTE. J.A. WITHAM,	10TH ESSEX.

1918

SGT. F.W. BARTON,	TANK CORPS.
PTE. F.A. BAILEY,	2ND G. GUARDS.
PTE. S.J. BOOGER,	2ND ESSEX.
PTE. G.W. DAY,	9TH NORFOLKS.
PTE. J. GREEN,	2ND R. FUSILIERS.
PTE. M.A.W. MASON,	11TH R. FUSILIERS.
SGT. H.H. MOSELEY,	LONDON R. BRIGADE.
PTE. F.E. NOBLE,	13TH YORKS.
PTE. J. SIMPSON,	DURHAM L.I.

97, The names of the men of Chigwell killed between 1914 - 1918 as they appear on the village war memorial.

98, St Mary's Church, Chigwell and the Village War Memorial 1925.   Copyright The Francis Frith Collection

99, The Cenotaph in Whitehall

100, The statue of Earl Haig in Whitehall in London

APPENDIX 1

Whilst the object of this book has been to describe the events surrounding those men listed on the Chigwell Village War Memorial killed during the First World War up until now the stories of two men not on the memorial have also been told. As previously explained Charles Alfred Reeves and Daniel James Trevett were included because upon their deaths their names were individually mentioned in the Chigwell Parish Magazine. During the course of my research however another name kept cropping up that is neither on the memorial nor in the parish magazine but was on a number of occasions linked with Chigwell and St Mary's Church via the Woodford Times and Essex Chronicle newspapers. In addition to this he is also mentioned as killed in action on his parent's gravestone inside St Mary's Churchyard, therefore for all of these reasons the story of the following soldier is also included.

JOHN WILLIAM DRAPER

John William Draper was born at Hackney in East London on 3rd November 1886 the eldest son of John and Julia Lovett Draper. John William had two older sisters, two younger brothers and a younger sister. The Draper family had lived in various places in and around London but by the turn of the century had settled at the Abridge end of Chigwell having bought a farmhouse and mill with farmland. Known locally as 'The Old Farm', John's father along with several employees ran the business. John attended Chigwell Grammar School from 1898-1902 and on leaving, along with his brothers and sisters, worked for his father. Sadly in 1907 John's father died suddenly aged 50, at this point we can only assume the Draper family continued as farmers and ran the business. John however in addition to working the farm at some point decided to join the Essex Yeomanry. It would appear that John enlisted in Loughton before the war seeing the Essex Yeomanry as a way of escape when he wasn't working. As already explained elsewhere in this book Yeomanry units were the mounted arm of the Territorial Force and in times of war, just like infantry units, could be called upon to serve alongside the regular army. On the outbreak of war in August 1914 the Essex Yeomanry was stationed at Colchester, later that month it moved to Melton in Suffolk. That September the unit created a second line formation based back at Colchester however the first line remained in training at Melton preparing itself for active service. The 1/1st Essex Yeomanry finally received orders to head overseas towards the end of November, as part of the first line formation John left his life in Chigwell and volunteered for service abroad, by the time his unit left for France he'd obtained the rank of Sergeant.

The 1/1st Essex Yeomanry along with Sgt John Draper sailed from Southampton on SS Anglo-Canadian at 7:30pm on 29th November 1914, the units strength was 25 officers, 468 other ranks and 513 horses when it arrived at Le Havre the following morning. On the 12th December 1914 the 1/1st Essex Yeomanry, commanded by Lieutenant Colonel Edmund Deacon, became part of the 8th Calvary Brigade along with the Royal Horse Guards and 10th Hussars, this brigade was attached to the 3rd Calvary Division commanded by Major General Sir Julian Byng. The next two months saw the men of the Essex Yeomanry training behind the lines southeast of St Omer; daily exercises were carried out along with instruction in trench warfare. Being an NCO Sgt John Draper would have found himself in charge of a section containing somewhere in the region of sixteen men. It would have been his job not only to look after his men but ensure all orders given to them were carried out whilst at the same time reporting regularly to his commanding officer. With the onset of trench warfare the men of the Essex Yeomanry found there was little need for horses except in the case of moving supplies and munitions between camp and the frontline. For most of the war the unit would hold the line dismounted and first went into the trenches near Ypres at the beginning of February.

Subjected to occasional shelling their first spell at the front was relatively quiet and they soon found themselves back behind the lines southwest of Hazebrouck. During March and April the Essex men remained in this area occasionally being called upon for work detail in the surrounding villages, daily training and exercise continued however ensuring the men remained fit and well in case ordered back to the trenches. Towards the end of April with the Second Battle of Ypres being played out the men moved up to Vlamertinge. Being only a few miles west of Ypres this put them within range of the German guns which meant they were regularly subjected to enemy shellfire. Over the next two weeks the men were moved between reserve lines and rear areas but some nights as was customary for troops out the line they found themselves called upon to form work parties. By 10th May Sgt John Draper and the 1/1st Essex Yeomanry were positioned in brigade reserve a few miles northeast of Vlamertinge occupying huts and dugouts at Brielen. That night saw the men on work detail south of Ypres, the following day was spent resting but again on the night of 12th May the men were called upon to form work parties. This time the men of the Essex Yeomanry were ordered forward to reserve line trenches, from here they proceeded on foot to dig communication trenches in positions north of Hooge east of Potijze in areas around the Bellewaardebeek Canal. Just before dawn the Essex men ceased working and returned to the reserve line. From here Sgt John Draper and the rest of the Essex men were due back behind the lines but whilst in reserve they came under intense shellfire as the Germans launched an attack on sections of frontline trenches (held by units of 7th Cavalry Brigade, 3rd Cavalry Division) some 1,000 yards away on Frezenberg Ridge. As a result of the German attack that morning some British positions along the frontline were captured by the enemy and had to be abandoned, by noon however orders were received that units of 8th Cavalry Brigade move forward and retake them.

The counter attack by 8th Cavalry Brigade started at 2:15pm on the afternoon of 13th May, the 10th Hussars held the left flank, the Essex Yeomanry some 320 men strong held the centre whilst the Royal Horse Guards advanced on the right flank. As units of 8th Cavalry Brigade rushed the German positions with bayonets drawn the enemy, under immense pressure, was forced to abandon its gains and return to its original frontline. The Essex Yeomanry along with the 10th Hussars occupied the trenches and held onto these frontline positions until dark having spent most of the afternoon subjected to constant shell, machine gun and rifle fire. The war diary of the Essex Yeomanry records that during their advance the regiment had lost touch with the Royal Horse Guards on their right flank. At roughly 6:00pm sections of Essex men retired westward to dugouts near the reserve line. Some men were kept in advanced positions occupying shell holes and ruined houses. It was their job to hold off further attacks which they managed successfully, they remained in position until after dark before retiring to join the rest of the regiment in reserve line trenches. The men of the Essex Yeomanry held their position until 9:00pm on the 14th May when they were finally relieved by units of 2nd Cavalry Division. As the surviving men of the Essex Yeomanry returned to camp south of Vlamertinge they had engaged in their first major action of the Great War, unfortunately 29 year old Sgt John Draper was not with them, he had been killed in the fighting.

Although it is impossible to know the exact part Sgt John Draper played in the fighting on 13th/14th May 1915 we can be left in no doubt that the counter attack carried out by 8th Cavalry Brigade certainly saved the allied lines east of Ypres being overrun by the enemy. In the days that followed the brigade commander expressed his sincere thanks to those units who took part in the action. The battalion war diary of the Essex Yeomanry states many men were wounded in the fighting, it lists actual casualties for this period as 5 officers and 29 men killed; SDGW puts the latter figure slightly higher at 52 men killed. The regiment CO Lieutenant Colonel Edmund Deacon was amongst those officers killed, his body was never found and his name is commemorated on the Menin Gate Memorial to the Missing. As for Sgt John Draper he is buried 2.5km south of Ypres in Enclosure 4, Plot III, Row C, Grave 6 at Bedford House CWGC Cemetery, it's almost certain he was initially buried elsewhere and moved here with other burials after the Armistice.

The first public report that Sgt John Draper had been killed in action appeared in the Woodford Times on 21st May 1915, the article simply says he was one of those killed in a recent heroic charge made by the Essex Yeomanry at Ypres. On 11th June another article appeared in the Woodford Times stating a memorial service for Sgt Draper would be held at Chigwell Church (St Mary's) on Wednesday 16th June at 7:00pm. This service was reported soon after in both the Woodford Times and Essex Chronicle, the latter carried a picture of Sgt Draper along with its report. At the service a choir sang and funeral marches by Beethoven and Handel were played, in attendance were relatives, friends and members of the Essex Yeomanry as well as the Cadet Corps from Chigwell Grammar School. Given that this service took place at St Mary's Church I find it puzzling that no mention of it appeared in the Chigwell Parish Magazine. Although mentioned on his parents gravestone having tried to work out why Sgt John Draper in not listed on the Chigwell Village War Memorial I came up with one theory. John's mother Julia died shortly after the war on 21st June 1920, the village war memorial was not erected until November 1921 therefore in the meantime if John's surviving relatives had sold the farm and moved away no one was around to put his name forward for inclusion. Having attended Chigwell Grammar School John's name does appear in the school memorial chapel; the motto that follows his name as chosen by Headmaster Ernest Stuart Walde is *'He giveth much who giveth all'*. Sgt John Draper was entitled to several medals, the 1915 Star, BWM & VM were sent out to next of kin sometime during the early 1920's.

101, The gravestone of Sgt John William Draper of the Essex Yeomanry at Bedford House CWGC Cemetery near Ypres in Belgium

102, Sgt John William Draper

103, Men of the Essex Yeomanry 1914-1918 (Picture courtesy of Caroline O'Neill and Essex-Yeomanry. org)

104, The gravestone belonging to John William Draper Senior situated inside St Mary's Churchyard in Chigwell

APPENDIX 2

According to SDGW the following men were killed in the Great War, their names do not appear on the Chigwell Village War Memorial however these soldiers were either born in Chigwell or Chigwell Row or at the time they enlisted lived in one of the two villages.

ANDREWS, William, 8th Buffs, DOW F&F 26/7/17 (born Chigwell)
BARNES, Charles Edward, 13th Essex, KIA F&F 28/4/17 (lived Chigwell)
BASS, Frederick Albert, 11th Essex, KIA F&F 8/10/16 (born Chigwell)
BASS, William Parker, 83rd Bde RFA, KIA F&F 6/8/17 (born Chigwell Row)
BOWSHER, Albert, 2nd Worcesters, DOW F&F 18/11/18 (born Chigwell Row)
BOYD, William, 4th Middlesex, KIA F&F 31/7/17 (lived Chigwell)
BROOKER, Frederick Natt, 6th Buffs, DOW F&F 20/5/17 (lived Chigwell Row)
CARFORD, Bernard Bright, 1st RMF, KIA F&F 22/3/18 (lived Chigwell Row)
CARTER, Walter James, 1st Essex, KIA F&F 20/5/17 (born Chigwell Row)
CAVILL, Walter George, RASC, Died Malta 8/1/17 (born Chigwell)
COLES, George Henry, 23rd Royal Fusiliers, KIA F&F 3/12/17 (born Chigwell)
FARROW, Levi, 1/5th DLI, DOW F&F 26/12/17 (lived Chigwell Row)
HALLS, Lewis, 10th Rifle Brigade, DOW F&F 2/12/17 (lived Chigwell Row)
HILLS, Thomas Frederick, 2/8th West Yorks, KIA F&F 26/03/18 (born Chigwell)
HOPKINS, William Henry, 1st West Yorks, KIA F&F 9/8/18 (born Chigwell)
INGRAM, Albert Cecil, RASC, KIA F&F 31/10/17 (born Chigwell)
JEFFORD, Samuel, 4th Bedfords, DOW F&F 30/9/18 (born Chigwell)
KNIGHT, Frank Herbert, 12th East Surreys, KIA F&F 2/8/17 (born Chigwell)
MARTIN, Charles, 10th Royal Fusiliers, KIA F&F 18/11/16 (born Chigwell Row)
MARTIN, Leonard Percy, RASC, DOW F&F 5/9/17 (lived Chigwell Row)
METSON, Frederick, 11th Essex, KIA F&F 22/3/18 (born Chigwell Row)
PAGE, Frederick Walter, 7th Bedfords, KIA F&F 21/11/15 (born Chigwell)
PAGE, Thomas Reginald, 11th Suffolks, KIA F&F 24/10/18 (born Chigwell)
RUMBLE, James, 2nd Northampton's, KIA F&F 9/5/15 (born Chigwell)
SHEPHERD, Thomas, 11th QRWS, KIA F&F 21/9/17 (born Chigwell Row)
SIMMONDS, Charles Alfred, 5th Yorks, Died F&F 22/8/18 (born Chigwell)
SMART, Alfred Willie, RASC, Died Home 27/3/15 (born Chigwell)
TAYLOR MM, Frederick Charles, 121st Bde RFA, Died F&F 5/11/18 (lived Chigwell)
TRIDGETT, Arthur Albert, 7th Bedfords, KIA F&F 1/7/16 (born Chigwell)
TRIDGETT, Frederick Charles, 8th Royal Berkshires, KIA F&F 18/8/16 (born Chigwell)
WAGSTAFF, Charles Edward, 16th QWR, KIA F&F 1/7/16 (lived Chigwell Row)
WATT, Kenneth Malcolm, 21st KRRC, KIA F&F 6/1/17 (lived Chigwell Row)
WILSON, Arthur Leslie, 2nd Devons, KIA F&F 31/5/18 (born Chigwell)
WOOLLARD, Herbert Alfred, 16th Middlesex, KIA F&F 10/7/17 (born Chigwell)
WRIGHT, John, 2/4th Gloucestershire Reg, KIA F&F 3/12/17 (born Chigwell)

According to SDGW the following men were killed in the Great War, their names do not appear on the Woodford Bridge Roll of Honour Plaque however these soldiers were either born in Woodford Bridge or at the time they enlisted were living there.

CHACKSFIELD, John Ernest, 2nd Essex, KIA F&F 23/10/16 (lived Woodford Bridge)
COYNE, James, 9th East Surreys, DOW F&F 16/10/18 (lived Woodford Bridge)
JOINER, Ernest Charles, 20th Middlesex, KIA F&F 4/9/16 (born Woodford Bridge)
ROBINSON, George Leake, 2nd East Surreys, KIA F&F 25/4/15 (born Woodford Bridge)
SHEPPARD, William, 7th East Yorks, KIA F&F 8/7/16 (lived Woodford Bridge)
STOWER, Walter Ernest, 16th Middlesex, KIA F&F 20/10/16 (lived Woodford Bridge)

APPENDIX 3

WOODFORD BRIDGE ROLL of HONOUR

At the junction of Manor Road and Chigwell Road on the wall opposite the White Hart Public House stands the Woodford Bridge Roll of Honour. The original Roll of Honour was erected in 1918 however over the years it deteriorated and a replacement was unveiled on 26th September 1993. The names on the memorial list all men from Woodford Bridge and District who served in the Great War and those who made the ultimate sacrifice have a + by their name.

Adams Frank
Allway Harold
Alston William
Amer John
Andrews Herbert
Bailey Charles +
Bailey Frederick +
Bailey Harry +
Baker Wilfred
Barrett Frank
Barton Frederick +
Barton Stanley
Barton T
Beaven William
Bellis Edward
Bellis George
Berrecloth Arthur
Berrecloth Cecil
Berrecloth Christopher
Birch E
Birch James
Birch William
Bird Alan Ernest +
Bird Henry Cecil
Bird Howard
Bird John
Bird Leslie
Bird Robert
Bird Rodger
Bird William
Blackmore N
Bloomfield Curtis
Blundel H
Blunt Alfred
Blunt Charles +
Blunt Frank
Blunt Geo Charles
Blunt Horace
Blunt Joseph
Bodger Sidney +
Boultard Charles
Bowtell Clifford
Bradbury Frank
Bradley H
Bradley William
Braithwaite William
Brittain F
Broad George
Brown Christopher
Brown Edward
Brown Harry +
Burgess E
Burroughs Arthur +
Burrows W
Butler Harry
Carter Ernest
Carter Walter +

Caward Edward
Chapman William
Chumbley William
Clack Frederick Harry
Clark A
Clarke Edward
Coleman Stanley
Coles Percy Lawrence
Cooper Sidney
Cooper Thomas
Coppen Charles
Cornwell Arthur
Cousins A
Cox Frank
Crisp Bert +
Curtis Edward James
Dawson Fred
Dawson Owen +
Diamond Frank +
Dodkins Thomas
Draper Walter
Eastwood Robert
Edwards C
Elliott Cecil
Elliott Samuel
Ellis Stanley
Evans Albert +
Ewens Charles +
Ewens George
Ewens Harry
Ewens Percy
Ewens Thomas +
Faggeter E
Feldwick William
Firth Sidney
Fitzgerald Patrick +
Flack Robert
Fogg Herbert
Foster Robert +
Fouracre Frederick
Freestone William
Froggatt W
Fuller George
Fuller Herbert
Fuller Stanley +
Gearing Joseph
Girling Albert
Girling Edwin
Girling Thomas Wm
Girling William
Grayston Francis +
Greaves H
Greaves J
Green George
Green Percy +
Gregory Alfred
Gregory Arthur +

Gregory George Joseph
Gregory Sidney +
Griggs Charles
Gumbley Arnold
Gumbley Charles
Gumbley Frank
Gumbley Percy
Gumbley Robert
Gunton Ashley
Gunton Harold
Hall William
Hannant Sidney
Hare Charles
Hare Frederick
Harris William
Harrup Charles +
Heasman Henry
Henshaw Fred
Herring Edward
Herring Ernest +
Herring George
Holcroft Allan
Holcroft Raymond +
Holland William
Holmwood W
Holt A
Honnor Leonard
Houghton James
Hudgell A
Humphreys William
Hyde L
Ingram Charles
Jackman Chas. John
Jackman George +
Jackman John
Jackman William
Jennings James H
Johnson Edward
Jasper William
Josey Alfred
Joyce C
Kelly Robert
Kent Ralph
King Denham +
King E
Ledgerton Eric
Ledgerton William John
Lemon H
Lemon W
Lindsay Ernest
Lindsay George
Lindsay Percy
Litchfield Harold
Litchfield Horace +
Long Lambert
Lucas J
Malin Henry

Mansfield Cecil
Mason James
Mason Matthew +
Maxwell Albert
Menhinick George
Menhinick Gordon +
Menhinick John
Menhinick Norman
Millman Charles
Millman Ernest
Millman Frank
Mitchell A
Moyler Arthur
Moyler Bertram +
Moyler John
Moyler Robert
Mulley Bert
Newman William
Nichols John
Oades Benjamin
Page Frederick
Parr Sidney
Parry Joseph
Partner Frank
Partner Fred
Partner George
Partner Harry
Peacock Frank
Pearce Henry
Penny George +
Pleasance Archibald
Pleasance Edward
Pleasance George +
Pocknell Albert
Poole Charles
Poole Frederick +
Porter G
Porter George
Pratt William
Price J
Rackham Cyril
Radley Albert

Radley John
Rainbird Edward
Rand T
Ranson George
Reason George
Redfern Roger
Reeves Charles Alfred +
Richards Alfred
Richardson Roland
Saye Charles
Schuman John
Scott Alfred
Scott P
Scudamore Stephen
Shaw William
Shaw George
Shephard Alexander +
Shephard James
Shephard H
Shuttle Edgar
Shuttle Harold +
Shuttlewood Joseph
Simpson James +
Skingley Charles
Skingley Ernest
Skipton A
Smallbone John
Smallbone Walter
Smith Albert
Smith Ernest
Smith Percy
Sole George
Stephens Walter
Street Edward
Such Walter
Sulley G
Surridge John
Surridge Thomas
Talbot William +
Taylor John
Thompson William +
Thurston John +

Toseland A
Trevett Daniel +
Trivett William
Underwood Joseph +
Vaughan E
Waites Alfred
Walledge William
Ward John Hallam
Warner Alfred
Warner James
Webster Ernest
Webster H
Wellman William
Wells Roderick
Wells Thomas
White H
White J
Wilcox Arthur
Wilcox Robert
Wilcox W
Willcox Horace
Wilshere C
Witham Albert
Witham George
Witham Henry
Witham James
Witham John +
Witham Robert
Wix Arthur Robert +
Wix George
Wood Albert
Wood Harry
Wood James
Woodford John
Woodford Reginald
Woodley D
Wright George +
Wright Herbert
Wright Stanley
Wurston Alfred

105, The Woodford Bridge and District Roll of Honour

106, The plaque commemorating the replacement of the Woodford Bridge Roll of Honour situated at the junction of Manor Road and Chigwell Road in Woodford Bridge

APPENDIX 4
ST PAUL'S CHURCH WAR MEMORIAL
(WOODFORD BRIDGE)

The following names appear on the Great War 1914 - 1919 Memorial situated in the North Aisle inside St Paul's Church, Woodford Bridge. Unveiled on the 17th October 1920 by the Reverend C E Waller MA of the forty five men listed ten also appear on the Chigwell Village War Memorial.

1914
Cpl Harold H Shuttle – 1st Bedfordshire Regiment
OS Joseph S G Underwood – HMS Pathfinder
Pte Fred E Poole – 2nd Manchester Regiment
Pte C Leonard Harrup – 1st Dorset Regiment
Pte C Alfred Reeves – 4th (Queens Own) Hussars
Pte Robert T Foster – 1st South Staffordshire Regiment

1915
Pte Owen S Dawson – 1st Cameron Highlanders
Staff Sgt Thomas W H Talbot – Army Service Corps
Able Seaman J Gordon Menhinick – Royal Naval Division

1916
Lt Raymond B Holcroft – 9th Devonshire Regiment
Pte Jack Goldsmith – 1st/3rd City of London Regiment
Cpl Arthur Gregory – 2nd/17th London Regiment
Lt George Penny – 8th West Yorkshire Regiment
Pte Sidney C Gregory – 3rd Suffolk Regiment
Pte George H C Jackman – Duke of Cornwall's Light Infantry
L/Cpl George H N Wright – 13th Essex Regiment
Gunner Thomas Baker – Royal Field Artillery

1917
Staff Sgt Stanley H Fuller - Royal Army Ordnance Corps
Pte George Pleasance – 2nd Essex Regiment
Lt B Aubrey Clapham – 1/4th Essex
Lt Thomas W Ewens - 13th Northumberland Fusiliers
Pte Harry M Brown – 1st Essex Regiment
Pte Frank Diamond – 1st Norfolk Regiment
Pte Walter J Carter – 1st Essex Regiment
Pte Daniel J Trevett – 13th East Surrey Regiment
Cpl Horace W Litchfield – 17th County of London Regiment
Pte Arthur Burroughs – 10th Royal Warwickshire Regiment
Pte Albert E Evans – 7th East Kent Regiment
Gunner Ernest H Herring – Royal Field Artillery
Driver Bertram Moyler – Army Service Corps
Pte Alec Shephard – 22nd Royal Fusiliers

1918
Pte Francis C J Grayston – 6th Royal West Kent Regiment
Lt Charles G Blunt MM – 3rd Rifle Brigade
Pte John J Thurston – 2nd North Staffordshire Regiment
L/Cpl William Thompson - 7th Duke of Cornwall's Light Infantry
Pte James Simpson – 20th Durham Light Infantry
Pte Sydney J Bodger – 2nd Essex Regiment
Cpl Frederick W Barton – 2nd Battalion Tank Corps
Sgt Bertie J Crisp – 10th Royal Fusiliers
Pte A Robert Wix – 19th London Regiment
Pte Alan E Bird – 2nd Royal Sussex Regiment
Pte J Arthur Witham – 10th Essex Regiment
Pte Percy E Green – Labour Corps
Pte Otto Marc – Royal Engineers

1919
Steward A Charles Ewens - Transport

'Greater love hath no man than this that a man lay down his life for his friends'

107, The St Paul's Church War Memorial Woodford Bridge

APPENDIX 5

The following Roll of Honour is taken from the book entitled 'A History of Chigwell School' by G Stott and records the names of 79 Old Chigwellians who gave their lives for king and country in the Great War, of those listed three appear on the Chigwell Village War Memorial.

1914
Hugh Stafford Northcote Wright
Richard Hutton

1915
Frank Potter
Hugh Galfrid Duplex Kemp
John William Draper
John Maurice Legge
Esmond Theodore Allpass
Frederick William Gray
William Henry Walker Moore
George Henry Reginald Mellers
George Archibald Percy Douglas
Ernest Charles Purchas

1916
Everard Francis Scott Henderson
Edwin Cyril Challoner
Harrington Douty Edwards
Frederick Christian Dietrichsen
Cyril Searancke
Frederick Wilford Wright
Neville Seymour
Frank Henry Charles Hickman
Thomas Henry Leman
John Leslie Fish
Edward Grantham
Henry Blythe King Allpass
Charles Edgar Holton Smith
Geoffrey Albert Pain
Sydney Michell
Albert James Harris
Edwin Ambrose Daniels
Guy Cheselden Reuell Atkinson
Cyril Brookes Ellis
Reginald John Wright
Arthur Goulburn Brooke
Noel Mitford Henson Atkinson

1917
Francis Herbert Heveningham Goodhart
Geoffrey Oliver Richardson
John Paul Chambers
Arthur Pole Godfrey
Geoffrey Robert Youngman Thurlow
Douglas George Challoner
Issac Hinton Scarth
Evelyn Charles Ellis
Horace Leonard Theak
William Charles Stringer
Howard Charles Brufton
Leslie Richard Hodge
Ronald William Aspden
Harold Frank Barclay Turner
Ralph Luxmore Curtis
Henry Clifford Lewis
Reginald Gordon Hill
Arthur George Elvin
John Hedley Trask

1918
Archibald McDowell
Gerald Edward Drake
John Cameron Gordon
Alfred Stuart Tween
Wilfred Ernest Harrison
Frederick Cecil Stovin
John Kennings Thurlow
Cyril Henry Underwood
Reginald Dell
James Herbert Jeffryes
William Francis John Prince
Edward John Barnes
John Dudley Bishop
John Arthur Paul Methuen
Leonard Victor Dennis
Edward Miller Ellis
Harold Hull Moseley
John Archibald Grove
Anthony Frederick Gray
Paul Locock Malton
William James Carter
Geoffrey England Taylor
Douglas Underwood Thomas
Basil Brocas Hardman
Roland Edwin Hill
Cuthbert Hickman

APPENDIX 6

The following names were added to the Chigwell Village War Memorial sometime around 1990 and commemorate those men from the village who gave their lives for king and country during the Second World War.

1940
L/Cpl Frederick William John Arnold - East Riding Yeomanry
Trooper William Anthony Chappell - 12th Royal Lancers

1941
Leading Seaman Arthur Petrie Apps - H.M.S. Juno (Royal Navy)
L/Cpl Leonard John Dodkins - 8th Royal Warwickshire Regiment
P/O Ralph Geoffrey Prior - RAF (Volunteer Reserve)

1942
Able Seaman Ernest Alfred Bickmore - H.M.S. Tamar (Royal Navy)
Sgt/Pilot Eric Charles Blackman - RAF (Volunteer Reserve) +
P.O. Edwin Sidney English - H.M.S. Quebec (Royal Navy)
P/O Brian Ernest Hawes - RAF (Volunteer Reserve)
Sgt Ernest William Holbrow - Royal Corps of Signals +
Sgt Eric Evans Kempton - 2nd Kings Royal Rifle Corps
Gnr Michael Joseph O'Meara - Royal Artillery (Maritime Regiment)

1943
Sgt Peter Frederick Hansen - 1st Battalion Rifle Brigade
F/Sgt Albert Joseph Horwood - RAF (Volunteer Reserve)
L/Bdr Ernest George Page - Royal Artillery
Sgt Wilfred Sharp - RAF (Volunteer Reserve)

1944
Cpl Brian Giles Allen - Royal Inniskilling Fusiliers*
Dvr Walter Edward Dace - Royal Corps of Signals
F/Sgt Harry George Newbery - RAF (Volunteer Reserve)
Pte Thomas Robson Nosworthy - Essex Regiment
Lt Phillip Nigel Pratt - 1st Coldstream Guards
Sgt Peter Eric Tuthill - RAF (Volunteer Reserve)
P/O Alan Ernest Williams - RAF (Volunteer Reserve)

1945
Lt Cdr Anthony McDonald Garland DSC - H.M.S. Formidable (Royal Navy)
P/O John Henry Haseldine - RAF

+ = CWGC says killed in 1943
* = on memorial as killed in 1945

The following information concerning Chigwell's Second World War casualties is taken from the records of the CWGC.

1, L/Cpl Frederick William John Arnold: 1st East Riding Yeomanry. Died on 18th May 1940 aged 20. Buried Cement House Cemetery, Langemarck Belgium. Son of Frederick William and Elsie Jane Arnold.

2, Trooper William Anthony Chappell: 12th Royal Lancers. Died on 28th May 1940 aged 20. Commemorated on column 3 of the Dunkirk Memorial, Nord, France. Son of William and Mabel Hilda Lucy Chappell of Woodford Bridge, Essex.

3, Leading Seaman Arthur Petrie Apps: HMS Juno. Died on 21st May 1941 aged 25. Commemorated on panel 47 of the Chatham Naval Memorial, Kent, United Kingdom. Son of Henry and Ethel R Apps of Chigwell, Essex.

4, Pte Leonard John Dodkins: 8th Royal Warwickshire Regiment. Died 25th July 1941 aged 26. Buried St Mary's Churchyard, Chigwell, Essex. Son of Leonard Johnson Dodkins and Alice Dodkins of Chigwell; husband of Winifred Dora Dodkins.

5, P/O Ralph Geoffrey Prior: RAF Volunteer Reserve. Died 8th December 1941 aged 26. Buried St Mary's Churchyard, Chigwell, Essex. Son of Harry John and Ethel Elsie Prior of Grange Hill, Chigwell, Essex.

6, Able Seaman Ernest Alfred Bickmore: HMS Tamar (lost in SS Lisbon Maru). Died on 2nd October 1942 aged 23. Commemorated on panel 53 of the Chatham Naval Memorial, Kent, United Kingdom. Son of Alfred William and Ellen Bickmore; husband of Ellen Rose Bickmore of Chigwell, Essex.

7, F/Sgt Eric Charles Blackman: RAF Volunteer Reserve. Died on 4th July 1942 (or 1943) aged 23. Buried Bergen-Op-Zoom Canadian War Cemetery, Noord-Brabant, Netherlands. Son of William and Susannah Blackman.

8, P.O. Edwin Sidney English: HMS Quebec. Died on 19th August 1942. Buried City of London Cemetery, Essex, United Kingdom. Husband of Phyllis Julia English of Chigwell, Essex.

9, P/O Brian Ernest Hawes: RAF Volunteer Reserve. Died on 28th July 1942 aged 21. Buried St Mary's Churchyard, Chigwell, Essex. Son of Ernest and Nettie Hawes of Chigwell, Essex.

10, Cpl Ernest William Holbrow: Signal Corps. Died on 26th January 1942 (or 1943) aged 24. Buried Fajara War Cemetery, Gambia. Son of Albert Ernest and Matilda Maud Holbrow of Woodford Bridge, Essex.

11, Sgt Eric Evans Kempton: 2nd Battalion Kings Royal Rifle Corps. Died on 3rd November 1942 aged 27. Buried El Alamein War Cemetery, Egypt. Son of Bernard and Minnie Florence Kempton of Chigwell, Essex; husband of Ethel Margaret Kempton of Chigwell.

12, Gnr Michael Joseph O'Meara: Royal Artillery (Maritime Regiment). Died on 10th November 1942 aged 23. Commemorated on panel 72 of the Portsmouth Naval Memorial, Hampshire, United Kingdom. Son of Michael and Harriett O'Meara of Chigwell, Essex.

13, Sgt Peter Frederick Hansen: 1st Battalion Rifle Brigade. Died on 4th October 1943. Buried Salerno War Cemetery, Italy.

14, F/Sgt Albert Joseph Horwood: RAF Volunteer Reserve. Died on 27th March 1943. Buried Berlin 1939-1945 War Cemetery, Berlin, Germany.

15, L/Bdr Ernest George Page: Royal Artillery. Died 20th June 1943 aged 24. Buried Kanchanaburi War Cemetery, Thailand. Son of George and Lily Daisy Page; husband of Barbara Isobel Page of Pitlochry, Perthshire.

16, Sgt Wilfred Sharp: RAF Volunteer Reserve. Died on 13th June 1943 aged 20. Buried Reichswald Forest War Cemetery, Kleve, Nordrhein-Westfalen, Germany. Son of Fred and Florence May Sharp of Woodford Bridge, Essex.

17, Cpl Brian Giles Allen: 6th Battalion Royal Inniskilling Fusiliers. Died on 15th May 1944 (Chigwell Memorial says 1945) aged 21. Buried Cassino War Cemetery, Italy. Son of Ernest and Florence Roberta Allen of Woodford Green, Essex.

18, Driver Walter Edward Dace: Royal Corps of Signals. Died 21st April 1944 aged 23. Buried Beach Head War Cemetery, Anzio, Italy. Son of Alfred Thomas Dace and Gertrude Maude Dace of Woodford Bridge, Essex.

19, F/Sgt Harry George Newbery: RAF Volunteer Reserve. Died 4th November 1944 aged 21. Buried Rheinberg War Cemetery, Kamp Lintfort, Nordrhein-Westfal, Germany. Son of Albert Harry and Marguerite Blanche Newbery, husband of Elizabeth Joan Newbery of Shottery, Stratford-on-Avon.

20, Pte Thomas Robson Nosworthy: Essex Regiment. Died 19th May 1944 aged 19. Buried Sangro River War Cemetery, Italy. Son of William Herbert and Emily Mary Nosworthy of Chigwell, Essex.

21, Lt Phillip Nigel Pratt: 1st Battalion Coldstream Guards. Died on 11th August 1944 age 24. Buried St Charles De Percy War Cemetery, Calvados, France. Son of Dr John Henry Pratt and Olive Lydall Pratt of Chigwell, Essex.

22, Sgt Peter Eric Tuthill: RAF Volunteer Reserve. Died 5th October 1944. Buried Rheinberg War Cemetery, Kamp Lintfort, Nordrhein-Westfal, Germany.

23, P/O Alan Ernest Williams: RAF Volunteer Reserve. Died 8th June 1944 aged 20. Buried Imphal War Cemetery, India. Son of Benjamin Walter and Daisy Williams of Chigwell, Essex.

24, Lt Cdr Anthony McDonald Garland DSC: HMS Formidable. Died 16th April 1945 aged 24. Commemorated on panel 2 of the Lee-on-Solent Memorial, Hampshire, United Kingdom. Son of John William and Hilda Drake Garland of Chigwell, Essex.

25, P/O John Henry Haseldine: RAF. Died 10th June 1945 aged 30. Buried Delhi War Cemetery, India. Son of Thomas George and Gertrude Haseldine; husband of Frances Glynis Haseldine of Chigwell, Essex.

1940
Tpr. F. Arnold, E. Riding Yeo.
Tpr. W.A. Chappell, 12th Lancers.

1941
Leading Seaman A.P. Apps, R.N.
L/Cpl. L. Dodkins, R. Warwicks.
P/O. R. Prior, R.A.F.

1942
AB. E.A. Bickmore, R.N.
Sgt/Pilot. E.C.D. Blackman, R.A.F.V.R.
P.O. E.S. English, R.N.
P/O. B.F. Hawkes, R.A.F.
Sgt. E.W. Holbrow, R. Signals.
Sgt. E. Kempton, K.R.R.C.
Gnr. M. O'Meara, R.A.

1943
Sgt. P. Hansen, Rifle Bde.
F/Sgt. A. Horwood, R.A.F.
L/Bdr. E. Page, R.A.
Sgt. W. Sharp, R.A.F.

1944
Dvr. W. Dace, R. Signals.
Sgt. H. Newbery, R.A.F.
Pte. T. Nosworthy, Essex Regt.
Lt. P.N. Pratt, Coldstream Guards.
Sgt. P. Tuthill, R.A.F.
P/O. A.E. Williams, R.A.F.

1945
Lt. Cdr. A.M. Garland, D.S.C. R.N.V.R.
P/O. J.H. Haseldine, R.A.F.
Cpl. B. Allen, R. Irish Regt.

108, The names of the men of Chigwell killed between 1939-1945 as they appear on the village war memorial

APPENDIX 7

The following is a complete list of all CWGC casualties buried within the area of Chigwell, Chigwell Row and Woodford Bridge.

Chigwell - St Mary's Churchyard:

Pte Thomas George Bird, 2nd Battalion West Yorkshire Regiment, Age 31, died 27th May 1915.
Pte Leonard John Dodkins, 8th Battalion Royal Warwickshire Regiment, Age 26, died 25th July 1941.
Cpl Conrad Francis William Fisher, RAF, 908 Balloon Squadron, died 29th October 1939.
Pilot Officer Brian Ernest Hawes, RAF Volunteer Reserve, 2nd Squadron, Age 21, died 28th July 1942.
Aircraftman 1st Class John Alfred Pluckrose, RAF (Auxiliary Air Force), Age 37, died 6th January 1941.
Pilot Officer Ralph Geoffrey Prior, RAF Volunteer Reserve, Age 26, died 8th December 1941.
Warrant Officer 1st Class Edmund Stearns, 17th County of London (Bermondsey) Battalion, Home Guard, Age 48, died 19th April 1941.
Sgt Henry Hilton Walker, RAF Volunteer Reserve, 53rd Squadron, Age 26, died 9th April 1941.

Chigwell Row - All Saints Churchyard:

Lt Claude Handley Trotter, (Canadian Infantry), RAF, 44th Squadron, Age 23, died 13th October 1918.
Cpl James Alfred Willis, RAF, Age 35, died 23rd February 1942.
Sapper Hilary Oswald Hugh Worley-Wells, Royal Engineers, 309 Battery – 28th Anti Aircraft Battalion, Age 27, died 9th June 1940.

Woodford Bridge - St Paul's Churchyard:

Sgt William Ronald Evans, RAF Volunteer Reserve, died 7th December 1942.
Pte Percy Edward Green, Labour Corps, Age 28, died 29th November 1918.
Pte Sidney Charles Metcalf, Royal Army Ordnance Corps, died 10th April 1945.

Woodford Bridge - Roding Lane Cemetery:

Aircraftman 2nd Class William Thomas Gawthrope, RAF, Age 18, died 6th December 1947.
Commander Leslie Griffiths DSO RD, Royal Naval Reserve, HMS Yeoman, died 19th July 1944.
L/Cpl Kenneth Arthur Light, Royal Corps of Signals, Age 17, died 20th October 1940.
Gunner William George Smith, Royal Artillery, 321 Battery (26th Searchlight Regiment), died 3rd December 1942.
Cpl Charles Edward Hugh Strudwick, RAF (Auxiliary Air Force), died 14th December 1942.
Senior Commander Evelyn Christine Summerfield, Auxiliary Territorial Service, Age 30, died 6th October 1947.

Chigwell Parish Magazine Roll of Honour

The following men of Chigwell served king and country in the Great War, this list was compiled by the Chigwell Parish Magazine in late 1915 with help from family members. Whilst some included lost their lives in the conflict others were fortunate enough to return home, where known unit, rank and number appear, although these changed throughout the war they were correct when the list was first published. It must be stressed not all men who appear on the Chigwell Village War Memorial appear in this particular Roll of Honour.

Frederick Allen
Frederick Bailey (1st Life Guards)
Frederick Barton
Stanley Barton
William Bass
William Bevan
George Bellis (4951 Royal Irish Rifles)
Edward Bellis (HMS Agamemnon)
Albert Edward Billett (London Rifle Brigade)
Edward Henry Billett (Royal Navy)
Alfred Bird
William Birch (13674 Machine Gun Section 7th Bedfords)
Charles Blunt (1560 2/1 East Anglia Siege Train)
John Brown
L/Cpl Edward Arthur Brown (12531 Royal Warwick's)
William C Bullock
John Burrows
Sidney E Cann
Driver Alfred Chew (162789 H M Trawler)
Alfred E Clark (7th Royal Berks)
William Chumbley DCM
Harry Coote
Charles Cook
Harold Roy Coombs
Albert Charles Cox (7th Norfolk's)
Leonard Cracknell
Edwin Daniels (HAC)
William Archer Daniels
Walter Dodkins
Henry C Durrant
Frederick Dunkley (3745 7th Buffs)
Gregory Faux (RFA)
William Filby (RGA)
John Leslie Fish (HAC)
Herbert Arthur Flack
Charles Alfred Flack (3066 7th City of London Regiment)
William Frank Gapes
Edward Green
Sidney Green
Stephen Greenaway
Charles Henry Griggs
William Griggs
Arthur Hall
Allan Hall
Percy Hannant (Veterinary Corps)
Sidney Hannant (RFA)
Frederick Harmour
Richard Harmour
Charles Harrup (1st Dorset's)
Frederick Harris
Capt Cyril Hatfield (18th Middlesex)
Cpl Sidney Hayter (12th Rifle Brigade)

Lt Arthur Edmund Hawker (RNAC)
George Herring
John Humphries
William Humphries
William Hudgell
Arthur Hunt
William Harold Hyde
Arthur Lionel Jennings
Charles George Joyce
Charles Arthur Kerner
Frederick Charles Kimber (RFA)
Edward King (19th Hussars)
Cpl Arthur Lambert (1/4th Essex)
Alfred Lines (2260 11th County of London Regiment)
Stanley Lowin (Essex Regiment)
Cpl Harold Moseley
Lt Maurice Austin Murray (11th Essex)
Cecil Murray (845 4th Essex)
Albert Lister Noble (89845 128th Field Coy RE)
Henry Noble
Charles Page
Herbert Charles Parry
John Pearson (7th Royal Berks)
John Radley
Major Robert Muriel Sanders
Charles Smith
Percy Smith
Alfred Smart DCM
Charles Smart
George Smart COM (7127 9th Kings Royal Rifles)
Harry Smart
John Smart COM (5003 13th Kings Royal Rifles)
Percy Smart
Rifleman Edward Scott (7941 11th Rifle Brigade)
Thomas Stephens (2448 Royal North Devon Hussars)
William Taylor
Frederick Taylor MM (16605 12th Essex)
George Thomas (Royal Engineers)
Charles Alfred Vince (7939 11th Rifle Brigade)
William Vernon Waite (Essex Yeomanry)
George Watts (1485 Reserve Battalion 4th Essex)
Capt Arthur Waugh (RAMC)
Lt Leonard Waugh (3rd Essex)
Stanley Waugh (Essex Yeomanry)
Roderick Wells
Horace White
Frederick Wilson (Bedfordshire Regiment)
Peter Winter (15637 Coldstream Guards)
William George Wood (The Buffs)
Dudley Woodley (RASC)
Albert Wright
Alfred Wursten.

ALSO

Hereward Cleveland (RAMC)
George Jull (31st Canadians)
Kingsley Jull (31st Canadians)

Alfred Savill
Edwin Lydall Savill
Eric Savill

Col James Anthony Stewart (Ordnance)
Capt Alfred Styles (28th Canadians)
Lt Francis Tibbs (RFA)

Lt Robert Tibbs (39th Garhwali's)
Lt Herbert Tibbs
George Robert Wallis (ASC).

At some point between 1914 and the Armistice the names of the following service men with connections to Chigwell also appear in either the Chigwell Parish Magazine or Woodford Times Newspaper:

Trooper Arthur Brown (Grenadier Guards)
Pte C Brown DCM
Pte Darkin (39th RFA)
Reverend M Davidson MID (Temp 4th Class)
S Fuller MM

Trooper Charles G Golding (2817 1st Life Guards)
George Lewin
Reverend W C Stainsby MID (Temp 4th Class)
Robert Tibbs
S Vale MM

CHIGWELL'S VICTORIA CROSS WINNERS

The Victoria Cross was constituted in 1856 and is Britain's highest military award for gallantry in the face of the enemy. At the time of writing 1,356 VC's have been awarded in conflicts spanning the Crimean War right up to the ongoing war in Iraq which started in 2003. During that time at least three men with Chigwell connections have received the VC, they are listed as follows along with an edited version of their citation that appeared in the London Gazette, the official newspaper of record.

Lieutenant John Watson VC

Born in Chigwell Row on 6th September 1829 Lt John Watson was awarded the VC on 14th November 1857 whilst serving with the 1st Punjab Cavalry at Lucknow during the Indian Mutiny. His citation appeared in the London Gazette on 16th June 1859:

"Lieutenant Watson, with his own squadron and that under another lieutenant, came upon a body of rebel cavalry. Their leader in command of them, with about half-a-dozen, rode out and confronted Lieutenant Watson and in the fierce fighting which ensued the lieutenant received several disabling blows and cuts from swords. He continued to defend himself, however, until his own men joined in the melee and utterly routed the enemy".

Lieutenant John Watson VC later achieved the rank of General as well as a Knighthood; he died on 23rd January 1919 and is buried at St James Churchyard at Finchampstead in Berkshire. His VC is held by the Ashcroft Collection, the largest collection of Victoria Crosses in the world

Private Thomas Edwards VC

Born at Brill in Buckinghamshire on 19th April 1863 Pte Thomas Edwards was awarded the VC on 13th March 1884 whilst serving with the 1st Battalion, the Royal Highlanders (The Black Watch) during the Mahdi Rebellion in Sudan. His citation appeared in the London Gazette on 21st May 1884:

"On 13th March 1884 at the Battle of Tamai in Sudan when both members of the crew of one of the guns had been killed, Private Edwards, after bayoneting two Arabs and himself receiving a wound from a spear, remained with the gun, defending it throughout the action".

Private Thomas Edwards VC later moved to Woodford Bridge and died there on 27th March 1952, he was subsequently buried at St Mary's Churchyard in Chigwell however the exact location of his burial is unknown. In March 2001 some 49 years after his death a headstone was erected towards the front of the churchyard in memory of Thomas Edwards, his VC is held by the Black Watch Museum in Perth in Scotland.

Lieutenant Colonel Augustus Charles Newman VC

Born in Chigwell on 19th August 1904 Lt Col Augustus Newman was awarded the VC during the Second World War. Whilst serving with the Essex Regiment and attached to the 2nd Commandos he took part in an attack behind enemy lines at St Nazaire in France on 27th March 1942. His citation appeared in the London Gazette on 19th June 1945:

"On 27th March 1942 in the attack on St Nazaire in France Lieutenant Colonel Newman was in charge of the military forces and he was one of the first ashore, leading his men and directing operations quite regardless of his own safety. Under his inspiring leadership the troops fought magnificently and held vastly superior numbers of the enemy at bay until the demolition parties had done their work. The colonel then attempted to fight through into open country and not until all the ammunition was spent were he and his men overwhelmed and taken prisoner".

Having been captured by the Germans Lieutenant Colonel Augustus Charles Newman VC didn't receive his award until after the war; he later went on to receive an OBE as well as the Legion d'Honneur and Croix de Guerre from the French government. He died at Sandwich in Kent on 26th April 1972 and was later cremated, his VC is not publicly held.

THE ALBERT MEDAL

Unlike the Victoria Cross the Albert Medal was a gallantry medal awarded to both military and civilian personnel alike for heroic acts carried out when not in the face of the enemy. Initially awarded to mariners and non mariners for heroic acts carried out at sea it came in two classes, 1st class gold and 2nd class bronze. The Albert Medal was later also awarded for heroic acts carried out on land and in 1917 the two classes were replaced by just the Albert Medal Gold and Albert Medal. In 1949 both types of Albert Medal stopped being awarded and were replaced by the George Cross. We know of at least one man with Chigwell connections who was awarded the Albert Medal during the course of the First World War.

Commander Francis Herbert Heveningham Goodhart DSO, AM Gold

Born in 1886 Francis Goodhart was the son of Reverend C A Goodhart M.A. and Catherine Elizabeth Warner. He attended Chigwell Boys Grammar School from 1893-1898 and on leaving joined the Royal Navy; he eventually rose to the rank of commander and married his wife Isabella Goodhart. On the outbreak of war in 1914 he commanded a submarine that bore the Chigwell school crest and motto *"aut viam inveniam aut faciam"*, a Latin phrase meaning *"Either I shall find a way or I shall make one"*. Undertaking dangerous missions in home waters and the Baltic Sea Commander Goodhart was personally decorated for his actions by Tsar Nicolas II and awarded both the Order of St. George, 4th Class (Russia) and the Order of St. Vladimir, 4th Class (Russia). On 30th January 1917 whilst serving aboard HM Submarine K13 in Gare Loch in Scotland Commander Francis Goodhart was killed whilst trying to save his crew when his submarine sank, for his actions he was posthumously awarded the Albert Medal in Gold by King George V. An extract from the second supplement to "The London Gazette" dated 23rd April 1918, records the following:

"Owing to an accident, one of H.M. submarines sank and became fast on the bottom in 38 feet of water, parts of the vessel becoming flooded. After several hours the only prospect of saving those remaining on board appeared to be for someone to escape from the submarine in order to concert measures with the rescuers, who were by this time present on the surface. Commander Goodhart, after consultation with the Commanding Officer, volunteered to make the attempt. Accordingly, after placing in his belt a small tin cylinder with instructions for the rescuers, Commander Goodhart went into the conning tower with the Commanding Officer. The conning tower was flooded up to their waists, and the high-pressure air was turned on; the clips of the conning tower were knocked off and the conning tower lid was soon wide open. Commander Goodhart then stood up in the dome, took a deep breath, and made his escape, but, unfortunately, was blown by the pressure of air against part of the super-structure, and was killed by the force of the blow. The Commanding Officer, whose intention it had been to return inside the submarine after Commander Goodhart's escape, was involuntarily forced to the surface by the air pressure, and it was thus rendered possible for the plans for rescuing those still inside the submarine to be carried out. Commander Goodhart displayed extreme and heroic daring in attempting to escape from the submarine in order to save the lives of those remaining on board, and thoroughly realized the forlorn nature of his act". His last remark to the Commanding Officer was: 'If I don't get up, the tin cylinder will'.

During his career Commander Francis Herbert Heveningham Goodhart was also awarded the DSO as well as the Chevalier of the Legion d'Honneur by the French government, whilst the whereabouts of his medals is unknown he is buried along with other crew members of Submarine K13 at Faslane Cemetery near Garelochhead, Dunbartonshire, Scotland. Having attended Chigwell Grammar School the name of Francis Goodhart also appears in the school memorial chapel, the Latin motto that follows his name as chosen by Headmaster Mr. Ernest Stuart Walde is *'Dominus dedit in mari viam'* meaning *'the lord has given way to the sea'*.

109, *The memorial to Pte Thomas Edwards VC situated inside St Mary's Churchyard in Chigwell*

110, *Pte Thomas Edwards VC*

111, *A Cap Badge of the Black Watch*

112, *The Victoria Cross*

NOTES

1914

(1) The battalions of both the 1st Brigade and 4th Brigade consisted entirely of Guard Regiments.

(2) By this time the 4th Division had arrived and prior to being attached to III Corps was temporarily under Smith-Dorrien's control.

(3) According to a book entitled 'Du Ruvignys Roll of Honour 1914 -18' (Volume 2 Part 3) which lists some of the casualties of the Great War Cpl Harold Henry Shuttle is incorrectly listed as having been killed in action on 9th September 1914.

(4) Most likely standing behind Charles Harrup in the queue at the recruiting office in Stratford was my wife's aunts grandfather Pte Harris Cassonman. Also in the army reserve and posted to the ranks of the 1st Dorset's his army service number was 7023. Harris Cassonman was killed on 21st April 1915 while holding the lines southeast of Ypres, buried at Woods CWGC Cemetery he was the only 1st Dorset killed that day and was 29 years old.

(5) On the 18th October 1914 Major General T Morland took over command of the 5th Division from Major General Fergusson.

(6) The Indian Divisions as part of the British Empire were used extensively on this sector of frontline during the early years of the war. As the conflict dragged on however it was decided they should be withdrawn from France and Flanders and sent to more suitable theatres such as Egypt, Palestine, North Africa, Mesopotamia and India.

(7) The 14th (Light) Division was originally called the 8th (Light) Division but at this time more Regular Army units were formed. These new units took priority over the 'New Army' and were therefore numbered the 8th Division. As a result of this change the 8th (Light) Division became the 14th (Light) Division.

(8) The 63rd Royal Naval Division was formed in September 1914 from the men who were in the reserves of the Royal Navy. These men for one reason or another could not be found jobs on ships and were therefore recruited into this division to fight alongside the regular infantry. The 63rd RND would see lots of action during the course of the war.

(9) Situated some 8 miles southeast of Armentières Lille had been occupied by the Germans on 12th October.

(10) Having been attached to 4th Division, following the BEF's re-deployment north to Flanders, the 19th Infantry Brigade was placed under the control of GHQ at St Omer. On 12th October 1914 it temporarily became part of 6th Division until May 1915 when the brigade was transferred to 27th Division.

(11) Rupprecht was a talented commander and later promoted to Field Marshal, his father ruled the southern German province of Bavaria.

(12) The other man lost was Corporal Arthur Bushell; he is buried at White City CWGC Cemetery in the village of Bois Grenier about 4km south of Armentières.

(13) The 129th Duke of Connaught's Own Baluchis to give them their full title were one of the first battalions attached the Indian Corps that served on the Western Front. They arrived just in time to participate in the First Battle of Ypres and would win the first Indian VC of the war.

(14) After the Armistice the body of Captain Kenneth Croft North was found and buried at Oak Dump CWGC Cemetery south of Ypres. Initially classed as missing his name also appears on Panel 5 of the Menin Gate Memorial.

(15) The 1/14th (County of London) Battalion TF (London Scottish) were attached to the Cavalry Corps and on 31st October/1st November they were the first Territorial troops to see action during the First World War. Whilst holding the high ground west of Messines known as Messines Ridge they suffered heavy casualties.

(16) It should be noted that at least five other members of HQ staff were also killed by the shell.

(17) The Germans first attacked Ypres with artillery on 22nd October.

THE WAR AT SEA
(1) Edith had a son Mr Leslie Prescott who was of tremendous help during the early stages of writing this book.

(2) The building was built in 1897 and completed in 1902, it consisted of a glass drill shed that was bombed in September 1917 causing many casualties.

(3) To date only three men have ever been awarded the VC twice; one of those men was the brother of HMS Pathfinder's captain. Surgeon Captain Arthur Martin-Leake was attached to the RAMC and won his first VC during the Boer War; his second was awarded during the First Battle of Ypres in October 1914.

(4) The first was during the Russo/Japan war of 1905-1906.

(5) As with Cpl Harold Henry Shuttle Du Ruvignys Roll of Honour 1914 -18 also records the death of Ordinary Signalman Joseph Samuel George Underwood. However instead of reporting that the ship he was on was torpedoed it states incorrectly that he was killed when H.M.S. Pathfinder struck a mine off the Northumberland coast.

(6) One of Von Spee's ships, the S.M.S. Emden, did not join the main fleet; instead it continued to operate in waters of the Pacific and Indian Ocean. It was eventually tracked down and half sunk on 9th November 1914 by the Australian ship H.M.A.S. Sydney, by that time however the Emden had sunk a large number of British merchant ships.

(7) The Royal Navy service record belonging to Harry Norman Bailey lists him as having been born at Epping; the 1901 census however states he was born in Chigwell.

(8) H.M.S. Falmouth was sunk by the German submarine U63 on 19th August 1916.

(9) As well as being listed on the Chigwell Memorial Harry's name also appears on the Roll of Honour at Woodford Bridge, a mistake however sees his name recorded as Henry Bailey.

(10) The youngest VC of the war was won at the 'Battle of Jutland' by 16 year old John Travers Cornwell. I feel this is worth mentioning as John was from Ilford - about five miles from Chigwell. He was awarded a posthumous VC for manning his gun when all around him had been either wounded or killed. He died of wounds at Grimsby on 2nd June 1916 and is buried at Manor Park Cemetery in East London.

1915
(1) According to an article that appeared in the Woodford Times in late 1914 upon the death of Cpl Harold Henry Shuttle the choir had raised £5.00 and sent it to the Prince of Wales Relief Fund.

(2) Whilst a brass plaque marking the event stands on a memorial stone near the corner of Manor Road and Hainault Road during the years following the Second World War the grave itself fell into disrepair. On the 30th anniversary of the event in April 1971 the grave was paved over and thirty years later to mark the 60th anniversary the grave, helped by sponsorship from the magazine entitled 'After the Battle', was completely refurbished and a rededication ceremony was conducted.

(3) SDGW records that Thomas was born at Romford in Essex.

(4) The CWGC lists Thomas as being part of the 3rd West York's, this was a reserve battalion that remained in England throughout the war. Although he may initially have been attached to this unit on re-enlistment he was later transferred to the 2nd Battalion.

(5) The 1/6th Cameronians (Scottish Rifles) joined 23rd Brigade during March 1915, they left three months later.

(6) The IWGC became the CWGC in 1960.

(7) The command of I Corps now fell to the newly promoted Lieutenant General Sir Hubert Gough.

(8) During the Great War Alfred served with the 7th Battalion Royal Berkshire Regiment and went on to survive the war.

(9) After the war various personal accounts of the conflict were published by men who had served on the Western Front but of these many were written by former officers. In 1969 however a former private with the 6th Battalion Queens (Royal West Surrey Regiment) and later the Machine Gun Corps called George Coppard published a well known book based on diaries he'd kept whilst serving in France entitled 'With a machine gun to Cambrai'. Given

that George Coppard had the service number 701 it would appear that both he and Henry probably enlisted at Croydon on the same day.

(10) SDGW lists their first casualty as being sustained on 26th June 1915.

(11) Today the village of Mill End falls within the county of Buckinghamshire.

(12) Reverend Thomas Marsden died in April 1913 aged 76.

(13) As previously mentioned some battalions had titles or area affiliations and this was true in the case of the 16th Battalion Middlesex Regiment, known also as the Public Schools Battalion it was established in London by Lieutenant Colonel JJ Mackay.

(14) A class system certainly existed in England at the time of the First World War and a Public School education would have almost certainly earned you a commission. Your average man in the street, regardless of his intelligence and even with a few years service under his belt, would have been lucky to achieve the rank of sergeant let alone become a commissioned officer. As unfair as this may seem it's just the way it was however this should in no way suggest that Maurice Austin Murray didn't deserve his commission, after all he'd attended Sandhurst and spent four years in the OTC. It must also be added that towards the end of 1914, due to those either killed, wounded or serving overseas, there was a real shortage of officers stationed in England available to train the volunteer armies.

(15) The 9th Norfolk's were to follow the 11th Essex in support on the left whilst the 8th Bedford's supported the 9th Suffolk's on the right.

(16) Later promoted to Lance Corporal, Albert Ernest Gosling was killed in action on 1st January 1917; he is commemorated on the Loos Memorial to the Missing.

(17) The total casualty figures for the 11th Essex that day according to their battalion war diary were 18 officers and 350 other ranks, according to SDGW 8 officers - 5 including Murray are wrongly listed as having been killed on 25th September - and 74 other ranks were actually killed. It should be noted however that from the figure quoted in the war diary many men were listed as wounded, whilst some would die over the following days many others were taken prisoner.

GALLIPOLI
(1) He was replaced by Admiral Sir John Jellicoe.

(2) Churchill having crossed the floor of the House of Commons from Conservative to Liberal was disliked by Tory leader Andrew Bonar Law and because of this it was felt any coalition, with Churchill still retaining his post, could be undermined. Fed up and dejected Churchill went off to command a Scottish battalion on the Western Front.

(3) The Essex Brigade contained the 1/4th, 1/5th, 1/6th and 1/7th Battalions of the Essex Regiment.

(4) During this action the battalion lost 2 officers and 11 other ranks. Whilst SDGW correctly lists the officer's as having been killed on 18th August 1915 in the case of the other ranks they are shown incorrectly as having been killed on 20th August 1915.

(5) The first married man lost had been Pte Charles Leonard Harrup back in October 1914.

(6) The 1/4th Essex were evacuated at 4:00pm on 3rd December 1915, they left the peninsular for Mudros eventually arriving back at Alexandria on 16th December 1915 where they were due to meet the remainder of 54th Division.

1916
(1) When I began writing this book, although not in its original position, this Union Jack still hung in the south aisle of St Mary's Church, following refurbishment however it has since been removed.

(2) In a further attempt to confuse the Germans as to British intentions both Plumer and Monro were ordered by Haig to make waves on their stretches of line to coincide with 4th Army's main attack on the Somme.

(3) This Reserve Army under Gough was created in the spring of 1916. Consisting initially of cavalry units in June 1916 three infantry divisions were added but then almost immediately removed and placed under the command of GHQ. These units were to be used to exploit any breakthrough created by Rawlinson's 4th Army.

(4) Following the death of Lord Kitchener in mid July minister of munitions David Lloyd George was made secretary of state for war followed a few months later by the aforementioned Lord Derby.

(5) Introduced in November 1915 steel helmets significantly cut down the number of men killed and wounded from head injuries.

(6) It's possible that two other sisters existed however their names are unknown, as for Eliza she went on to have a son called Frank after her father. The child was raised by his grandparents and as a result took the surname of Gapes. Eventually the young Frank Gapes married and had children of his own; as a result at the time of writing his eldest son is Mike Gapes and Labour Party MP for Ilford South.

(7) The youngest British soldier killed in WW1 was just 14 years old.

(8) In addition a battalion of the Warwickshire Regiment from 48th Division was attached to the 10th Brigade and 11th Brigade and fought alongside them that morning.

(9) The explosion created what's known as the Lochnagar Mine Crater, positioned just outside La Boisselle it exists today as a tourist attraction and every year on 1st July a ceremony is held at its edge in memory of those men who fought and died on the Somme.

(10) Harry also served as a soldier during WW1 however where and who with is unknown. Whilst serving at the front he was exposed to the effects of gas poisoning and suffered from this for the rest of his life, he died prematurely on 14th February 1939 aged 44 and is buried in the churchyard of St Mary's in Chigwell. In addition it also appears that Frederick and Harry's father Joseph was at the Prince of Wales Pub on the night of 19th April 1941 and was subsequently reported to be one of the casualties.

(11) The medal roll at the NA lists his number as G/3745 as does SDGW, the CWGC however lists him as G/3744.

(12) A well documented story that took place on the first day of the Somme battle concerns the 8th East Surreys and the action of one of its officers. Captain W P Nevill - serving with the 1st East York's but attached to the 8th East Surreys - whilst home on leave bought footballs for each of his platoons and offered a prize for the first one to kick a ball into the German lines as they went over the top that morning. Unfortunately Captain Nevill was killed in the advance before he could award the prize. Two of the balls were later recovered and one is on show at the National Army Museum at Chelsea in London.

(13) Like many outlying villages Wanstead has now become a suburb of London.

(14) The commanding officer of the 12th (Eastern) Division upon its arrival in France was Major General F Wing; mortally wounded soon after the Battle of Loos in September 1915 he was replaced by Major General A Scott on 3rd October 1915.

(15) John's death was reported in the Chigwell Parish Magazine in November 1916.

(16) Also buried in the cemetery at Ovillers is Captain John Lauder, son of Sir Harry Lauder a popular Scottish Music Hall entertainer of the time, Captain Lauder was killed by a sniper on 28th December 1916.

(17) A list of these names can be found at the back of this book in Appendix 5.

(18) The Field Ambulance was a medical unit consisting roughly of 250 men and should not be confused with a modern day motorised vehicle. Each division had several Field Ambulance units (usually three) and each of these was usually numbered after the brigades within the division. The Field Ambulance units were mainly situated close to the frontline and their men saw the horrors of war up close.

(19) A later resident and pupil of Forest School was the Military Historian and Professor Richard Holmes CBE who amongst other things has written many books on the Great War several of which have been referred to whilst writing this book.

(20) Also Buried at Carnoy in Row E Grave 28 is Captain W P Neville who bought footballs for the 8th East Surreys to use on 1st July 1916.

(21) Leonard Victor Waugh joined the army before the war and initially served with the Essex Regiment; he injured his leg in a riding accident and never fully recovered so when war broke out he requested a transfer to the Army Service Corps. This request was denied and in November 1914 he was sent to France to serve as a Second Lieutenant with the 2nd Royal Berkshire Regiment. In May 1915 Leonard was court martialled for cowardice

however he was acquitted of all charges, senior officers concurred he was unfit for active service and sent him back to England. Leonard retained his rank and in June 1915 was posted to the 3rd Essex, a reserve battalion based at Harwich. On 21st October 1916 he married Mabel Beatrice Pinchin at St Mary's Church, Chigwell and almost a year later their son Victor Marshall was born. Lieutenant Leonard Victor Waugh remained with the 3rd Essex in England until 1919 when he was demobilised; he remained on the Officers Special Reserve list until 1928. The army service record of Lieutenant Leonard Victor Waugh survives and can be viewed at the NA in file WO339/9142.

(22) A sunken lane quite simply is a road with high banks on either side, in much the same way a trench would it was able to afford those who sheltered in it protection from enemy activity, many such roads can be found in and around the Somme region.

(23) The 11th Rifle Brigade had been unlucky with its commanding officers; back in March 1916 their original commander Colonel H C Petre had relinquished his command. Then a Major Starky became CO but was wounded northeast of Ypres in June 1916 so he was replaced. Major J Harrington DSO then took command but he too was wounded this time in late August whilst the battalion were in support at Delville Wood, from there Major Cotton took command.

(24) Both officers are commemorated on the Thiepval Memorial to the Missing.

(25) Also buried in this cemetery is Lieutenant Raymond Asquith, the eldest son of the then Liberal Prime Minister Herbert Asquith, Raymond was shot in the chest during an attack on 15th September 1916. Ironically on the same date the leader of the Labour Party Arthur Henderson lost his son Captain David Henderson during an attack at High Wood.

(26) On the Chigwell Village War Memorial Alfred's initials are incorrectly engraved as AG and not AC.

(27) During the early months of the war the position of CIGS was held by several people however by September 1915 Sir Archibald Murray held the post, Sir William Robertson took over three months later and Murray was sent out to Egypt to command the EEF.

(28) The 9th Battalion Rifle Brigade was attached to the 14th (Light) Division as part of 41st Brigade, at the time this division was also in training at Winchester.

(29) Although Edward and Alfred didn't join up until January 1915 they would have still been at Winchester whilst Sidney was there.

(30) The MIC belonging to Sidney Hayter at the NA in Kew points to 3rd May 1916 but its unlikely this is correct, on this date the 12th Rifle Brigade reported a quiet day whilst out of the line in billets.

(31) T/Capt and Adjutant Alfred Furze is commemorated on the Thiepval Memorial to the Missing.

(32) This area known as 'The Quadrilateral' should not be confused with the Redoubt of the same name situated southwest of Serre as described in the events surrounding the death of Pte William Frank Gapes on 1st July 1916.

(33) The man in question was Cpl Albert Yates, in a later battle he was wounded and died of his injuries on 2nd June 1917. As another matter of interest 'C' Coy's commander Second Lieutenant Reginald Ruddle was later in the war awarded the Military Cross for bravery, he was killed in action on 24th June 1918 whilst attached to the 3rd Battalion Rifle Brigade.

(34) By April 1918 four former pupils of Chigwell Council School had been awarded the Military Medal; of those four two including Sidney Hayter were killed during WW1.

(35) In Central London on the corner of Grosvenor Gardens and Hobart Place in Victoria, SW1 there stands a memorial dedicated to the 11575 officers, NCOs and men of the Rifle Brigade who fell in the Great War.

(36) That day at Ilford Albert enlisted with at least three other men however it's unclear if they were all friends. They were 19560 L/Cpl Arthur Sargent, 19561 Pte Percy Roberson and 19562 Pte William Witham. Albert Cox was given number 19563. Witham was killed in action during April 1916 and the others including Cox would all be killed on the same day in October 1916.

(37) During the night of the 11th/12th October the 41st Division was relieved by battalions from 30th Division, come the morning of the assault the 7th Norfolk's 'A' Coy would find the 2nd Royal Scots Fusiliers positioned on its left flank.

(38) Their eldest son - named William after his father - also served in the forces during the Great War, as far as is known he survived the conflict.

(39) The South Lancashire Regiment was also known as the Prince of Wales Volunteers.

(40) The 7th Brigade had been part of 3rd Division however during October 1915 it swapped places with 76th Brigade from 25th Division.

(41) The war diary also states:

Officers: 6 wounded + 1 missing
Other Ranks: 85 wounded + 42 missing.

(42) According to SDGW Charles enlisted at Chigwell, his service record still exists however and says the City of London.

(43) Later in the war the brigade Machine Gun Companies of each division were joined together and formed into battalions, this battalion then took its number from the division it was attached to: e.g. 4th Division = 4th Battalion MGC.

(44) Six men were also wounded.

(45) The other men killed along with Charles that day were Pte Benjamin Leyland and Pte Joseph Stacey; their NCO Sgt Archibald Macey was also killed and is the only one with a known grave.

1917

(1) The Chemin des Dames is a road that runs through an area of high ground north of the River Aisne northeast of Soissons, translated it means 'Ladies Way'. The road and its name dates back to the time of Louis XV whose daughters used to enjoy horse and carriage rides through the area.

(2) When George was born in 1889 Hampstead came under the county of Middlesex; today it forms part of the London Borough of Camden.

(3) Archibald and Herbert were also soldiers in WW1, the units they served with are unknown but both men survived the war.

(4) After the disastrous start of the Somme offensive the 4th Division moved north to the Ypres Salient in order to refit, it moved back to the Somme at the beginning of October 1916.

(5) Towards the end of March the second Chigwell casualty of 1917 was sustained, the man was not killed on the Western Front and his story is told in the following chapter.

(6) Sir Henry Horne took over the command of 1st Army from Sir Charles Monro during the autumn of 1916 when Monro was sent to India.

(7) Edward Brown served with the Royal Warwickshire Regiment in WW1; despite being seriously wounded in June 1917 he survived the war. It is also possible that another brother called Christopher existed although I've been unable to confirm this. Pte Christopher Brown served with the Royal Engineers and was injured as many as four times before being awarded the DCM for telephone work in 1917.

(8) The 1st Essex had been stationed in Mauritius in August 1914; they returned to England and joined the 29th Division in February 1915.

(9) The 1st Newfoundland's also joined the 29th Division in February 1915 but still had companies designated A through D, as did the Worcester's and the Hampshire's.

(10) The creeping barrage was a method developed by artillery units whereby they moved targets forward at timed intervals in conjunction with infantry units as they advanced. By doing this it gave attacking troops vital time to head over the top and reach their objective before enemy troops could emerge from their dugouts and man their guns. In some cases when attacking troops were held up the effects were disastrous as men were shelled by their own guns. On another note the standing barrage was a method developed whereby guns were concentrated directly on a specific target in order to cause maximum devastation.

(11) This report comes courtesy of a book entitled: The Essex Regiment 1st Battalion by J.W. Burrows.

(12) According to SDGW:

4th Worcester's: 0 Officers + 9 Other Ranks KIA
2nd Hampshire's: 0 Officers + 5 Other Ranks KIA + 2 DOW

(13) Of the 24 mines originally laid by the British two were discovered by German miners and destroyed whilst 3 others were not blown and later dismantled by British units. Of the 19 detonated on 7th June 1917 two failed to explode and their positions were lost; one blew up during a storm in 1955 and the other remained missing for many years until its location was discovered in 2003. To this day the mine still lies buried under Petit Douve Farm southwest of Messines; experts suggest that trying to move it would be too dangerous.

(14) Bantam Battalions, Brigades and Divisions initially consisted of men who were under regulation height but otherwise fit for active service, an official order at the beginning of 1916 stated that only men between 5ft 1″ and 5ft 4″ were eligible. As the war went on standards dropped, units were replaced and Bantam units were eventually diluted with men of regulation height. Without his service record or a photograph it is impossible to know if Daniel Trevett was in fact a Bantam or not.

(15) Casualty figures for the 13th East Surreys during this action according to their war diary were:

3 Officers + 26 Other Ranks KIA
8 Officers + 152 Other Ranks wounded and 10 missing

(16) This battalion was also part of 120th Brigade; the other two battalions being the 14th HLI and the 14th Argyle and Sutherland Highlanders.

(17) There is some confusion about when Daniel Trevett actually died. The CWGC say 13th July but SDGW say 15th July. After consulting the battalion war diary I am convinced he was wounded on 13th July and died on the 15th July.

(18) Like with the Somme battles Third Ypres was divided into several actions all of which after the war were given their own names. Only the last two of these actions actually formed the battles for Passchendaele village itself however most people incorrectly refer to the whole Third Ypres campaign as 'The Battle of Passchendaele'.

(19) Although now classed as a suburb of southwest London Twickenham was and still is situated in the county of Middlesex.

(20) Next door to 57a Farringdon Road - outside the building of 59-61 Farringdon Road - is a plaque on which appear the following words: These premises were totally destroyed by a Zeppelin Raid during the World War on September 8th 1915 (Rebuilt 1917). This incident was carried out by Zeppelin L13 commanded by Captain Mathy, the most respected German airship officer of the war.

(21) The 2/6th London's were sent to France in January 1917.

(22) These brigades were also known as the 4th, 5th and 6th London Brigades whilst the 1st, 2nd and 3rd London Brigades were the 167th, 168th and 169th Brigades attached to 56th (London) Division.

(23) The reader should note the difference between City of London and County of London battalions. City of London battalions were generally based within the Square Mile whilst County of London battalions were based in what we would call today the Central London area i.e. those areas with a Central London postcode.

(24) SDGW puts casualties for the battalion on this day at: Other Ranks 2 KIA + 1 DOW.

(25) A mistake on the Chigwell Village War Memorial sees Charles initials appear as G E and not C E.

(26) Having tried it has not proved possible to find out what the 'M' stands for.

(27) The Royal Munster Fusiliers consisted of eleven battalion's altogether. The 1st and 2nd were Regular, the 3rd was a Reserve Battalion, the 4th and 5th were Extra Reserve Battalions, the 6th to 9th were Service Battalions and the last two (formed in 1917) were the 1st (Garrison) Battalion and 2nd (Home Service) Battalion.

(28) The two other brigades within this division were the 47th Brigade and 49th Brigade.

(29) Captain Wallace lived for about 1½ hours before dying of wounds, his body was not recovered and his name appears on the Tyne Cot Memorial to the Missing.

(30) The Poplars offices at 66 Tredegar Road were destroyed in the Blitz during World War Two.

(31) In most cases a wounded man on recovery would report to the home service battalion of his regiment and would remain there until such time as he was deemed fit to rejoin his original battalion at the front. In George Belchers case it was the 3/17th London's which was formed in early 1915.

(32) According to the CWGC all commonwealth nations with the exception of New Zealand whose men were killed in the Ypres Salient after 16th August 1917 and have no known grave are commemorated on the Tyne Cot Memorial to the Missing. This said sometimes exceptions are made which is not surprising given the numbers involved. One such example where this occurs is the case of L/Cpl George Charles Belcher and his fellow Poplars who although killed after this date find their names appear on the Menin Gate.

(33) Before the war the Royal Fusiliers consisted of four regular battalions, two reserve battalions and an extra reserve battalion, by the end of the war the regiment had a mixture of over forty battalions.

(34) Originally the 21st Division consisted of the 62nd Brigade, 63rd Brigade and 64th Brigade, after the change over it consisted of the 62nd Brigade, 64th Brigade and 110th Brigade.

(35) SDGW lists casualties as: 2 Officers + 26 Other Ranks KIA

(36) Most of the shells that were fired during this period failed to explode effectively; they just hit the mud and stuck in the ground. As a result most have lay undiscovered for many years and today when the fields are ploughed they still turn up with alarming regularity.

(37) Although Guards units have already been touched on at the beginning of this book a further explanation of the Guards Division can be found in the story of Frederick Arthur Bailey during the chapter entitled '1918'.

(38) As has been mentioned elsewhere in this book all heavy guns were operated by the RGA and all mobile guns by the RHA.

(39) Austria invaded Serbia in August 1914 and over the months that followed heavy fighting developed between the two sides especially around the Serbian capital Belgrade. Eventually Austrian and German forces along with Bulgarian forces, whose country entered the war on Germany's side in September 1915, drove Serbian forces out of their homeland and down through Montenegro and Albania where, during the spring of 1916, they were rescued by allied ships and taken to relative safety at Salonika.

(40) Ernest's grandparents on his father's side are also buried in the graveyard; Edward Herring senior died in 1895 whilst his wife Catherine died in 1908.

(41) Those divisions that went to Italy were the 5th Division, 7th Division, 23rd Division, 41st Division and 48th Division.

(42) In order to recap on those Brigades within 18th (Eastern) Division the reader may wish to refer back to the story of Pte Frederick Dunkley.

(43) According to their battalion war diary casualty figures for the 10th Essex that day were:

Officers 1 KIA + 6 wounded
Other Ranks 36 KIA + 187 wounded and 23 missing.

(44) Having started out as a junior officer Major T M Banks would eventually achieve the rank of Lieutenant Colonel and command the 10th Essex after Lieutenant Colonel Frizell was subjected to gas poisoning in April 1918, during the war he was awarded both the DSO and MC.

(45) Each division had two sometimes three Field Companies of the Royal Engineers attached and it was their job to help infantry units improve positions and communications etc. Working close to and on the frontline the men of these companies were often involved in the fighting. The 18th (Eastern) Division had two Field Companies of the Royal Engineers attached; they were 79th Field Coy RE and 80th Field Coy RE.

(46) This turns out to be incorrect as previously explained James Witham was not in Salonika but in Italy.

(47) At the Battle of Arras Sir Julian Byng had been in command of the Canadian Corps and successfully captured Vimy Ridge. After the Battle of Arras 3rd Army's commander Sir Edmund Allenby was sent off to command the EEF and Byng was brought in to replace him.

(48) One such man was 19 year old Pte Henry Alexander Shephard from Gainsborough Road Woodford Bridge who served with the 22nd (City of London Regiment) Royal Fusiliers. Killed by a shell during in heavy fighting at Bourlon Wood on 28th November 1917 his name is commemorated on both the Cambrai Memorial to the Missing and Woodford Bridge Roll of Honour Plaque.

(49) This technique was to have two main advantages, not only did it save ammunition being wasted as guns tried to find their targets but it also meant that the enemy had no idea an offensive was in the offing until it started.

(50) Although bells were rung throughout the country its unknown if they were rung in Chigwell or neighbouring villages.

PALESTINE

(1) Prior to this attack over the preceding months small scale clashes involving the troops of both sides had occurred but as a result nothing major happened.

(2) As mentioned previously in this book Murray had held the position of CIGS before being sent to Egypt to command the EEF.

(3) The 74th Division was made up mainly of dismounted Yeomanry units.

(4) As previously mentioned in the chapter entitled Gallipoli 161st Brigade consisted of the 1/4th Battalion, 1/5th Battalion, 1/6th Battalion and 1/7th Battalion of the Essex Regiment.

(5) This information comes courtesy of the book entitled Essex Units in the War 1914 – 1919, Volume 5 by J W Burrows.

(6) The reader should remember that Gordon Road, Ilford where Pte William Hyde enlisted was also home to 'C' Coy of the 4th Battalion Essex Regiment, this point is previously explained in the chapter entitled 'Gallipoli'. With this in mind but with no concrete evidence to back it up we can only presume that Pte William Hyde was attached to 'C' Coy.

(7) Lieutenant Colonel Edmund Jameson DSO died of wounds the next day and is buried at Dier El Belah CWGC Cemetery in Israel.

(8) The commanding officer of the 1/5th Essex, Lieutenant Colonel T Gibbons, was wounded as he led his battalion forward however his injuries turned out not to be life threatening.

(9) Among them was Lieutenant Barnard Aubrey Clapham from Woodford Bridge, although not killed instantly he died of wounds on 27th March 1917. Buried at Gaza CWGC Cemetery his name appears on the Great War 1914 – 1919 Memorial situated inside St Paul's Church in Woodford Bridge (see Appendix 4 for details).

(10) All except for the garrison holding out at Medina.

1918

(1) Although by this time the United States had some troops in France its army was tiny, by mid 1918 however it numbered a million men and by the end of the war that number had doubled.

(2) In April 1918 a new law would come into force that allowed men aged 41 to 50 to be conscripted.

(3) Just to recap the British armies on the Western Front were positioned as follows: 4th Army commanded by Sir Henry Rawlingson held the northern sector around Ypres, 1st Army commanded by Sir Henry Horne held the area from Armentières to Vimy, 3rd Army commanded by Sir Julian Byng held the sector just north of Arras southwards in front of Bapaume and 5th Army commanded by Sir Hubert Gough held the remainder to the River Oise. During this period 2nd Army commanded by Sir Herbert Plumer was in Italy, it would return to France on 17th March 1918.

(4) Although the British referred to the opening phase of actions as the March Offensive it was also referred to as the 'First Battles of the Somme 1918', under this banner individual actions were also named and the actions that took place between the 21st March and 23rd March were later known as the Battle of St Quentin.

(5) The Crozat Canal is technically still the St Quentin Canal and runs from the River Somme, at its junction east of Ham, southeast to the River Oise at Tergnier, its construction was financed by and named after Antoine Crozat, an 18th Century rags to riches banker..

(6) The 1911 census may shed some light on Matthew's profession however it's not available to the public until 2011.

(7) Prior to being disbanded in February 1918 the 12th (Service) Battalion Middlesex Regiment were also attached to 54th Brigade.

(8) In total the 18th (Eastern) Division suffered 46,500 casualties during the course of the Great War of which 13,730 died, the division was awarded eleven VC's.

(9) The Italian campaign has briefly been mentioned in the chapter entitled '1917'.

(10) As previously mentioned elsewhere in this book the other division sent back to France was the 5th Division in which John Witham's father James was serving.

(11) SDGW lists 12 other ranks killed in action.

(12) The original 4th Army that Rawlinson had commanded on the Somme in 1916 was renamed 2nd Army and stationed at Ypres when Plumer's troops went to Italy in November 1917. On Plumer's return in March 1918 the 2nd Army reverted back to being 4th Army (incorporating on 2nd April what remained of 5th Army) and his troops once again became known as 2nd Army.

(13) Germany declared war on Portugal on 8th March 1916 and her troops fought alongside the allies.

(14) It should be remembered that Pte Daniel James Trevett had served with the 13th East Surrey's (120th Brigade, 40th Division) until he was killed in July 1917. In the reorganisation of the British Army in February 1918 his former battalion was transferred to 119th Brigade and 120th Brigade went on to consist entirely of Highland Regiments.

(15) Its unknown if this was the same address on Hainault Road that Frederick's mother and sister lived at.

(16) As we know from the story of Lieutenant Maurice Austin Murray the 11th Essex went to France in August 1915, the 16th Welsh crossed the Channel four months later in December 1915.

(17) SDGW incorrectly lists him as Private 34596

(18) The Yorkshire Regiment is also known as the Green Howard's, the name dates back to 1744 and commemorates the then CO and the colour his men wore.

(19) Given the state of confusion at the front during this period it could, and in this case did, take months for news of individual losses to be relayed to families back home.

(20) Although at this stage of the war the fighting in France seemed desperate for the allies up in the sky they were starting to gain the upper hand. On 1st April 1918 the RFC and RNAS were amalgamated to form the RAF and given the efficiency of flying schools and factories in England a steady supply of men and machines were produced. Still not to be underestimated enemy aircraft at times were capable of giving the allies a run for their money however as the war continued German flyers found themselves hampered by shortages. Another point worth mentioning is the fact that on 21st April 1918 the German air ace Baron Manfred Von Richthofen, also known as 'the Red Baron', was shot down and killed over the Somme, a hero in Germany with eighty confirmed kills to his name this came as a massive blow to German moral.

(21) The two other infantry battalions attached to 71st Brigade were the 1st Battalion Leicestershire Regiment and the 2nd Battalion Sherwood Foresters (Notts and Derby Regiment).

(22) Casualty figures sustained by the 9th Norfolk's for the period 15th – 18th April 1918 according to SDGW were 2 officers and 113 other ranks.

(23) Adjacent to Pont-De-Nieppe Communal Cemetery stands a large German Military Cemetery, one of only a few in this area of the Western Front.

(24) As explained elsewhere in this book the 4th Division contained the 10th Brigade, 11th Brigade and 12th Brigade. Throughout the war the latter contained various battalions and from February 1918 onwards consisted of the 1st Battalion Kings Own (Royal Lancaster) Regiment, 2nd Battalion Lancashire Fusiliers and the 2nd Battalion Essex Regiment.

(25) According to SDGW 2 officers and 69 other ranks were killed in action whilst 10 other ranks died of wounds and 1 other rank died.

(26) With the exception of 1st July 1916 when both William Frank Gapes and Frederick Dunkley were killed the 18th April 1918 was the only other day during the course of the war that Chigwell lost two men on the same day.

(27) Between the 21st March and 29th April 1918 the Germans suffered overall casualties in the region of 350,000 whilst the allies lost 305,000 the majority of whom were British, these figures come courtesy of a book entitled 'The First World War' by Anthony Bruce.

(28) A brief explanation regarding the role of the Household Cavalry appears in the chapter entitled '1914'.

(29) This is the same CCS where Sgt Sidney Hayter MM was treated and died of wounds.

(30) In guards battalions the rank of Guardsman was equivalent to that of Private.

(31) Trench Mortar Batteries are explained in a little more detail later on in this chapter.

(32) The only son of author Rudyard Kipling had served as an officer with the 2nd Battalion Irish Guards and was killed at Loos in September 1915, Kipling never got over the death of his son and after the war wrote a volume of books entitled 'The Irish Guards in the Great War'.

(33) Although its unknown if he too was part of the wiring party according to SDGW it appears that on 4th May the 2nd Grenadier Guards also had one other rank killed in action.

(34) Built and unveiled in 1926 a memorial commemorating all units of the Guards Division stands in Central London on the west side of Horse Guards Road SW1.

(35) The First Battle of the Marne took place in early September 1914.

(36) In the process the Germans had 25,000 men taken prisoner and lost tons of supplies and munitions.

(37) This process of reorganisation has already been touched upon at the start of this chapter.

(38) The first British casualty of the Great War on the Western Front came on 21st August 1914 when Pte John Parr of the 4th Battalion Middlesex Regiment was killed whilst on cycle patrol near the Belgian town of Mons.

(39) All tanks belonging to 'C' Coy rallied however 'B' Coy had started with one tank short due to engine trouble, during the first phase of attack it lost a further two tanks to land mines and two to direct hits by enemy shellfire.

(40) A memorial dedicated to the officers, NCO's and men of the Tank Corps stands on the Albert to Bapaume Road near Pozières.

(41) The death of Sarah Moseley was reported in the 11th August 1916 edition of the Woodford Times Newspaper.

(42) Trench Mortar Batteries didn't exist in the early years of the war and came into play in the spring of 1916. By June 1916 they were assigned to Infantry Brigades defining themselves by the number to which brigade they were attached (e.g. 169th TMB was attached to 169th Infantry Brigade). In simple terms the role of the TMB was to support the infantry by way of silencing hostile machine guns and snipers, at various times they were also brought in to destroy barbed wire entanglements and bombard enemy strong points.

(43) Before and after the war the HQ of the 12th Battalion London Regiment (The Rangers) stood on Chenies Street off Tottenham Court Road in Central London. Today whilst the building no longer exists a fine memorial stands on the north side of the street opposite Alfred Place commemorating men of all ranks who served with the battalion.

(44) On occasion the Chigwell Parish Magazine refers to Cpl Harold Hull Moseley as Sgt Harold Hull Moseley; whilst there's no evidence of promotion the higher rank also appears on the Chigwell Village War Memorial.

(45) It should be remembered how Gough's 5th Army suffered greatly during the German Spring Offensive of March 1918 and following his dismissal that same month Rawlinson took over what remained renaming it 4th Army. In May 1918 however a new 5th Army was constituted, commanded by General Sir William Birdwood who had commanded the Anzacs at Gallipoli it took over positions on the Lys that July.

(46) The other infantry brigades within 29th Division were the 87th Brigade and 88th Brigade whilst in addition to the 2nd Battalion Royal Fusiliers the other infantry battalions within 86th Brigade were the 1st Battalion Lancashire Fusiliers and the 1st Battalion Royal Dublin Fusiliers.

(47) Throughout the war and especially in 1918 St Omer was a considerable hospital centre.

(48) A brief account of events in Salonika has already been told in the story of Ernest Herring.

(49) Prior to his dismissal the German Chancellor had been Count Von Hertling, his replacement was Prince Max of Baden second cousin to the Kaiser who was sworn in on 3rd October.

(50) Wilfred Owen was born in Shropshire in March 1893 and joined the army in October 1915, less than a year later he was commissioned into the Manchester Regiment and in October 1918 whilst serving with the 2nd Battalion he was awarded the Military Cross. Whilst much of his poetry was published after the war his most famous poems are probably *'Dulce et Decorum Est'* and *'Anthem for Doomed Youth'*. Lieutenant Wilfred Edward Salter Owen was killed in action whilst crossing the Sambre and Oise Canal with the 2nd Battalion Manchester Regiment on 4th November 1918; he is buried in Row A, Grave 3 at Ors Communal Cemetery in France.

(51) On 10th November 1918 the Kaiser fled to neutral Holland where he lived in exile up until his death on 4th June 1941.

EPILOGUE

(1) In January 1919 another man from Woodford Bridge died that I feel is worth mentioning. The name A Cousins is recorded on the Woodford Bridge Roll of Honour and in the early stages of writing this book I met somewhat briefly a lady called Alice Frost who turned out to be his daughter. Mrs Frost informed me that before the war her father worked at the Police Station in Woodford Bridge prior to joining the navy, unfortunately its unknown if this was the Royal Navy or Merchant Navy. Having survived the war however in January 1919 Mr Cousins contracted tuberculosis and died soon afterwards, sadly nothing further is known and no listing exists within the CWGC database.

(2) Not far from the Cenotaph and also on Whitehall stands a statue erected by parliament of Field Marshal Earl Douglas Haig seated on horseback. As CIC of the BEF from 1915 until the Armistice Earl Haig as he became in 1919 spent most of his post war life working vigorously to help war disabled as well as their families. Instrumental in creating the Royal British Legion funds raised by their Poppy Appeal rolled out every autumn go to help ex servicemen, born in Edinburgh on 19th June 1861 Haig died somewhat suddenly on 29th January 1928 aged 66.

(3) Opposite Victoria Station on the north side of Buckingham Palace Road, near the corner of Grosvenor Gardens, stands a statue of General Ferdinand Foch, allied CIC from April 1918 until the end of the war.

(4) Born in August 1853 Lieutenant General Sir Francis Lloyd G.C.V.O., K.C.B., DSO commanded the London district of the Grenadier Guards for much of the Great War, the great grandson of Admiral Sir Eliab Harvey, he retired in September 1918 and lived at Rolls Park in Chigwell until his death in 1926.

(5) The windows inside the Lady Chapel have been replaced due to a bomb which exploded near the churchyard wall in 1941; one of the yew trees in the churchyard still shows signs from the blast.

(6) Sometime around 1990 the names of those men from Chigwell killed in the Second World War were added to the memorial the details of which can be found at the back of this book in Appendix 6. When these names were added the following words were also added to the rear of the base of the memorial: 'At the going down of the sun and in the morning we will remember them'. These words represent a famous line from a poem entitled 'The Fallen'. Written by Lawrence Binyon in September 1914 they are repeated at Remembrance Day services all over the world.

(7) At the time of writing the pictures of two soldiers from the First World War hang in the Dining Room of the Kings Head Public House however it has not proved possible to determine if in fact these are men of Chigwell killed in the conflict whose names appear on the village war memorial. A copy of the pictures of these men - one of whom is a corporal - can be found on Page 190 of this book.

BIBLIOGRAPHY

Apart from consulting The Chigwell Parish Magazine, The Woodford Times Newspaper, The Essex Chronicle Newspaper, The London Gazette and the East Kent Gazette throughout my research I have consulted the following books and sources and would like to take this opportunity to thank both the authors and publishers for all of their help.

ADDISION WILLIAM, Epping Forest (J.M. Dent & Sons)
ARTHUR MAX, Forgotten Voices of the Great War (Ebury Press)
ASHWORTH TONY, Trench Warfare 1914-18 (Pan Books)
BANKS ARTHUR, Atlas of the First World War (Leo Cooper/Pen and Sword)
BROPHY JOHN & PARTRIDGE ERIC, The Long Trail (Sphere)
BROWN MALCOLM, The Imperial War Museum Book of 1918 Year of Victory (Pan Books)
BRUCE ANTHONY, The Last Crusade (John Murray Publishing)
BRUCE ANTHONY, The First World War (Michael Joseph)
BURROWS J W, 1st, 2nd, Territorial and Service Battalions - The Essex Regiment Volumes 1 to 6 (Burrows & Son - Southend on Sea)
CARLYON L.A, Gallipoli (Doubleday)
CARVER LORD, Turkish Front 1914-18 (Pan Books)
CHELL Capt R A and Lt Col T M BANKS, With the l0th Essex in France (Naval & Military Press)
CLARK ALAN, The Donkeys (Pimlico)
CLAYTON ANN, Account of Francis Martin-Leake & HMS Pathfinder
COOMBES ROSE, Before Endeavours Fade – A Guide to the Battlefields of the First World War
COOPER CAROL & DURRANT TONY, Chigwell Hall – A Brief History
COPPARD GEORGE, With a machine gun to Cambrai – (HMSO 1969)
EVANS MARIX MARTIN, 1918 The Year of Victories (Capella)
FILBY JENNY & GEOFF CLARK, 'Not All Airmen Fly' the story of RAF Chigwell, (Epping Forest District Council 1994)
FOX, CULL, CHAPMAN, McINTYRE, WEBB, Arras to Cambrai - The Kitchener Battalions of the Royal Berkshire Regiment 1917.
GRAVES ROBERT, Goodbye to all that (Penguin Books)
GODFREY E G, The Cast Iron Sixth (Naval & Military Press)
HANSON L. NINA, Memories of Chigwell
HARGREAVES REGINALD, Great Land Battles (Hamlyn)
HARRIS J.P, Amiens to the Armistice (Brassey's 1998)
HART LIDDEL, History of the First World War (Pan Books)
HAYTHORNE and WAITE, The World War One Source Book (Arms & Armour)
HOBSON CHRIS, Airmen Died in the Great War
HOLMES RICHARD, Riding the Retreat (Pimlico)
    The Western Front (BBC Books)
    Tommy (Harper Perennial)
HOLT MAJOR & MRS, Battlefield Guides to: SOMME (Leo Cooper)
    YPRES (Leo Cooper)
    GALLIPOLI (Leo Cooper)
HOWARD MICHAEL, The First World War (Oxford University Press)
JAMES E.A, British Regiments 1914-18 (Naval & Military Press)
JOLL JAMES, The Origins of the First World War (2nd Edition) (Longman Publishing)
JONES-DERVICHE Lt Col A D, History of the Post Office Rifles (Gall & Poldes 1919)
KELLEY'S DIRCTORY, Essex editions for 1907, 1908, 1913 and 1917.
LOUGHTON & DISTRICT HISTORICAL SOCIETY, Newsletter No.161 (April – May 2004)
MACDONALD LYN, They called it Passchendaele (Penguin)
MACKSEY KENNETH, The Shadows of Vimy Ridge (William Kimber)
MARTIN DAVID, A History of RAF Fairlop
MAUDE H ALAN, The History of the 47th (London) Division (Naval & Military Press)
McCARTHY CHRIS, The Somme – The Day-by-Day Account (Brockhampton Press)
McCARTHY CHRIS, Passchendaele – The Day-by-Day Account (Arms & Armour)
MIDDLEBROOK MARTIN, First Day on the Somme (Penguin)
MOOREHEAD ALAN, Gallipoli (Wordsworth)
PETRIE HUGH, Chigwell Photographic Memories, (The Francis Frith Collection)
PEWSEY STEPHEN, Chigwell & Loughton Old Picture Postcards Library (European 1996)
PONSONBY FREDERICK SIR, Grenadier Guards in the Great War - Volume 3 (Macmillan &Co)
RAWSON ANDREW, Battleground Europe – Loos/Hill 70 (Leo Cooper)
SIMPKINS PETER, Chronicles of the Great War

STOTT G, History of Chigwell School (Cowell)
TATTERSFIELD DAVID, A Village goes to War (Dewsbury Publishing)
TAYLOR A.J.P, The First World War (Penguin)
TERRAINE JOHN, Mons (Pan Books)
WILCOX RON, The Poplars, History of the 1/17th London Regiment Poplar & Stepney Rifles (Doppler Press Brentwood Essex)
UNKNOWN AUTHOR, The 54th Infantry Brigade 1914 - 1918 (Naval & Military Press)

INDEX

A

Abdul Hamid II, Sultan, 59,
Achi Baba, 61, 62,
Aisne, Second Battle of the, 107,
Ajax House, 132,
Albert, Battle of, 184,
Albert, King of Belgium, 17, 186, 188,
Albert Medal, 222,
Alexandria, (Egypt) 65, 66, 227,
Alexandria (Chatby) Military War Memorial Cemetery, 66,
Allenby, Gen Sir Edmund, 20, 31, 69, 71, 103, 145, 232,

American Army,

ARMIES

First Army, 185,

DIVISIONS

33rd Division, 173, 176, 180,

American Navy, 41,
Amiens, the Battle of, 172, 173, 181,
Ancre, the Battle of the, 94,
Ancre Heights, the Battle of, 91,
Ancre River, 69, 77,
Anzac Cove, 61,
Arabia, 146,
Armentières, the Battle of, 29, 31,
Armistice, 189, 195,
Army Cyclist Corps, 174,
Arras, the Battle of, 103, 232,
Arras Memorial to the Missing, 107, 135, 157, 191,
Asquith, Herbert Prime Minister, 26, 48, 97, 229,
Asquith, Lt Raymond, 229,
Asset Farm, 183,
Aubers Ridge, Battle of, 46,
Australian Light Horse Reg, 64,
Austria – Hungary, 17, 107, 128, 155, 186, 188, 232,

B

Baboon Camp, 131,
Baden, Prince Max of, 189, 236,
Baghdad, 147,
Bailey, Pte Charles Ernest, 111, 136, 168,
Bailey, Pte Frederick Arthur, 168, 192, 232,
Bailey, AB Harry Norman, 39, 42, 111, 168, 226,
Bainbridge, Maj Gen E, 91,
Baker, Lt Col E M, 182,
Balfour, Arthur, 62,
Banks, Lt Col T M, 131, 132, 232,
Bantam Battalions, 231,
Barton, Cpl Frederick William, 21, 173, 192,
Basilique, (Albert) 71,

Basra, 147,
Beaumont Hamel, 73, 94,
Beaurevoir Line, 186, 187,
Beck House, 116,
Bedford House CWGC Cemetery, 206,
Bedfordshire Regiment, - see H H Shuttle, M A W Mason and F W Barton
Beersheba, 141, 145, 146,
Belcher, L/Cpl George Charles, 120, 124, 136, 232,
Belgian Army, 31, 186, 187,
Belgrade, 188, 232,
Bellewaerde Ridge, 121, 122,
Bellewaardebeek Canal, 205,
Bellicourt Tunnel, 102, 186,
Béthune, Battle of, 165,
Bienvillers CWGC Cemetery, 170, 192,
Binyon, Lawrence, 236,
Bird, Pte Edwin, 30, 36, 44,
Bird, Pte Thomas George, 30, 44, 50, 57,
Birdwood, Gen Sir William, 62, 181, 185, 187, 235,
Birr Cross Roads, 122,
Blucher Offensive, 170,
Bodger, Pte Sydney James, 166, 191,
Bois Grenier, 159, 160,
Bonar Law, Andrew, 62, 227,
Borry Farm, 116,
Bosphorus River, 59,
Bosnia – Herzegovina, 17,
Bourlon Wood, 133, 185, 233,
Braithwaite, Lt Gen Sir Walter, 186,
Bray CWGC Cemetery, 102,
Brest-Litovsk, Treaty of, 151,
Brickstacks, 96,

British Army,

ARMIES

1st Army, 44, 47, 48, 50, 52, 69, 103, 151, 159, 160, 166, 181, 184, 185, 187, 188, 230, 233,
2nd Army, 44, 47, 69, 103, 107, 113, 117, 120, 122, 123, 125, 127, 160, 162, 163, 181, 182, 185, 186, 187, 188, 233, 234,
3rd Army, 48, 69, 71, 72, 103, 124, 133, 145, 150, 155, 157, 163, 168, 181, 184, 185, 187, 189, 232, 233,
4th Army, 69, 71, 72, 74, 88, 103, 107, 157, 171, 172, 175, 181, 184, 185, 186, 187, 188, 189, 227, 233, 234, 235,
5th Army, 91, 103, 107, 113, 117, 123, 125, 127, 130, 149, 151, 155, 157, 171, 181, 185, 187, 188, 233, 234, 235,

Reserve Army, 71, 91, 227,

CORPS

Anzac/Australian Corps, 59, 62, 122, 123, 127, 171, 172, 176, 185, 186, 187,
Canadian Corps, 103, 127, 130, 173, 184, 185, 187, 232,
Cavalry Corps, 133,

I Corps, 20, 21, 33, 34, 189, 226,
II Corps, 20, 21, 24, 26, 115,
III Corps, 29, 77, 88, 89, 152, 172, 173, 175, 176, 180, 186, 225,
IV Corps, 46, 52, 155,
VI Corps, 33, 103,
VII Corps, 103,
VIII Corps, 72,
IX Corps, 52, 54, 63, 186,
XIII Corps, 75, 123,
XIV Corps, 82, 83, 88, 89, 116, 125,
XV Corps, 79, 88, 89, 90,
XVII Corps, 103,
XVIII Corps, 116, 118,
XIX Corps, 116,

DIVISIONS

2nd Australian Division, 175,
3rd Australian Division, 175,
4th Australian Division, 175,
5th Australian Division, 175,
Cavalry Division, 20, 31,
1st Cavalry Division, 31,
2nd Cavalry Division, 31, 33, 34,
3rd Cavalry Division, 31, 34, 205,
4th Canadian Division, 92,
Guards Division, 52, 54, 87, 127, 168, 232,
New Zealand Division, 185, 189,
1st Division, 20, 33, 34, 52, 54,
2nd Division, 20, 21, 33, 52, 54, 169,
3rd Division, 20, 21, 24, 26, 230,
4th Division, 22, 29, 72, 73, 101, 125, 127, 166, 168, 225, 230, 234,
5th Division, 20, 21, 24, 26, 83, 125, 130, 232, 234,
6th Division, 29, 80, 87, 163,
7th Division, 33, 34, 46, 52, 54, 74, 79, 127, 130, 232,
8th Division, 46, 47, 116, 225,
9th (Scottish) Division, 27, 52, 54, 109, 183,
10th (Irish) Division, 27, 63, 64,
11th (Northern) Division, 27, 63, 64, 116, 118, 119, 120, 125, 127,
12th (Eastern) Division, 27, 48, 50, 77, 79, 89, 105, 173, 180, 228,
13th (Western) Division, 27,
14th (Light) Division, 27, 152, 225, 229,

15th (Scottish) Division, 28, 52, 54, 108, 116, 128,
16th (Irish) Division, 28, 83, 84, 115, 116,
17th (Northern) Division, 28,
18th (Eastern) Division, 74, 92, 115, 130, 152, 173, 176, 179, 180, 232, 234,
19th (Western) Division, 93, 113,
20th (Light) Division, 82, 83, 84, 86, 116,
21st Division, 52, 54, 124, 232,
23rd Division, 163, 232,
24th Division, 52, 54, 80, 81, 124,
25th Division, 80, 91, 122, 230,
29th Division, 44, 59, 61, 62, 64, 73, 105, 114, 116, 125, 127, 159, 182, 230, 236,
30th Division, 74, 89, 229,
31st Division, 73, 184,
32nd Division, 96, 169,
34th Division, 74, 159, 160,
36th (Ulster) Division, 28, 74, 92, 115, 116,
37th Division, 124,
38th (Welsh) Division, 28,
39th Division, 92,
40th (Bantam) Division, 108, 109, 159, 234,
41st Division, 89, 90, 113, 155, 229, 232,
42nd (East Lancashire) Division, 62, 64, 157,
44th Division, 124,
46th (North Midland) Division, 71, 72, 187,
47th (London) Division, 52, 54, 111, 121, 123, 173,
48th (South Midland) Division, 116, 118, 120, 130, 228, 232,
49th (West Riding) Division, 127, 164,
52nd (Lowland) Division, 141, 143,
53rd (Welsh) Division, 141, 143,
54th (East Anglian) Division, 64, 65, 141, 143,
55th (West Lancashire) Division, 159,
56th (London) Division, 71, 72, 115, 178, 231,
58th (London) Division, 94, 120, 152, 173, 176, 178, 180,
59th (North Midland) Division, 164,
61st (South Midland) Division, 109, 118,
63rd Royal Naval Division, 28, 59, 225,
66th (East Lancashire) Division, 127,
74th (Yeomanry) Division, 141, 233,

Broodseinde, the Battle of, 124,
Brown, Pte Christopher, 230,
Brown, L/Cpl Ely, 51,
Brown, Pte Harry Mark, 105, 135, 184, 198,
Bruce-Williams, Maj Gen H, 125,
Bryce DSO, Lt Col E D, 175,
Buffs, (East Kent Regiment) – see F W Dunkley
Bulgaria, 128, 186, 188, 232,

Byng, Gen Sir Julian, 32, 103, 133, 151, 157, 181, 185, 187, 189, 205, 232, 233,
C
Cairo, 139,
Cambrai, the Battle of, 133,
Cambrai Memorial to the Missing, 233,
Camisole Switch, 152, 153,
Canal du Nord, 133, 185,
Cape Helles, 61, 62,
Caporetto, the Battle of, 107, 155,
Carnoy CWGC Cemetery, 82,
Cassonman, Pte Harris, 225,
Caterpillar Wood, 75,
Celery Copse, 183,
Cenotaph, 197, 203,
Chatham Naval Memorial, 39, 40, 42,
Chemin des Dames, 101, 107, 167, 170, 230,
Chief of the Imperial General Staff, 85, 149, 229,
Chigwell Council School, 13, 14, 85, 105, 141, 152, 173, 177, 181, 198, 229,
Chigwell Grammar School, 13, 14, 77, 79, 91, 94, 177, 181, 198, 205, 206, 222,
Chigwell Hall, 14, 80, 82, 162,
Chigwell Junior Football Club, 43,
Chigwell Rifle Club, 77,
Chipilly Spur, 180,
Chlorine Gas, 46, 51, 53,
Christ's Hospital, 177,
Christmas Truce, 35,
Churchill, Winston, 33, 37, 59, 62, 134, 227,
Cite Bonjean Military Cemetery, 50, 57,
Clapham, Lt Barnard Aubrey, 233,
Clark, Pte Henry John, 48, 57,
Claybury Hospital, 14, 37, 118,
Coldstream Camp, 131,
Colombo House, 132,
Colvin MP, Brig Gen Sir Richard Beale, 14,
Constantine of Greece, King, 128,
Constantinople, 41, 59, 140,
Coppard, George, 226,
Cornwell VC, John Travers, 226,
Cousins, A, 236,
Cox, L/Cpl Albert Charles, 50, 89, 229,
Cox, Pte James Edward, 50, 77, 89,
Creeping Barrage, 230,
Cromer Village War Memorial, (Norfolk) 79,
Crozat, Antoine, 233,
Crozat Canal, 152, 233,
Curfew House, 183,
D
Dallas, Maj Gen A G, 143,
Damascus, 146,
Daniels, Capt Edwin Ambrose, 91, 100, 198,
Dardanelles Straight, 59,
Dardanelles Committee, 62, 66,
Daubeny DSO, Lt Col G B, 128,
Day, Pte Charles William, 162, 181, 191,

Day, Dvr William, 163,
De Wippe Camp, 132,
Deacon, Lt Col Edmund, 205,
Delva Farm, 116,
Delville Wood, 79, 81,
Derby, Lord, 69, 228,
Derby Scheme, 69, 105, 108, 111, 130, 142, 155, 159, 162,
Derviche-Jones DSO MC, Lt Col, 179, 180,
Desert Column, 141,
Dickens, Charles, 13,
Dier El Belah CWGC Cemetery, (Israel) 233,
Dive Copse CWGC Cemetery, 180, 193,
Divisional Troops, 124,
Dogger Bank, 41,
Dorsetshire Regiment, - see C L Harrup
Draper, Sgt John William, 205, 207,
Drocourt – Quéant Switch, 103, 185,
Dud Corner CWGC Cemetery, 56,
Dunkley, Pte Frederick William, 74, 86, 152, 232, 235,
Dunkley, Harry Cecil, 198, 200, 228,
Durham Light Infantry, - see J Simpson
E
Eastern Force, 141,
Edward VII, King, 17,
Edwards VC, Pte Thomas, 221, 223,
Egypt, 61, 139,
Elgar, Edward, 198,
Elmslie, Lt Col W F, 76,
Epehy, Battle of, 185,
Erquinghem-Lys Churchyard Extension Cemetery, 163,
Essex Regiment, 27, also see J E Cox, D G King, M A Murray, W F Gapes, G Pleasance, W H Hyde, H M Brown, J A Witham and S J Bodger
Essex Yeomanry, 205, 207,
Euphrates River, 147,
F
Fairview Hospital, 14, 79, 82,
Falkenhayn, General Erich Von, 24, 85, 88, 102,
Fanshawe, Maj Gen R, 118,
Faubourg-d'Amiens CWGC Cemetery, 107,
Felixstowe Military Hospital, 155,
Ferdinand, Franz Archduke, 17,
Festubert, (attack) 48,
Fielding, Maj Gen G, 168,
Fifteen Ravine, 109,
Fins New British CWGC Cemetery, 109,
Fish, Lt John Leslie, 77, 80, 89, 98,
Fisher, Lord, 59, 62,
Fitzgerald, Pte Patrick, 117, 137,
Flack, Pte Charles Alfred, 94, 174,
Flers-Courcelette, the Battle of, 85,
Flint Cottage, 14, 91, 93, 100,
Foch, Gen Ferdinand, 23, 157, 158, 162, 172, 181, 185, 187, 189, 236,

Fogg, Pte Frank M, 114, 136,
Foster VC, Cpl Edward, 108,
Franco-Prussian War, 17, 69,
French, Field Marshal Sir John, 3, 20, 21, 23, 44, 47, 48, 50, 54, 56,
French Army,

ARMIES

First Army, 20, 172, 173, 187, 189,
Fourth Army, 171, 185,
Fifth Army, 20, 171,
Sixth Army, 23, 171,
Ninth Army, 23,

CORPS

French First Cavalry Corps, 24,
Twenty-First Corps, 24,

DIVISIONS

45th Algerian Division, 46,

Frezenberg Ridge, 116, 205,
Frizell DSO MC, Lt Col C W, 131, 232,
Frost, Alice, 236,

G

Gallipoli, 41, 44, 47, 59,
Gapes MP, Mike, 228,
Gapes, Pte William Frank, 72, 94, 98, 101, 166, 229, 235,
Garnet, Sir Guy, 198,
Gaza CWGC Cemetery, 233,
Gaza, the First Battle of, 141, 143, (Picture) 148,
Gaza, the Second Battle of, 145,
Gaza, the Third Battle of, 146,
George V, King, 17, 65, 94, 112, 142, 197, 222,
Georgette Offensive, - see Lys Offensive
German Offensives, (Map) 150,

German Army,

ARMIES

First Army, 23,
Second Army, 23, 172,
Third Army, 22,
Fourth Army, 22, 33, 160,
Sixth Army, 30, 33, 159,

CORPS

First Cavalry Corps, 33,
Fourth Cavalry Corps, 33,
Fifth Cavalry Corps, 33,
Seventh Corps, 24, 30,
Nineteenth Corps, 30,

DIVISIONS

Third Bavarian Division, 106,
Sixth Bavarian Reserve Division, 34,
Eighth Division, 22,
Thirteenth Division, 25,
Fourteenth Division, 25, 26, 30,

Twenty Fourth Division, 30,
Twenty Fifth Reserve Division, 30,

German Navy, 37, 41, 189,
Gneisenau Offensive, 171,
Gommecourt, 69, 72,
Goodhart, Commander Francis H H, 198, 222,
Gordon Road, (Ilford) 65, 142, 233,
Gorringe DSO, Lt Gen Sir George F, 111, (Maj Gen) 147,
Gough, Gen Sir Hubert, 31, 52, 71, 77, 85, 91, 103, 107, 113, 117, 123, 127, 149, 151, 157, 226, 227, 233, 235,
Graff Von Spee, Vice Admiral, 39,
Grandcourt, 92,
Grand-Seraucourt CWGC Cemetery, 154, 190,
Graves, Robert, 96,
Green Hill, 143,
Green Howard's, 234,
Green, Pte John, 181, 193,
Green, Pte Percy, 197, 200,
Grenadier Guards, 168, 236,
Grierson, Gen Sir J M, 20,
Groener, Gen Wilhelm, 188,
Grove Town CWGC Cemetery, 88,
Guards Division Memorial, 192, 235,
Guards Museum, 168,
Gueudecourt, 89,
Guillemont, 69,
Guillemont, Battle of, 82, 83,
Guillemont Road CWGC Cemetery, 84,
Gunners Farm CWGC Cemetery, 51,

H

Haig, Sir Douglas, 3, 20, 33, 44, 47, 48, 50, 52, (Field Marshal) 56, 69, 77, 85, 91, 101, 102, 109, 117, 127, 130, 133, 149, 151, 157, (Order of the Day) 160, 172, 181, 184, 187, 188, 189, 203, 227, 236,
Hainault Farm Airfield, 11,
Halton Park Camp, 142,
Hamel, (attack at) 171,
Hamilton, Gen Sir Ian, 59, 62, 66,
Hansen, Nina, 159,
Harrup, Pte Charles Leonard, 24, 30, 36, 227,
Harsnett, Samuel, 13,
Harvey, Admiral Sir Eliab, 13, 236,
Hayter, L/Cpl Albert, 85, 90, 91, 100,
Hayter, Sgt Sidney MM, 85, 90, 100, 198, 229, 235,
Heard, Daniel, 94,
Heath CWGC Cemetery, 176, 192,
Heilly Station CWGC Cemetery, 91,
Hejaz Railway, 146,
Hell Fire Corner, 122,
Henderson, Arthur, (Labour Party Leader) 229,
Henderson, Capt David, 229,
Herring, Gnr Ernest Handy, 128, 137, 236,
Hersing, Capt Otto, 38, 39,
Hertling, Count Von, 236,
High Wood, 79, 81,

Hill 60, 107,
Hill 70, 52, 54,
Hindenburg Line, 102, 133, 157, 185, 186,
Hindenburg, Field Marshal Paul Von, 88, 102, 186, 187, 188,
Hitler, Adolf, 195,
HMS Hampshire, 71,
HMS Kestrel, 40, 42, 111, 168,
HMS Pathfinder, 37, 38, 39, 42, 226,
Hohenzollern Redoubt, 121,
Holmbury St Mary, (Surrey) 88,
Holmes CBE, Prof Richard, 228,
Honourable Artillery Company, 77, 91,
Horne, Gen Sir Henry, 103, 159, 160, 166, 181, 184, 185, 187, 230, 233,
Houthulst Forest, 131,
Hughes MC, Lt Col WW, 122,
Hundred Days, 181,
Husey, Lt Col R H, 178,
Hussars, - see C A Reeves
Hussein, Prince, 139,
Hussein, Sherif, 146,
Hyde, Pte William Harold, 141, 148,

I

Ilford War Memorial, 11, 12,
Imperial War Graves Commission, 48, 226,
Indian Corps, 46, 225,
Indian Lahore Division, 26,
Indian Meerut Division, 86,
Inglefield, Maj Gen F, 65,
Isandhlwana, Battle of, 20,
Israel, State of, 147,
Italy, 107, 130, 155, 186, 188, 233, 234,

J

Jackson, Maj Raphael, 168,
Jaffa, 141, 146,
Jagger, Charles Sargeant, 129,
Jameson DSO, Lt Col Edmund James, 65, 144, 233,
Jassby, 2nd Lt Harry Walter, 11, 12,
Jellicoe, Admiral Sir John, 37, 227,
Jerusalem, 141, 146,
Jerusalem CWGC Cemetery, 145, (Picture) 148,
Jerusalem Memorial to the Missing, 145, 148,
Jihad, (Muslim Holy War) 140,
Joffre, Gen Joseph, 20, 23, 44, 50, 69, 96,
Johnson, Lt Col R N, 178,
Jordan River, 146,
Jutland, Battle of, 41, 226,

K

Kaiser Wilhelm II, 17, 19, 21, 37, 103, 186, 187, 188, 189, 236,
Kaiserschlacht, (Kaisers Battle) – see March Offensive
Kelly's Directory, 114,
Kemal, Mustafa, 64,
Kerry, Pte William Albert, 124, 137, 169, 178,
King, Pte Denham George, 64, 142,
Kings Head Public House, 13, 14, 190, 236,
Kipling, Rudyard, 74, 235,

Kiritch Tepe Ridge, 62, 64,
Kitchener, Lord Herbert Horatio, 20, 23, 26, 50, 59, 62, 69, 71, 228,
Kluck, Gen Von, 21, 23,
Krithia, First Battle of, 62,
Krithia, Second Battle of, 62,
Krithia, Third Battle of, 62,
Kut el Amara, (Siege) 147,

L
La Bassée Canal, 121, 159, 167,
La Bassée, the Battle of, 24,
La Boisselle, 74, 228,
La Ferté-Sous-Jouarre Memorial, 22, 36,
Labis Farm, 184,
Lagnaz, Marguerite Blanche, 65,
Langemarck, the Battle of, 114,
Lanrezac, Gen Charles, 20,
Lauder, Sir Harry, 228,
Lauder, Capt John, 228,
Law, Andrew Bonar, 62, 227,
Lawe River, 160, 165,
Lawford, Maj Gen S, 155,
Lawrence, Maj T E, (Lawrence of Arabia) 146,
Le Cateau, the Battle of, 21, 22,
Le Grand Beaumart CWGC Cemetery, 162, 191,
Le Transloy, the Battle of, 88,
Leipzig Redoubt, 92,
Lemnos, 65, 66,
Lesage Farm, 183,
Lesseps, Ferdinand de, 139,
Leuze Wood, (Lousy Wood) 83,
Lewis House, 126,
Lisle de, Maj Gen H, 105,
Lloyd George, David, 48, 62, 71, 97, 101, 107, 130, 141, 145, 149, 158, 188, 228,
Lloyd, Lt Gen Sir Francis, 198, 236,
Lochnagar Mine Crater, 228,
Lockwood MP, Col Amelius Mark Richard, (First Baron Lambourne) 14,
Logeast Wood, 157,
London Gazette, 86, 221, 222,
London Regiment, - see C A Flack, C E Bailey, G C Belcher, (London Rifle Brigade) H H Moseley
Longuenesse (St Omer) Souvenir Cemetery, 184, 193,
Loos, the Battle of, 50, 52,
Loos, Memorial to the Missing, 56, 57, 167, 191, 227,
Louis XV, King of France, 230,
Louvois Farm, 132,
Luce River, 172,
Ludendorff, Erich Von, 88, 102, 149, 151, 155, 157, 162, 167, 177, 185, 186, 187, 188,
Lusitania, (Sinking of) 41,
Lutyens, Sir Edwin, 197,
Lynde Farm, 183,
Lys Offensive, 158, 162, 167,

M
Macedonia, 186,
Machine Gun Corps, 94, 96, 135, 174, 230,
Mallard Wood, 180,
Mametz, 75,
Mametz Wood, 79,

March Offensive, 151,
Marden, Maj Gen T, 163,
Marne, Miracle/First Battle of the, 23, 235,
Marne, Second Battle of the, 171,
Mars Offensive, 157,
Marsden, Reverend Thomas, 52, 227,
Marshall, Sir William, 147,
Martin-Leake VC, Capt Arthur, 226,
Martin-Leake, Capt Francis, 39,
Mason, Pte Matthew Amos Wesson, 152, 190, 198,
Maude, Maj Gen Sir Stanley, 147,
Maxwell, Maj Gen Sir John, 139,
McMahon, Sir Henry, 139,
Meggy, Lt Col A R, 65,
Menin Gate, Memorial to the Missing, 34, 36, 123, 136, 206, 225, 232,
Menin Road, 122,
Menin Road Ridge, the Battle of, 123,
Mesopotamia, 147,
Messines, the Battle of, 108, (Lost Mines) 231,
Meuse-Argonne, 185, 187,
Michael Offensive, - see March Offensive
Military Medal, 86, 100,
Millbrook, 77,
Moltke, Gen Helmuth Von, 19,
Monash, Lt Gen Sir John, 171,
Monchy-le-Preux, 103, 105, 184,
Monck-Mason, Lt Col R H, 115,
Monoury, Gen, 23,
Monro, Gen Sir Charles, 35, 48, 66, 69, 227, 230,
Mons, 20, 149, 187, 189, 235,
Mont St Quentin, 185,
Montauban, 75,
Montreuil, 69,
Mormal, Forest of, 19, 188, 189,
Morval, Battle of, 88,
Moseley, Cpl Harold Hull, 177, 193,
Moseley, Headmaster Mr John R, 43, 85, 177, 181,
Murray, Gen Sir Archibald, 141, 145, 233, 229,
Murray, Reverend Frederick Auriol, 52, 56, 65, 69, 197, 198,
Murray, Lt Maurice Austin, 52, 57, 159, 167, 227, 234,

N
Nazi Party, 195,
Neuve Chapelle, Battle of, 44,
Nevill, Capt W P, 228,
New Armies, 27, 28, 48, 69, 72, 74,
Newman VC, Lt Col Augustus Charles, 221,
Nibrunesi Point, 63,
Nivelle, Gen Robert, 96, 101, 102, 107,
Nixon, Gen Sir John, 147,
Noble, Pte Frederick Elliot, 159, 191,
Norfolk Regiment, - see A C Cox and C W Day
Norman, Lt Newman F, 80,
North, Capt Kenneth Croft, 34, 225,

North DSO, Lt Col P W, 155,
North Staffordshire Regiment, - see A J Waugh

O
Oak Dump CWGC Cemetery, 113, 136, 225,
Oise River, 149, 152,
Old Contemptibles, 21,
Oliver, Bill, 181,
Ors Communal Cemetery, 236,
Ottoman Turkish Empire, 17, 59, 139, (army surrender) 147,
Outer Amiens Defence Line, 173, 177,
Outtersteene Ridge, 183,
Ovillers, 77,
Ovillers CWGC Cemetery, 79, 228,
Owen, Lt Wilfred, 189, 236,
Owls Wood, 132,

P
Palestine, 139,
Panama House, 132,
Parr, Pte John, 235,
Pasha, Djemal, 139,
Passchendaele, 111, 137, 162,
Passchendaele, First Battle of, 127,
Passchendaele, Second Battle of, 130,
Penn, William, 13,
Pershing, Gen John Joseph, 185,
Persian Gulf, 147,
Pétain, Gen Philippe, 107, 110, 151, 157,
Petit Douve Farm, 231,
Piave River, 155,
Pilckem Ridge, the Battle of, 113,
Pleasance, Pte George, 101, 135, 166, 198,
Pleasance, Congressional Minister James, 101, 102, 198,
Ploegsteert, Memorial to the Missing, 31, 162,
Ploegsteert Wood, 51,
Plumer, Gen Sir Herbert, 47, 69, 103, 107, 113, 117, 120, 127, (to Italy) 130, 160, 162, 163, 181, 182, 185, 186, 187, 227, 233, 234,
Poelcapelle, the Battle of, 127,
Poll Hill Camp, 131,
Polygon Wood, the Battle of, 123,
Ponsonby, Maj Gen John, 159,
Pont-De-Nieppe Communal Cemetery, 165, 191,
Poplar & Stepney Rifles, 27, 120, 232,
Portugal/Portuguese Army, 159, 234,
Post Office Rifles, 27, 178, 179,
Pozières, the Battle of, 89,
Prince of Wales Public House, 14, (destroyed) 16, 43, 57, 152, 165, 228,
Princip, Gavrilo, 17,
Pulteney, Gen Sir William, 29,

Q
Quadrilateral, (Serre) 73, 229,
Querrieu, 71, 77, (Wood) 175,

R
Race to the Sea, the, 24,

Radclyffe, Lt Col, 55, 56,
RAF Chigwell, 198,
Rangers Memorial, 235,
Rasch DSO, Lt Col G E C, 169,
Ravelsberg Ridge, 162,
Rawlinson, Gen Sir Henry, 33, 46, 52, 69, 71, 77, 79, 85, 88, 91, 103, 107, 157, 167, 171, 172, 184, 186, 189, 227, 233, 234, 235,
Red Baron, (Baron Manfred Von Richthofen) 234,
Reeves, Pte Charles Alfred, 33, 108, 205,
Reims-Marneschutz Offensive, 171,
Richardson, Lt Col A J, 93,
Riding, Mr. Henry, 48, 198,
Rifle Brigade, - see E S Scott, A C Vince and S Hayter
Robertson, Gen Sir William, 85, 149, 229,
Rolls Park, 13, 236,
Royal Army Medical Corps, 80,
Royal Field Artillery, 128, (Memorial) 129, 136,
Royal Flying Corps/Naval Air Service/Air Force, 11, 198, 234,
Royal Fusiliers, - see W A Kerry, M A W Mason and J Green (Memorial in Holborn) 127,
Royal Munster Fusiliers, - see F M Fogg
Royal Navy, 37, 59, 62, 110, 146, 147, 188, 222,
Rupprecht, Crown Prince, 30, 225,
Russia, 17, 59, 101, 103, (Revolution) 134, 141,
Ryecroft, Maj Gen W, 96,
S
Sadleir-Jackson DSO, Brig Gen, 152,
Salonika, 128, 186, 188, 232, 236,
Sambre, Battle of the, 189,
Sanders, Gen Liman Von, 59, 60, 64,
Sandringham, 65,
Sarajevo, 17,
Sari Bair, Battle of, 64,
Savill, Alfred, 80,
Scapa Flow, 37,
Scarpe, First Battle of the, 103,
Scarpe, Second Battle of the, 107,
Scarpe, Third Battle of the, 107,
Schelde River, 188,
Schilliber, George, 13,
Schlieffen, Count Von, 19,
Schlieffen Plan, 19,
Schwaben Redoubt, 74, 92,
Scott, L/Cpl Edward Stephen, 82, 85, 86, 99, 198,
Selle River, 187,
Sensee Canal, 185,
Senussi Tribe, 140, 143,
Serbia, 107, 186, 188, 232,
Serre, 72, 73,

Serre Road No. 1 CWGC Cemetery, 74,
Shaw, Norman, 80,
Shephard, Pte Henry Alexander, 233,
Shuttle, Cpl Harold Henry, 21, 36, 173, 187, 226,
Simpson, Pte James, 155, 166, 191,
Sinai Peninsular, 139,
Smeaton Road, 14, 21, 24, 37, 108, 130, 133, 166,
Smith-Dorrien, Sir Horace, 20, 44, (Replaced) 47,
Solferino Farm CWGC Cemetery, 129, 137,
Somme, the Battle of the, 69,
South Lancashire Regiment, - see E A Daniels
Spanish Flu, 195, 197,
Springfield Farm, 119, 120,
St Bartholomew's Hospital, 80,
St Mihiel, 185,
St Omer, 69, 184, 236,
St Quentin, Battle of, 233,
St Quentin Canal, 102, 133, 186, 233,
Steenbeek River, 113, 118,
Stevens, Rt Rev Thomas, (Bishop of Barking) 198,
Stirling DSO, Lt Col G, 72, 74,
Stonehenge, 82,
Stopford, Gen Sir Frederick, 63,
Stormtrooper Battalions, 134, 151,
Stuff Redoubt, 92,
Stuff Trench, the capture of, 92,
Suez Canal, 139,
Suffolk Regiment, - see J L Fish
Sulman MC, Lt Col A E, 153,
Sulva Bay, 62,
Surrey Regiment, Royal West – see H J Clark, East – D J Trevett
Sutton Veny Camp, 111,
Sykes-Picot Agreement, 146,
Syria, 146,
T
Tank, 85, 167, 171, 173,
Tank Corps, 133, 174, (Memorial) 192, 235,
Tara-Usna Line, 184,
Territorial Army, 27, 111,
Thiepval, 69, (Wood) 184,
Thiepval Memorial to the Missing, 76, 84, 90, 93, 96, 98, 229,
Thompson, Lt Col R N, 166,
Three Jolly Wheelers Public House, 13, 14, 128,
Tigris River, 147,
Tomkinson, Lt Col J M, 119,
Tower Hamlets, 125,
Townsend, Maj Gen Sir Charles, 147,
Training Reserve, 163, 181,
Trench Mortar Batteries, 168, 178, 235,
Trevett, Pte Daniel James, 108, 135, 205, 231, 234,

Trones Wood, 81,
Tsar Nicholas II, 17, 103, 134, 222,
Turkish Fourth Army, 139,
Turkish Navy, 41,
Tyne Cot CWGC Cemetery, 116,
Tyne Cot, Memorial to the Missing, 116, 120, 126, 132, 136, 137, 231, 232,
U
Underwood, OS Joseph Samuel George, 37, 40, 42, 226,
United States, 149, 158, 171, 233,
Unknown Warrior, the Tomb of, 197,
V
Valenciennes, 188,
Vampir Farm, 116,
Vancouver Farm, 119,
Verdun, Battle of, 69, 96,
Versailles, Treaty of, 195, 197,
Vesle River, 172,
Victoria, Queen, 17,
Vieux-Berquin, 182, 183,
Villers-Plouich, 108, 109,
Vimy Ridge, 103, 232,
Vince, Pte Charles Alfred, 82, 86, 90, 99,
Vittorio Veneto, Battle of, 188,
W
Wadi Ghazze River, 143,
Walde, Headmaster Ernest Stuart, 79, 94, 206, 222,
Waller MA, Reverend C E, 212,
Watson VC, Lt John, 221,
Waugh, Capt Arthur John, 80, 98, 99,
Waugh Family, 80, 99,
Waugh, Lt Leonard Victor, 99, 228,
Waugh, Walter, 80, 162,
Western Desert, 140,
White City, 96,
White Hart Public House, 209,
Wilkins Farm, 72,
Wilson, President Woodrow, 103, 149, 187, 188, 189, 195,
Winnipeg Farm, 119,
Witham, James, 130, 232, 234,
Witham, Pte John Arthur, 130, 137, 152, 234,
Worcester Regiment, – see P Fitzgerald
Wytschaete, (Whitesheet) 108,
Y
Yorkshire Regiment, - including Yorks & Lancs Regiment and West Yorkshire Regiment – see E Bird, T G Bird and F E Noble
Ypres, First Battle of, 24,
Ypres, Second Battle of, 46,
Ypres, Third Battle of, 110, 111, 130, 137,
Z
Zeebrugge, 41, 110,
Zeppelin Raid, 136, 231,